Waking to Mourning Doves
A Memoir

Caryl Crozier

WingSpan Press

Copyright © 2011 by Caryl Crozier

All rights reserved.

No part of this book may be used or reproduced in any manner
without written permission of the author,
except for brief quotations used in reviews and critiques.

Printed in the United States of America
Published by WingSpan Press, Livermore, CA
www.wingspanpress.com
The WingSpan name, logo and colophon
are the trademarks of WingSpan Publishing.

First Edition 2011

Personal memories, childhood diary entries, quotes from family
journals and books form the basis of this book. The author's recollection
of events may not be consistent with what others remember.

Publisher's Cataloging-in-Publication Data

Crozier, Caryl.
Waking to mourning doves / Caryl Crozier.
p. cm.
ISBN 978-1-59594-455-9 (pbk.)
ISBN 978-1-59594-407-8 (hardcover)
ISBN 978-1-59594-771-0 (ebk.)

1. South Dakota—Biography. 2. Farm life—South Dakota. 3. South
Dakota—Social life and customs. I. Title.
CT275.C89 A3 2011
978.3`092—dc22

2011940947

Dedication

Mom gave me a crewel embroidery with the words, *TO LOVE SOMETHING IS TO GIVE IT ROOM ENOUGH TO GROW*. It reflects her philosophy of life and raising a child — me.

This memoir could be entitled *A Love Story*, because two people in my life gave me that room to grow: Mom, as she made sure I had all the opportunities denied to her, and my husband, Sherm, who patiently stood by my side and encouraged me to explore, experiment and become the person I am today.

Most mothers try to protect their children, and I think Mom was comfortable "giving" me to Sherm. At the end of her life, she seemed worried to leave me. When Sherm repeatedly assured her he would take care of me, I know she died at peace.

It is to these two most important people in my life that I dedicate this book.

Acknowledgments

Thanks to our daughters' (Michelle Kegler and Cherise Barnes) curiosity in knowing what my parents and extended family were really like, I felt compelled to tell their story and mine.

Since my husband Ed (Sherm) Crozier had published his memoir, I knew it was achievable. My diaries and journals and family encouragement helped the laborious process along. Fortunately, I had finished the early childhood and rural school sections before Mom's (Elvera Kinkner) death in 2009, so she had input too.

By writing my mother's Friendly Hour Club story in 2006, I began writing in earnest. Michelle's request to have my book completed by her 50th birthday in 2011 was a stimulus.

Suggestions and input from our daughters, and from Harriet Duerre, Harriet Dukelow, Juanita Carpenter, Carol Sheggeby and my AAUW writing groups were helpful. Childhood friends Lois Norling, LaVonne Young, Janet Helgaas, Karen Olson and Alice Harrington also offered memories and suggestions.

Granddaughters Rachel and Claire Barnes contributed some of their writing and Rachel helped with cover design and graphics. Sherm helped with typing, editing, layout and photographs. Michelle and Cherise provided photographs and journal entries.

Maxine Jacobson, Doug Henderson and Ruth Jones contributed ideas and editing. John Hickman did the final edit and preparation for publication.

The family portrait is by Bonnie's Impressions of Beresford. Scott Sharkey provided the Mourning Dove cover photograph.

Preface: Waking to Mourning Doves

Waking to the soulful call of a mourning dove shortly after my mother's death gave me the inspiration for my book title. Their plaintive cooing evokes nostalgic reminders of my life growing up on rural South Dakota prairies in the 1940s and 1950s, a memory of the simpler times of my youth. Soft spring mornings, gentle breezes stirring the curtains and a cacophony of birdsong and farm animal sounds define contentment to me. Their cooing still evokes the same feeling that all is right with the world.

Mourning doves are unassuming, not flashy and don't push and shove or bully other birds out of their space. They have adapted to blend into their surroundings, just as the women who settled the Great Plains did. Their nests and homes aren't fancy, but they have survived and thrived, just like my immigrant ancestral families.

Furthermore, they symbolize much of the happenings of my life and the experiences that have molded it, for they are like the soft-spoken ladies that surrounded me in my childhood: women who helped form my character and outlook on the world. These ladies were strong women and full partners in life, but with the polite, gentle demeanor of mourning doves.

My book is built around excerpts from my personal diary entries from ages ten to twenty-one, adult journaling and my memories. Dated diary entries and family journals are printed verbatim and expanded upon.

It is obvious from this book that I have an interest in preserving family history. My husband and I have published seven family-history books that describe our ancestors as far back as we can find records. Many go back hundreds of years and dozens of generations to our northern European roots. In addition to the history of our ancestors, I wish to pass on to my descendants my own personal history.

It is my hope that this memoir will inspire readers to record their own life experiences.

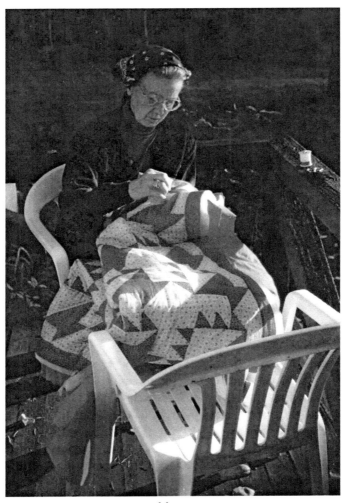
Mom

WAKING TO MOURNING DOVES

PROLOGUE 1

    Country Roads 3

PART I - EARLY MEMORIES 9

    1. Tinker Toys and Tea Parties.................................11
    2. Barns and Biffies 20

PART II - FAMILY...27

    3. Room Enough to Grow.................................... 29
    4. Reflections in a Cracked Mirror 38
    5. Grandma's Time Capsule.................................. 46
    6. My Chautauqua Grandma.................................. 56
    7. The Daughter They Never Had........................... 66
    8. My Swedish Bachelor Farmer Uncle.................. 74
    9. Aunt Hazel's Miracle 78

PART III - PALS 85

    10. Playhouses and Paper Dolls............................ 87
    11. Cuddles, Buster and Ginger 95

PART IV - FARM CHORES 101

    12. Chicken Chores.. 103
    13. Alfalfa and Cockleburs 108
    14. Threshing Runs..112
    15. Wringer Washers and Flatirons 119
    16. Heirloom Gardens.. 121
    17. Funnel Clouds, Blizzards and Jackrabbits...................... 123

PART V - BRANCHING OUT 127

    18. Frozen Creeks and Drifting Snow – And Christmas!..... 129
    19. 4H-Head, Heart, Hands, Health....................... 142
    20. Ode to Daisy Dewey..................................... 149

PART VI - CLIMBING FENCES 153

    21. My One-Room Country School........................ 157

22. Beresford Watchdogs, '50s Era 174

23 Choices 194

24 Following My Dream 204

25 Missouri River Summers 208

26. Contusions and Crutches 214

27. Mapping My Future 218

PART VII - NAVIGATING THE RIVERS OF CHANGE 223

28. Just Keep Paddling 227

29. You'll Be a Cute Mama 238

30. Mothers and Daughters 245

31. Country Calico 251

32. Wood Ticks, Woodcock and Wildflowers 260

PART VIII - SHIFTING GEARS 269

33. Do You Know Ed Crozier? 271

34. And He Had No Feet 276

35. You Are the Geranium 281

36. PR in a Pressure Cooker 284

37. From Good to Great Neighbor 291

PART IX - BEYOND OCEANS 297

38. Horsey Rocks to Houseboats 299

39. Was Great-Great Grandma a Polygamist? 309

PART X - SANDWICH GENERATION 313

40. A Void In My Heart 315

41. Hollywood Comes to the Farm 322

42. Goodbye to Dad and Mom 327

EPILOGUE 337

43. Still Paddling 339

PROLOGUE

Kinkner Home

Grandpa Kinkner's Barn

Walt & Effie

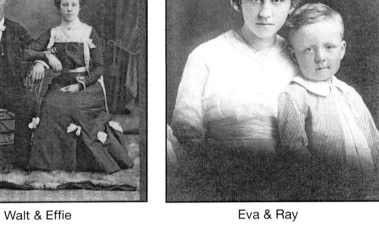
Eva & Ray

Dad

Mom

Country Roads

Many say that home is a state of mind, but physically holding on to the place that sheltered me much of my life seems essential to me now that only the spirits of those who came before me remain. The mere thought of selling it is like selling my very soul. My childhood home east of Beresford, South Dakota has been occupied by my family for over 110 years and now it has been entrusted to me.

Beresford grew from its first settlement in 1872 to incorporation in 1884 in what was then Dakota Territory. By 1889, when South Dakota became a state, I am sure this sturdy little house had been built by pioneer merchants and withstood the bitter blizzard of 1888, the year the Jones side of my family arrived to homestead.

Renovation and renewal describe the phases this old family home has undergone. Like me, it started out small, expanded its walls and weathered the storms and changes, and emerges now a bit weathered, but girded with the strength to face an unknown future. Sure, the windows to the world need a little repair like my growing cataracts, and the porch is sagging like some of my body parts. While the slowly decaying house mirrors my aging body, the memories are as fresh and alive as when we were both in our prime.

The house and its contents speak to me of times past. A faded brittle newspaper clipping found in my grandmother Nan's well-worn Bible states,

> *At one o'clock last Sunday (Sept 30, 1900) at the home of the bride's parents, Mr. and Mrs. Henry Jones, in Gothland, there occurred the marriage of Mr. Walter Kinkner and Miss Effie Jones.... About 30 relatives of the happy pair were present and many and useful and valuable were the presents received. The bride and groom have both grown to maturity in Gothland and are known and respected by everyone. We know of no couple to whom congratulations are more in order so we extend a full measure of good wishes. We understand that the new home will be made on the farm of Mr. Kinkner's mother, which will be vacated when she moves to Beresford this fall (Stark place).*

By age 31, my grandpa Walt had acquired a little nest egg, but not quite enough to build on the 80 acres he purchased in 1900. For a few years he and

Nan rented the nearby Stark and Gardner farms, both owned by Canton, South Dakota relatives. This allowed them to squirrel away enough money to move a small house from Beresford to their own 80 acres two miles east of town. A long, tortuous driveway accessed the home-site atop a small hill. A deep clear creek flowed through the adjacent pasture and flooded the driveway after heavy rains.

Nan recalls, "The men put the house on skids and pulled it to the farm site by four horses the winter of 1905." Come spring they moved their sparse furnishings to their own land at last.

The land east of Beresford is a gently rolling landscape, empty to the unfamiliar eye, but life sustaining for the current occupants. Originally, the land cover was tall prairie grasses and herbaceous flowering plants that had existed for centuries, providing food and cover for a great variety of wildlife ranging from butterflies to buffalo. The landscape was treeless except for a few trees along the small creeks and an occasional savanna where a few oaks were scattered over a prairie-covered hillside.

Today, the landscape topography has not changed much except the prairie grasses are all gone now and there are tree groves scattered about. The grasses were plowed under when the land was settled by newly arriving Europeans. Many of the first settlers came from Norway, Germany and Sweden. On the rolling hills around the family farm, the Swiss settled. The white population grew slowly until the Sioux Indians were gradually defeated and railroads were built across the land. Then settlement of the area increased dramatically with the "Dakota Boom" from 1870 to 1880.

Farmsteads appeared on the land, usually four to a square mile, since each homestead was about 160 acres in size. Earlier, U.S. government surveyors had surveyed the land. While the land was still covered with prairie grasses and there were only Indian and buffalo trails across the land, these surveyors staked out each square mile and sometimes each half-mile . The first settlers found these stakes and made their claim on their homestead, usually 160 acres, which was sometimes sold into smaller farm tracts, like the first Kinkner owned land. Gradually, roads were built around each section as someone had the foresight to set aside right-of-way along each of these section lines.

The land most suited for agriculture was converted to cropland, while the land that was wetter and less suited for crops was retained in grass and used as pasture for cattle and horses. The first settlers planted trees around their homes and out-buildings, so today, nearly every square mile section generally has a small farm grove in each of its four corners. Now many of those buildings have disappeared, as the smaller farms have been replaced by the larger, corporate-size operations that farm thousands of acres.

The early farmers planted a variety of crops including corn, wheat, oats, and alfalfa. This type of self-sustaining farming was transformed after the 1960s when the farming of a great variety of crops and livestock gave way to a monoculture of very large fields of corn and soybeans with fewer farms and less livestock. Thus, even the remaining grasslands disappeared and were also replaced with giant fields of corn and soybeans. Some individual crop fields are, by themselves, the size of the original farms and few farms still have livestock. The topography is still gently rolling and to the untrained eye, not much different. The land is still covered much of the year with plants, but of a different nature than the prairie grasses.

The identity of the builder of the house in town that sold the family farmhouse to Grandpa has been lost in the passage of time, but we know my small family has called it home for over 100 years.

I can almost hear the walls reverberate as my grandparents' precocious three-year-old daughter Eva Lillian dashed about exploring her new home. If she behaved anything like her great grandnephew Nate, the walls said, "Oh boy, this family will be lively."

As the farm prospered, two more bedrooms, a large wrap-around front porch and a utilitarian screen porch at the back door were added. By the time my father entered the world in this house in 1911, an imposing, crimson board-and-batten barn, two chicken houses, a machine shed and an outdoor two-seater toilet dotted the hilltop farm.

My dad's cousin Blanche recalls: *Oh, Eva was mad when the new baby was a boy cuz she wanted a sister. Uncle Walt had to pull her out of the shed when she was pouting so bad. Then she ran down home to our place a half-mile away and cried and cried. Later she learned to love him, though. Being the only child for nine years she became a little spoiled, dontcha know.*

Did those walls listen to my dad as a contented or colicky baby — who knows? I only know his cousin described him as a little hellion. I am sure they listened to Nan's birthing screams while Aunt Ida was there as a midwife. As my Aunt Eva excelled in school and honed her skills on the piano, I am sure she found her little brother annoying, but in all my memories and tales I heard she was his mentor and protector.

Gothland School opened its doors in 1880 and my grandmother Effie finished her eighth grade education there while Grandpa Walt completed his eighth grade education in Illinois and Iowa. Since Grandpa Jones still chaired the Gothland school board, it was only natural that Eva should attend school there. Oddly enough, my mom's father joined the school board by 1910 and the two men disagreed often, one being slightly Bohemian and the other a staid conservative Swede.

I can imagine Nan rushing about every morning, getting Eva and busy toddler Ray dressed, packing lunch pails, hitching the pony to the buggy and driving the two and a half miles to the Gothland school. Mornings got even busier when Dad started at Silver Lake School in 1917 and Nan first drove Eva to high school in town and then took Dad in the opposite direction to Silver Lake.

The barn, a necessary building for any rural church or schoolhouse, housed horses during services and classes. Rows of black buggies lined up outside barns at church services. The Silver Lake School barn was a large red wooden vertical-slatted building with grey wooden shingles. The dark interior housed rows of horse stalls — individual compartments for horses enclosed on three sides with a deep trough at the front for hay. A huge sliding door opened to provide space to park buggies or store bikes. Five generations of children played exciting games of hide-and-seek and cemented lifelong friendships near those barns. The majority of students from 1885 to 1970 were descendants of the first German, Swiss, Norwegian and Swedish settlers to the area.

Dad probably had many similar thoughts to mine as we both walked or rode the same roads to Silver Lake School. Gravel and blacktop on country roads arrived in the late 1940s. Prior to that time, dirt roads mired in mud and deep ruts hindered rapid travel. Washboard bumps dotted the hills and I remember my teeth chattering as our old Chevy negotiated the gravel roads. Swaying flocks of birds, tall waving grasses and fast moving clouds provided a ballet as magical as the Bolshoi ballet we saw in Russia in 2004. I know that glimpses of nature I experienced along these roads inspired my family, as they took the time to teach me to see the beauty, too.

The building that became my childhood home sheltered my Dad's family of four until 1933, the year my parents married. Each day from 1905 to 1933 bustled with activity: farm chores, food preparation and preservation, and fields to till or harvest. Most Sundays, relatives gathered at Nan's home for a groaning table of fried chicken, mashed potatoes and gravy, preserves, thick slices of homemade bread and freshly churned butter. No one pushed away early from her table. They knew her flaky apple or cherry pies or sour cream raisin and coconut cream with thick meringue would soon appear.

As the meal was being prepared, someone kept the wood stove stoked with corncobs and wood as the homegrown Kennebec potatoes boiled away.

"Oh don't throw away the potato water, I need it for gravy," Nan would say as she put the last of the crispy fried chicken on the platter. "Lottie, could you dish up the peas and Blanche maybe you could slice that bread. Eva, you get the butter out of the icebox on the porch. Ray, get your dirty fingers away from that ground cherry jam. Go wash up now before we sit up."

"We can sit up now" brought our family to the table before the mandatory prayer. Carefully ironed white damask tablecloths with matching napkins rarely caught a spill, as company used their best Sunday manners. Fragile sherbets and goblets set off Nan's finest china. Fresh or dried flowers or fruit adorned the center. Nan loved to cook and entertain, so it's no wonder her home became the family gathering place.

After dinner the women gossiped while washing dishes and the men discussed the crops and weather. Later, competitive games of croquet made room for homemade freezer cranked ice cream and Nan's date cake.

DATE CAKE

1 cup sugar	1 cup boiling water (pour over dates & soda)
1 egg	1/2 cup nut meats
1 or 2 heaping tablespoons butter	1 1/2 cups flour
1 cup dates chopped	1 teaspoon vanilla
1 teaspoon soda	a pinch of salt

Mix and bake at 350 degrees till toothpick inserted in center comes out clean. About 30 minutes.

As I look at old photos of my grandparents' friends and relatives taken on the open wrap-around porch, I remember their quirks and personalities. I can still hear them laughing and teasing each other. The men wore striped blue-and-white bib overalls and wrinkled suit coats, while the ladies wore their Sunday best. Feed-sack aprons sewn by Nan protected their dresses as they helped in the crowded kitchen.

Change came to the Kinkner home with the onset of the Depression in 1929. Eva was now working as a linotype operator for the local newspaper, The Beresford Republic, and sharing a portion of her meager income of twenty-one dollars a week with the family. She continued to give support to her family during the early '30s as the Depression deepened.

Meanwhile, my dad's days of courting my mother led to a marriage proposal in February of 1933. August and Edla Erickson, my mother's parents, must have been shocked and disappointed when Aunt Eva broke the news to them that Ray and Elvera planned to get married the next day at the Kinkner home.

I can imagine August saying, "Well, how's he going to support her, he just lives with Walt and Effie."

"Well, when you are in love not much else matters," my parents must have thought as they meekly entered the new Erickson home after Eva's announcement. According to Mom's diary, they went to town and she bought a wedding dress.

Mom writes: *February 5, 1933 – Became the Bride today.*

Hazel Erickson and Ragnar Ostenson, Eva's husband to be, stood with them as Reverend Harper from the Congregational Church read their vows in the parlor of this home I know so well.

I remember my Dad saying, "I was sweating so much from nerves, and that kerosene space heater just behind us made matters worse."

The parlor doors, which usually remained closed in the frigid South Dakota winters, welcomed the small wedding party as they marched in to Eva's music on the piano. Dad pulled a narrow silver band from his pocket and placed it on Mom's left finger and her life changed forever. She left behind her sheltered life with her conservative Evangelical Lutheran parents and siblings and entered a new hardscrabble existence during the '30s Depression years. Mom's father was noticeably absent from the wedding, withholding the approval that sister Hazel and Grandma Edla readily gave from the start.

Dad later said, " I guess old August thought I was okay when he saw I could support her."

Mom joined the liberal Congregational Church and enjoyed the dancing, parties and card games that the Erickson family found somewhat sinful.

A month after their wedding, in March 1933, my parents and grandparents, out of the necessity to support two families, moved three miles to the northeast to rent a 320-acre farm owned by Grandpa's relatives from Canton. Grandpa rented his 80 acres and house to another family. For nine years, they farmed together through the Depression, crop failures and dust storms.

It is into this scene that I made my arrival on August 1, 1938.

PART I: EARLY MEMORIES

Parents and Me

Grandpa and Me

Four Generations

Me

1941 Home

Farm Yard

CHAPTER 1

Tinker Toys and Tea Parties

Mom gave me a priceless gift on our 40th wedding anniversary. She wrote her story about my life in a memory book, which I will quote throughout this memoir.

> Mom begins: *Caryl was born August 1, 1938 on a Monday at 11:30 A.M. in Lydia Nelson's home in Beresford weighing 7# 13 oz. We stayed at the place 13 days. Lydia was a wonderful person to us both and always gave lunch to whoever came to see us and her mother would come upstairs and sit by us too.*

> *We went home to the Deane Farm where we lived with Ray's folks and your Grandpa was so delighted to have you there, coming in at noon no matter how hot or tired he was. He loved to hold you, walk with you and also liked to rock you.*

> *Your great grandma Clarissa came and stayed with us often and she loved you dearly, and Grandma Effie also loved to hold and take care of you. Your Grandma Erickson was always so pleased when we came to see her; she would hold you while she rocked and hummed. Then she would usually have something for you. You took to her right away, and also to Hazel and Clarence.*

> *For your first Christmas, the Erickson gathering was at our house and Ruth, your cousin, had a bad cold. Well, a few days later you came down with a severe cold. Your dad and Effie went some place for something in the PM and when they came home, I said you were not feeling at all good, so we called Dr. Leitzke and he came out. He recommended steaming you. We had a little burner we used that night and made a paper funnel for steaming. Then Eva said to come in as it would be warmer and better at her house, so Effie and I stayed and we steamed you every half hour all night. Then the Doctor came at noon the next day. Your nails were even*

Waking to Mourning Doves

turning dark and he said this is the turning point, one way or the other. Thank goodness it was for the better and you improved so quick. Your dad was with us too, so this brought great joy to all of us. Grandma was staying with Walter when we were gone and when they heard the good news, they could hardly wait for us to come; even started down the driveway to meet us.

Things went pretty good, only you cried a lot and to find out, you weren't getting enough milk, so you were put on the bottle. Grandpa was so good about holding and rocking you, trying to keep you from crying. All changed after getting the bottle.

Eva and Ragnar came most every Sunday mainly to play and be with you. When we went to town to shop when you were walking, you always carried your brown teddy bear and wore a blue snowsuit.

We had a great dog named Fritz and a pet lamb, which we let in the house to feed it with the bottle. Caryl would hold the bottle sometimes. We let it in one time too many and it went on the living room rug. Sometime later the lamb was found dead; overfed or something. We kept it in the brooder house.

One winter we hired Jim Hanson and Elmer Patnoe to pick corn. They really made a fuss over you and you liked them, especially Jim. Elmer smoked a pipe and you would pull it out of his mouth.

Emma Schietler was a teacher who stayed with us for four years. She was from Garretson. One winter day when the roads were so cold and you were out, you started walking up the road and were going to Emma's school.

You weren't quite three years old and we moved over to our 80-acre home in 1941 where we still lived. We moved over to the new farm across from George Voegeli.

So where were my parents during my early formative years? They lived with my grandparents on a rented 360-acre farm trying to survive the Depression, clouds of greedy crunching grasshoppers and choking dust storms of the dirty thirties. These hard times were punctuated when Grandpa deposited $400 in the local bank after selling a load of hogs. The bank closed the next day, devouring Grandpa's earnings. Maybe that's why I still find moldy old dollars stashed away in my mom's damp basement. Trust in banks dissipated in the '30s, just like hope in the future. Mom and Dad even skinned a skunk to sell the pelt for 25 cents. Times were tough, but they never tried that again.

I made my unplanned arrival in the midst of this, so everyone living in the gigantic drafty old house had a hand in my upbringing: parents and grandparents, plus the hired man and the rural schoolteacher who boarded with us. All the men competed with Grandpa for my attention and they often won. Now I wonder how my dad felt when other adults monopolized most of my time. I can still conjure up the sights and smells of the hired hand, Palmer, in his multi-patched, frayed-cuff bib overalls. Little traces of cow manure and straw clung to the turned-up cuffs and when he unrolled them in the house, all kinds of debris fell out: weed seeds, burrs, dirt and straw.

Nan scolded and said, "Clean off your pants with that old broom by the back door before you come inside or you can sweep the floor yourself."

A man sweeping the floor? Unheard of!

Emma, the pretty schoolmarm that boarded with us for four years, became my mom's good friend and they corresponded into old age.

Mom relates, "You took a shine to her and always wanted to go to Emma's school."

At Pleasant Hill school, Emma taught all eight grades to thirteen students. It was the custom to board with the family that lived closest to the school. She walked the half-mile from our house to school every day. Only rarely did a schoolteacher own a car.

One bright sunny day in the middle of winter, Mom bundled me up in my wooly blue snowsuit and heavy, three-buckle boots and I took off running for the road before she could get her own outdoor clothes on.

"Wait, where do you think you're going honey?" Mom shouted.

"To Emma's school," I replied, as I tumbled into the deep soft snow in the ditch.

Well, I didn't get there by myself that day, but Emma loved the story and hugged me tight every time she told about it. All I remember about her is her easy laughter, frequent hugs and playing fierce games of carom with the family in the parlor by the wood-burning stove.

I have a few snippets of memory from my first three years, mostly traumatic events like the big old floppy-winged geese chasing me or cranky

Waking to Mourning Doves

roosters jumping at me. One time an angry hissing old gander chased me across the yard when I was alone exploring. My three-year-old stubby legs couldn't go fast enough as he gained on me inch by inch.

I must have thought, "Why pick on me? I'm only interested in seeing your new gosling family."

As my stumbling legs raced across the barnyard, I could see safety ahead up the steps to the woodshed. Just as I heard the swish of his wings and that hissing beak brushed my sun-suit, I was suddenly swooped up by strong arms. My grandpa swung me high in the air as the gander crashed against his legs.

Through the years, Grandpa swung me across deep, chocolate-mud creeks as we got the cows home and rescued me from all sorts of problems. He patiently played along with his fiddle as I tried to learn to play the piano by ear. He protected and loved me even when I was naughty by licking the cow's salt block or pedaling away on his whetstone blade sharpener. What I really mean to say is that he was my guide, my protector and a man to measure all others against. He died when I was only eight years old, but I learned unconditional love from him.

Why do memorable events often involve urine? Crying at the top of the stairs when I was two years old, because I had wet my pants or feeling sorry for the orphan pet lamb that wet on Nan's good carpet leaving a permanent yellow spot are vivid memories. Dad always laughed when he told how I wet on the floor when we had a houseful of company. He said I went out and got the mop from the kitchen and said, "Up the pee" as I tried to clean it up. Thankfully, I don't remember the laughter or the event.

The Christmas when I was two, my Uncle Clarence, acting as Santa, handed me a cloth-bodied composition face doll and Tinkertoys. Bob Larson, Uncle Ragnar's nephew, sat on the floor and helped me make a windmill out of the Tinkertoys. Well, he made it and I watched in fascination and I hero-worshipped him for years. That afternoon I named the doll Gracie for a favorite fat and jolly Deane relative from whom we rented the 320-acre farm. I liked her because she fussed over me and brought sweet treats.

The old farmhouse on the Deane place seemed very large, not insulated, and drafty. Water froze in the glasses in the upstairs bedrooms where my parents and I slept. On the coldest nights, I snuggled in bed with Mom and Dad, but usually slept in the baby crib under heavy quilts. My daughters and granddaughters all slept in that same crib when they were small. Now it is considered dangerous because the slats are too far apart and a baby's head might get stuck between them.

We always had cats, and I remember a black one with a white stripe on his face that loved being in the house. A photo of me standing by the cat in my new purple coat and bonnet from the Sears catalogue shows a prim and proper little girl posing for the camera.

In 1941, when I was two and a half years old, Grandpa encouraged and helped my parents buy 80 acres a half mile north of his original 80 which had been rented to another family for nine years. Inflation has now increased the value from $80 to $5000 an acre. After nine years of living together, my parents and grandparents finally lived in separate homes. Nearly every day though, Grandpa drove his team of horses from his farm to help Dad. I like to think he came to see me too.

I missed the daily contact with the hired men, Emma and my grandparents when we moved to our own farm in 1941, but almost three years with this extended family made me secure in knowing I was loved.

My memories from the time I was three after we moved to the present farm place, two miles east and one mile north of Beresford, are in clearer focus than the first two and a half years spent on the Deane place we rented three miles east. Moving day is vivid; boxes everywhere and the happy confusion of moving into a new place. Our new neighbor, Hertha Voegeli, brought baked beans and something else for our dinner. We ate off paper plates while surrounded by piles of boxes and orange crates in the kitchen. I thought Hertha was wonderful and best of all, she had a daughter and two sons that I could play with. They were older than me, but became the closest thing I ever had to siblings.

This white clapboard house had an entry porch, kitchen and pantry, long narrow dining room, living room and bedroom on the first floor. The upstairs had two bedrooms and a storage attic and very steep narrow stairs leading from the ground floor. We hung our clothes on a rod at the end of a long spooky hall. There were no closets, so we put our clothing in drawers or on hangers behind the doors or in wooden wardrobe closets.

Mom quickly chose new wallpaper and refurbished and scrubbed all the rooms in the house. Mom and I poured over wallpaper sample books at the Gambles store in town and ordered our favorites. Sometimes I influenced the decision. My relatives made their own wallpaper paste, but the recipe is a mystery to me. I think they used some kind of starch. I can still smell the thick starchy paste and see Mom on the top rung of a step-ladder balancing the floppy wallpaper as she stuck it on the ceiling with Nan handing her brushes and coaching encouragement. As a team, they hung wallpaper in other friends' homes too. Since the coal burned in furnaces made the walls sooty, applications of wallpaper or washing walls in the spring was necessary. Cracks in the plaster in those old houses had to be repaired with strips of old sheeting soaked in paste and stuck on the damaged surface.

Waking to Mourning Doves

As an only child, I learned to enjoy solitary activities at a young age. My dolls, cats and books kept me company. If I wanted to play house, my tiny red table and rocking chair held my china dish set from Grandma and made a fine setting for pretend tea parties with my dolls. Tinkertoys, alphabet blocks, pull toys and a plate-sized train on a track are antiques now, but I had many happy hours playing with them. I loved my Red Flyer wagon and hauled cats and dolls all over the bumpy yard. Mom remembers that I liked to play in the dirt and sand with a pail and shovel, and play store using a toy red cash register and telephone. I positioned my small ironing board and flatiron next to Mom's heavy metal board to pretend I was ironing. Many children played with my toys after I outgrew them, and they show significant wear and tear. I think grandchildren Rachel, Claire and Nate enjoyed playing with them almost as much as I did.

Mom, my grandmas and aunts read stacks of books to me from the time I was small.

Some that I recall are *Mother Goose, Jack in the Beanstalk, Three Little Pigs, Little Red Riding Hood,* and *Grimm's Fairy Tales.* I loved books, their crisp new smell and all the adventures I could read about. I never traveled far from home in South Dakota, but my books took me to exotic places and times in my imagination. Relatives always gave me the classics like *Heidi* and *Little Women.* Later, I was hooked on the Nancy Drew mystery series as well as comic books and movie star magazines, all of which are collectible today. The city library became a wonderful resource and I always joined their summer reading program encouraged by my aunts, Lily and Eva.

A paper farm set with animals, a big barn, silo, house and outbuildings got many hours of use, especially during the winter. My parents helped me assemble the buildings, which I strung out all over the living room. I made such a mess that they must have been glad they had only one child. Now the cardboard farm set is tattered and torn from use, but I enjoy setting it up and pretending with grandchildren.

A small shed east of the house that we called a cob house, stored corncobs and firewood for use in the kitchen stove. When nearly empty, I used it as an indoor playhouse. My outdoor playhouse and shelves were behind the cob house. At various times, it was a pretend house, grocery store or ice cream store and restaurant. Sometimes I had three different area playhouses going, and spent many hours playing alone or with friends. I also played on top of the cob house with my cats and dolls, climbing one of the surrounding Chinese elm trees to reach the roof.

We obtained water from a wind-powered windmill or from a cistern by the house. Eaves fastened to the house caught soft rainwater that ran through

Caryl Crozier

a coal filter unit into the cistern, a cement-lined chamber below ground level. The cistern was a frightening deep pit of dark water for which I had profound respect and fear. Adults guarded children from ever playing near it or removing the top. A pump unit covered the cistern hole and as you cranked it, a rotating loop of cups brought water from deep in the cistern into the spout and water poured out. We never used this water for drinking because my parents feared contamination.

Looking back, living as we did seems pretty primitive. We didn't have electricity or refrigeration other than an icebox that had to have ice replenished every week. Kerosene lamps provided dim light in the evenings until the Rural Electric Association (REA) brought electric lines to farm homes on our road in 1946. We had to wait our turn. We finally got running water and an indoor bathroom in 1951 when I was 13 and my parents moved Nan's house to the north 80 and remodeled it. This seems unimaginable to my grandchildren!

> Mom writes: *We moved houses, Effie's house up to our place and the old one to her place. We remodeled the house. We put the kitchen where a bedroom was; we put two windows in and made them flat in the old dining room. Then we built a bedroom on the east side of the house which was a great task. We had Reiersons living in the old house when we moved it. We put a full basement and a hall and bath room in the remodeled house and enclosed the front porch.*
>
> *June 15, 1951–The men came to move our old house–2 men, there will be 4 tomorrow.*

In 1951, after my Aunt Eva died, Nan wanted to move her house to our farm, just a half mile away, remodel it, and have us all live together. Mom preferred to build a new house, but Nan and Dad overruled her. Workmen put our old two-story house up on moving blocks and moved it into the yard, where we lived while they moved Nan's house to the site. Later, the old house was moved to the "south 80", completing the exchange of houses. What a strange sight to see a huge house rolling up the road. I rode in the house while it was being moved; a dangerous venture no moving company would allow today. The crew dug a new basement and laid concrete blocks to form the foundation. What a change from the old, dirt-wall and partially floored basement we had.

Nan's house was flip-flopped in direction from what it had been on her farm. It was always a bit confusing when we talked about the north or south bedrooms. A couple of carpenters from Hawarden did the project, Ernie

Packard and someone else whose name I can't remember. They had a sweet deal going: Mom made all their meals and my parents helped the carpenters who assigned Mom and Dad all the dirty work. The carpenters were paid by the hour and worked very slowly. Dad occasionally chewed them out, but as far as I could tell they never picked up their pace.

November 15, 1951–Worked at the other house today–varnished, filled holes and applied oil.

December 4, 1951– Cupboards arrived and the men came to put them in tonite.

December 9,1951–Ida, Lucille and Mom papered my room. Men came to fix cupboards. Ida stayed tonite.

December 15, 1951–25 degrees below zero and moved to new house today. Got all rooms but living room settled–fun bed making. Ragnar brought me candy.

January 2, 1952–Went to Alcester and got new electric range and deep freeze.

I watched in amazement as interior walls were relocated and a bathroom put in where the kitchen had been. Nan's former bedroom became the new kitchen with birch built-in cupboards. I was sad when the beautiful wide oak woodwork and parlor doors were taken out and replaced with cheap pine. I liked the old look, so I was allowed to keep it in my bedroom. Mom and Dad decided to build an additional bedroom because Mom said I should not share a room with Nan. Thank goodness she stood up for me in that regard.

July 7, 1952–Ma's varnishing the porch floor, I helped.

Carpenters enclosed the old rounded porch and it became a place to store extra stuff. Mom fought that idea too, but I know she was thankful for the expanded space later. I loved that porch and it served as my retreat. I spent hours and hours reading on the old mohair couch and sewing on the treadle machine. After I left home in 1956, it morphed into a catchall space. I am still struggling to sort and clean it out in 2011.

February 23, 1952–Worked at our old house for Reiersons to move in on Tuesday.

May 5, 1952–Moved the old house to Nan's farm today.

Caryl Crozier

The Reierson family lived in the old house on our farm until it was moved to Nan's farm on the "south 80" later in the year. I think they paid something like $200 a year rent and lived there for many years.

I was thrilled to have modern conveniences in this newly remodeled house. Best of all, we had an indoor bathroom with a bathtub, hot and cold running water, a new electric stove and freezer and a cement floor in the basement where I could roller skate. It felt like living in luxury. The house today is like a time capsule – still very much like it was in 1951.

CHAPTER 2
Barns and Biffies

Who would ever believe you could teach a cow to shake hands (hooves)? Mom did just that in our cavernous red barn after twin coal-black calves Peg and Meg were born. She made an extra effort nurturing and playing with them. As a result, they bonded to her and she taught them to lift their front leg and shake hands. Even as 15-year-old milk cows, they lifted their front leg and sidled up to Mom. She cried when Meg was sold and put the $200 from the sale in her bank safety deposit box labeled Meg. We found it there after she died. I guess she just couldn't bear to lose her last tie to her pet cow. Now, I need to spend it for something special. Maybe it will be used to promote the Hollywood film about the Friendly Hour Club and farm life in the '30s (*Prairie Sonata*). Mom would like that.

My parents always monitored young heifers when they gave birth in case they needed help. Dad usually knew when a birth was imminent and kept the cow in the barn. Occasionally, a renegade cow surprised him and delivered her calf in the pasture. Dad had to go and carry the new calf home since it was too far for a wobbly calf to walk and he didn't want a coyote or other predator to get it.

One time, when Dad was gone, Mom called the veterinarian to help an exhausted heifer deliver her calf. As the vet reached his arm in the birth canal, he declared, "It's breach."

That's bad news. It means the calf is feet first unlike a normal headfirst delivery. The heifer had struggled too long, so he reached in, put a chain around the calf and pulled it out. As Doc Cotton fell to the ground, the calf and all the afterbirth plopped on top of him. Mom and I tried to restrain our relieved laughter as he got up, soaked to the skin.

Mom rushed in to help clean the calf when the heifer collapsed, too tired to lick her newborn. An animal bonds to whoever stimulates and feeds it at birth, and this calf bonded to Mom. We called her Clover and she followed Mom around like a puppy. The heifer survived, but Clover never liked *her* mom as much as she liked *my* mom!

Our A-shaped or double-sloped, classic-style barn was primarily devoted to raising cattle. The large haymow was set up for using a pulley system to move large bundles of alfalfa hay inside. Farmers mowed and raked hay into windrows in the field and then loaded it with three-pronged pitchforks onto horse-drawn racks pulled into the front of the barn. Loose hay was hoisted from the racks in huge roped bundles, pulled up into the second-story hayloft by a team of horses at the business end of a series of ropes and pulleys.

Haylofts in barns provided farm kids with places to play away from the watchful eyes of adults. We played hide and seek, exchanged a few smooches and did daring tricks on rope swings. Swinging across the cavernous barn loft on a rope that had a big knot tied on the end scared even the most adventurous kids. We landed in a soft pile of hay if we were lucky. Woe to the kid with allergies when dust exploded from the dry hay. Sometimes we found baby kittens hidden in the hay piles. If we got too intrusive, the mother cat moved her brood to another hiding place, but we always had a way of finding them.

The ground floor of the barn had a middle aisle with cow stanchions on one side and horse stalls on the other. A calf-holding area was on the side near the cow-yard entry. Those first days of sucking the thick colostrum from the cows gave calves a healthy start, but after five days they were separated so my parents could milk the cows. The new calves always bawled for their mothers for days after weaning. The cows bellowed and tried to reach the calves when brought in for milking and this cacophony was deafening. Mom taught the calves to drink milk from a pail by sticking her fingers in the pail .The calves must have thought it a substitute for teats, as it worked. With stubborn calves, she straddled the calf to force it to drink. She never gave up and we never lost a calf for lack of food. I felt sorry for the calves and a few times I sneaked to the barn and opened the door to let the mother cow back in to her calf. That only made matters worse! I got scolded for my actions, but never spanked.

Swallows loved the barn and insisted on building their nests right above the cows. My parents sat right under the nests when milking and got "spilled" upon more than once until the nests were knocked down. I didn't want Dad to knock the nests down because the cats always pounced on the featherless baby birds, which was probably just as well because they would have died anyway.

Life and death can be cruel on a farm. It is easy to become attached to farm animals, and the harsh reality of selling or butchering them for food is a lesson farm kids learn early.

Dad pitched manure daily, out the two barn doors onto huge aromatic piles. Hogs rummaged through the droppings and recycled them again. In the spring, Mom and Dad pitched manure from these piles and the chicken house into a manure spreader to distribute onto the fields. Dad didn't use commercial fertilizers; only natural animal by-products replenished the soil. They also did crop rotation with oats, corn and alfalfa, which helped keep the soil healthier and less prone to weed infestations. This is what they call sustainable farming now.

Our family farm site seemed crowded with small buildings, most being related to chickens. A two-room lap sided building was the only chicken house on the farm when we arrived in 1941. My parents soon purchased a brooder house, a small building designed to house baby chickens. Eventually five buildings were devoted to chickens. Not too surprising, because the chicken flock produced income that Mom used for groceries and necessities.

The hog house, a pleasing inverted U-shaped building with red overlap siding and faded grey wood shingles, had a central alley with hog pens on each side. In the spring the sows gave birth and the hog pens were wriggling with red, white and spotted piglets, usually ten or twelve to a litter. They had proper names like Poland China, Hampshire and Chester White, but I identified them by color. When learning the facts of life, Dad tried to tell me the little pigs came out of the sow's ear, but I knew better because I snuck into the hog house and watched the birth while Mom and Dad milked cows. There is no way to hide the facts of life from a curious child on a farm. When Dad felt I was old enough, he let me watch litters of little pigs come into the world.

The bullet-riddled pig weather vanes once atop the hog house now have a resting place on my fireplace mantle.

April 21, 1952–My sow had pigs.

Sometimes we brought newborn runt pigs in the house and placed them in a box on the oven door of the wood cook-stove to keep them warm. Birthing and breeding on the farm left little doubt in a young girl's mind about the "birds and bees." My older cousins were quick to fill in any unknown details. Little or no knowledge was out-sourced by parents in those days. They must have just been too busy or uncomfortable talking about sex.

Dad rarely used the hog-yard cistern, originally meant for holding water, but cautioned me to stay away from the dangerous deep hole. Sometimes he threw trash in there and it eventually filled up making it much safer. One time he euthanized some unwanted baby kittens and threw them into the pit. I cried and cried, as I never thought we had too many cats. Twenty-five or more, in retrospect, does seem excessive. The hog yard where the pigs could run freely eventually became Mom's best garden site.

The machine shed had red, narrow vertical siding and sliding doors. It had three large oat bins and open storage for machinery. Oats and ground feed or corn were kept in the bins and each bin had a little chute from which we could fill our pails. Sometimes, I furtively opened the chute and gave extra grain

Caryl Crozier

to my favorite animals, but not the chickens. I detested chickens. Dad kept the grain binder, wagons, tools, grain seeder, tractor and a car in the shed. It always seemed like a disorganized mess. Dad would use a tool and then drop it wherever he worked. Only much later, he built a proper workbench in the barn, but since neatness wasn't one of his virtues, not much changed.

Old setting hens hid their clutches of eggs under the grain binder or in inaccessible corners in the machine shed. What a thrill it was to find a clutch of twenty eggs in a pile. If fertilized, Mom let the hens set and hatch baby chicks; but most of the eggs were not fertilized and rotted. If you gently shake an egg you can tell if it is rotten. My friends and I liked to throw the rotten eggs at a target and exclaim about the stench. Sometimes though, an old setting hen surprised us and proudly displayed her new family in the yard. Those free-range chicks always seemed smarter than the ones we purchased at the hatchery. When we bulldozed the rickety machine shed in the 1990s, I discovered a pile of eggs that had to be at least ten years old because Mom quit raising chickens in the '80s. They were buff colored, dried out and light as feathers.

We had a typical two-seat outhouse near the house. Going out to use it in the dark before bedtime was spooky. On cold winter mornings I wished for fur seat covers. When I was younger, we used a chamber pot that had to be emptied and cleaned every morning. Bedside stands were designed with a door in which to hide the " thunder pot" as it was called. We still have two of the cabinets: a maple set from my childhood room and an oak set of Nan's.

I was excited when Dad decided to build a concrete silo near the cattle yard beside the wooden stock water tanks. Day by day the workers added blocks until it towered over all the buildings on the farm. I thought it made our farm look prosperous, and I guess it was needed for a self-sustaining farm. Silage is fermented roughage made from chopped green corn stalks harvested in late summer. My Uncle George owned a silage-cutting machine, so Dad joined a work group called a "run" in order to fill our silo. Silage supplemented the hay given to cattle in the winter. I always thought cows loved it because it's warm and smells good.

Our silo was a circular concrete structure with an exterior ladder from top to bottom. On the chute side were wooden doors that could be fastened in while filling the silo, but then removed one by one as the silage was pitched out down the chute to a feed bunk where the cows were waiting.

Later, laborsaving electric unloaders were invented to unload the silage. But in my time on the farm, Dad always had to climb up the chute and pitch the silage down by hand. This was hard labor. He seldom asked me to help or to do this task for him. Many silos had a domed metal cover. Ours didn't.

Waking to Mourning Doves

I liked to climb those long ladders to peer inside. Dad didn't allow me to step on the slippery silage as it could dangerously slide out from under one's feet. He used great caution, but I worried about him anyway.

I have often wondered how long these monuments to family farms will stand. I love driving the countryside to see the many different types of silos commemorating the era of milk cows sustaining families so alive and happy on their little farms. It's fun to imagine the children doing their chores and helping with the house and yard work so that they could have time to play the games that children today have never heard of.

Eventually, Dad had a two-car garage built close to the house. Unfortunately, money ran out before a cement floor could be installed and it still has a bumpy dirt floor through which hardy climbing vines grow.

The structure I loved the most on our farmstead was the windmill. It is long gone, but a portion of the steel blade fan serves as a background in my cottage garden. Only a few of these silent sentinels remain near Beresford. I still get goose-bumps seeing the beauty of a windmill silhouetted against a South Dakota sunset.

Heine Henle, Beresford's well driller, drove his rig to our farm to drill a new water well, which we connected to our tall windmill. I guess that profession is gone too, and that's too bad. A windmill is one of the most energy efficient and ingenious ways ever devised to pump water from the ground. A windmill captures the energy of the wind with the large circular fan or blade wheel located at the top of the tower. When the wind blows, the fan rotates, catches the wind and is connected to the long rod moving up and down which connects to the mechanical gears that power the cylinder pump located deep underground in the aquifer. It makes sense harnessing the renewable power of the wind and using that energy to lift water to the surface for agricultural and other uses. In the United States, the development of water pumping windmills was the major factor in allowing the farming and ranching of vast areas of land which was otherwise devoid of readily accessible water. Windmills occurred where connection to electric power lines was not a realistic option.

The windmill pumped fresh, cold water into our stock tanks. The cattle made a beeline for the water tanks when they ambled home from a day in the grass pasture. The tanks often got slimy looking from cattle drool, but my friends and I still liked to jump in that tank on scorching summer days. Dad soon chased us out because he said it stirred up the slime so the cattle wouldn't drink. He never said we were in any danger of contagion! Once we threw a chicken in the tank to see if it could swim. It couldn't! Someone braver than me rescued it and we never told Mom. We kept goldfish in the tank and they reproduced like crazy. We watched the tiny fish grow to ten inches long. Dad must have thinned them out occasionally. I didn't like the feel of the fish slithering by and nipping on us when we sat in the tank. Finally, Dad gave up and bought a metal tank just for us kids.

Some of my family members climbed windmills without a trace of fear. Mom climbed to the very top to oil or fix the fan blades while Dad and I watched from the safety of the ground. I dared climb to the first rung, but that was it! My four-year-old cousin, Howard, climbed to the top of their windmill and his nine-year-old brother, Norman, climbed up and brought him down safely. I can imagine how terrified their parents must have been watching them.

PART II: FAMILY

Ragnar, Eva & Me

Parents & Me

Grandma Erickson

Nan Kinkner

Family Quilting

Claire & Clarence

Aunt Hazel

CHAPTER 3
Room Enough to Grow

A crewel embroidery made by my mother had the title, *"To love something is to give it room enough to grow."* It was a philosophy practiced by my hardworking parents as well as my extended family. In addition to giving me room to grow, they also imbued a strong work ethic. Idle hands were seldom seen in the Erickson and Kinkner families. If the women weren't doing household or outdoor chores or cooking, their hands were busy with a crochet hook, knitting needle or embroidery, crewel or quilting needles. Patching and mending along with beading and other crafts were a way to make do with what they had. The women inspired one another and taught and encouraged their daughters. The men kept busy maintaining farm machinery and doing the multitude of tasks necessary on a self-sustaining farm. A strong work ethic was passed down from generation to generation and we can see it in our daughters and granddaughters today.

Expressions of love, though rarely verbal, were readily apparent in family interactions. We cousins never doubted that we were loved and cherished by the whole extended family. Feelings ran deep but were seldom expressed, very common for Swedish families. Dad's Yankee family was a little more demonstrative, but I don't remember many hugs. My grandfather's German father died of alcoholism when Walt was 12 years old, so learning how to be a good father probably didn't happen for Grandpa. He was sometimes moody and never gave my father much credit or encouragement. For example, even later in life he didn't think my dad had the skill to plant corn. According to family legend, he always favored his daughter, Eva.

Mom says her father was stern, unforgiving and unapproachable, just the opposite of her mother. My parents were the youngest in their families and both of their mothers were over 40 when they were born. They both said they had happy childhoods, however, and were surrounded by lots of cousins, siblings and friends. My parent's relationship is a bit difficult to describe and be objective. They had known each other since childhood and lived only one mile apart as children. Neither ever lived farther than three miles from where they were born. They began dating in high school and didn't date many others. Being married at ages 19 and 20 in the middle of the Depression molded them into a hard working team to just survive. They lived with Dad's parents for nine years, which could not have been easy. Mom's diary indicates that

Waking to Mourning Doves

Dad got peeved easily and didn't always want to socialize with her family or friends. She often felt blue.

The pressure of being poor and living with parents as a young married couple would be difficult for anyone, but from the time I can remember, Mom and Dad had a pretty good marriage. They worked together on a daily basis, had common goals and did occasionally socialize with friends at dances and card parties. Dad's pet name for Mom was Verie and he often gave her a smooch while she was cooking or doing dishes. Women always wore housedresses and sometimes he tucked the back of her dress into her panties as she stood at the sink. He became much more affectionate and expressive as he got older, even after his stroke in 1985. Although he said mean things to all of us after the stroke, he often told me how he cared about me and appreciated my help.

Sometimes my parents argued, but it would be over quickly and neither seemed to carry a grudge. Volatility was what I got used to and it never seemed like a problem, and today I get over most things quickly myself. My parents never had to exert much discipline over me and knowing their high expectations kept me in line. I can't remember any threats, spankings or discipline. I just wasn't a troublemaker and I was eager to please my family.

As an only child, I was close to my mother and other adults because I spent so much time with them. Mom taught me many skills and her attitude through example formed my personality today. She was extremely social, though soft-spoken and reserved. I knew people liked her. " Sweet" sounds like a trite word, but I have heard many describe her that way. She went out of her way to help others. She served lunch to whoever came to her door, including workmen and salesmen from Watkins's, Fuller Brush and McConnen. Hospitality and kindness were ingrained in her personality.

Mom wore housedresses and aprons for most household tasks. She often had her fine brown hair up in bobby pins with a bandana knotted at the top of her head with the ends tucked underneath. For chores of milking and feeding chickens and field planting or cultivation, Mom wore jeans. Until the late 1940s, she always wore housedresses and aprons in the house, often faded and patched. She didn't use makeup except when she went out socially. A lotion, loose powder and rouge were carefully applied. Dad and I always waited patiently in the car while she slowly applied makeup and got dressed. Dad honked the Chevy's horn for her to hurry up, but we both knew it never did much good.

Dad wore striped bib overalls, often patched and stained with grease from his farming tasks. His shirts, light denim blue, showed wear around the collar, frayed cuffs and rips and tears that Mom patched. His caps, blue and white striped to match his overalls, covered his forehead to give him the recognizable "farmer's tan." In later years a collection of seed corn and farmers' elevator caps crowded the entry porch shelves. He must have had thirty or more and never threw any away. Sturdy rubber five-buckle boots allowed him to keep his feet dry in the mucky cow and hog yards after spring thaw or hard summer rains.

Dad had thick brown hair and deep, morning-glory-blue eyes. Mom's eyes were green as are mine. I was the only girl in the Kinkner and Erickson families that had blonde hair. Quite a few blonds turned up on the Jones side of the family, so it doesn't appear to be a Swedish trait in our family.

Garrulous might be a word that aptly describes my father, especially when talking to strangers. I took my parents on trips in later years, and Dad readily took up endless conversations with complete strangers. We literally had to start the car and attempt to leave before he'd quit. As a child, I often went to town with him to get gas or equipment repaired or to the grain elevator. His conversations seemed absolutely endless to an impatient child. He especially liked to talk to old Tim, the gas station attendant, where he bought his Copenhagen chewing tobacco. With spit and drool coming out of their mouths, Tim and Dad discussed everything from the state of the world to local gossip. My only compensation was an Orange Crush drink from the pop cooler or a penny's worth of peanuts and Boston baked-bean candy from the old-fashioned dispenser.

Although Dad sometimes balked at attending my school events and upset me at times, he usually came to the really important events in my life. I think he lacked some social confidence in larger groups, maybe due to the fact that his father didn't think he'd ever amount to anything and said so, a rather typical assessment of a wild teenage boy. After his marriage to Mom, he apparently proved himself capable and Grandpa Kinkner became his helper, not his boss.

When I was older, Dad, Mom and I worked as a team on the farm. There was rarely a lull in the table conversation, as we went over the events of the day and made plans for the next day's tasks. We always knew and understood each other's work and it made for a camaraderie that is unknown to young families these days. Our lives were more blended and most of the time it was positive. We did negotiate jobs, however. I much preferred driving the tractor, cooking, baking and gardening to milking cows and taking care of the chickens. There was so much work to do that shirking duties wasn't an option.

January 1950—We played canasta all the time about.
April 19, 1951—Went to the Little Oscar show and it was the best I'd ever seen.

Waking to Mourning Doves

May 22, 1952—Went to "Wabash Avenue" with Mom and Dad- a Betty Grable movie.

As a family, we had a lot of fun together. In the evening, after chores, we often played catch with a softball, tossed horseshoes and played croquet or cards. Dad always played with (teased) the dog a while and then came in for supper which often consisted of fried or creamed leftover potatoes, and eggs, either fried or deviled. Dad liked to eat raw onions. For breakfast, he liked peanut butter and mustard on bread, which he dipped in his coffee. Yuk! Another favorite was popcorn and milk and sometimes we made a supper of that.

We often went to a movie in town or to the Legion Hall where a traveling band called Little Oscar's put on plays and dances. Entire families attended and danced well into the night. I chuckle every time I remember my husband, Sherm, calling Little Oscar's his favorite music group in a high school interview. He hadn't been exposed to a lot of musical culture.

Mom writes: *I helped Dad farm in many fields and this could be on a Sunday after dinner too. We often worked late at night if it was getting late in the season. I drove the Massey Harris tractor for most of the time and I pulled the disc and drag and mower and I plowed with the tractor. I shocked grain and also picked corn by hand. I had never used a tractor before. Once when we picked corn by hand Dad hit me in the head with an ear of corn he was throwing in the wagon.*

My parents shared fieldwork and chore duties. Both drove tractors for plowing, cultivating, seeding and mowing. Both milked cows and pitched hay and manure. Mom usually did the "chicken chores" and Dad carried countless buckets of corn, oats and ground feed to livestock. He hoisted the heavy corrugated metal bushel basket up on his shoulders and dumped it in the bins to impatient squalling livestock. The pigs came running in a brawling squealing mass when he called, "souie, souie, souie." Their greedy behavior was predictable. They soon devoured the corn leaving piles of cobs we later gathered for the cook stove. We had a two-ring slatted corn crib near the barn from which Dad carried buckets to feed the pigs all winter. That was when corn was picked by hand instead of with large mechanized combines that harvest and shell in one operation.

Mom and Dad were a good team on the farm and they both worked very hard, yet had time for fun. They loved going to dances in Sioux Falls or to local dances. Mom's parents didn't approve of dancing, but Dad taught Mom when they were dating and it was a lifelong passion for them. They looked good on the dance floor, taking long strides in time with their favorite big band music. They even danced to the Lawrence Welk band at the Ritz Ballroom south of Beresford when Welk was just getting started. They were equally at ease at the large Arkota Ballroom in Sioux Falls or at the Beresford Legion Club or Ritz. Another couple or two usually joined them: Warren and Millie Reierson, Wayne and Lucille Wastell or Stanley and Ethel Smith.

I loved watching my parents get ready to go dancing because that is when they seemed the happiest. Mom tied a scarf on her brown hair, holding pin curls in place while she hurried to finish the milking and chicken chores. Dad dressed up in a suit and tie, put pomade Vaseline on his hair and slicked it back. Mom wore one of her better dresses, always asking Dad what he thought she should wear. He liked red, so she had several red dresses and skirts. After selecting a dress and straightening the seams in her nylons, she combed her hair and applied powder and rouge. Powder came in a box, Max Factor being her favorite brand. She dusted it on with a powder puff, so her nose wouldn't look shiny. What is wrong with a shiny nose, I will never know! Next, Mom straightened Dad's tie and they were ready to drop me off at one of my grandmother's or Aunt Eva's for the night. I never had a baby sitter at our house while growing up. I think they liked the privacy of having me gone once in a while.

November 24, 1952– Dad is teaching me to dance.

Dad taught me how to dance in our living room as we waltzed to the scratchy Philco phonograph. When company came, we occasionally danced too. Several of my friends danced their first tentative steps on our non-glide carpet. My parents loved dancing and missed going to dances after Dad's stroke in 1985. They had their first and last dances together, the last at my daughter Michelle's wedding in 1987. When Dad stumbled, Mom steadied him, just as she had in many aspects of their lives.

I learned to drive our tractor at age ten. It didn't have today's comforts of a radio, phone, computer, or an air-conditioned enclosed cab. Farmers were out in the elements, rain or shine. We farmed land a couple miles away and that tractor ride could be long, slow and cold, or scorching hot in the summer with only a floppy umbrella for sun protection. Criss-crossing the fields all day could be boring, but having a breakdown or getting stuck miles from home was what I most feared.

A 1949 Ford was the first car that my parents bought brand new. It was several years after World War II ended and people were feeling prosperous again. I tagged along when we went to the garage in town and walked up and down the aisles looking at the shiny new cars. We chose a light grey four-door

Waking to Mourning Doves

sedan. It had a push-button starter and a shift on the floorboard. It seemed sleek, rich and luxurious to me after the clunker Chevys we had been driving. The rich dark grey upholstery was something I could sink down into. It didn't have running boards and was the beginning of a new look in cars; not that stubby rounded look, but a beginning of the longer-line, finned atrocities that were in vogue a few years later. Dad had the car painted a light celery green a few years later and bought flashy white sidewalls and mud flaps which never served any purpose that I could see.

February 14, 1951–Went to town with Dad and I drove.

It was an easy transition to drive a car, since I was familiar with shifting and using a clutch on the tractor. At eleven years old I was allowed to drive the 1938 Chevy in our yard and pasture, but I longed to get behind the wheel of our new car. In less than a year, I got my wish when Dad let me drive the country roads to town if he was along. Little did he know that I had been driving the Chevy to town when he thought I was going to my grandparent's house!

The 1949 Ford eventually became my car when I drove to high school, summer jobs and college. That little car responded to my heavy foot as I drove 90 mph over well- oiled country roads. It had its advantages being built high off the ground when I drove over muddy dirt or flooded roads and into stubble fields as a part of my summer extension job in 1957.

There is nothing to compare to Mom's old wood cook stove on crisp fall days. A soft crackling of cobs and kindling burning gave promise of warmth and security, and the teakettle making a faint whistling sigh was sheer comfort. I was always amazed at how Mom knew just how to build a fire for whatever use she planned for the stove. Cold mornings called for a fast hot fire that would heat up the kitchen and get water boiling quickly. As it cooled down, she might slap pancakes right on the stovetop using the coal-black surface as a griddle. Pans placed on top of the firebox heated quickly and slow cooking was provided further back. The reservoir held warm water. The warming oven at the top of the stove held potholders as well as food to be kept warm. Bread left there while dinner was being prepared would be warm and tender.

The cob container stood near the stove firebox and had to be filled daily. I often gathered cobs from the shelled corn, which was piled in a rosy red, cone-shaped heap, surrounded by slatted burgundy snow fencing. As a winter of snow and ice came, it became more difficult to pry the cobs loose. The best cobs were in the hog yard, leavings of the noisy pigs that had just had their supper. Grandma Erickson liked to gather cobs in the hog yard and she always asked me to come along and help, often to hold the basket. I think she liked to spend the time alone with me. We had wonderful conversations as the farm sounds and pungent smells surrounded us. She always treated me like I was an interesting person, as did most of the adults in my life.

The house felt cold on winter mornings even though the wood furnace was banked carefully by Mom the night before. When I was little, I stayed in bed until it sounded like the kitchen fire was going and then I dashed down the stairs and got dressed by the warm stove. Mom stood me on the open oven door and dressed me; complete with an undershirt and long brown stockings held up by a garter belt. I always loved the way that wood stove heated up the kitchen so quickly in the morning. I hated those ugly brown stockings though! I only wore white stockings "for good."

We had a wood and coal-burning furnace in the basement for heating the house and I feared the belching popping noises it made. The spidery arms (heat chutes) emanating from the furnace heated the first floor pretty well, but only a couple of heat registers in the ceilings allowed the heat to rise upstairs where we slept. Water often froze in the glasses at night. Mom always stoked and banked the furnace before going to bed, so coal and wood held some residual heat until morning.

Mom has always been an extraordinarily good cook in the basics. Sherm married me expecting me to be able to make gravy like she did, but that has rarely happened. Using rich, separated cream never hurt any dish (except for cholesterol watchers, I suppose). I especially liked her creamed peas, asparagus, cabbage, corn, potatoes and homemade ice cream. Still some of my favorites to eat or make. She made great lemon meringue pie, white bread and chocolate pudding as well as many specialty desserts. She let me experiment and cook by her side and didn't seem to mind my messes. I had a toy baking set with small cookie cutters and a rolling pin and Mom let me use real cookie dough with them.

Baking bread in a wood cook-stove was well regulated by Mom. After breakfast she mixed up the dough using potato water saved in the icebox from the day before. The bread was set to rise in a big enamel dishpan on the back of the stove and covered with a damp flour sack or embroidered dishtowel. As it rose and was punched down twice, a yeasty smell gave promise of things to come. At last the dough was ready to put in pans to become cinnamon loaves or rolls, small buns for company dinners and loaves of rich, thick crusty bread. Mom threw in wood to fire up the cook-stove to 350 degrees. Keeping the heat steady, the bread was soon sending out irresistible odors and was ready to take steaming out of the pans. Mom slathered the loaf tops with home-churned butter to keep the crusts soft. I preferred them crusty! I could barely wait to grab a thick slab to spread with my favorite wild grape jelly.

We made cottage cheese with whole milk from our cowherd. Mom mixed rennet tablets with the milk and put the mixture on the back of the stove for several days. Then she separated the curds from the whey and a fine, slightly sour-tasting product emerged. I have never found that taste duplicated in commercial cottage cheese.

One night when Mom and Dad were out milking cows, I made chocolate cupcakes. No measurements, just dumping in what I thought Mom usually used. I fired up the cook stove and had them baked for supper. They were awful. Too much soda and salt, but Dad ate two of them just like they were the best he had ever tasted. Encouragement and support like that was important to me and Daddy knew it. In my 4-H days I baked and baked, as we got "credit" for it in our foods projects. Dozens and dozens of baking powder biscuits, cakes and cookies were charted on my 4-H check sheet.

> *April 2, 1950–George's, Grandma's, Harold Nelson's, Elmer's, Eva's and Nan came to Ma's b'day- she got an electric mixer.*

Getting our first Hamilton Beach mixer in the '50s was like a miracle and we tried all the recipes in the accompanying book. All cakes and baked goods were made from scratch then. I still prefer that method. Box mixes are quick to make, but never taste quite as good. That old mixer still works perfectly.

Small appliances were built to last – and so were relationships.

> *February 2, 1958–Mom and Dad celebrated their 25th anniversary at church- lots of guests and it went over well- Janet O and I played duets and Lily made a cute poem.*

The church where the celebration was held was the United Church of Christ in Beresford. Since they had had a small wedding, we celebrated their 25th as we did later for their 40th, 45th and 50th anniversaries with open houses at the church. I felt happy wearing my new red wool dress, playing piano duets with Janet, and entertaining all of their friends and neighbors. Mom wore a silver grey suit with a corsage and looked young and pretty. I was always proud of her slim figure and good looks. Dad looked pretty snappy in his new blue double-breasted suit too. I was glad that Hazel and Ragnar, their wedding attendants, attended the festivities.

Looking back, I can see that life with my parents programmed my career, attitudes and values. I thought Mom let Dad have his way too much and I was determined to never be a doormat as a wife. Maybe that's why I became strong-willed, not always a virtue. It is not too difficult to see how my ideas of a life/marriage partnership were formed. Sherm's mother, as well as mine, were dominated by their husbands and the wives catered to every whim and wish. Ella even had to quit a job she loved because Ed didn't want her to work as a school lunch cook.

Independence was something I'd tasted, especially by working as an Extension Home Economist for two summers during college. During most of my childhood, there were plenty of confidence-building experiences such as 4-H, spelling contests, good grades, music performances and high school activities. I viewed marriage as a partnership in which my opinions and input were equal to my husband's. Well, sometimes I overdid that, but Sherm wasn't comfortable with conflict due to his childhood experience of seeing family avoid it, so he may have given in to my desires rather than argue.

The women of my generation have very different lives from our mothers'. For one thing, we got college degrees and worked outside the home and became more independent. Granted, what we observed in our parents' and grandparents' marriages influenced us, but we were a transition generation. Now our daughters work and are independent too. How much their marriages are influenced by observing ours, I don't know, but their husbands bring a whole set of values and ideas that have to be blended too.

CHAPTER 4

Reflections in a Cracked Mirror

When it came time to bury my grandpa, my grandma had to ask his natty, alcoholic brother, Fred, for a suit jacket in which the neighbors could view him at the wake.

Throughout his life Grandpa said, "Why on earth would I want a suit, the horses and cows think I look just fine in these patched, old striped bib overalls. No one complains if I wear clean overalls to church on Sunday."

After years of watching his father destroying his life with alcohol and dying of cirrhosis of the liver at age 38, Grandpa vowed to escape the stranglehold that alcohol had on his father. He succeeded, whereas his brother did not. Grandpa, with the assistance of two maternal uncles, had to drop out of school and begin farming for family survival at age 12. Consequently, Grandpa became a no-nonsense, frugal father-figure to younger siblings.

Clutching the handles of a single-bottom, horse-drawn plow as the deep black soil turned over must have been difficult for my 12-year-old grandfather, while he tried to become the man of the family. Losing his father was difficult, as was leaving school to plant, cultivate and pick corn, cut, shock and thresh grain, pitch and stack hay, and keep invasive weeds cut and controlled. There was wood to be cut and split for fuel as well as animals to care for. His little brother and sisters weren't much help as he tried to do a man's work.

Years of youthful hard labor in the fertile fields of Illinois hewed my grandpa into a strikingly handsome man with a six-foot willowy frame of solid muscle topped in later years by a thick shock of white hair. His square jaw and well-proportioned features made those magical brown eyes sparkle. To me, his only grandchild, he was perfection, with large gentle hands that always sought mine, and his unending patience with the questions and exuberance of a little girl who never wanted to leave his side.

"Why does it look like rain tomorrow? I can't see it."

"Why do I have freckles and you don't?"

"Why can't I milk that cow?"

"Why doesn't Nan have whiskers?"

These questions were always answered as if they truly mattered.

My mother often told me, "Walt became a different person after you were born."

Thoughtfully, she said, "He used to be moody and go off by himself for a day or two at a time, but he could hardly wait to get to the house after chores to play with you. Walt was the one who walked the floor with you at night, fed you the bottle and rocked you to sleep." No wonder I bonded to him so early.

In 1941, Grandpa mortgaged his farm and helped my parents buy 80 acres. For many years, they took out new mortgages in the spring to buy seed and supplies and paid it back in the fall after harvesting the crops. After nine years of living together, we finally lived in separate homes. Living only a half mile apart, though, we saw each other often.

One sultry summer afternoon, Grandpa and Dad labored putting up a wooden seated swing between two giant ash trees in our yard. The free-range chickens and I watched in suspense as they climbed wobbly wooden ladders and placed the long metal pole between two parallel branches. Finally the ropes were in place and I climbed on. Flying through the air clinging to the ropes and learning to pull myself higher and higher brought cheers and encouragement from the special men in my life.

When I was in second grade, Grandpa and Dad took me to town to choose my new Monarch – a wide-tired, sapphire-blue bike. My happiness was almost too much to contain. Sweating, struggling, flopping sideways, and yes, swearing under my breath, I learned to ride my bike on our uneven dirt yard that day. Overhearing the occasional cuss word from the menfolk had enlarged my forbidden vocabulary.

Worried, Grandpa said, "She's going to get overhet." Those were his words. "She should quit for a while but she's too stubborn to quit."

Fortunately, it was a girl's bike, so planting my feet on solid ground was easy when tipping and swerving began.

Walking the half mile from home to Grandpa's farm gave me time to gather clutches of wildflowers from the ditches to give Nan: mayflower, wild prickly roses, daisies, black eyed Susan, vervain, mullein, clover and delicate, early-spring pasque flowers. Sometimes a couple of faithful cats followed me anticipating a snack from Nan or maybe a tasty mouse or gopher caught on our trek.

Nan thrust freshly made, tart lemonade in the summer or hot chocolate with marshmallows in cool weather into my waiting hands upon arrival at their house. We sat around the table and talked, munching whatever treat emerged from Nan's oven and then I climbed on Grandpa's lap in the big oak rocker and read Dick, Jane and Sally to him. One would think it was Richard Burton reading Shakespeare as he listened to my halting efforts.

Grandpa might be described as a Renaissance man. He played rousing

Waking to Mourning Doves

fiddle tunes for waltzes and jigs at community dances accompanied by my grandma on piano or steel-string guitar. Neither of them had training or lessons, but music and rhythm were a part of their lives. Teaching me to play the piano by ear and chord accompaniment let me join the family band after the years of Nan and Grandpa's "roll back the rug" house parties of the early 1900s. In the 1940s Mom played banjo and Dad ukulele as I joined them jamming by lamplight after chores were finished.

One momentous day, representatives of the Rural Electrical Association (REA) came to our country road, and we hooked up to the miracle of electricity in the late 1940s. I still remember the electrician crawling under the houses in the dirt crawl spaces stringing wires and the thrill of the first flash of electric lights when he threw the switch.

Grandpa had many interests including an amazing collection of good books for someone who only completed the eighth grade. Stacks of 78-RPM records ranged from classical to the silly one I loved the most, *The Whistler and His Dog."* How I loved winding up that old Victrola record player on the library table in Grandpa's bedroom and choosing a stack of favorite records to play.

When Grandpa and I went to town, he visited with all the shopkeepers and whomever he met on the street. I was proud of him, as folks seemed to like him and ask his opinion and best of all, he didn't go to the saloon and smell of alcohol like his brother, Fred. There was always an extra nickel in his pocket for a Hershey bar or a cherry nut ice cream cone for "my little girl" as he called me.

My grandparent's families settled in southeast South Dakota arriving while it was still a territory in the 1880s. Both families attended the rural Gothland Congregational Church and that's where they met. Grandpa, being 13 years older than Nan, must have noticed her Chautauqua personality and quick wit when she was 18 and he, 31. They were a good match: Grandpa's stoicism and Nan's one-woman, life-of-the-party sideshow persona. The minister read their wedding bans in that quiet little wooden church beneath the largest cottonwood tree in the county. A simple, no- fuss wedding ceremony was held in the house where I spent my formative years. I go to the deserted Gothland Cemetery now to visit ancestors' graves, and the native prairie grasses thrust up and cling to ancient gravestones. My roots go as deep as theirs to that former endless native prairie I call home.

Grandpa must have thought having a suit and tie vital in his younger days, as in his wedding portraits he appears in a dark suit, white shirt and matching white bow tie. In the photos his bushy drooping mustache reminds me of the countless times I stroked it, teased him about the food or beverage nesting there or the delight I took in seeing him drink from his mustache cup. Even now I can close my eyes and imagine running my hands or comb through his thick mane of white hair. I loved to style his hair with metal curlers and bobby pins, wave set, barrettes and ribbons and he endured it all as if he were in a fine beauty salon. Sometimes his short stubble of white beard brushed my cheeks and made me giggle in delight. Other times he'd purposely slurp Nan's thick creamy potato onion soup so that remnants would stick to his beard. Grandpa could balance a row of peas on his dinner knife blade and somehow get them in his mouth without dropping a single one — a trick I still can't master. Lathering up his face from the worn brush in his pewter shaving mug, he'd grin at me, take out his straightedge razor blade, sharpen it on his leather strop, and the whiskers would come off in a single stroke. I still have the cracked mirror in which I loved seeing his reflection, and now my wrinkled face and hair match his.

Tagging along behind Grandpa was pure joy as he painstakingly brushed, curried, fed and talked to the huge workhorses each evening. Goldie's caramelized honey color contrasted with Babe's warm violet black coat.

"Well, Babe and Goldie, we got half that field plowed today. How 'bout a bucket of oats in your trough. I'll go to the haymow and throw down some timothy and alfalfa hay. You just rest there awhile."

Grandpa sidled between the two horses and murmured, "I'll curry the burrs off your legs and tail. Maybe Caryl will bring you some carrots or sugar cubes. She might even ride on your back when we go out to get another drink from the well."

Whistling happily, he suddenly stopped and sighed, "Oh, Goldie why didn't you do that when we were outside, oh well, I'll just get the shovel and scoop it up."

Uttering low comforting sounds he whispered, "That's a girl. Steady now. Let's check your hooves. Looks like we need to give you a new horseshoe in the morning. Maybe we can finish that field tomorrow before the rain comes. Steady there now. Let me get between you and brush off your backs. I know it's hard for you to reach."

As he heard Nan coming to the barn to help milk the cows, he muttered to the horses, "I'm not going to let you out tonight to roll in the pasture. I'm tired too, and there's still the milking chores to do."

"C'boss, c'boss, are the cows all in, Ma? Here comes your little friend. She's holding out something in her hand for you."

My legs stuck straight out when Grandpa hoisted me onto Goldie's steaming back as he led the horses to the water tank for a drink. My clothes got sopped, dirty and horsy smelling, but no one seemed to mind. I giggled

Waking to Mourning Doves

with pleasure as we ambled back to the barn and Grandpa gave me a hug and whisker rub as he plopped me on the ground.

Farming with horses was Grandpa's preferred mode and he never learned to drive a tractor very well, always preferring his animal friends. He taught me to love and care for all animals, everything from grooming to pitching pungent manure. He tried driving a car a few times, but after hitting barbed wire fences, wooden gates and driving in and out of a few too many ditches, Nan and my dad convinced him to stick with the horses and buckboard wagon for transportation. One might call him a distracted driver. A recurring nightmare of mine is being in a car with Grandpa as a little girl and having to commandeer the steering wheel when he couldn't drive. Thank goodness it was only a dream.

Walking through the pastures and woods with Grandpa was as sweet as the ambrosia for which Nan won a cooking contest. Temptations popped up everywhere. Grandpa didn't encourage a little girl like me to climb on the seat of the whetstone on which he perched to sharpen knives and mower blades, but I did it anyway, pedaling as fast as my short stubby legs could go. When Grandpa wasn't looking, I'd spit on the salt block set out for the cows, rub it clean with grubby hands and take a few licks for myself.

Nan scolded us saying, " Pa, you need to watch that girlie. She'll get sick. Why does she do that? Maybe we should tell Verie." (My mother, Elvera, was often called Verie by the Kinkner family).

Grandpa and Nan had a German shepherd, Fritz, who was adored by everyone. One day while he was expertly herding cows by nipping their heels, a skittish cow kicked and mortally wounded him. It took a long time for Grandpa to think about replacing him. When he finally did, the new puppy, Bowser, suffered the same fate. I watched as big tears rolled down Grandpa's face when Bowser had to be put down. We marked his grave near the mound of stones that had been removed from the fields. Grandpa vowed to never own and get attached to another dog. .

Using a flat stone boat (an eight by ten foot wood or metal container on skids) pulled by Goldie, the whole family trudged through the plowed fields picking up the glacial stones that rose up to the surface each spring like popcorn. I loved being outside on those first balmy days of spring and felt useful as I dashed over the plowed clods of dirt picking up stones. Hearing them clunk as they collided on the stone boat made a sharp staccato accompaniment to the red-winged blackbirds' angry outbursts as we approached their nesting sites.

In Grandpa's later years, he slowed down as Dad and Mom assumed more of the strenuous farm work. During corn picking time, he strapped the leather and metal corn picking husker to his palm and insisted on joining my parents in the harvest. His strong hands never forgot the rhythm of breaking off the ripe ear, running the iron shank down the side of the ear, removing the husk in one quick twist and tossing the clean ear against the wagon sideboard. A steady drumbeat of 60 bushels per acre in a good year filled the wagon to the brim. Corn picking machines were not available until the late 1940s. Today, the farm produces up to 200 bushels per acre and is harvested by combine in a matter of hours instead of days.

One crisp fall morning after the corn, still on the cob, was neatly stowed in the crib, Grandpa grabbed his milking pail and headed for the barn.

I was hurrying to pull on my new red boots to follow him when it happened. In a panic, I shouted to Nan, "Grandpa fell down by the barn door and he's not getting up."

We ran to the barn, scattering chickens as we went and Nan shouted, "Go call your daddy and tell him to get Doc Lietzke. If someone is talking on the line, tell them you need the phone, cuz I think Grandpa just had a stroke."

At only five years old, I had never ever called anyone on this old crank phone, but observing Nan countless times, I knew what to do. Amidst tears and panic, I rang the operator on our party line and screamed, "23F111," my parent's number and nobody answered.

On party lines everyone picks up and listens and Hertha, our neighbor lady, heard me crying and asked, "Caryl, sweetie, is that you? What's wrong?"

I blurted out, "Get my folks and call Doc Lietzke cuz Grandpa maybe had a stroke and we need help."

Hertha took over and soon the doctor and most of the concerned neighbors who had listened on the 15-family party line rushed up the long driveway to assist. A couple of burly farmers carried Grandpa into the house on strong shoulders and placed him in the guest bedroom. In the 1940s, stroke victims were kept at home and rarely got therapy. Their total care fell on family members. Nan asked Grandpa's favorite cousin, Lida, to help and together they slowly and tenderly nursed him back to health. Weakness was the major long-term effect of the stroke. His hard-working days were ended, but the silver lining was that he had more time to spend with me.

Some time later Nan said, "Honey girl, you're the light of his life and he wanted to get better so he could play with you."

For three more years we were pals in quieter activities: reading, listening to records on the old wind-up Victrola, or just sitting on the open porch watching the day go by and listening to the lullaby sounds around us.

Sticky blood cells build up and clog veins and arteries and the potential is always lurking and waiting to attack again.

One day Dad came to pluck me from my 4th grade class and said, "Grandpa wants to see you." He spoke very softly and looked sad.

"What's wrong?" I fearfully asked, grabbing my coat and lunch pail as we walked to the car.

Dad said, "Doc Leitzke came this morning and there's a blood clot in Pa's leg."

"Well, can't they fix it?" I asked, thinking doctors could fix anything.

"No," Dad replied. I knew he felt too choked up to say more.

Before the days of Coumadin and blood thinners, the choices with a blood clot were amputation or fear that gangrene would set in bringing a painful death. At age 77, Grandpa chose not to have an amputation, and gangrene did set in quickly and we watched him fade away. His last two days, he tried to eat ice cream and swallow water to please me, but the toxins soon built up and claimed his life.

When Grandpa died, the undertaker quietly took him away in his long black hearse. The next time I saw Grandpa, he seemed peacefully asleep lying on a flat surface covered with a garish green/gold patterned coverlet. We have a photo of that scene and it still gives me the shivers I felt as a child. Nan wanted me to touch him. He felt firm and ice cold. As a child growing up with animals, I saw death often, but my first experience of losing someone I loved was totally different.

I remember getting ready to go to Grandpa's funeral. Mom took pride in fastening a big white bow atop the curls she made in my straight blonde hair. I dreaded dress-up events that required curly hair. To make curls Mom stuck the metal curling iron in the lamp chimney to heat it. Cringing as the hot iron approached my scalp may be the reason I am still squeamish with electric curling irons.

Funeral parlors have a way of casting a spell over mourners. Strange smells bombard the senses. Is it the distasteful chemical smell or is it the combination of flowers, tobacco smoke, body odors and the tearful expressions of grief? Somber background music played as friends and neighbors hugged and expressed sympathy to my family. These same folks brought mounds of cakes, pies, breads and hot dishes to our houses after his death.

As if in a time warp, I can place myself in that room as if it were yesterday. I felt isolated as the only child at the wake and didn't quite understand or accept the finality of death. As I sat there in that dimly lit funeral parlor all dressed up in my curly hair, turquoise velvet jumper, white long stockings and new patent leather shoes, several ladies told me, "You look so pretty, honey, you're going to miss Grandpa aren't you?"

As we sat in that dim barren funeral parlor Nan said, "Grandpa's in heaven now."

I didn't like that idea and thought, "No, he's right here with me and he always will be."

Now I'm only a few years younger than he was in 1947 and indeed he still is with me. You never lose the people you love. Grandpa taught me that lesson at an early age.

Chapter 5

Grandma's Time Capsule

Intense grief over the loss of her 26-year-old daughter, Edna, caused my Swedish grandmother, Edla Erickson, to abandon her sewing basket in 1937. As I look at this small chestnut wicker basket now, Grandma's hand seems to be on my shoulder urging me to tell her story 73 years later. I am one of the last to remember. It brings tears to my eyes thinking I am the first to touch this forgotten basket since my Grandma's hands put it away. Although I was born after her death, family anguish of losing their beloved Edna seeped into my psyche long ago.

For decades Grandma's sewing basket lay silent waiting for someone to discover the artifacts that tell of joyous family times and unthinkable sorrow. Its contents – some I could recall vividly and others I could only imagine – compelled me to unlock its secrets.

In 1998 when Mom and I helped prepare for the Erickson estate sale, we discovered the basket in a dark corner of a storage closet. We uncovered its contents layer by layer. Needlework activities of 30 years by the four Erickson sisters and their mother came alive in the vintage fabrics and clippings.

The trauma that closed the basket for so long is reflected in the faded brownish funeral flowers wrapped in crumbling cellophane that sealed the basket with the same finality as Edna's coffin. Carnations, rose petals, daisies and ferns have the lingering fragrance of exhausted potpourri, and dry petals fell like tears onto my lap.

Under the flowers was a hand-sewn quilt block in shades of brown and coral. Was this a quilt block Edna had been piecing? Since I have seen all of the quilts the Erickson sisters completed, this one is a mystery. Maybe it is a memento of Edna's last sewing project. Perfectly stitched, it shows the skill of an accomplished quilter.

Tucked under the quilt block were four postcards from 1935–37, and the basket also contained a treasure trove of other postcards. I found four tucked inside a Christmas card from Valeria, the teacher who replaced Edna at the Gothland School and boarded with the Ericksons for several years, sharing a room with my Aunt Hazel.

There's a postcard of Pinecrest Tourist Campgrounds, Deadwood, South Dakota dated September 2, 1933, and postmarked Sturgis, SD. Edna writes, "Dear Mother, Enjoyed a good rest last nite as we stopped early. I decided not to go to the Bell's as that would take most of this day there and then I wouldn't be settled at all. The picture is of the camp where we stayed Thursday evening and yesterday we saw Crystal Cave which was neat and we also went through the gold mine at Lead. With love, Edna."

My Uncle Clarence drove his sisters Alice and Edna to teach in western rural schools in South Dakota where they boarded with families in desolate areas. My mother married in 1933 and missed the opportunity of travel and adventure with her siblings. Clarence, Alice and Edna also drove to the Chicago World's Fair in 1933.

Two more postcards from Mayo Clinic in Rochester, Minnesota dated June 22 and 24, 1935 from Hazel tell the frustration of getting her face treated after Doctor Hoard in Beresford tried to cure her acne in 1935 and severely burned her. She writes, "I am at the Worrall Hospital now for treatment. Came here about 1:30 p.m. and will be here for a week or so and after getting out hard telling how long I'll have to stay. If I only get over this I won't care. Dad was supposed to get in to have treatments too, but they are so filled up at the hospital."

The Mayo Clinic is two hundred miles from Beresford, a long drive by slow cars of the '30s. Grandpa Erickson was in the Colonial Hospital at Mayo getting treatment. I'm not sure what his problem was, but he had fallen from a tree and injured his back, causing problems for several years before his death in 1938.

Later, Hazel writes, "We have already been gone a week and it seems much longer. I had my first light treatment this morning and my face has been awfully sore. I am not in bed, just staying in my room with packs on my face; Edna and Alice came back from Minneapolis last night."

Hazel's burned face never improved and she spent her life somewhat disfigured and self-conscious around strangers. Her fun-loving personality made her everyone's favorite aunt and she was like a second mother to her seven nieces and nephews.

Edna moved home to teach at Gothland rural school in 1936 and after experiencing several months of debilitating headaches, took the train to Mayo Clinic accompanied by her brother, George.

A postcard dated Friday, March 26, 1937 from Edna reads " I have been at the clinic today and still have a test for tomorrow. I have a tumor back of the eyes so will have to have an operation next week."

Edna died after surgery on March 31, 1937 with her devastated family by her side. Shattered, Grandma, Mom and Uncle George gathered her belongings and accompanied her lifeless body home on the train. Edna's clutch purse, which I found, contains her Mayo appointment records, an embroidered handkerchief and a powder compact with two letters she had written to her mother. A silent memorial that still carries the aroma of her face powder.

Buried deeper in the sewing basket, coral Indianhead fabric showcases sampler stitches that Edna learned with her mother and sisters. These embellishments later appeared in Edna's embroidery projects, and I recognize some stitches that became the basis of my mother's crewel embroidery. The Erickson sisters' rich history of creating embroidery, crochet and quilting pieces inspire their descendants today. Cousins Gwen, Ruth, Janice, and I learned from these women and have tried to pass their skills to our daughters and granddaughters.

The next layer of the sewing basket holds two crocheted pieces made by my grandmother; a floral top for a camisole undergarment and a square with a star design. Were these for Edna? We will never know.

Grandma didn't follow patterns when crocheting or cooking. She looked at an item and then made it. Likewise, no handwritten recipes exist from her, as she cooked by taste and memory. I remember European style rye, wheat and white breads and crunchy rusks made from biscuits served with sharp cheese. Grandma's specialties were lutefisk, thin pancakes and ost kaka, a cheesecake made from fresh cream and rennet tablets. Mom remembers barrels of fresh frozen herring purchased in town. Links of homemade beef and pork sausage stuffed into clean intestines were packed in the snow bank for winter storage. My family still made potato sausage until the last years in the 1990s. Homegrown organic foods gave Grandma's six children a healthy start and her daughters became incredible cooks.

Although a petite lady standing less than five feet tall, Grandma Erickson had the strength of steel as she guided her family through hard times. Her frugality is a trait that became ingrained in her descendants. Nothing speaks to that more clearly than the nylon stocking repair kit and a tiny spool of silk thread from the basket. Delicate weaving is a challenge and hand darned socks are an example. I still think I should darn socks with holes in the toe or heel and I learned that skill from Mom.

Cardboard quilt templates and scraps of fuchsia and yellow fabric match several quilts on my quilt rack made by Mom or Grandma. Her crochet hook and tatting shuttle represent skills I wish I could have learned from her.

A November 1929 Household magazine page advertises chic, flapper-fashion patterns to order. The reverse page is titled "Patchwork Attuned to Modern Home." The Friendship basket pattern deeper in the pile is Mom's friendship wreath quilt pattern, her first bright pink and calico quilt used by my eldest daughter Michelle. Mom thought the hot pink was garish. Another

Household magazine page shows colored patterns Grandma admired. Patterns were 15 cents each or two for 25 cents.

The reverse side advertises Uneeda Bakers Nabisco sugar wafers. Nostalgic feelings overwhelm me as I close the basket with the faded flowers. Who will open it again when I am a dim memory? Maybe a great grandchild will read my story and feel Grandma's presence too.

So what made Grandma Edla memorable? To me, her adventurous spirit and grit stand out. Born one of five children in Normlosa, Osterjutland, Sweden in 1870, she told me of her happy childhood days as we sat at the breakfast table in the 1940s. She sucked her coffee through a sugar cube as I listened to my Rice Krispies snap, crackle and pop.

She took great delight in teaching me to count to twelve in Swedish and how to say butter and little girl and little boy. As I remember it, the numbers sound like *"en, twoo, thray, feda, fam, sax, whough, ott, neea, teeah, elve, tar."* Butter was *schmarr* in Swedish, and *litta flika* and *litta pike* are little girl and boy. She never lost her thick Swedish brogue. Hazel, Clarence and George also carried an accent, as they didn't learn English until they started school. As the surprise child Grandma had at age 43, my mother wasn't included in the children's family portrait, nor did she acquire a Swedish accent. She could, however, recite a table prayer in Swedish and she reluctantly said that prayer at our family gatherings in Minnesota until August 2008, her last visit. I wonder if Mom still felt slightly embarrassed to be born of immigrant parents or if she just didn't like to be the center of attention. The Erickson siblings were not encouraged to retain Swedish ways. They were Americans and proud of it.

How I wish some of Grandma's adventures had been written down, but her love of Sweden and its traditions inspired me to travel there in 1983 and find her ancestral home, as well as research and teach adult education classes in crafting Swedish straw and wood curl ornaments and other Swedish traditions. I think Grandma would have approved.

Losing her father to heart problems as a six-year-old child in 1876 must have been difficult for Grandma. Her mother, with the help of her two brothers, struggled to keep the family together and eke out a living on a small farm. Little sisters, Clara and Christine, died in infancy. Another sister, Emma, was born just after her father died.

The children walked across the meadows to church and school in Normlosa, sites my husband and I visited in 1983. Wildflowers she described grew in profusion in fields and ditches and brilliant red poppies dotted the landscape. I felt Grandma's presence guiding us as we found her home still inhabited by her uncle's descendants. A photo from one hundred years ago

Waking to Mourning Doves

looked the same; even the birch trees were in the same location. The small front porch had been removed and stored behind a barn.

Grandma's older brother, Andrew, emigrated to America in 1882 and Grandma and brother, Carl, came in 1888, to join Andrew in Clarinda, Iowa. Bible verses noted in her Swedish Bible dealing with fear indicate a frightening journey by sea on the Alaska ship. This same ship hit an iceberg and sank on its way back to Sweden. Grandma and her Carlson siblings planned to bring their mother, Johanna, and sister, Emma, to America, but they died within a year of the children's departure: the mother of a heart attack and Emma of tuberculosis. A floral picture woven from their brown hair and a somber photo is the only physical connection we have to them.

After working in Dayton, Boone and Des Moines, Iowa as a hotel maid and for a family (Bergquist) whose son later became the governor of Minnesota, she followed her brother, Andrew, to the Brooklyn Township area near Beresford in 1895. Per August Erickson and Grandma were married on Christmas day 1897, and they farmed in the Komstad area until they purchased the family farm in 1898, for $25 an acre from my father's Grandpa Jones. These families have been intertwined for several generations in churches, schools and marriages, not always having the same viewpoints on many things.

The Kinkner-Jones families were more unrestrained boisterous folks who enjoyed having a good time and attended the liberal Congregational Church. They enjoyed parties, dancing and Nan's brother, Henry, even operated a pool hall in which beer was sold.

My Dad said, "Grandpa Jones was a lot of fun, but he sure wasn't a financial manager." Oddly enough, the Erickson family often purchased land the Jones family lost due to poor management.

The Ericksons, on my mother's side of the family, were strict conservative Evangelical Swedish Lutherans and followed what I felt were the restrictions of their church faithfully. Grandpa Erickson's stern no-nonsense demeanor clashed repeatedly with Great Grandpa Jones on the Gothland School board according to family lore. Mom said her father was as cold and unapproachable as her mother was warm and loving. Maybe these long feuds with the Jones family were part of the reason Grandpa Erickson refused to attend Mom's marriage to my Dad at the Kinkner home. I never met Grandpa Erickson, but it is difficult to imagine how his sons and grandsons could be men that I adored, if he was that distant. Granted, he denied Mom piano lessons and a college education, but she may have been more of a hell raiser than her three sisters. It is hard to imagine that as I knew her. He probably thought her chances of

Caryl Crozier

marriage and a man to support her would only waste a college education, similar to opinions voiced by my dad as I approached college years.

I can only speculate on the relationship between my grandparents, because Grandpa died before I was born and the family rarely talked about him. I can only surmise that he was a strict disciplinarian and a typical unexpressive Swede. His father died young and he and his brothers and sisters lived a hardscrabble life as lumberjacks in the northern Swedish forests in Varmland, thus their immigration to America in the late 1800s. Grandpa came to the Swedish settlement near Beresford and worked as a hired man until his marriage to my grandmother ten years later. He worked hard and expected the same from his children. Four brothers, three sisters and their mother, Karin, left Sweden and scattered to Texas, Canada and Minnesota. One brother was killed in a logging accident in Sweden. Only Grandpa and one sister remained in Beresford their entire lives. My Great Grandmother Karin is buried in the Beresford Brooklyn Evangelical Lutheran Church cemetery.

The 1890s photos of Grandma with her family and cousins show a strikingly pretty, petite young woman who looks like she is about to get into mischief. Pictures of my mother and granddaughter Rachel at the same age show a remarkable resemblance, from cheeks and eyes to shapely figures. All three have an amazing athleticism, too. Playing tag or running foot races with her seven grandchildren wasn't beyond Grandma's capabilities.

For such a tiny person, that deep hearty laugh was infectious and my cousins remember giggle sessions with Grandma. She laughed at the antics of her grandchildren till tears came to her eyes.

She always made time for each of her grandchildren and asked about our activities. Frequent overnights with cousins at Grandma's house gave us an opportunity to know her well. We loved seeing her untangle her waist-length silver hair from a bun fastened with hairpins and tortoiseshell combs. One hundred brush strokes each night kept her hair silky and manageable. When she allowed me to run a brush through those long strands, it made me yearn for hair as long and beautiful as hers.

Grandma contentedly swaying back and forth in her small rocker, cutting old clothes into strips to make utilitarian braided rugs, is a vivid picture in my mind. She let us wind the strips into balls ready for crocheting or weaving and we were proud to be so helpful. Her busy nimble fingers seemingly always held a crochet hook, quilting or darning needle or a piece of embroidery.

The thought of making cutout sugar cookies or bread and buns with her brings to mind rich, sensory pleasures. Carefully chosen shapes of hearts, flowers and animals were sprinkled with sugar as we placed them on a cookie sheet. Grandma stuck her arm in the wood-fired cook stove oven to see if it

Waking to Mourning Doves

was hot enough to bake. If not, she added a few more fast-burning corncobs or kindling wood. Waiting for those melt-in-your -mouth cookies to cool enough to eat was torture. If any cookies were left, she made colored powdered sugar frosting for us to express our artistic talents in decorating. Sneaking raw cookie dough or licking the frosting spoon was allowed. I liked a brown sugar penuche topping better than candy from the Ben Franklin Five and Dime.

My grandchildren and I use her tin cookie cutters and flour and sugar canisters when we bake sugar cookies together. My favorite cookie cutter is a three-inch, fluted-edge circle. I can still feel Grandma's spirit by my side when I roll and cut the dough with that antique cutter.

Grandma made everything fun. Tagging along behind her while she fed and watered the chickens, turkeys and guinea hens became an adventure, as she'd stoop to find a four-leaf clover as if by magic or show us how to suck the sweet petal base of a purple or white clover. She made a game of gathering corncobs from the hog yard or picking up sticks from the lawn to see how quickly we could fill a basket. A faithful dog followed her everywhere.

Only rarely did we see Grandma without a coverall apron. All kinds of smudges covered that apron: children's tears, cooking spills, garden soil, strawberry stains or signs of whatever activity Grandma had accomplished that day. The apron came off for church services, but was quickly donned as she got home to begin the Sunday noon meal. The whole extended family converged on Grandma's at least monthly. Birthday parties held in the celebrant's home always meant great food and presents and time to play with cousins. Strangely, the sons-in-law's birthdays were rarely observed. Dad and Uncle Elmer must have felt left out, because Uncle Clarence and George's birthdays were always observed. Sometimes Dad balked at attending the frequent family gatherings, as the brothers and sisters were close and clannish. Dad and Alice's husband, Elmer, often drifted off for a smoke or a beer behind one of the farm buildings, a no-no in the Erickson family. I wonder if George's wife, Dorcas, ever felt like an outsider, as Mom, Alice and Hazel shared the same viewpoints on everything down to food preparation, identical lamps, television sets, gadgets, and games.

I loved being in the vegetable and flower garden with Grandma. Long white icicle radish, peas in the pod, plump June strawberries and searches for asparagus by the fence line are the most memorable. Tasting food right in the garden made all of us cousins gardeners for life. Vibrant hollyhocks grew in profusion in one corner of Grandma's garden. The adjacent grassy area became the perfect setting for wedding parties of hollyhock dolls. The full flower became the skirt and a bud peeled back and stuck into the hollowed-out underside of the blossom became the head with two tiny "eyes" and a full-upswept head of "hair." Why do little girls always play weddings, dress up and make playhouses? Girls' play was so different from boys' activities in the mid-1900s.

Grandma's immigrant trunk held fragile vintage clothing in which we kids would play dress-up. We never tired of prancing around in the beautiful garments worn by our grandma and aunts. Hazel's makeup stash was hard to resist and she usually laughed at our amateurish attempts to look glamorous.

Like our mothers and aunts before us, we made elaborate playhouses in wooded areas with the leftover scraps of lumber and household items we found. String wound around ash and box elder trees defined our rooms and broom-swept paths gave us a labyrinth of an imaginative settlement complete with ice cream parlors, grocery stores and homes. Mud pies decorated with meadow wildflowers dried in sunny areas and sometime real oatmeal cookies provided by Hazel and Grandma were stashed in our make-believe refrigerator boxes. Not many children today know the simple thrill of creating mud pies. We beat soil and water to just the right consistency and poured it into discarded metal canning jar lids or small shallow containers, decorated it and set it out to dry. Rolled Sears catalog pages became pretend ice cream cones when we plopped a blob of mud inside. Sometimes we added a stolen egg from the chicken house or a bit of skim milk to our soupy mixture.

How many grandmas would think of buying a new small chicken house (called a brooder house) as a playhouse for grandchildren? We couldn't believe our good luck as we set up housekeeping with kitchen cast-offs and divided the space into rooms. Our dolls and a few lazy cats helped us in our make-believe games. Old mail order Sears or Montgomery Wards catalogs provided pictures for us to cut out and play store. Dolls, art supplies, paper dolls, games like checkers and dominoes, puzzles, croquet, marbles and outdoor play equipment kept us occupied for hours.

After a day of playing outside, Grandma filled a washtub with water heated on the wood-burning cook-stove and gave us a scrubbing. Splashing was fun, but her determined scrubbing was not!

Visiting the outdoor toilet before bedtime required a lot of nerve when Grandma sent us alone. All kinds of imaginative dangers lurked and our weak flashlights barely pierced the dark. Some outdoor biffs had small holes cut for children's use, but not Grandma's. The two-seater toilet had holes cut to accommodate a 300-pound person or so it seemed to us. I always hung on to a person or something on the wall because of my fear of falling in. The toilet had been built in 1931 when her children were grown and a new house was built on land they owned a half-mile away, so that my Uncle George and his new wife could live on what they called "the home place." Grandma, Grandpa, Hazel

Waking to Mourning Doves

and Clarence spent the remainder of their lives in the new house. Mom, Alice and Edna lived there for a short time also. Alice and Elmer's wedding was held on the well-manicured lawn near a patch of lily-of the-valley, Grandma's favorite flower. Some of those roots thrive in our gardens, just as her spunky spirit resides in all of her descendants.

The Erickson's picturesque red, hip-roofed barn on the new place they built in 1932 had a cavernous upstairs haymow where we were allowed to play. Fresh piles of meadow hay provided places to slide or play hide-and-seek. Neatness and order must be a Swedish trait, as the barn was as clean and orderly as a barn could be. The cow stanchions kept the cows in place for the twice-a-day milking chores. Horse stalls and neatly hung horse harnesses lined the other side. Occasionally a litter of new kittens was discovered and we cousins considered it our job to tame them.

Grandma never learned to drive a car, so Hazel drove their Model T Ford as her chauffeur. If an emergency occurred or help was needed, Grandma and Hazel came within minutes of a call for help. My Aunt Dorcas never liked dealing with emergencies and often called Grandma to tend to her children's boo-boos. My cousins, Gwen and Ruth, like to tell stories of how their mom relied on Grandma Erickson. Once Gwen fell from the attic haymow in the barn onto a horse and got a bit shaken up. Dorcas panicked and called Grandma, whose common sense approach calmed many a crisis such as this. I think Grandma liked to feel needed and enjoyed helping her family. I know she lent money even to distant relatives. With hard work, she and August prospered and purchased surrounding farmland.

Mom, Hazel, Clarence and George were soft-spoken, but in later years, Grandma and all the Erickson siblings suffered hearing losses, and loud voices and several unrelated conversations going on at once became the norm. My granddaughter Claire called Aunt Alice "Mrs. Shout" because she talked very loud.

Maybe my memories of Grandma are seen through rose-colored glasses. She died from a stroke in 1951 when I was just 12 years old. As a teenager there is a tendency to be more critical of a grandparent, but Grandma will always be her sweet, giving self in my memory.

Being the only child can be lonely, but with neighbors and friends and a large extended family nearby, I was rarely alone. My extended family provided a rich childhood for me and it was great being surrounded by this strong, happy family in my formative years.

Our daughters experienced a taste of this extended family when we visited Beresford from our home in the Twin Cities. The eulogies written about Mom by Michelle and Cherise echoed similar relationships that I had with my grandmother. Living only four miles from our grandchildren has allowed us to be part of their lives too, but suburban living is very different from the small-town, rural life of my childhood.

Hopefully, our grandchildren will remember visits to our lake cabin and some shared experiences such as learning to sew baby things for Nate, their baby brother, and making lefse and krumkake. I hope some family traditions can be kept alive for them to know they have a diverse heritage from both sides of their families. Often the traditions handed down are from the female side, but I hope they integrate customs from their father's families, too. Thankfully, some of those customs are recorded in Sherm's own memoir, *Dream Hunter*.

CHAPTER 6
My Chautauqua Grandma

Nana — a word with so many layers of meanings in our family. It is a two-year old's shorthand for Grandma, but how did it start?

Our grandchild Rachel, at age two, couldn't say grandma, so I am Nana for all time to her and her siblings Claire and Nate. I suppose that's how my dad's mother, Effie Jones Kinkner, became Nan, or maybe it was to differentiate her from Grandma Erickson.

Living with Nan for the first three years of my life and then never being more than a half mile from her home while growing up gave us a closeness that some grandchildren never experience. I am thankful for the many years of interaction with grandparents, aunts, uncles, cousins and extended family growing up in Beresford. Even though 50 years has flown by, living in Wisconsin, North Dakota, Illinois and Minnesota, a large part of me has never left my family in South Dakota.

Memories and reminders, especially of Nan, are a part of my daily existence to this day. I constantly use her household furnishings, which bring warm feelings knowing that Nan's spirit is always with me. I can see her kneading dough and rolling out flaky piecrusts on the Hoosier cabinet we have in our great room.

Brushing flour from her nose she'd coax, "Come over here, girlie, and get your hands in this bread dough. It's ready to knead now."

Eagerly, I donned a feed sack apron decorated with rickrack that she had sewn for me and plunged my hands into the pliant dough. Kittens nursing at their mother's breast imitate my first efforts, but soon Nan taught me to push and turn the dough. "Here sweetie, just take this hunk of dough 'cuz it's not so big and you can make your own loaf."

As we kneaded bread in that warm corner of the kitchen, Nan regaled me with stories of her childhood in Racine, Wisconsin and Dakota Territory where she had arrived in 1888 with her parents and two sisters. How I wish now that I had recorded all those stories that she delighted in telling me. Although I have forgotten most of them, she succeeded in planting the seeds of my obsession to record family history and write my memoir for future generations.

Our daughters ask, "What were Grandma and Grandpa really like?" Since

Caryl Crozier

I am the last person to know, it feels good to capture their essence and in so doing realize how those hardy people are a part of who I am today.

So, how can I adequately describe Nan? Her rich sense of humor and ready laugh charmed folks who called her a Chautauqua kind of woman. Her vast repertoire of card tricks, parlor games and jokes still amazes me. I loved watching her in her role as the life of the party. How did her quick wit and sense of humor evolve? Maybe her family dynamics played a role. Lily, the oldest sister, a prim and proper intellectual lady, never stooped to do outside chores. Ida, the second sister, became a capable, down-to-earth, lovable woman who delivered babies, did custom sewing and joined Beresford's version of high society with equal ease.

Nan, as the youngest sister, had to compete for attention and I think took a cue from her parents. The tales I remember depict them as fun loving, often silly, yet hard working folks.

My dad recalled, "Grandpa Jones could jump up in the air and click his heels three times before landing." How I longed to see that as a child, but he died before I was born. He seemed magical in my imagination.

The incident that makes Great Grandma Clarissa Jones come alive for me was her response to a church circle lady's opinionated statement, "No woman can do three things at once." Grandma quickly retorted, " I can pick up cow chips, take a pee and call the men to dinner at the same time." Now, there is a woman I can love with that earthy sense of humor that must have influenced Nan's personality! Maybe Nan developed her sense of humor to get her share of attention in the family.

I remember Nan saying, " Ida and I were the ones to pitch the shit from the barn, Aunt Lily couldn't get her hands dirty." Nan and Ida married farmers and both could milk cows, work in the fields, or pitch manure with ease as well as entertain and become immersed in church and social groups.

I adored Aunt Lily, as did all of the nieces and nephews. She coaxed wild squirrels to eat from her hand, saying, "Come Flurry, come Flurry," as several gray squirrels rushed from the tree branches to her perch on the second floor balcony of the funeral home where she worked. How spookily exotic to be the hostess at a funeral home! Being a Unitarian and later cremated set her apart and I loved her spunk and intellectual leanings. No wonder she married a Renaissance man, Clark, an artist and sometime handy man who died young, a man ahead of his time and not equipped to cope in Depression times.

Nan inherited some genes for height as she stood inches above her two sisters and younger brother, Henry. She appears tall and slim in early photographs and always described herself as a bit fleshy. Watching her struggle into a full body corset and pull the laces tight fascinated me as a

Waking to Mourning Doves

child. She rolled her chestnut brown hair into a bun and fastened it with black hairpins. Sometimes she let me brush her thick hair when I stayed overnight with her. Before going to sleep at night, we knelt beside the bed and said a prayer and then repeated the 23rd Psalm and the Lords Prayer. Naming all of the US Presidents or quizzing each other on state capitals comprised our bedtime chatter. My favorite ancestor stories revolved around Nan's maternal grandparents' lives in the frontier village of Raymond, Wisconsin. Her voice inflections enhanced tales of panthers and wolves lurking in the tall woods.

Nan became my elocution teacher and sought opportunities for me to perform at church and social gatherings. Since storytelling and entertaining became her niche, her coaching skills focused on me. She enjoyed finding little "pieces," as she called them, for me to recite. Naturally, they were humorous and she reveled in helping me get the voice inflection and timing just right. Her wide range of vocal imitations accented the humor. In one long poem about an "oatmobile," she taught me to speak in a Swedish accent. It started, "Aye yust vent up to Minneeesota to see an oatmobile, dat ben da name ya call. And you kin take a ride on him vitout von horse at all." She also helped me dress in a costume to fit the poem. The ladies in her numerous clubs and social groups always encouraged my recitations and shaky piano solos.

I especially like a poem called *Two Little Kittens* that she had me recite. Her notes on the worn folded paper I found in her Bible read, "For Shirley (my second cousin). Caryl was about her age when she learned it. If she learns it, I want to hear her speak it."

Two little kittens a black and a brown,
And Grandma said with a frown,
It will never do to keep them both,
The black one, we will drown.
Don't cry my dear she said to Bess,
One kitten is enough to keep.
Now run to nurse for it's rather late
And time you were fast asleep.
When morning dawned rosy and bright
Came little Bess down from her nap,
And nurse said run to Grandma's room
And look on Grandma's lap.
Come here, my dear, called Grandma
From the room wherein she sat.
God has sent you two little sisters,
Now what do you think of that?
Bess looked at the babies for a moment

Caryl Crozier

With their wee heads yellow and brown
When to Grandma she said bravely,
Which one are you going to drown?

Nan's natural talent for music intrigued me. She played by ear and picked out melody or accompaniment unhindered by the lack of formal training. When Grandpa picked up his fiddle, she was right there chording on her Segerstom piano or steel string guitar in whatever key he chose. By age four, my fingers picked out *Peter, Peter, Pumpkin Eater* on the black keys just like I tried to teach my grandchildren.

At age five, my rendition of *Silent Night* at the church Christmas program prompted the audience to clap and I announced, "I am not done yet."

The congregation laughed and clapped again after I confidently played *Jesus Loves Me* by ear. Never since have I felt so proud of my musical talents!

Nan's creativity took many forms. Her scrap basket of fabrics ranging from men's wool suit samples to worn housedresses evolved into quilts with exotic names like Drunkard's Path, Nine Square or Shoo Fly. Her utilitarian, heavy-wool, tied quilts kept us warm on bitter cold nights. I loved sifting through her steadily growing pile of colorful fabrics and choosing pieces for doll quilts. Octagonal shaped pieces hand-sewn together with tiny stitches blended a riot of patterned bits and pieces of discarded cloth into a no-nonsense coverlet. Adding a thick wool batting and flannel backing, she quickly tied the three layers together with red yarn. A Victorian style crazy quilt with frayed pieces of silk and velvet now adorns my quilt rack. This quilt became her labor of love and she embellished it with fancy blanket stitches and embroidery. Nan rarely "saved things for good" to use later and her quilts show wear and tear. She patched the early 1900s crazy quilt with my sewing projects scraps. Quilts reflect the generations in my family – from Great Great Grandma Lucinda Lower's homespun wool fabrics to my granddaughter Rachel's self-designed Green Star quilt.

Chicken feed came in brightly colored fabric bags from which frugal housewives created aprons and clothing. Nan dutifully washed sugar and flour sacks to become dishtowels. Coarse grey feed sacks cleaned men's dirty, greasy hands after fieldwork and threshing and were also used daily to wash and wipe the cream separator.

Nan maintained an enormous garden. I loved watching her don her apron and faded straw sun hat and gather pans to pick strawberries. I tagged along to help as she filled her apron and pans with sweet June strawberries. What a treat it was to pour cream on my heaping bowl of berries.

Mom reminisced, "No matter how tired or sick Nan felt, she always had the energy to pick strawberries."

Nan's brow perspired as she plopped down on the red fainting couch on the screened porch. With a wet washcloth on her forehead, her hand-held rattan fan rhythmically cooled us both. While Nan rested after gardening we carried the garden's produce to the front wrap-around porch, one of my favorite places.

We often sat on her porch shelling peas, hucking strawberries, peeling apples or husking sweet corn. She made chokecherry jelly, apple butter, plum jam and wild grape jelly from the trees, bushes and vines growing in profusion along the edge of her flower garden. She and Mom canned and preserved all that they grew, even canning beef and pork raised in our pastures. Our farms were almost totally self-sufficient. Milk, eggs, meat, fruits and vegetables were all consumed right where they were produced: grass-fed beef, corn-fed pork and free-range chickens. The expensive organic foods of today were what I grew up eating. Field crops were used to feed the livestock, and oat and garden seeds were saved for planting the following year.

Countless childhood dreams were spun on Nan's open-columned porch. The east-facing section provided spectacular sunrises and cool respite on hot summer days. The south and west porches provided afternoon warmth and big sky sunsets.

Pale pink and crimson red June roses wafted a heavy scent through the air after the lilacs and yellow honeysuckle finished blooming. Heirloom purple and yellow iris, phlox and later freckled orange tiger lilies provided a colorful backdrop to the endless green prairie fields and blue sky. Fluffy clouds drifted into shapes ripe for a child's imagination. Once in a while, ragged bluish-black storm clouds rolled in with threats of hail and sharp lightning. My great grandmother taught her daughters to love the drama and beauty in the sky and that was passed on to me by my Great Aunt Lily and Nan. To farmers, the soaking rains were welcomed and hailstones became brief ice cubes – a rarity from my childhood.

My father and grandpa and assorted relatives watched the sky and talked about the weather from that open-air porch. "Yep, it sure looks like rain there in the west. The corn sure as hell needs it now if it's gonna make it knee-high by the 4th of July."

I loved to sit on the porch protected from the rain and storms until Nan coaxed me into the house. "C'mon in girlie, you'll get chilled and catch a cold sitting out there so long. Supper is ready now."

Grandpa's assortment of roan and Hereford cattle grazed away the quiet days, and an occasional spring calf frolicked and kicked up its heels in the soft grass and meadowlands. Doves provided the background music for red-headed woodpeckers drumming on the fence posts. Nan's cranky setting hens explored the flower gardens seeking insects and seeds, clucking encouragement to their small darting broods of chicks the colors of Mexican corn.

Nan kept a watchful eye over Grandpa and me as we walked hand in hand to the pasture to encourage the ambling cows through the deep rutted lane to the barn for evening milking. Sometimes he swung me over the creek as I shrieked in delight and landed on the other side or sometimes I just waded in the squishy chocolate mud. No fancy swimming pools for me, but I had the creek in which to dangle my feet to cool off on hot summer days or a secluded spot to shakily learn to ice skate in the winter. Icy air frosted my cheeks as I plopped on my rocket sled to coast down the long hill from the porch.

Gliding along the wooden porch floor on my clip-on roller skates made me feel as fleet as the wind. I spent hours pushing doll buggies filled with dolls or cats dressed in doll clothes to imaginary destinations. Sometimes mud pies dried in the afternoon sun or friends joined me to play. Most of all, I loved curling up with a good book or daydreaming.

The enormous cottonwood tree under which I would one day become engaged towered south of the porch about 100 feet. Its cool shade provided respite on hot days and the leaves and cotton fluff made good mud pie decorations. A couple of twig chairs invited us to sit a spell. Sherm knew my sentimental attachment to that majestic tree and at the stroke of midnight on October 7, 1959 placed a diamond ring on my finger beneath that golden-leafed tree.

A long treacherous dirt driveway led to the white house set upon the hill. Nan, Grandpa and I watched from the porch as cars of visitors struggled through the mud and ruts of the driveway. The pasture often flooded after heavy rains and the whole bottomland became a lake. Since the driveway was adjacent to the pasture, it flooded too. Sometimes cars detoured through a gate in the pasture or drove higher up on the hillside going onto corn or oat fields.

Not a lot of traffic used the existing gravel road which passed our farms, just the neighbors and an occasional delivery truck or a parade of tractors and farm machinery. The rural mail carrier deposited the day's mail in a box at the end of the long driveway. Nan was an avid letter writer and had a lively correspondence with friends and relatives from Wisconsin to California. She liked to sit on the porch and write and read the mail and newspapers.

Gene, my pet tiger cat, made daily visits from my parents' farm to Nan's house and always got leftover treats. He liked to lounge and purr on the porch, too. Nan didn't have cats, so I often brought one along. Gene met his demise on one of his jaunts and Dad found his mangled body alongside the road. Cars

Waking to Mourning Doves

didn't always slow down for animals. We buried him north of my parent's house and yellow iris still mark his grave.

On both farms, my friends and I loved exploring creeks, pastures, fields and ditches to learn about the mysteries of nature. Each spring I found a meadowlark nest in the tall grass in the ditches and eagerly awaited a peek at the new baby birds, being careful not to disturb the nest or visit too often. Red-headed woodpeckers were common as there were plenty of wooden fence posts and tree snags in which to make nests. Hungarian partridge, pheasants, robins, sparrows, swallows, pigeons, blackbirds and goldfinches, which we called canaries, were the most common birds. We went to sleep hearing their songs. Best of all was waking to a new day to the soulful call of Mourning Doves.

Nearly every weekend my parents enjoyed dancing at the Arkota Ballroom in Sioux Falls while I stayed overnight with Nan. We played cards — rummy, hearts, 500 — and I built fragile card towers as she listened to her radio soap operas. Sometimes I played on the porch as she leaned her left elbow on the oak wooden phone box that now hangs on our basement wall, a reminder of her endless phone conversations. There is a shiny worn spot where her arm rested.

Preparing supper, usually fried potatoes and eggs, sometimes became adventurous as we descended into the storm cave to get a jar of pickles or sauce to complete the meal. Deep dirt storm cellars were dug on most early 20th century farms to give protection from tornadoes and dangerous storms, as well as to provide cool storage for canned goods and garden produce.

Spiders, toads and creepy crawly bugs called Nan's cave home, and I clung to her apron strings as we descended the steep stairs into the cave. "Wait for me, wait for me," I whispered. "Oh no, there's a big toad over there. I'll get warts if he touches me."

Rows of shelves held blue Mason jars filled with pickles, preserves, and home canned fruit. Bins of potatoes and root vegetables lined the dirt walls. After a half century of abandonment, the cellar is still sturdy, but stands as the last useable remnant of the now deserted farmstead. Now the lilac and honeysuckle bushes bloom and century-old purple and yellow heirloom iris add a dash of color in the spring. The grove is a tangled mass of broken branches and fallen trees with scattered rubble piles where unthinking people have dumped trash, something which is commonly done on abandoned farmstead sites.

Tiptoeing beside Nan in the damp grass, I delighted in seeing grasshoppers jump and fireflies sparkle as we approached the outdoor toilet. "How come the fireflies' back ends light up, Nanny? Can we catch one and put it in a jar?"

Caryl Crozier

"Sure you can, honey, but you have to let it go before you go to bed."

Indoor plumbing was considered a luxury on the early farms and wasn't available in our home until 1951 when we moved Nan's house to my parent's farm, a half mile to the north, and remodeled it. Outdoor toilets had a variety of labels; outhouses, johns, or biffs to name a few. Peach wrappers and pages from Sears catalogs were commonly used as toilet paper. Leisurely strolls to the biffy in warm weather were infinitely more pleasant than cold dashes in the winter. Chamber pots sometimes solved the cold weather problem, but no one enjoyed emptying the night's accumulation from the so-called honey buckets the next morning.

A washstand in Nan's kitchen held the white pitcher and bowl in which we washed up before bedtime. In the winter, Nan placed at our feet a towel wrapped in soapstones she'd heated in the oven. As I snuggled up next to Nan in my flannel pajamas, I felt safe and content.

Since I was her only grandchild, Nan wanted to be my favorite Grandma. Once she asked me, "Who is your favorite Grandma?" Without knowing any better at age four, I replied. "Grandma Erickson."

Seeing the hurt look on her face taught me my first lesson in tact, and I still feel sorry about it seventy years later. A good lesson, but maybe not a good question to ask a child. I loved them both, but I had just spent a fun weekend with Grandma Erickson and maybe that influenced my answer.

On Sunday mornings we usually attended Sunday school and church. Nan laced up her corset, slipped on one of her dark-print pongee dresses, a dark straw hat, nylons and granny shoes. I liked to choose the hat to complete her outfit – feathers, flowers and veils decorated her collection and I was thrilled when she let me wear them for playing dress-up. How did Nan manage to do early outdoor chores and get a big Sunday noon meal started before church? She was amazing.

Seeing the world as a self-centered teenager left little interest in relating to Nan. I suppose my teenage granddaughters have a similar ambivalence toward me. Hopefully, they will have a few positive memories. Seeing or talking to Nan nearly every day of my life until I left for college in 1956 made her as familiar as my parents. Childhood memories of her have come more readily than from the time she lived with us when I was thirteen to eighteen years old.

Nan positioned her platform rocker where she could observe every room in the house. I felt she was spying on me. From her bedroom window she watched and listened as my dates walked me to the door. I considered this a huge invasion of my privacy and didn't hesitate to tell her so. At times I resented Nan's questions and interest in my teenage life. Now, with an adult's

Waking to Mourning Doves

perspective, I know she was only interested in my welfare, but it seemed like meddling at the time.

I now know she tried to fit into our family life as quietly as possible, but it was difficult for three generations to see eye to eye all the time. Arguments broke out now and then, with Dad usually defending Ma, as he called Nan. Fortunately, no one brooded long and we quickly got over the spats. Mom and Nan shared a household for nearly fifteen years and Mom told me they usually got along pretty well, considering the circumstances.

I remember a little rhyme that Nan often snidely said to my mother when they were having an argument, "A daughter's a daughter all of her life, but a son's a son till he gets him a wife."

Mom's quick retort was usually, "Well, your daughter told me she pitied me for having to live with you the rest of your life."

Now, of course, I regret any unkind words I said to Nan, but I am comforted by the fact that she knew I loved her and my words were all a part of growing up and becoming independent.

Mom and Dad were farming over 300 acres in the 1950s, which was a lot at that time. This required Mom to be heavily involved in fieldwork, driving the tractor and working in the fields. Nan prepared meals, washed dishes, and helped with yard and garden tasks. As her problems with congestive heart failure worsened, she slowed down. Washing chicken manure off eggs without gloves made fungus infections in her fingernails worsen. My friends asked why she painted her nails and why her nails sometimes came off. I was embarrassed for her when she had a hurt look when people asked about them. People never wore latex rubber gloves then.

Nan enjoyed playing cards, croquet and Chinese checkers. We spent hours playing Monopoly, dominoes or canasta. Poring over my stamp collection with her holds nice memories for me. Her interest in history and geography piqued my interest in learning more. She never failed to attend school events which were important to me: plays, concerts, and special activities. She loved listening to my piano and accordion practices and performances. Her pride in my achievements in school and 4-H was apparent in many letters she sent to relatives. Some of these letters were saved and given to me many years later.

Hope chests, repositories for a girl's preparation for marriage, were still in use in my generation. Nan helped me choose a blonde-finish, Lane cedar chest for Christmas 1955, and together we stashed embroidered linens and dishtowels made by Nan, Aunt Eva, Mom and me. She encouraged my needlework projects and gave me pillowcases or linens to embroider. A photo of Nan and me at Christmas in 1955 by the new cedar chest and Morse electric sewing machine shows her bursting with pride for her only grandchild.

Her health declined the summer of 1956 and she often spent nights sitting up in her comfortable platform rocker. Congestive heart failure took its toll and a month after I left for college she passed away quietly in the night. Thankfully I had spent the weekend prior to her death at home talking to her about my future plans. As usual, she gave me encouragement to become anything I wanted to be and told me how proud she was of my accomplishments. Her funeral service is a blur to me now. I felt sad and stunned to lose her, as she had always been there for me. A large part of her still lives through me and I have her to thank for helping shape my values and confidence. I hope a little of that Chautauqua personality rubbed off on me. My friends tell me it has.

CHAPTER 7

The Daughter They Never Had

People say that I remind them of my Aunt Eva, my father's sister. Granted, there is a physical resemblance, and based on my adoring memories of her, I hope it goes beyond that. I have never heard of anyone who didn't like her. She readily shared her time and talents as a community leader. Townspeople remember her clear, soprano voice as an inspiration at the community events and funerals at which she sang. As a little girl sitting in church, I never squirmed when she sang as the lead soprano in our Congregational Church choir. I felt mesmerized and proud of her.

She had no children, so I was like the daughter she never had. As long as I can remember, Eva and her husband, Ragnar, were always there for me. Eva married later in life at age 34, three years before I was born. I can visualize the setting of their 1935 marriage from their wedding write-up in the Beresford Republic where Eva worked as a linotype operator. A few old black-and-white photos help, too.

Kinkner-Ostensen

In a lovely ceremony performed by Rev. W.S. Harper Wednesday evening at the home of the bride's parents, Mr and Mrs. Walter Kinkner, east of Beresford, Miss Eva Lillian Kinkner became the bride of Ragnar Ostensen. The groom is a son of Mrs. Lawrence Ostensen, of Stavanger, Norway.

The Bride wore a tailored navy blue rich knit dress with matching accessories, and a shoulder corsage of Johannah Hill rose buds and orchid astors.

The bridesmaid, Miss Gladys Duncan, wore a tailored orchid crepe dress with a shoulder corsage of orchid and peach sweet peas.

Mr. Ostensen was attended by his brother, Osten Ostensen.

Before the single ring ceremony, Miss Grace Collings sang, "Love's Old Sweet Song" and "I Love You Truly." She was accompanied at the piano by Miss Edna DeRemer and on the violin by Robert DeRemer, both of Alcester.

As the wedding party came down the stairs, Miss DeRemer and her brother, Robert softly played the Wedding March from Lohengrin. The bride and groom took their places before a beautifully decorated window trimmed in the bride's chosen colors of orchid and peach. A large white wedding bell centered the arch and tall tapers were placed on either side. Baskets of rose buds, snap dragons and gladiolas formed the background. The rooms were candlelit.

After the ceremony, a four-course wedding dinner was served at tables beautifully decorated with orchid and peach favors and corresponding tapers. A three tier wedding cake centered the bride's table. Waitresses were Miss Emma Scheitler, Miss Olga Ellertson, Miss Olive Jones, and Miss LaVonne Forbes. They wore white dresses with orchid and peach aprons and caps.

The date of the wedding was the wedding anniversary of the bride's parents who were married 36 years ago in the same house.

Both the contracting parties are well known throughout the Beresford community. Mr. Ostensen has been employed by the South Dakota Public Service company for more than a year. His bride, a graduate of Beresford High School, has been employed by The Republic for the last 15 years.

They will reside in the Albert Larson home on West Spruce Street.

Dad told me that Eva was present at my birth in 1938 and was not a bit calm or helpful. He said she was hysterical and crying when Mom was having labor pains and giving birth. She took her big-sister role and empathy a bit too seriously. She also helped Mom steam me through the night when I had a pneumonia crisis as a baby.

I spent a great deal of time as a little girl with Eva and Ragnar. Mom said they visited us several times a week. As I grew, Eva was determined that I had access to all the books, music and amenities that a child in a small town

Waking to Mourning Doves

could have. They both doted on me, bringing books and treats and playing outside with me. Coaching me in spelling, reading and music, Eva reveled in telling her friends stories about me. Mostly, she bragged. One time, though, she hurt my feelings enough to make me cry when I pronounced my first piano song "Buggles" instead of "Bugles." She corrected me and told all her friends about it as a joke. Sure, it is funny to me now, but I didn't like being embarrassed in front of her friends. She never did it again.

She took me to Saturday afternoon matinees at the Vogue Theater. I cried through the Lassie series, *Song of the South* with Uncle Remus, *Bambi* and other Walt Disney movies.

Eva sat me on her lap and said, "Honey, I don't want to take you to the movies if it makes you cry." All the other pre-teens sobbed in the sad parts too. I loved those movies snuggled up against my pretty Aunt Eva.

> *April 17, 1949–I went to church- Eva's for dinner- Ragnar took us in 3 states- Iowa, SD, Neb.- went across Missouri R. bridge.*

My parents never ventured far from home because of all the farm chores. I never felt deprived, since most of my friends never traveled either. So, it was a big deal for me when Ragnar drove across the borders to Iowa, Nebraska and Minnesota on Sunday drives. Even so, I never traveled more than 100 miles from Beresford until my 1956 trip to Chicago during my freshman year in college.

Growing up in Norway, Ragnar became a skilled fisherman as a child. He and his siblings grew up one block from the sea where his father was the postmaster and ran a fishing business. At 13, Ragnar ran the fishing boat and kept the books while going to school. When living in South Dakota after marriage, he and Eva made Minnesota and Canadian fishing trips and brought back coolers full of Northern Pike, Walleye and pan fish, which they shared with us. I looked forward to their return, primarily because they always brought me a small, usually practical gift. Most memorable was a brass fingernail file featuring a pelican standing on an anchor from Pelican Lake in Minnesota. I longed to go along on their fishing trips, but they never asked me. Unfortunately, Eva died about the time I was old enough to go.

Eva tried everything to make me stop biting my fingernails in third grade. Colorful fingernail polish, monetary incentives and cajoling never worked, but somehow that new nail file did the trick. I carried it everywhere. I stopped biting my nails because I wanted to use that file and show it off to friends. Most of all, I wanted Eva's praise and approval.

Nearly every weekend my parents went to a dance somewhere and I

Caryl Crozier

stayed with either Nan or Ragnar and Eva in their home in town. I luxuriated in their indoor bathroom, spending hours soaking in the claw-foot bathtub. We didn't install indoor plumbing on the farm until I was 13. Sometimes Eva made up a bed for me on the sofa, which wasn't nearly as comfortable as the room I had of my own in the upstairs of her house when she finally decided I was old enough. She helped me decorate and choose the curtains and a quilt from her cedar chest collection. I loved the privacy of hanging out with my friends in my home away from home.

I usually stayed at her house during Vacation Bible School. She lined up playmates from the neighborhood for me, none of whom I liked too much because they were all younger. I much preferred spending time with her and Ragnar, searching for asparagus along the country roadsides, going pheasant hunting, gardening or just talking. They both seemed to think what I had to say was important. They would have made terrific parents, but were married when Eva was 34 years old, and in the 1930s that was considered too old to start a family. I also learned later that she had an obstruction that prevented her from conceiving a child. I didn't mind being their substitute. Eva was pleased when people said I looked just like her and called me "Little Eva."

Eva and Ragnar displayed more affection with each other than my parents did. They never left the house without a goodbye kiss and an expression of love. They both were tall, good-looking and nearly perfect in my opinion. Eva was always conscious of her figure and carried her weight below her waistline. I often watched her take a wooden rolling pin and vigorously rub it up and down her hips and thighs, I guess to break up cellulite. She struggled into a corset, but I never thought she needed one.

Aunt Eva did beautiful handwork, both crochet and embroidery. I treasure an heirloom ecru, crocheted bedspread, a pink crocheted baby quilt, and linens and dishtowels that she made. Sometimes Eva and I sat and embroidered together as we listened to records on her radio/phonograph player. It was an expensive, quality set for its time, and her proudest possession. We played records by the popular Inkspots quartet and the Big Band era. She always listened to the *$64 Dollar Question* radio program and the 10 o'clock news. Sometimes I perused their piles of Life and Time magazines, which they never threw out.

During World War II, the Germans were the enemy and I was afraid of their next-door neighbors who were of German ancestry. When I told her this, she promptly took me with her to visit them. She gently taught me that you couldn't judge people because of race or nationality. Of course, the German neighbors' home then became a favorite "cookie stop." We didn't have any Japanese families in Beresford, but if we had I know she would have taken me to visit them to see that they were not the "dirty Japs" that everyone in our town called them.

Eva had many friends and was active in Eastern Star and Rebecca Lodges, church choir and study clubs. Once she took me to a secret installation of the Lodge and members questioned her judgment. She insisted that I stay. I was spellbound watching the parade of ladies in their long white gowns. I never told anyone of their secret proceedings either.

Eva and Ragnar were active in the American Legion activities. Sometimes I climbed up on a chair in their bedroom to look at a long, narrow-framed photograph of a group of WWI soldiers. I liked finding Ragnar perched in the second row among hundreds of soldiers posing in front of a French building. In 1914 at age 26, he had immigrated to America with his brother. He went into the military service in 1918 and served in World War I, thereby gaining his citizenship. He paraded with General Pershing in New York City and Washington, DC and was in the 1st Division, 3rd Machine Gun Battalion, Co. D. He saw duty in Europe in France, England, Belgium and Holland, and in Canada. He was never injured or in combat on the front lines. Still, he reluctantly talked about the pure hell of war and the terrible gas and useless deaths. At the time, I couldn't imagine being so far from home, but I enjoyed visiting those places later in my life.

Ragnar and Eva had a lengthy courtship after the war and during the Depression. I don't think they felt they could afford to get married because he worked at a filling station and Eva earned a meager salary and needed to help her parents. He described the Depression as "just plain hell, terrible. People didn't have anything – they had enough to eat and that's all." He spent a couple of winters living with my parents and grandparents in the big old Deane farmhouse as a hired man before his marriage to Eva.

Eva and Ragnar's yard and garden in town produced a bounty of flowers and vegetables. I helped harvest a bumper crop of Whitney apples from their tree every year, and tried to assist Mom, Eva and Nan in making apple pickles, sauce and pies. Basement shelves sagged with canned and preserved garden produce that lasted all winter. I liked exploring every nook and cranny in the basement while Eva washed clothes and hung them on the lines to dry inside in the winter. At the time, Mom's washing machine was on a cold-entry porch and I was glad to be in school on Monday mornings so I didn't have to help with the laundry.

Ragnar's hybrid tomatoes and roses were legendary: the best in town. His garden was perfectly manicured, mulched and productive. Pansies, lilies-of-the-valley and a mock-orange bush joined the peonies and lilies blooming in profusion near the house.

Eva possessed a beautiful soprano voice and was an accomplished pianist. I enjoyed playing piano and singing duets with her. I still have stacks of her sheet music, which I eventually learned to play on the piano. I wish she had lived long enough to hear me play some of her favorite songs. She would have been so proud.

Eva operated the linotype for the Beresford Republic newspaper for 25 years. I loved to watch her set type on that big old clanking machine. Once she typed in my name and gave me the metal type. My friends all envied me. What a laborious way to produce a newspaper, setting all those little metal pieces in trays! She earned $21 a week in the early years and she used some of that money to help my parents and grandparents during the Depression.

January 16, 1949–We went to Eva's for dinner and I watched a fire at the Free Methodist Church.

I tasted new foods at Eva's table. My first glass of buttermilk was an unwelcome surprise. She didn't tell me what it was and I took a big gulp expecting nice cold pasteurized milk, different from the kind we had at home. I sputtered and spit it out on my plate. I was quickly taught a lesson in manners, but to this day I still don't like buttermilk! She fried eggplant and told my grandfather it tasted just like steak. He took one cautious bite and was unimpressed! She always kept ice-cold water in a green bottle in her refrigerator. Having ice cubes and chilled water was a treat for me, because we only had an icebox until rural electricity came to our farm in the late 1940s. I also tasted new foods going to church lutefisk dinners with her. Ragnar always had tasty Norwegian meats and cheese for us to snack on.

Ragnar served as councilman and mayor in Beresford for many years, but what I remember most clearly is that he was also the fire chief. He would switch on the siren on his 1932 Oldsmobile when he rushed to a fire. My most vivid fire memories are when the elementary school burned (classes were held in church basements until a new school was built) and when a church just a half block from Ragnar and Eva's house burned. Eva clung to me as we watched the flames leaping from the roof of the church from her kitchen window. I tried to comfort Eva whenever Ragnar was called to a fire, as she worried that he would be injured. He was always first on the scene and performed more than a few daring deeds and rescues.

While on a fishing trip to Minnesota in 1950, Eva became ill and was hospitalized. Doctors discovered inoperable ovarian cancer during surgery in Sioux Falls. I was devastated as was the whole family. She wasted away quickly and died at the age of 48. She was brave and loving during this time and spent her days saying goodbye to friends and family. I couldn't believe

Waking to Mourning Doves

that she would not always be in my life. Since I was so much like her, I was just certain that I would die at age 48 too. That fear turned out to be unfounded, but I was very relieved that my hysterectomy at age 40 eliminated the fear of ovarian cancer.

My diary entries chronicle the speed with which we lost Eva.

July 9, 1950–Eva went to the hospital today.

July 13, 1950–Eva had operation today- we were up morn and aft- she has cancer- Nan and Ragnar stayed here tonite.

July 22, 1950–We drove up to Sioux Falls and brought Eva home.

October 17, 1950–Eva passed away at 3:45 a.m.

October 19,1950–Went to Eva's funeral today and was there ever a big crowd- church basement packed, stood outside, $250 in memorials.

There was some animosity after Eva's death in regard to the fact that she left no will. Therefore, her inheritance of half the Kinkner 80 acres became Ragnar's. Grandpa Kinkner had willed the farm to his two children instead of his wife. Nan and Dad got a lawyer and tried to change things, but after a year, Ragnar made a very low offer for Dad to buy him out. It was a relief to Mom and me who had continued to see Ragnar during the feud.

Nan had been living with Eva and Ragnar during the winters. They had planned to move her farmhouse to town and remodel it so they could all live together in it. Instead, the house came to our farm in 1951 and Nan lived with us.

January 1, 1951–Went to a Lutefisk supper with Ragnar.

March 1952–Ragnar brought us a box of candy.

When relationships improved with the estate settlement, Ragnar spent a great deal of time with our family. He took me to many social events, church suppers, pheasant hunting and provided transportation for me when I needed a ride all during my high school years.

Seven years after Eva's death, Ragnar married Wave, who was the Director of Nursing at Methodist Hospital in Sioux City. She looked like Eva and we all liked her very much. My family and I visited them whenever possible through the years as did my parents.

An article in the Beresford Republic about Ragnar reads in part,

> *He was such a quiet, unassuming man, always there for his friends in good times and bad. Did he have an enemy? I doubt it. Ragnar was not a pushover. If he had a conviction on anything he would dig his heels in and be stubborn as a mule.*

The writer also remembers Ragnar's friendly grin, his sparkling blue eyes and the ever-present aroma of cigar smoke. So do I. Our family was fortunate to have him in our lives until his death in 1980.

Rarely does a day go by that I don't think of Eva and Ragnar, thankful for their influence in my life. Their photograph on our family photo wall continually reminds me of them.

Chapter 8

My Swedish Bachelor Farmer Uncle

Uncle Clarence was a true man of the soil, having lived and worked on a farm his entire life. His oversized hands symbolized the manual labor that dominated his life. He wrote his own biography in 1985, at age 84, in a tattered Sioux City Stockyards notebook and entrusted it to my mother. Clarence lived his entire life on the two farms in Prairie Township southeast of Beresford, making his home with his mother and sister Hazel. He grew up with one brother and four sisters. The three older children, George, Clarence and Hazel, didn't know a word of English until they started rural school. I tried to imitate their Swedish brogue without much luck.

Uncle Clarence loved farming with horses, feeding cattle, and doing outside chores. He attended school through the sixth grade and then quit to help farm. His words, complete with spelling errors, give us an idea of what he wanted us to remember about his life. I like the phonetic spelling and think he might feel right at home with brief text messages on an iPhone today.

April 26, 1985

When I was young, I road a bike around. When winter came we head fun kosting, ice skiting. When it stomed, it was so much snow so to water the cows we card water to them in barn. We head lots of horses in the barn so we hald straw in the barn. When it was fair day we hald maner. In the spring we work in the field. We put four horses on the disk. Then to drag put four horses ther. Then when we planted corn two horses. Then caltivator the corn one row cultvate. Then later years we two cultvator 4 horses. Then in the faul we plowed two bottom plow. Six horses for that.

We milked 16 cows and one night I was lone and 16 cows to milk by hand. That was a long night for me.

Then in 45 I got the first tractor. I went hard ships. This was in the 1911. I plow with three horses when I was 10 years old.

We stak hay with stacker that took two horses and to buck the hay that took two horses. I was in the stack. Then to hall it home in the hay rack that to pitch from the stack on rack then to pitch in the manger. To cut grain with binder four horses. Then shocke to dry

Gorge and I head a thrashing machne so we thresh in stake. Then to hol the grain in wgon and shovel

We picked corn by hand. We head to skupe it of by hand. Then chorse in the morning and then at night that was work work.

My uncle head steme threshing machen. It took a water wagon. Three man for the machene. That was in 1909.

I was very young when started to milk cows. I head smal pail. Then carry the milk to house to seprate the milk. We made are owne butter. The skim milk for the calves and for the pigs. We baked our owne bread. That was good.

Losing his hearing and his sister Hazel later in life left Clarence in an isolated world from 1984 until his death in 2000. At age 96, having spent little time at a doctor's, he was still wiry and strong because of hard work and staying slim. He lived alone on the farm with his white Spitz dog, Trixie. His grocery lists were never very long and always under $10. He bought frozen bread dough, lemonade, cheese, cereal, milk, wieners and bacon, dog food, cookies and ice cream. Fortunately, Mom and nephew Norman's wife, Karen, supplemented his diet weekly with hot dishes, baked goods and meals at their homes. Mom used her barber set to trim his hair monthly and he always slipped her a few dollars to say thank you.

Uncle Clarence fell and broke his hip at age 95 and had a blood clot in his leg. The doctors didn't hold out much hope for his recovery, but his strong constitution pulled him through. He woke up the morning after surgery, in good spirits and hungry, asking for oatmeal. We couldn't believe it! He spent the last four years of his life at Bethesda Nursing Home enjoying the socialization that had not been as frequent for him after sister Hazel died in 1984.

Clarence loved kids. A child brought a smile to his face that literally spread from ear to ear. We seven nieces and nephews adored Uncle Clarence. He spent many hours playing with us, pulling us on sleds or Red Flyer wagons and even ice-skating on the creek (pronounced crick by many Midwesterners). He never refused a game of croquet, dominoes or board games. We cousins

Waking to Mourning Doves

tagged along behind him when he did farm chores and were rewarded by the loving attention he always gave us. We tamed the wary kittens that lived in his barn and spent hours looking at the multiplying goldfish in the stock tank. We helped him pick up sticks in the grove, which he kept clean as a whistle until he fell in 1996. Sometimes we sauntered down the pasture cow lane with him to sprinkle salt on the noxious bull thistle weeds to kill them. I loved to take off my shoes and wade in the creek. If I was lucky, we might find a stone Indian arrowhead in the creek bed. Clarence had a whole collection of them. I thought it was unbelievable that Indians had hunted his pasture a mere 50 years before.

I remember him as "Uncle Clink," a nickname the family gave him at a young age. He often exclaimed, "by jinx" or "jiminy crickets" when he got excited about something.

When he was a young man, we teased him when he got all gussied up to go out on Saturday nights. I don't know if he ever dated anyone, but Hazel told me that her friend had a crush on him. Whether he was too shy to date or just felt his responsibility was to take care of Hazel and Grandma, I don't know. I do know that I loved to spend time with him as a child and throughout my life.

Clarence took meticulous care of his spirited pony, Goldie. If we begged, he hoisted us up on Goldie's back and led us around the yard. Clarence was protective of us nieces and nephews and didn't want us to get hurt playing on machinery, in the haymow, or by getting too close to the livestock. Although we cousins played in Hazel's room with her possessions all the time, Clarence's bedroom was off limits and we steered clear of it.

The loud, piercing whistle Clarence made through his teeth enthralled me. Much as we cousins tried to imitate it, he was the sole possessor of that talent. He whistled as he worked and was always a cheerful and optimistic person. He did some woodcarving and whittling, but never let us touch his carving tools.

Clarence had a special way with animals, especially horses. He lovingly worked with and cared for them all during his lifetime, even boarding a few horses and colts after he retired. He farmed with horses before there were tractors, and he never learned to like driving a tractor as much as farming with horses. He loved the little colts and said he was lonely after horses were no longer used in farming. I know he liked farming with his brother, George, and nephew Norman.

He spent a lot of time cutting wood with the chainsaw to burn in the house furnace. He used the chainsaw long after he should have stopped. I think he hated to give up doing the tasks he enjoyed, even as his body weakened. He and my parents worked together cutting wood with the buzz saw, as both families heated their houses with wood-burning stoves.

When he was 50 years old, Clarence and his brother, George, were working together putting a roof on the corncrib when he had a terrible fall. He was up in the tractor front-end loader bucket when the bucket tipped and he fell 15 feet onto the tractor. I remember my mother's panic when she heard the news. The doctor didn't expect him to survive, but he was rushed to the hospital and recovered after a long stay. He wore a brace on his neck for a long time and also broke his elbow. One time Clarence asked my dad to remove his neck brace and shave his whiskers. The nurse walked in and scolded them both for this dangerous effort. Luckily, no damage was done. He also lost his hearing in one ear as a result of the accident, and his arm was stiff for a long time.

The Erickson family planted many evergreens in front of the house, and Clarence carried endless buckets of water from the well to keep them alive. He loved flowers, especially peonies, and brought them into the house and kept them long after they had dried up. His garden included tomatoes, beans, radishes, carrots, potatoes, watermelons, and a prolific patch of asparagus. He also froze rhubarb, mulberries, apples, and sweet corn. He picked wild grapes for my mother to make into jelly.

Clarence kept immaculate farm records and was very frugal. He was also a saver in every way. When we cleaned out his house for sale, practically every birthday card and valentine he ever received was in a big box along with napkins from social events. I treasure those valentines and postcards.

He made early and wise investments in the stock market, in bank certificates of deposit and in war bonds, none of which he ever cashed out. Frugality was ingrained in him, but he died a millionaire from farming and conservative investments. Leaving his investments to his sisters after his death helped them to pay their nursing home bills. I think he saw his role as a caretaker to his family.

I am grateful to have had this kind, stereotypical Swedish bachelor farmer as my uncle and friend.

CHAPTER 9

Aunt Hazel's Miracle

Don't ask me how, but it happened. Mom's colon cancer diagnosis and surgery at age 65 left scant hope for her survival. Dad, Hazel and I held a vigil at her side as the doctor's prognosis became clear.

I remember Aunt Hazel lamenting, "Oh I wish it could be me, Elvera has so much to live for." Ten years older than Mom, Hazel took her big-sister role seriously. Always Mom's protector, confidant and best friend, she supported and sustained Mom throughout their lives.

After the 1978 surgery, Mom was declared cancer-free and lived another 30 years to the very day of the invasive procedure. Within a year of Mom's diagnosis, Hazel had colon cancer herself, and she lost her battle in 1984. Despite surgery, chemo and rigid diet restrictions I think Hazel died happy knowing that her little sister could enjoy her life and family and grandchildren cancer-free.

One might believe that Hazel's celibate life was a tragedy after Dr. Hoard burned her face while treating acne. I am not so sure that is true. Surrounded by her four siblings and seven nieces and nephews who adored her, she had a family without the responsibility of raising children herself. I always considered her my second mother. Her caregiver personality mirrored my mother's.

As the eldest daughter with three younger sisters and two older brothers, Hazel learned responsibility early in life. Born of Swedish immigrant parents, she spoke only Swedish until she started school. She and her two brothers only finished eighth grade because they were needed to help with farm work and caring for younger siblings.

The whole family participated in cutting and stacking native prairie meadow hay, milking cows and caring for animals. Hazel held a more prominent role in household duties and cooking than her sisters. I know she was proud of her culinary skills, being the best cook in the family. She also sewed Halloween and Christmas costumes for her sisters from crepe paper, a popular idea at the time. It was inexpensive and disposable.

In her late teenage years, Hazel worked as a hired girl for a family in Sioux City, Iowa. Her letters to her bachelor brother, Clarence, revealed distaste for a servant's role.

As a teenager, she enjoyed 4-H club, piano lessons, church activities and

Caryl Crozier

socializing with friends. She, her mother and sisters enjoyed designing and piecing quilts. Every scrap of fabric was turned into heirloom quilts that we treasure today. I wonder if Hazel dreamed of marriage and a family when she worked on creating her masterpiece in the late 1920s, a double wedding-ring quilt . Maybe her hopes were dashed for that future when her face was burned and disfigured by Dr. Hoard's treatment for acne. Not even a desperate trip to the Mayo Clinic doctors at Rochester, Minnesota could restore that hope. She never finished the quilt.

Hazel must have felt both pride and disappointment when her two younger sisters, Alice and Edna, finished high school and college. She knew her future didn't hold such promise.

Meanwhile, she watched my pretty mother, the surprise youngest child whose birth wasn't even recorded, be denied piano lessons and college. My mother dated, was vivacious and popular and didn't quite fit the staid, conservative mold of her Swedish family. None of the older sisters dated, so Grandpa must have thought they needed a profession to support themselves in case they didn't get married. Mom wanted to go to college and become a Home Economist, as I later became, but Grandpa refused to further her education. I guess he thought she would just get married and an education would be wasted. Mom made sure that I got every opportunity she was denied. Just as Mom lived her dreams through me, I think Hazel shared some of those dreams, too.

Hazel stood by my mother's side as she exchanged wedding vows in 1933, a wedding boycotted by their father. I can only imagine their thoughts.

Hazel and Mom and a few young, neighbor-lady friends organized the *Friendly Hour Club* in 1934. The club provided life-long friendships and an outlet for sharing talents and learning new skills. Hazel felt comfortable and accepted in the club even as she withdrew from church and community activities.

Self-conscious after her disfigurement, she shopped for groceries and gifts for nieces and nephews in nearby towns, but ordered her clothing and other necessities through the Spiegel, Alden's and Sears's catalogs. I remember poring through those thick "wish book" catalogues with her. On the few shopping excursions to a larger town, I knew she felt self-conscious when people stared. Mom said my Aunt Alice didn't want to be seen in public with Hazel. That must have hurt, and it makes me sad to think about it even now.

Aunt Hazel gave me constant love and support her entire life and hosted my baby and wedding showers. I would like to think I was her favorite, but I know she had enough love to go around to all seven of us cousins. We all thought we were the favorite. We four girls loved to stay with Hazel overnight because we got to share her room with her, listen to records on the old Victrola, and play "dress-up" with her trunk full of vintage clothing.

She often played the piano for our sing-alongs, and I especially liked a song, *Oh I Want a Paper Doll To Call My Own, a Doll That Other Fellows Cannot Steal.* We sang at the top of our lungs as she played the popular songs of the era. Church hymns we didn't like so much and neither did she. She had stacks of popular sheet music to select from. Practicing my piano lessons on her piano gave me some needed variety, and Hazel gave me compliments when I played.

When Hazel was older, she sold the family upright piano to a guy who loaded it into his pickup and drove off. A mile from the Erickson home the unsecured piano toppled out of the pickup and rolled end over end into the ditch. Mom and Hazel mourned for that old piano for years and talked about how someone had later stolen all the ivory keys from the keyboard. The piano endured rain and vandalism until the county road crews must have cleaned up the remains.

Hazel liked to drive and I think she felt free and in control behind the wheel. I stood between Mom and Hazel at age three in the Model T Ford speeding down the country dirt road on the steep hill where the wild pasque flowers grew. I said, "We're going a whooping away."

She laughed over that comment for years and reminded me of it often. I think she felt pride in her fast-driving skills.

The Neighbor Lady and Art Linkletter radio shows provided entertainment and stories for Hazel. She faithfully copied the recipes the Yankton, South Dakota radio hostess Wynn Speece dictated. Wynn, a Martha Stewart type, had an avid following of ladies and produced folksy recipe booklets with her family photos.

My favorite food memories from Hazel are Ost Kake, a Swedish cheesecake, chocolate chip pie, whipped lime Jell-O with pineapple, and Rice Krispie bars with peanut butter frosting. Mom, Dad, Hazel and Clarence nearly always had Sunday dinners together and that continued with Uncle Clarence and Mom after Dad and Hazel were gone, in 1995 and 1984 respectfully.

AUNT HAZEL'S PEANUT BUTTER RICE KRISPIE BARS

½ cup sugar and ½ cup light syrup — Mix and bring to boil
Add and melt ½ cup peanut butter
4 cups Rice Krispies — stir into above mixture

Press in 9x9 pan and top with 1 cup chocolate chips and 1 Tablespoon peanut butter melted.

Hazel was always at Mom's side helping whether it was quilting, canning garden produce, cooking for the threshing run, or making cookies and fancy little sandwiches for my wedding reception. It was Hazel who quickly drove to the farm to retrieve the fancy waitress aprons I'd sewn and forgotten to take to the reception.

Quilting, a skill the Erickson sisters shared, benefited our daughters when Aunt Alice, Hazel and Mom made embroidered animal baby quilts for new babies in the family. Together, they spent years making a variety of quilts. This must have brought them memories of their enjoyment of gathering around a quilting frame in their youth.

For my parents' 45th anniversary, Hazel helped me coordinate the effort to gather embroidered squares made by their friends and family. The designs represented a meaningful event or relationship each had with my parents. Hazel embroidered a violet — Mom's middle name. I wonder if that middle name was her idea in 1913 when her sister, Elvera, was born.

Tatted snowflakes on our family Christmas tree remind us of Hazel's skills. She tried in vain to teach me to do tat and crochet but said, "Caryl, I can't believe you can't do that. You can do everything else so well."

Maybe that was why. I did too many other things and rarely to the perfection my aunts and mother achieved. Whenever Sherm and I came back to Beresford, I showed Mom and Hazel my latest craft or sewing project and they always looked forward to new ideas to share with the *Friendly Hour Club.* I loved their new ideas, too.

Hazel and I exchanged frequent letters and like Mom, she saved most of mine through the years. In 1983 Hazel provided the information to help me find ancestral homes in Sweden. She had carefully kept letters from Sweden, which led us to the parishes from which her parents had emigrated in the 1880s.

Aunt Hazel treasured photos and tales of our travels to her parents' homes in Varmland and Ostergutland, Sweden. She kept them on her bedside table along with a photo album of her family. She loved taking family pictures with her reddish-brown, box Kodak but managed to stay in the background when group photos included her.

As the colon cancer took control of her frail body, she had numerous stays at the hospital. Mom always accompanied her and I often did, too. One time made me angry when the emergency room staff treated her as a disposable entity. Old and having a fatal disease may explain staff attitude, but I didn't share the view. I remember demanding medication and attention for her. I was a trained nursing home administrator by this time and knew the medical

Waking to Mourning Doves

jargon and procedures. I knew how to be an advocate, a skill every hospital patient's family members should have.

When Mom and Dad celebrated their 50th wedding anniversary in 1983, Hazel was in the hospital and the doctors wouldn't release her for even a few hours. She was devastated and so were we. I contemplated kidnapping her, but did the next best thing by recording and taping the program, and taking the slide show and recorded greetings from friends to her in the hospital. She shed tears as we held hands and listened together.

As the cancer progressed in the summer of 1983, she hurried to finish an ecru crochet project of my favorite pattern for my August birthday. She rode to our home in Burnsville with my parents so she could give it to me in person. Her last visit was special for all of us. We visited the rose gardens and the tallest building in downtown Minneapolis at the time (IDS Tower) and laughed about our visit to the shorter Foshay Tower in 1966. So many years had gone by since Hazel had looked down from the then-tallest building in Minneapolis at Mom holding toddler Cherise in the parking lot below.

Fortunately, our daughters had some experiences with my beloved Aunt Hazel. We always spent time while they were growing up with Hazel and Clarence on our frequent visits to South Dakota. Hazel's home was filled with photos of her great-nieces and nephews, and she followed their activities just as she had done for my cousins and me. She cuddled them as babies and played with the youngsters, as she called them.

As insidious cancer cells invaded her body she suffered in silence and resignation, just as she had borne her disfigurement.

I knew Hazel wouldn't be with us much longer as she and Clarence, my parents, Sherm and I watched Beresford's 1984 July 4th parade. After another short hospital visit, Mom and I stayed with Hazel all night at her home and realized that she needed constant nursing care. The next day we arranged for her admittance to the Bethesda Nursing Home. I stayed a couple of days, skipping the big farewell party that was planned for me at Horizon West Nursing Home where I had been an interim Administrator for four months. It is a decision I don't regret.

During Hazel's illness I tried to do a "life review" with her, something I learned in training to become an administrator. Validating one's life is important, and I tried to tell her what a positive impact she had had on my life.

Always self-effacing, she said, "You give me too much credit."

Hazel died quietly in her sleep a month later, and I was glad to have spent the time with her. After the funeral, Mom and I helped sort her things and found a neatly organized genealogy packet complete with old Swedish letters, photos and all the family records she had collected. I knew it was up to me to continue that family history project, and I did, starting with the Erickson and Carlson family history books.

Unworn items of lingerie that I'd sewn for her filled a corner of her neatly organized oak dresser drawer. Well-worn, double-knit polyester dresses and pantsuits Mom had sewn hung on closet hooks. I guess she kept the lingerie items "for good" which never came, much like my mother did.

Hazel would be pleased to know that her dear little sister didn't suffer for years from cancer as she did. The hospice nurses kept Mom's pancreatic cancer, which gave her pain only the last two weeks of her life, under control.

As we left our home in Burnsville for what we knew would be our last visit with Mom, three brilliant VIOLET-colored cosmos bloomed on one plant in my garden. They were the only cosmos blooms all season. To me the message was clearly stated as if by her three sisters: "Caryl, you can let her go, we will take care of her now."

Most skeptics would say, "Just a coincidence." Maybe, maybe not.

Hazel would be flabbergasted but flattered to know that her life story touched the hearts of a Hollywood film director and producer. I am working with them to make a fictional film based on her life and the *Friendly Hour Club*. Playing my grandmother in the '30s portion of the film *Prairie Sonata*, I can imagine myself in a time before I was born.

PART III: PALS

Paul & Me

Buster & Me

4th Birthday

Cousins

Lois & Me

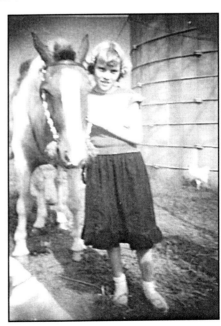

Ginger & Me

CHAPTER **10**

Playhouses and Paper Dolls

The children of my parents' friends were my earliest playmates. When we moved to the new farm in 1941, the neighbor children quickly became my friends.

> Mom writes: *Caryl celebrated her 4th birthday party having Donald and Dennis Stuessi and Paul Voegeli and Linda Wells. Caryl liked to dig in the dirt and played with dolls and cats and helped in the garden pulling weeds and came to the barn when we milked cows. She enjoyed going to Grandma Erickson's and Effie and Eva and Ragnar's and stayed with them a lot and we went to the Arkota. Dad and Grandpa put a swing up east of the house for her.*

My new friends and I played outside exploring the creeks, meadows and fields. Safety never seemed a concern of our parents, but maybe we just weren't aware of it. I loved making play houses in the groves and building forts and dugouts of scrap lumber or tree branches and logs. We liked to form clubs, climb trees, swim in the stock tanks if we thought we could get away with it, and play hide-and-seek in all the buildings. We especially loved the barns and sliding in the hay, jumping from rope swings onto soft, aromatic piles of hay. We kept busy exploring every nook and cranny of each other's barns, always observed by flocks of cooing, nesting pigeons that you didn't want to be standing under.

> *September 194–Gail, Marge, Mary and I started our club. We also have dues of 3 cents.*
>
> *April 7, 1949–Went home with Mary first and then on the way home stopped at Stuessi's and played till 8.*
>
> *September 1949–Mary came down and we started a clubhouse. We dressed up and played cowboy. Thrill!*

Nearly every Sunday we got together with Mom or Dad's families. This always included a big meal. We celebrated birthdays with gifts, games and angel food cake. There was at least one birthday every month. One strange thing is that on the Erickson side, the sons-in-law rarely had their birthdays celebrated with a clan gathering nor were they given gifts. The seven cousins usually had birthdays close to one of the grown-ups, so birthdays were frequently celebrated together.

> Mom writes: *Grandma Erickson, George and family, Dorcas, Gwen, Ruth, Howard and Norman, Alice, Janice and Verlyn and Elmer, Hazel and Clarence, Caryl, Elvera and Ray often got together on Sunday to celebrate birthdays or holidays. We played games such as croquet, jarts, and dominoes. Sometimes we planned a pot luck dinner or picnic. We often served mashed potatoes, beef, gravy and creamed peas, pickles, homemade breads and had cake, pie or sauce.*

We seven cousins — Gwenneth, Ruth, Howard, Norman, Janice, Verlyn and I — all grew up within a few miles of each other and spent so much time together it was like having six brothers and sisters. We stayed overnight at each other's houses as much as we could and never ran out of ways to get in trouble and have fun. We especially enjoyed playing in the playhouses we made and producing mud pies decorated with all the prairie flowers and grasses. Ruth, Norman and I sneaked cream and eggs from the storm cellar to make our mud pies creamier and smoother. Aunt Dorcas didn't catch us until Gwen squealed on us. I suppose we chanted our favorite tattletale rhyme, but not loud enough for our parents to hear us.

Tattletale, Tattletale, hanging on a bull's tail, when the bull takes a pee you'll have a cup of tea, when he takes a poop, you'll have a bowl of soup.

> Mom writes: *Caryl had a 7th birthday party. Gwen, Linda, Lois and Ruth. She often stayed overnight with Ruth and Gwen and played out in the grove and played on the hay bales and barn haymow. The girls stole eggs and cream from the cave to make mud pies until Gwen squealed on them. They got up on the roof and dressed up and made up plays and songs. They put the lines on the old buggy and dressed up pet cats and played in the play house. Caryl put up stores, bakeries and houses outside and she played there a lot. When friends came they made mud pies decorated with weed seeds. We gave her pots and pans from the house.*

At home, my playhouse with a store and soda fountain featured concoctions of mud balls, water, weeds and flowers for sodas and sundaes. Mom was my best customer and visited often. Our daughters and granddaughters were not so enamored with this activity, although I did provide the supplies for them. One photo I took of Rachel and Claire looks like they are saying "Why is Nana forcing us to make mud pies?"

> *September 17, 1950–Eva, Ragnar and Nan came out for dinner and supper and we played canasta and piano and sang and had fun.*

> *March 11, 1951–We're having quite a blizzard. Voegelis came over tonite- George and I beat in canasta.*

We had a lot of company, card parties and neighborhood gatherings in those days. We played cards and sometimes that mysterious "table up" game which was the closest thing to contacting spirits we ever did. Four people crowded to one side of a card table placed on the linoleum tile floor, interlaced fingers and chanted, "Table up, table up, table up." With the slow pressure of everyone's hands, the energy of the moment or whatever, the opposite two table legs lifted off the floor. When we asked the table questions, it tapped the answer. Yes and no questions or numbers-related ones like, "How old is Caryl?" worked best.

Everyone exclaimed, " No, I'm not forcing the table to tap," so it became a huge, hilarious mystery to everyone. It seemed to work best after an oyster stew dinner shared with the Voegelis while a blizzard raged outside.

Parlor games were fun, too. In one game, someone sat in a chair. Two other people held their breath and counted to three while waving their arms up and down. Then, with only two fingers under each arm of the person, they were able to lift the seated person off the chair. Sounds impossible, but I saw it happen several times and always begged to see it again.

Nan was masterful at conducting parlor tricks and had an entire repertoire. Her cousin called her a Chautauqua kind of woman. I loved watching her perform. In one trick, she balanced two forks on a match, placed them on a water-glass edge, burned the match — and the forks remained balanced on the glass! Her card tricks were varied. The one I remember is about using a jack and telling a story by the way the cards were placed. For example, the jack went out and got "treys" (3s) and had friends (king, queen and jacks). Nan taught me how to arrange the cards and tell the story with proper emphasis, but now I can't remember the card sequence or the details of so many of the other stories she told. If only I had written them down.

We kids were included in most community activities. The custom of a "chivaree" happened soon after a wedding. The goal was to surprise the newlyweds and get them to promise the rowdy crowd a party at a later date.

Someone would find out where the couple were and made hurried phone calls to neighbors to make a plan. Sometimes everyone met at another farm and drove in a line without car lights as a surprise tactic. In the early evening after chores, a large group converged on the targeted house banging on pots and pans, honking horns and making as much noise as possible after the house was surrounded so the couple couldn't escape. After a lot of shouting and teasing from the crowd, the newlyweds came to the door and agreed to what the crowd wanted. One time they wheeled the bride down the main street of town in a wheelbarrow, but usually the friends just requested a party.

I always got to go along on the chivaree surprises, but never the parties. I think they served beer or whiskey, so kids were not allowed.

> Mom writes: *Caryl would walk down to the creek to try and skate and there wasn't enough ice to learn. We often went on Nan's hill and coasted and once in a while on Jake Voegeli's hill. Sometimes Kenneth, Paul and Caryl made snow forts and houses and we brought food out to them.*

In the winter, we coasted, tried to ice skate on isolated small ponds and the creek, built forts in the snow banks, and played fox and geese. Winter provided sledding, ice skating and just playing in the snow making forts and tunnels. We had huge snow banks, as the wind in South Dakota rarely subsides and a small snowfall can produce deep drifts.

July 1, 1949–Jan here and we were playing in the tank.

Splashing around and cooling off in the wood-sided livestock water tank was a forbidden pleasure on a hot day. It stirred up the slime and moss that formed on the bottom and then the stock didn't want to drink. For a while we had a big, tin stock water tank that we used just for "swimming" and that was a favorite neighborhood spot. I grew up in the polio era, so was not allowed to use the Beresford pool to swim for fear of catching the disease, for good reason, as many children from Beresford did and there was no vaccine at that time. Lakes were scarce in South Dakota and I didn't learn to swim until I was a freshman in college.

I still have a shoebox chock full of paper dolls from the '40s. They range from cats and puppies with clothing to movie stars to Dick, Jane and Sally from first-grade readers. I begged for new books of cut-out paper dolls on trips to town and Mom usually relented. I spent hours cutting out doll clothing and planning elaborate scenarios and activities. When Mom and Dad did chores, I spread my paper dolls out over the sofa and living room floor. They preferred that I entertain myself in the house rather than go outside in below-zero weather with them. My friends and I often played together with our paper dolls, the Barbies of the '40s. Sometimes we made our own paper dolls and outfits from catalogue cutouts or crayon drawings. I liked to play "store" with friends either cutting pictures out of magazines and catalogues or using cast-offs.

I have been a collector all my life and learned the habit at an early age. Old magazines and Sears catalogues provided items to cut out for scrapbooks or playing store. I pasted pictures of cats, dogs and movie stars — as well as napkins and pen pal letters into theme scrapbooks. We made paste from flour and water and it worked surprisingly well.

I took pictures of cats and school friends to put in my photo album. Black-and-white photos mounted with little triangle art corners in a book have stood the test of time, unlike color photos taken in the '50s.

> Mom writes: *Caryl and her friends liked to dress up. Caryl had my banquet Jr. Sr. white dress on sometimes. They even got Dennis to put clothes on. Caryl Marge and Marion played wedding and danced and the cousins loved to use Hazel's make up and dress up in Grandma Erickson's clothes. They made wedding parties from hollyhock dolls. About every year, we gave her a new doll. She put water on their heads.*

My friends and I enjoyed dressing up in old clothes, hats, shoes and jewelry when we were younger. The Erickson cousins loved to play dress-up from an old trunk of Grandma's clothes. We helped ourselves liberally to Hazel's make-up, too. Whenever Mom bought new dresses, I couldn't wait till we could play with them. Sometimes we convinced the boys to play dress-up, but they preferred card games, comic books, listening to radio program adventures or outdoor activities. Most kids in the '40s liked dominoes, checkers, tiddlywinks, Parcheesi, Monopoly and card games like old maid, canasta, rummy, and hearts.

When we neighborhood girls gathered to play in each other's houses, we made up elaborate scenarios with dolls, parents' old dress-up clothes or paper dolls. We liked to play "doctor" and cut out a doll's stomach "voice box" and pretend we were removing her appendix. Then we sewed her up again. Putting wet compresses on dolls' heads did little for their rather fragile composition faces. I had a rubber "drink and wet" doll in the late '40s. She wasn't as cuddly and versatile as the composition or cloth dolls and got hard and brittle in only a couple of years.

In addition to pretending to bake and play house, I was a plant nut from a very young age. In the fall I dug up plants like petunias, coleus and marigolds and put them in cans of dirt wrapped in tinfoil on the wide windowsills of the south and east dining-room windows. Pruning wasn't one of my skills, and the plants grew long and scraggly. Mom let me keep them long after they should have been tossed. Sometimes I picked box elder bugs off plants and put them into a can of kerosene. I can still hear that sizzle as they succumbed. We had a big old box-elder tree close to the house. I suppose the loathsome bugs lived there, but my parents never cut it down until a windstorm tore it apart. I missed it because the spring seeds looked great on mud pies.

Mom taught me how to embroider and do other handwork. I still have my first project, a cross-stitched donkey on a white dishtowel. I remember laboring over it for hours and the sense of pride I felt when I finally finished it. Girls in the '40s made embroidered items for their hope chest. Mine had an abundance of pillow cases, dish towels for every day of the week, potholders and some small tablecloths. Some are in mint (unused) condition today.

Mom spent many hours mending stockings, Dad's overalls, shirts, and long underwear. Socks Mom mended were perfectly woven and comfortable to wear. Patches on jeans and overalls were quite durable and seem charming to me today. I made quilts for my grandchildren using these mended jeans as well as jeans from other members of the family. I put a pair of Rachel, Claire and Nate's size-one jeans in the center. Mom taught me to darn socks using a wooden darning egg and I still know how, but consider it a waste of my time. Oddly enough, I still feel wasteful throwing away a sock with a hole in the heel.

August 1949–At Sunbeams roller skating party- Ruth and I rode with Stuessi's. I roller skated with all the boys except 4.

My friends and I looked forward to skating at the Canton roller rink, and we all became pretty good skaters. The town of Canton was 20 miles from home, so we didn't skate there as often as we wanted to. Churches and schools sponsored skating parties for whole families to attend, but we all hoped our parents wouldn't go along and skate. As we got older, it was our first touch of romance if a boy asked us to skate during couples only when the lights dimmed. Beresford eventually allowed us to skate in the old Legion Hall where we also held class plays and dances, but it wasn't as good as the Canton rink. The advantage of skating in Beresford was meeting more kids from the area. One time I fell at the end of a crack-the=whip line, sat down painfully hard on my tailbone, and moved slowly for days.

July 6, 1951–What a nite. Lois and I laughed all nite. Went to Florence V for dinner and to town on our bikes.

Caryl Crozier

January 1, 1952–Saw Vonny, Janet and Karen and Marcene in town fun tearing around.

I met several girls from town when I was in seventh and eighth grades. I think they initially wanted to be friends with me because I had a couple of cute boy cousins and was a classmate at Silver Lake School of a boy several girls had a crush on. For whatever reason, we became friends and went to parties and became teenagers interested in boys. Going to town on Saturday night and "cruising" was our favorite weekly ritual. I met friends and walked up and down the same one block on each side about 30 times a night. Sometimes we shopped at Moons Variety Store, checked out the dresses or used the bathroom at the K & K store. We ate a lot of ice cream from Ryger's dairy bar or the soda fountains at the two drug stores. Bruehlers had booths and fantastic chocolate malts. Our introduction to soft-serve ice cream was called Whirl-a-Whip. By putting a chunk of hard ice cream in a noisy machine, it came out soft and whipped. A delicacy. We couldn't go home without buying bags of popcorn from Bessie Keifer's old-time popcorn wagon. Most families that I knew made this a tradition.

For nine cents, kids twelve and under could see a movie at the Vogue, an Art Deco style theater. Most of us tried to get by as under twelve until we started high school and then the jig was up. I am sure the ticket sellers knew our ages, but the theatre owners liked kids and let us get away with it. Fifty cents for the adult price seemed like a lot of money to us. We usually stopped at Macs Cafe after the movie for cherry Cokes and French fries with ketchup. The Main street cafe became our teenage hangout.

I expanded my friendships to town kids as I got older. I think it was because some of us were getting interested in boys, and the grass looked greener on the other side of the fence. So, we set out to make new friends, both girls and boys. LaVonne and Karen are still good friends. Helen began having boy-girl parties in 7th grade. I was thrilled to be invited to the town kids' parties. We danced (she had a great 45 rpm record collection), ate good food and played spin the bottle and post office. Although it seemed a bit risqué to me, we were always well chaperoned by Helen's parents.

4-H members Janet and Marcene became lifelong friends and we did many things together in elementary and high school years. They attended Augustana Academy (a Norwegian-Lutheran high school in Canton), but we were together in 4-H as well as dating in later years.

Dating started for some of us in 9th grade, usually in groups or on double dates. We went to football and basketball games, school plays, dances, roller skating, movies, house parties or just driving around in Beresford or the nearby towns of Centerville, Canton and Alcester.

Waking to Mourning Doves

All rural families were on party telephone lines of about 15 families each, and about that many receivers went up when our number rang: short, long, short. Our phone number was 23F111. The entire community knew my social life and friends and openly "rubbered" (eavesdropped) and then teased me about what they had heard. This seems invasive to me now, but those neighbors provided support systems that we don't have living in a large city.

CHAPTER 11

Cuddles, Buster and Ginger

Mom writes: *Grandma Erickson gave Caryl a white kitten and she called her Whitey and as time went on she had kittens and we looked and found them in the barn, so that was the start of our kittens. She played and played and played with them. Caryl and her cats were inseparable at times. She would put them on shelves and boxes and wrap them up. She would put them in the doll buggy and wheel them around like dolls. She put them on Grandpa and he wouldn't like it, but went along with it. She also gave them to Effie and she didn't care. She would lay them by her dolls and the cats didn't move or care. She even tamed the neighbor's cats as wild as they were. No cat was too wild for her to tame and train.*

Cats were by far my favorite farm animals. Our entire feline lineage started with Whitey, a female kitten that Grandma Erickson gave me. Her first five-kitten litter, born in a horse stall in the barn, filled me with wonder. They were so tiny, soft and helpless. I sat in the manger watching them for hours as their miniature paws massaged Whitey as they nursed. Mom taught me how to determine what sex they were, and I learned that females are rarely as brightly colored as the males, but they are more likely to survive. Two female kittens from this first litter survived to become the mothers of generations of my best playmates. Susie, a soft grey tiger cat, was best of all. Susie was a gentle, very pretty cat that lived to a very old age and bore Flippy, who lived over 15 years and mothered two batches of kittens each year. Flippy also adopted any other kittens that were abandoned. Finally, there was Trixie, a dark grey cat with a white stripe on her face. Trixie was somewhat of a renegade, and always hid her kittens more, usually upstairs in the hog house. Her offspring were never as good at mothering as Susie and Flippy.

April 18, 1950–Trixie had her kittens, 5 of them- 1 dead- so that makes 4.

April 21, 1950–Tomcat killed 4 kittens-Trixie's- she is with Flippy.

Waking to Mourning Doves

May 24,1949–I brought the kittens up to the cob house today.

The mother cats hid their kittens as best they could and usually gave birth to them in the horse stalls tucked under feed troughs or in hay piles in the loft.

In spite of the mothers' secrecy, a marauding tomcat often found and killed the whole batch of kittens. I suppose they weren't his offspring, and the mother would come into heat again to give him a chance for breeding. My parents tried to hide the mangled kitten bodies from me, but I always wanted to conduct elaborate burial ceremonies for them. Mother cats moved the kittens to different locations by grabbing them by the nape of their neck, carrying them one at a time to a new home. I sometimes helped by moving them into the cob house close to our house.

The roof of the cob house was flat and easily accessible by a ladder or by climbing the nearby tree. I spent hours up there with my menagerie of cats. I dressed them up in doll clothes and put them in their bed boxes and they stayed there as long as I did. Very rarely did one climb down the tree fully attired in a diaper, top or gown. They even lay under my doll blankets and kept bonnets on their heads and booties on their feet. There was no food incentive to spend that time with me, they just liked the attention and even tolerated being pushed around in doll buggies.

No matter how wild and uncooperative a cat was, I managed to tame it somehow and I also worked on taming the neighbor's cats too.

September 2, 1950– Cuddles got sick

September 26,1950–Cuddles is about the same today. I hope she gets better

Mom writes: *Cuddles had distemper and Caryl forced her back to health.*

When they weren't killing kittens, the male cats usually ran off or died of distemper. Vaccinations weren't available then, and half the new kittens didn't live through the winter. If they lived a year, they were usually healthy. I force-fed some and got them through their illnesses, as they would have starved if I hadn't. I held the cat's mouth open with one hand and used a teaspoon or eyedropper to force milk down its throat with the other hand. That was not a pleasant experience. My favorite kitten, Cuddles, was a success and she lived a normal lifespan after her illness.

A few memorable male cats, always more vividly colored, survived

Caryl Crozier

and became house pets. Gene, a beautiful, wide-striped tiger cat with a friendly disposition, was a family favorite. He usually spent the night at my grandparents' a half-mile away. A local photographer, Oscar Graverson, wanted to have a portrait of him, but Gene went ballistic when we tried to get him in the car. He met his maker on the road on one of his forays to my grandparents' house.

Whiskers, a male black cat with a white striped face and whiskers, managed to spend a large part of his life in the house during my high school years. He was always sleek and clean. Odysseus, a gold and white tiger cat, was not above rudeness. He gave his opinion of Sherm the first night he stayed at our house by using the deep pile rug next to Sherm's bed as a toilet.

After I went away to college, Mom still had a pet cat in the house. Her last one was a kitten that was apparently abandoned near her home. Kitty became her constant companion after Dad died. After Mom's stroke, Kitty spent a year with us until we found her a good home.

The dogs we had were tolerable, but were really Dad's and Mom's pets. Buster was my favorite. He was a bulldog-terrier mutt that slept under the porch, usually surrounded by a couple of litters of kittens that liked to shelter there waiting for handouts from the kitchen. Buster loved to ride on the tractor while Dad did fieldwork and trotted across the fields to pick up his ride if he was left behind.

Mitzi, a black-and-white spotted rat terrier, was too yippy for me to appreciate. Once she was run over by a car tire, but Dad breathed in her mouth and she survived many more years. Their later dogs, Ginger and Sugar, were wonderful companions for them after I left home.

April 21, 1952–My cow had a calf.

My Grandpa Kinkner gave me a red heifer calf called Red. She bore a red and white spotted heifer that I called Cherry. I tried to milk her once just before she was due to have a calf. We didn't realize she was about to give birth, and she stuck her foot in the pail and tried to kick me, spilling the milk on the ground. I soon decided that milking cows wasn't my forte, and my parents must have agreed. Mom and Dad always milked many cows (10-12) by hand. I can still see Dad struggling across high snow banks carrying big cans of milk to the house to run through the separator, which divided the milk from the cream. Chores like this, day after day, kept them tied down at home morning and night. They tried milking machines for a while, but found them more work than milking by hand. When I was little, I would either go along to the barn and watch or be left in the house playing with my paper dolls on the sofa. I was afraid in the house alone, as the big old belching wood furnace

Waking to Mourning Doves

in the basement made noises that I imagined to be everything from burglars to fire. Several times when I got scared, I scurried to the barn in blizzards and got scolded, but luckily not lost. More than once I rushed to the barn and told my parents the basement was on fire, so they always had to go and check to quell my fears.

Occasionally little goslings or ducklings were brought into the house to keep them warm. The geese began nesting in the spring, making the gander ferociously protective and cranky guarding his family. When the goslings hatched, Mom put them in small buildings for shelter from predators and weather. I scoured the lawn picking dandelion greens and grass to feed them and loved watching them peck at oatmeal and ground chicken feed.

In earlier generations the Kinkners were known to be horse traders, both professionally and for enjoyment. After what seemed like years of begging, Dad finally took me to see Miles Merrigan, the local horse trader, where we selected a pony for me. We liked a particular brown and white pinto, so Dad rode her first and then let me try. Ginger was the one! She soon became an important part of my life, and I spent some of the happiest times of my youth grooming her and riding her in the fields and pastures and on the roadways. For years, I saddled her up after getting home from school and rode her down the lane to get the cows from the pasture. Cleaning up her stall wasn't the most pleasant chore, but it became my responsibility.

> Mom writes: *Caryl and her pet horse Ginger were great pals; traveled a little all over. She went to the saddle club and rode several places. Ginger was a good mare; rode her all over in the country; she sometimes rode with friends and sometimes over to see Janice.*
>
> *April 27, 1952–I rode Ginger 11 miles.*
>
> *July 15, 1951–rode Ginger into saddle club, but don't think I'll join. Did I ever get sunburned.*

Although riding with friends was enjoyable, the best times were spent in solitude on Ginger with only the open skies, bird songs and the constant prairie breeze. I tried riding Ginger with the Beresford Saddle Club, but neither of us was into synchronization or sweat. We rode in a hot Fourth of July parade once, and she didn't care a bit about being in line or keeping up with the other horses. No amount of prodding seemed to change her mood. She also bucked if she didn't like two people on her back and managed to throw my friend Lois off a time or two.

Caryl Crozier

August 15, 1951– Went horseback riding at night with Paul.

August 13, 1952–Rode horse with Jim, Gerald and Mary. Dad came after me fooey!

Most of my neighbor friends had horses too, so after chores many of us got together and rode on the country roads at dusk. I rode Ginger to visit friends, too. It wasn't unusual for me to ride eight to twelve miles in a day.

March 2, 1951–What a blizzard. I didn't go to school. Pop went to pasture for Ginger.

I didn't ride Ginger much during the winters, and she roamed freely in the stubble fields and pasture and became quite wild and woolly by spring. One winter one of the workhorses kicked her in the nose and she had a bump and drainage for quite some time. Catching her in the field was tricky. I used oats for bait and hoped I could quickly slip a halter or bridle on her. A loving horse shouldn't be so contrary, but she was. A few times I got lucky and was able to jump up on her back from a fence.

When I departed for college, Dad sold her to a family with children without telling me beforehand. She only lived a year after that. I felt sad and angry, but the sale helped finance my college education.

Dad had a team of workhorses, Goldie and Blackie. Goldie, a beautiful golden horse, got stuck upside down in a hole in the deep part of the creek one winter. She had struggled a long time trying to get out by the time we discovered her in the icy cold creek. The neighbors brought their tractor loader over, and somehow pulled her up and out by her tail, a horrifying sight. In spite of administrations of medicines by the veterinarian, Dr. Cotton, she died a couple of days later. The men had belted her into a supported standing position and gave her rubdowns, but the shock had been too much for her.

When animals died, Otto Muhlenkort brought his rendering truck to pick them up. They only lived 3/4 mile away, and awful smells sometimes wafted over from his rendering plant in the middle of his field. I never knew what was done with the by-products of all those rendered animals.

Growing up with so many animals to play with and take care of was wonderful and has given me a life-long love and appreciation for all animals. There has hardly been a time in my life when we haven't had pets. After we were married, it was primarily hunting dogs kept in outdoor kennels. The two golden retrievers, Maize and Caper, each had two litters of pups. Our daughters enjoyed dressing them up in doll clothes and pushing them around in a doll buggy, just like I had done as a child with the cats.

PART IV: FARM CHORES

Me

Dad & Ginny

Mom & Genie

Dad & Mom

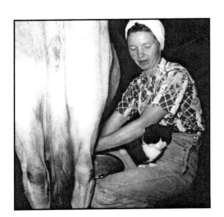

Mom & Dad

Mom & Whiskers

25th Anniversary

CHAPTER **12**

Chicken Chores

Our family farm site seemed crowded with small buildings — most being related to chickens, my nemesis. Had it not been for a mid-20th Century farmwoman's duty to take care of chickens, I might have ended up a farmer's wife. No way was it in my playbook to be surrounded by repulsive chickens the remainder of my life. Ironic, because Mom's "chicken money" helped finance all the extras for me. Piano lessons, nice clothes, books, sewing fabrics and supplies all contributed to my quest for a wider world.

A two-room lap-sided building was the only chicken house on the farm when we arrived in 1941. One side held nest boxes for the hens to deposit eggs, and there was a five-level bar roost at the other end. Chickens, like other birds, have the ability to perch on a bar or branch and doze the night away. Maybe it's an innate characteristic to be off the ground and safe from predators. The only predators that I experienced in the chicken house were the tiny black flea-like chicken mites that got on my body and made me itch. Although Mom doused the chickens with some kind of flea powder, the repulsive mites survived and reproduced. I avoided that side of the building at all costs. For a few years the other section only held baby chicks or young roosters ready for slaughter. Mom filled our freezer or the rented town locker unit with "spring chickens" and also sold "dressed chickens" to a few customers.

My parents soon purchased a brooder house, a small building designed to house baby chickens. Mom always purchased several hundred chickens in a variety of breeds: Leghorns, Red Rock, and Cornish. She kept them in a brooder house that was heated with a huge, hooded lamp, which the new chicks huddled under to keep warm.

When I was four years old, Mom bought me fifteen red baby chicks of my very own, which we housed in the brooder house north of our house. Having not yet been exposed to the distastefulness of chicken work, I was excited to get the box holding my baby chicks home from the hatchery in town. I carefully lifted each fluffy chick out of the box and watched it scurry to join the other hatchlings. Mine were easy to pick out from the other yellow chicks. I spent hours sitting and watching them dash out from under the brooder stove heater to get feed from trays strategically placed on the soft, spongy peat moss on the floor. We provided water in a quart jar inverted over a special glass-drinking container that let out more liquid as the chickens drank. Mom put some kind of de-wormer drops in the water. I loved to shuffle-step in among the scurrying chicks. One sad day I accidentally stepped on one of my red chickens and it died. I cried inconsolably most of the day and never felt quite the same about chickens after that.

Sometimes disasters struck with the rather dangerous brooder stoves. One time, Uncle Elmer and Alice's brooder house and chickens went up in smoke and flames. The same thing happened to my parents' brooder and it caused a great deal of distress. Insurance didn't pay for the losses.

July 6, 1949 – Mom went out to the chicken yard at night and 130 chickens were dead.

Another time, Mom went out to check on the chickens, and 130 were dead in the outside chicken pen. I think they became frightened, piled on top of each other and smothered each other trying to reach safety through a small opening into the chicken house. Chickens are really stupid, and in a rainstorm, they just pile up and die. Whenever it rained, we always rushed to get them to safety whether they were in the yard or loose under the evergreen trees.

The roosters were fearsome as they grew older. They chased me and flew at me and flapped their wings wildly if I invaded their territory. I walked around and behind buildings to avoid them. Only rarely did I venture into the yard without carrying a stick or broom to swat them away. I also couldn't stand chickens following me too close for their food. Most kids that grew up on a farm hated roosters.

I even avoided gathering eggs when possible. Sometimes the chickens had mites that got on me, and the setting hens pecked at me when I reached under them to get eggs. I couldn't avoid the daily chore of washing eggs that were soiled. We packed them in egg crates clean for sale and trading. Sometimes the eggs were cracked; Mom used those in baking or as fried eggs for supper. Maybe I ate too many fried eggs as a child, because I still can't fry an egg properly, nor do I want to even try.

When we wanted chicken for dinner, Mom took a special, long wire hook she had made to snare one by the leg. She deftly grabbed the unlucky chicken by the neck and with her strong hands, twirled it round and round till the head was released from the body. This is called "wringing its neck." The body flopped about the yard in its last nerve reaction, not realizing it had been decapitated. The cats eagerly awaited a chance to pounce on this easy prey, but never succeeded. The chickens were just too much larger than the other birds they stalked. Besides, Mom moved fast and they feared her swipe at them if they tried to grab the meal she had planned for the family.

Then came the most disgusting part: dressing. Mom slit the body cavity and pulled the entrails out in one bloody mass. She retrieved the heart, liver and gizzard to fry along with the rest, as our family considered them delicacies. Next, Mom plunged the headless corpses into a pail of boiling water so the feathers could be more easily plucked. The smell was indescribable: hot, wet feathers. I was very squeamish about plucking foul-smelling feathers from freshly scalded carcasses. I couldn't stand this operation and rarely helped dress chickens. If I did, it was to gingerly pick off pinfeathers when Mom had most of the job finished. Mom then singed the chicken by holding it close to a kerosene flame in a flat sauce dish. This burned off the very fine hair which remained on the skin after plucking the feathers. I preferred it when she skinned the chickens and yanked off the skin, feathers and all. In one deft operation with slits of her sharp butcher knife in just the right places, she cleaned the gizzard. This was the most fun to watch. She tried to cut the meat not breaking the grisly, grainy, disgusting bag in the middle. If she cut too far, it exploded in a foul-smelling manure-like mixture of partly digested grains.

Sometimes we butchered and dressed twenty young roosters at a time. I was very thankful that Aunt Hazel or our neighbor Hertha helped. Some of these dressed chickens were frozen for our use later and others we sold. Free-range chickens like we raised had a lot more flavor than the ones we buy at the supermarket today. But considering all the unpleasant work involved in manually processing chickens, maybe the factory farm model makes sense after all.

Mom made wonderful fried chicken coated in flour and then pan-fried in home-rendered lard. When browned, she added water and popped it in the oven. The best gravy in the world served over mashed potatoes was the culmination of the process.

All the chicken feed was housed in a small shed near the chicken coop. Dad supplemented the expensive commercial chicken feed that came in colorful print bags with ground corn and oats harvested from our fields. He had a grinding machine powered by the tractor and a pulley belt. Sometimes a couple of neighbors worked together to grind feed. Completing farm work in cooperation with neighbors made farming easier.

> Mom writes: *One Christmas we gave Caryl a cowboy outfit and clamp-on roller skates. She could roller skate in the new chicken house on the new cement floor. One night she had a party; Paul, Kenneth, Don, Dennis, Marion, Margie, Leon, Lois, Paul and Lowell and I fixed lunch for them, which they enjoyed. They often went to the roller rink in Canton.*

After the 1949 tornado blew away our original chicken house, my parents

Waking to Mourning Doves

had a larger one built, complete with a concrete floor. I hosted a "chicken house housewarming" roller skating party for the neighborhood kids that spring. I must have been desperate to roller skate!

> *September 21, 1949–My roller skating party was tonight. Dennis, Zweifels, me and Thompsons were there. We had a weiner roast. Real fun!*

My girlfriends and I spent days decorating the walls and planning the party. We deemed it a success when the boys we invited came too. I think they came because they knew Mom provided a great lunch. And she did! We clamped steel wheeled roller skates to our sturdy oxfords and whizzed, well maybe clomped, around under crepe paper streamer decorations. Skating on concrete was noisy and rough. We couldn't even hear the music from the radio while we skated.

Soon my enchantment with the new chicken house ended. With a couple hundred laying hens settled in the building, the piles of manure and molting feathers, and the invasion of rats under the building, made it just plain gross.

With all the grain stored on a farm, rats are a common problem. Dad always tied twine around his pant legs while mechanically shelling corn or grinding feed. It took only one rat running up his pants leg to teach him a lesson in precaution and prevention. Rats dug tunnels and lived under the new chicken house, a ready source of ground corn and chicken feed concentrate.

Occasionally, my parents decided to drown out the rats and hired the man who owned the water hauling truck to come out and force water under the chicken house. Pitchforks in hand, overalls tied tight with twine around the leg bottoms, and their rat-killing dog by their side, Mom and Dad performed a ballet of slaughter plunging their pitchforks into the rats as they scurried out from the flooded tunnels under the building. Mom moved fast and often had three or four rats impaled on her pitchfork at one time. Sometimes a couple of neighbors joined in the "fun." I watched from the safety of the car with closed windows. The cats feasted on the dead rats for days. This operation went on for years and years and my daughters witnessed it with the same aversion that I had. I think my grandson Nate would have loved to join in the fracas.

> *July 17, 1949–Jezebel hatching her chix-7 chix so far- 11 eggs-3 more will hatch.*

We had one pair of red and brown Bantam chickens. They were about half the size of our other chickens and were considered ornamental and somewhat useless by most farmers. Jezebel, our hen, hatched eleven active chicks from a nest hidden in the flowerbed. Jezebel and her chicks were very tame and

Caryl Crozier

weren't afraid of humans, but would have been a tasty snack for an owl, coyote or cat. Therefore, we put them inside the cob house every night. We brought out a wooden bushel basket and Jezebel clucked her chicks into the basket so we could carry them into their shelter. Very unusual behavior for a chicken, but she seemed to know we were protecting her babies. Her mate, on the other hand, lived in the chicken house most of the time with the big hens. Sometimes he was one frustrated rooster!

CHAPTER 13

Alfalfa and Cockleburs

The following diary entries summarize some of my duties — and attitudes toward my duties —on the farm.

June, 1951–Painted cistern and screens and worked in the yard.

April 15, 1952–Cleaned in yard and had a wiener roast.

May 17, 1952–I cleaned house, went to the field a while and Ma and I went to town.

May 27, 1952–Mowed lawn and put up fence and pulled weeds.

June 19, 1952–Slept till 11:45, made cake, pulled weeds, mowed lawn PU. Got skirt and silverware in the mail.

June 26, 1952–Read a book, chased pigs, cleaned house and picked and cleaned mulberries.

August 9, 1952–PU cut cockleburs all day and got $2.50 and huge blisters. Then went to Hazels to help clean house.

July 27, 1950–I helped Mom today mostly. Also cutting alfalfa.

If the acrid sweetness of a freshly mown alfalfa field could be bottled, I think everyone who grew up in the Dakotas would use it as a room freshener. I know I would. The scent of a newly swathed alfalfa field permeates one's clothing and nostrils. Of all the crops Dad grew, this was my favorite. Dad and Grandpa rotated alfalfa, corn and oats in our fields to enrich the soil. Alfalfa is a hardy, deep-rooted perennial plant that fixes nitrogen into the soil and helps prevent soil depletion. Farmers didn't use commercial fertilizers when I was growing up. Instead, crop rotation and livestock and chicken manure spread on the fields provided the necessary nutrients.

Caryl Crozier

We had to be careful to keep the cows out of the alfalfa fields because they went berserk eating, tearing and chewing alfalfa leaves until they bloated. I sympathized with my parents' despair when a favorite roan cow got loose overnight in the hay field and ingested too much alfalfa and bloated. The vet couldn't save her and had to put her down. The financial impact of losing a cow from our small herd was significant.

Southeastern South Dakota receives enough yearly rainfall to harvest three or four cuttings of alfalfa each summer. After Dad and Grandpa cut the hay, raking it into windrows was my favorite field job. I rode high on the seat over the tongs of the hay rake that Dad pulled with the tractor. When I pushed a foot lever, it created long rows of freshly bunched alfalfa, which is then easier to pitch into a hayrack to move to the barn or haystack.

Hen pheasants find alfalfa fields ideal places to nest. If the first alfalfa cutting comes before the eggs hatch, disaster can occur. Hens stay on their nests till the very last moment and sometimes don't escape the sharp sickle blade of the mower. Dad and Grandpa felt sad when it happened and told about it in hushed tones at dinnertime so I wouldn't hear. I did hear, though. The birds were abundant in my childhood because habitat had not been destroyed by the "clean" weed-free farming of today. Fencerows between farms provided plum thickets and long prairie grasses for nesting. We frequently saw busy pheasant broods tagging along after the hen. Pheasant nesting areas disappeared as farms grew in size, fences were removed and the low areas and pastures were drained and converted to cropland for the monoculture of soybeans and corn.

In 2008, we began converting the 80 acres of corn and soybean land I inherited to native grass to provide wildlife habitat. Now it is not unusual to stir up 25 pheasants and small herds of deer. A chorus of birdsong now fills the air on our farm, just as it did in my childhood.

In the '60s, baling machines tied the hay in compact bundles and our old-fashioned dump rake method fell by the wayside. The aesthetic appeal of a dump rake is still strong for me. Now, an old dump rake sits among the daylilies on the edge of our woods, reminding me daily of times from my childhood.

I liked driving the tractor for harvesting, mowing or raking hay. I especially liked driving the tractor while Dad sat on the binder. Mom shocked the oat grain bundles with Dad's help — much harder work than sitting on the tractor! We wore ugly, wide-brimmed straw hats to keep cool, but didn't worry then about exposure to ultraviolet rays. I repeatedly got sunburned and peeled. Mom wore long-sleeved shirts to prevent sunburn.

Weed control before herbicides and sprays required backbreaking work.

Waking to Mourning Doves

I dreaded the job of hand-cutting cockleburs in the cornfields. Armed with a sharp, machete-like corn knife, I trudged through my four assigned corn-rows hacking and chopping off noxious cockleburs at the base. Sharp-edged corn leaves cut my exposed skin and rivulets of sweat ran down my back. The thought of a cool drink of water from the burlap-wrapped Red Wing crock jug at the end of the field row kept me going. Watery blisters formed on my hands despite the gloves Mom made me wear. It took Mom, Dad and me several days from dawn to dusk to complete the job. I hated it.

One summer, I wanted to join a seed-corn detasseling crew, but my parents said no. I guess they needed me for farm work at home. They paid me an allowance of $2.50 a day to cut cockleburs, but I refused offers to help other neighbors.

It seemed we had every noxious weed on the planet on our farm. Fields, gardens and flowerbeds required constant weed control, which usually meant pulling them out by hand. If we weren't diligent, our gardens and flowerbeds got choked with pigweed, ragweed and a sharp thistle plant called buffalo burr . Prickly cockleburs, sandburs, beggar's tick and thistles invaded fields, pastures and ditches. Seeds spread by attaching to our clothing or animals' fur. Sandburs were the worst in my opinion, because they grew everywhere I wanted to explore. Picking them off my socks and pants cuffs was a painful operation. And they *really* hurt if you stepped on them barefoot.

Canadian thistles were and are troublesome. Uncle Clarence dispatched them by pouring salt near the root. Our friend Steff trained his cattle to eat thistles by putting molasses on them. The cows like the taste and eventually chow down on the weed without molasses! Nowadays, we are mandated to mow or use environmentally harmful herbicides to eliminate patches of thistles from our restored grasslands. The sprays are not good for pheasants and other wildlife, so it is better to mow before the seeds mature.

A variety of weeds provided mud-pie decorations. Dandelions and pigweed are beautiful garnishes. Ripe brown dock resembled coffee grounds, so we made pretend coffee with it. Ragweed had pretty leaves, but was the true culprit for allergy sufferers, not the stately goldenrod. All farmers hated creeping jennies, a vine-like weed that climbed and strangled plants, but as a child I rather liked them: The flower resembles a tiny white morning glory and looked great on mud cakes.

Tumbleweed, sometimes called Russian thistle, grew on flat dry saline soils and is known for its wind-blown seed dispersal. In late fall, strong South Dakota winds uprooted and propelled tumbleweeds across roads and onto fence-lines, sometimes making a long solid screen. A few times, Mom and I searched for the bushiest specimen and sprayed it with artificial snow. Small multicolored glass balls made it a perfect Christmas decoration! Somehow, Dad was not impressed.

Wild marijuana grew in the fenced cow lane between the pasture and barn. We ignored it, and by the 1970s it was a virtual forest. My parents got the old corn knives and scythes out and hacked it off to burn. I was never there when they burned it, but I wonder if they got high! The closest Sherm and I ever got to smoking pot was at a 1960s Leo Kottke 12-string guitar concert where people near us passed a joint back and forth. My lips felt strange, kind of sticky and sweet just by inhaling the haze in the air.

During WWII, people collected milkweed pods, fluffy down-like seed carriers, to make stuffing for life vests. Farmers didn't like milkweed infestations, but we all liked the butterflies that depended on the plants for food and chrysalis incubation. Our grandkids love watching a monarch butterfly emerge from its chrysalis.

My favorite farm chore was riding my horse, Ginger, to the pasture to herd the cows home in the evening. The cows rarely could be trusted to come home on their own, so we either walked or rode to get them. The pasture was marshy in the places the cows preferred to graze, so it was good to be on horseback. The grassy hummocks made by the cows grazing in wetlands gave me the creeps. I called them swamp stumps.

Dad developed a strong upper torso and a strong heart through so much physical labor, as did Mom. Mom's hands and arms at age 96 were still remarkably strong. As much as I loved the farm as a child, I came to the conclusion that living on a farm was probably not the life for me, and planned my life goals accordingly.

CHAPTER 14
Threshing Runs

Between the Dust Bowl and the invention of mechanical combines, threshing grain was an annual event for all who lived in the country in the Midwest. I have met many old gents through the years who reflect on those times with the fondest of memories. As a child, helping the women bake and prepare sumptuous harvest meals became a highlight of the summer. I looked forward to the cycle of work in which I could participate. By the Fourth of July, the oat fields were turning from green to golden yellow, and my favorite part of the summer had begun. Starting when I was 12, I drove the tractor during the threshing run for six years, usually working in tandem with two men who pitched the bundles into hayracks (large wagons pulled by horses or tractors).

The soft swishing sound of South Dakota prairie winds nudging our oat fields as they ripened is a sound I can still hear when I close my eyes in our native-prairie restoration. Big bluestem, switch grass and Indian grass now send down deep roots in the fields where Dad rotated oats, corn and alfalfa. The monoculture of today's endless fields of corn and soybeans in southeastern South Dakota didn't exist in my childhood. This monoculture slowly replaced the self-sustaining, diversified farming in the 1960s and '70s.

My parents harvested the bounty of our fields to feed livestock, including cattle, pigs, chickens and a few sheep and geese. By the time Dad had finished cultivating the cross rows of corn three times, it was the first of July. Weeding with a four-row attachment on the tractor was slow but effective. If corn was knee high by the Fourth of July, it was a good sign in that era. Today, commercial fertilizers and herbicides have replaced organic farming and cultivating, resulting in higher crop yields. Most corn now stands six feet tall by the 4th of July where I grew up.

In the 1940s, when he had stacked the second cutting of alfalfa, Dad pulled the binder out of the machine shed to swat the oat fields. He fussed and swore as he made the necessary annual repairs, and I stood by hoping he would let me help use the grease gun that I called a squirt gun. More than once Dad scolded me for using the squirt gun as a toy to douse tools and machinery with oil. It was more fun than a water gun, and the sticky black oil lasted longer.

July 9, 1952– Drove tractor on the binder.

Caryl Crozier

A binder has sharp sickle blades that cut the 24- to 30-inch tall grain near ground level. A rotating paddle fells grain onto the canvas rollers that propel it to the apparatus that ties twine around a bundle of oat stems. Thus, the name "binder." Dad rode high on the seat over the binder operation and pushed a foot pedal to dispel the bundles in long rows back onto the ground while Mom or I drove the tractor that pulled the binder. Sweltering summer sun beat down on us as we circled the endless fields. I liked getting a glorious tan, but Mom wisely protected her skin with lightweight clothing. We had a small umbrella over the tractor seat, but it didn't provide much shade.

I loved seeing the patch of uncut grain dwindle as I drove the tractor around and around the 40-acre field. It took at least two days to cut the grain and then a couple more days to stack the bundles into rows of shocks. When Dad decided we needed help, we hired men to shock the grain, but mostly the three of us did the work ourselves. We worked until dusk or early in the morning to avoid the midday heat. Mom had beads of sweat running down her face and back while she struggled to make shocks of the oat bundles. She grasped two heavy bundles and stood them together, teepee fashion, then added four more bundles to stabilize and complete the shock of six oat bundles. The standing shocks allowed the oats to dry. The bundles were heavy, and my job was to carry stray bundles to my parents. My shocks usually fell down, and I never tried very hard to get the correct technique.

Harvesting the oats began in late July, when all the farmers had cut and shocked their grain. A group of farmers worked in a "run," cooperatively harvesting from farm to farm. Our neighbor George Voegeli owned the threshing machine – an enormous, tin, dragon-like contraption.

Soon after the maintenance check of his machine, George hooked up his powerful, fire-engine red Massy Harris tractor to the thresher and pulled it to the first farm on the run. If I lay down on my tummy on the grass, I could feel the ground vibrate as the enormous machine rumbled by.

George annually rotated where the threshing run started to give all the neighbors an opportunity to get their grain in the bin first. I remember watching him grease and oil every nook and cranny of that huge machine, and once in a while he let me climb up to look into its mysterious caverns. He lived right across the road from us and always tolerated my endless questions and interest in his machine. His children were a bit older than me, and I think he liked to have me tagging along behind him. His gentle ways reminded me of my Grandpa Kinkner, who died when I was eight years old.

July 21, 1952–Started threshing, driving for Dad and Ken at Voegelis- 8 racks- Jimmy is quite a worker.

Waking to Mourning Doves

Since about ten farmers joined each run, it took nearly three weeks to complete the harvest, spending two or three days at each farm. Threshing time fell at the most sweltering part of summer and the farmers both dreaded and anticipated it. The camaraderie of the team effort almost made up for the backbreaking work of pitching the bundles of grain into the yawning hayracks. Bundles had to be pitched into the hayracks high above the men's heads and stacked just right so the rack wouldn't tip over in the hilly fields. An unspoken contest existed to see who could stack the fastest and best. Muscles bulged and dirt, sweat, and prickly oat hulls covered the men as they labored ten hours a day. I was proud of Dad, as he had the reputation of being a hard worker and his racks were packed properly. Woe to the reputation of the farmer whose rack tipped over because he hadn't balanced the load. I saw that happen more than once and was glad it wasn't my dad or someone I drove the tractor for.

Farmers pitched the oat bundles into the chute from two hayracks positioned on either side of the feeder belt and fed the grain into the thresher, which chewed, grated, sifted and spewed out the oats separated from the straw as the end result. Nothing was more fun than climbing on that newly threshed straw pile, prickly and slippery as it was.

My uncle Clarence, at age 85, wrote, "My uncle had a steam threshing machine. It took a water wagon and three men for the machine. That was in 1909." His tales and fond memories of the early days fascinated me. Although I can't remember many of the stories, old black-and-white photos tell the tale of early 1900s farm life, which wasn't much different from my own.

Being a gofer was my primary threshing-time job in grade school. Mom and others would say, "Caryl, go get the butter and eggs from the cellar," or, "Caryl, go ask George if the first crew is ready to come to dinner."

As I grew older, my threshing-run responsibilities escalated. I always helped set up the wash area for the men, helped set up and clear tables, and washed and dried dishes. I liked being the waitress and interacting with the men and often helped at other farms as Mom and the neighbors exchanged help. It wasn't until I turned twelve that I started driving the tractor.

As a small child I loved watching Mom, Aunt Hazel, Nan, and our neighbor Hertha working as a team preparing enormous meals for the threshing crew. Mom used our homegrown beef and pork from the commercial deep freeze locker in town and butchered several chickens. The crankiest old roosters that chased me usually eluded Mom's hook. They would have been too tough to eat anyway. Her ample garden produced most of the food served, but a trip to the grocery store got last-minute flour, yeast, sugar, chocolate chips, oatmeal and raisins for baking.

Baking all the cookies and cakes ahead of time kept our kitchen steamy-hot for days. The first job I can remember is chopping walnuts in a small metal food chopper. I poked the walnuts into the chute at the top and turned the crank while watching the metal teeth grind and drop the walnut pieces into the glass container below the grinder. Sometimes we cracked and used black walnuts from my Uncle Clarence's trees. They were the best. Yummy white cupcakes or oatmeal cookies filled with black walnuts are a treat to remember.

Mom and I spent several days baking mounds of cookies before the crew arrived. The aromas from the oven kept me close by so I could snitch a sample as they came out of the oven. The ravenous threshing crew consumed cookies by the handful at morning and afternoon lunches: chocolate chip, oatmeal raisin, peanut butter, ginger snaps, pineapple drop, and sugar cookies.

Mom preferred paper-thin sugar cookies for entertaining, but the men liked thick ones made with Grandma's three-inch diameter cookie cutter. I loved to cut and sprinkle sugar on the cookies after Mom rolled out the dough on our Hoosier cabinet. I must have learned a lot at Mom's elbow, because my first 4-H blue ribbon at age eleven was for my sugar cookies using Grandma's antique cutter.

Mom had the ability to stoke our cook stove with wood and cobs to reach just the right temperature for baking. She stuck her arm in the oven to test the heat. It must have been a good method, as perfection emerged from that oven every time.

Each cook tried to outdo the other to become the best cook on the "run." I think Mom had the reputation of being one of the best cooks, because Dad said the men really hurried to get the threshing rigs to our farm by ten a.m. so they would be served the noon dinner there. I was proud of her ability and wanted to have that reputation myself someday. The crew usually finished their long days by six p.m., but often stayed till dusk if a job was close to completion.

The wives made enormous meals, and morning and afternoon lunches were taken to the threshing crew. Cooking over the hot, wood cook-stove in 90-degree weather was necessary to make the pies, meat and hearty meals the men required and expected. Most farm families ate five meals a day: breakfast, morning lunch, dinner at noon, afternoon lunch, supper and sometimes a bedtime snack.

Food for a threshing crew was a sight to behold; not gourmet, but every inch of the table was filled with the hearty foods the men needed for the intense labor they engaged in. Even 2000-calorie/day meals could not sustain their efforts. and the wives spent days preparing high-energy foods. They

Waking to Mourning Doves

must have burned 5000 calories a day at least. The ladies always prepared two kinds of meat, and mounds of mashed potatoes sprinkled with paprika and dots of butter for garnish along with the most flavorful gravy I have ever tasted.

"Long slow moist heat is the secret to making perfect gravy stock," my Aunt Hazel said as she added flour thickening to the chicken drippings. "A little dash of thick cream helps, too."

Fresh garden vegetables creamed or buttered, along with macaroni and cheese, navy beans and corn, nestled in the pools of gravy. As a child, I liked to watch how much the men piled on their plates and marveled at how they could eat so much. Carbs were needed to fuel their bodies for the hard work. No wimpy lettuce salads for these hearty eaters; instead sweet jello or fruit and maybe coleslaw with a large variety of pickles, jams and relishes along with loaf after loaf of homemade bread was consumed. Apple, cherry or coconut cream pie topped off the meal and sometimes the men ate a generous slice of all three. Mom's pies were perfection, and her secret was using home-rendered lard for the pie crust. I can still make perfect crusts, but I rarely do so anymore. Pillsbury pre-made piecrusts are so much easier.

We always set up a shady wash area outside on laundry table benches, complete with a mirror hung on a tree, clean combs and gritty Lava soap. We used towels made from feed sacks because Mom didn't want to stain her best towels. Men washed up and ate in shifts after they had unloaded their creaking hayrack loads into the threshing machine feeder.

August 2, 1952–At Grahams and Jakes- drove for Jim alot and had fun with him and Paul and Ken.

Much teasing and laughter accompanied dinner and the rest period afterwards. Weary, sweaty men flopped down on the grass or straw bundles and regularly had noon siestas.

Harlan quipped to my dad within earshot of all the crew, "Ray, I think Jimmy is sweet on your daughter." I blushed and tried to ignore the knowing looks and laughter.

Someone added, "Yeah, she's pretty cute, and sassy too." I didn't know what to say or do, but I liked the attention.

Giggling and flirting with the opposite sex was a handy skill I learned on the threshing run. I was glad there weren't many other girls participating those six summers, but I enjoyed the girls that did. Other neighbor boys too young to load hayracks helped by driving the tractor as I did to load hayracks or haul wagonloads of oats to be put in oat storage bins.

Minutes after serving dinner to the third shift of sweaty men, the women began making afternoon lunches: thickly sliced homemade bread sandwiches filled with ground meat and homemade egg salad and pickles, cheese or cold meat and peanut butter, always several choices. Rich moist chocolate cakes made with sour cream with creamy fudge frosting or spice cake with brown sugar caramel frosting (penuche) were the favorites. Steaming pots of egg coffee and freshly squeezed lemonade washed down handfuls of cookies.

When the threshing crew was at other farms, Dad always came home late and tired from the day's work, so Mom and I often did the farm chores alone. (I drove tractor at other farms but could leave the run earlier when my last farmer had his rack filled.) Mom milked ten cows by hand while I fed the cattle and chickens. Sometimes Dad got home in time to help finish milking and carry the milk pails to the house to separate the cream from the milk in our hand-cranked DeLeval separator. I was glad to escape the dreaded chore of washing the separator discs by hand every morning when I left early for the threshing run. We often worked until 10 p.m.

Noise from the tractors, threshing machine and men's loud voices was a sharp contrast to the usual dead silence in the country. Background sounds of birds singing and animals grunting and rummaging were a lullaby compared to the clamor of the threshing run. I relished coming home, getting clean and watching the silent fireflies frolic on our lawn as dusk fell while crimson, sapphire and amethyst sunsets lit the sky.

After two or three weeks of work, a threshing party was held to compare labor hours and "settle up" financially. I earned about $20 from each employer and thought I had hit the jackpot. I couldn't wait to go and buy some new clothes for high school with my earnings. I remember buying a red hat, full slip and a red sweater for ten dollars at the local K&K department store. Packrat that I am, I still have those bargains.

Sometimes the threshing run brought me the extra bonus of getting to know guys I drove tractor for and later dated.

After the men sat around a table in George's porch joking and completing business, they scattered to play croquet on the brightly lit lawn. George's sons, Kenneth and Paul, usually spent the afternoon stringing lights in the trees and clothesline for the three sets of fiercely competitive croquet games to follow.

As we left the porch that summer of 1952, Jimmy, one of the hired town boys helping on the threshing run, had other ideas and grabbed my hand as we left the porch. He said he had something to give me for my birthday. My heart beat faster because I had developed a huge crush on him while driving the tractor for him while he pitched bundles in the hayrack that summer. He

Waking to Mourning Doves

had carrot-red hair and freckles and flirted with me all three weeks of the threshing run.

Laughter and lights from the grassy croquet court pierced the orchard as we sat beneath the bountiful apple tree. Jimmy pulled a little box from his pocket and gave me a heart-shaped necklace with a rose in the center. At the time I thought it was beautiful.

"You're so sweet," Jimmy murmured as his arm tightened around me. He drew me closer and in the shadows of the grove, I experienced my first real boy-girl kiss.

"Whew what was that all about?" I thought. Sure, I'd exchanged a few furtive pecks with other boys, but this was totally different. Growing up might be interesting after all! We quickly returned to the party thinking we wouldn't have been missed, but the knowing looks and my blush told it all.

When the party ended at midnight, I still felt like I was walking on air. I fell asleep at home with the necklace clutched to my heart.

CHAPTER 15

Wringer Washers and Flatirons

On farms and towns throughout the Midwest, Monday heralded washday, rain or shine. On Sunday night, Mom sorted piles of linens, whites, bedding, light-colored items, darker clothing and Dad's denim overalls and caps. She soaked items coated with grease or dirt overnight with strong homemade lye soap. Sometimes she scrubbed Dad's clothing on the washboard, a ribbed tin or glass implement, before putting them into the washing machine. Before she owned a washing machine, Mom's diary entries quote how she "rubbed her hands raw" from the strong soap and friction.

Before milking chores on Monday morning, Mom carried pails of water from the cistern and stoked the old cook stove with wood and cobs. She used cistern water because the soft rainwater worked better than well water for making soapsuds. A cistern held rainwater collected from the roof in a deep, cement-llined chamber below ground level. A chain loop of rectangular cups dipped into the water, bringing it to a surface spout as you cranked the handle on the case above the cistern. Mom filled the copper boiler, a twelve-gallon tub with handles on the ends, to heat on the stove. After she finished the milking, she filled the Maytag wringer washer with steaming hot water and homemade lye soap, or with P&G or Fels Naphtha bar shavings. She used lukewarm water in the two rinse tubs.

Since soft rainwater was somewhat scarce on a farm and dependent on rainfall, Mom used the same water for the entire process, washing light loads first and the dark-colored items last. The hard rubber washer rollers squeezed out some of the soapy water from the clothing. I had a healthy fear of those rotating traps. The wrangler arm that housed the wringer rotated around to the rinse tubs and then to the laundry basket. Sometimes Mom let me use a stick to raise items from the washer's hot water to propel them through the wringer. I had countless warnings to be careful about getting my fingers too close to the wringers.

I helped hang sheets and nice linens on the roadside edge of the clothesline for public view. Everyone hung the unmentionables and overalls on the backside lines. A warm, breezy day brought a wonderful, fresh smell to the laundry, but early spring and late fall, our fingers got numb handling the wet and frozen clothes. South Dakota is known for strong winds, and often clothes flapped so hard the clamp clothespins came undone. We often

Waking to Mourning Doves

scrambled to retrieve the clothes from the lawn and flowerbeds nearby. Some hardy neighbors hung clothing out in the winter, but Mom used a wooden drying rack and lines strung in the basement. By evening, most items were dry, so we took baskets and clothespins bags outside and folded sheets and towels as they came off the line. We put fresh sheets on the beds weekly. In my opinion, nothing compares to the luxury of crawling into bed between fresh, air-dried sheets.

Mom stashed clothing and linens to be ironed in a basket for sprinkling the next morning. She sprinkled the clothes by filling a 7-Up bottle with water, then capped it with a cork-and-metal sprinkler head. The sprinkler head had to be wrapped in rags so it tightly fit the bottle. Items to be ironed needed to be sprinkled and set an hour or two before ironing. We didn't have steam irons in the 1940s, so sprinkling was essential. I still like to sprinkle linens that need ironing because the moisture permeates the fabric and makes it perfect for ironing.

Mom spent most of Tuesday mornings ironing. Before we got electricity, she heated flatirons on the wood stove and changed irons as they cooled. Handles were attached to the iron base that she put on the stove to heat. What a hot, labor-intensive job! Sometimes she even ironed the sheets and Dad's boxer shorts, a task I never viewed as necessary.

I wanted to use an iron just like Mom's. My toy ironing board and iron sufficed until she deemed it safe for me to use the real thing. Why the eagerness to iron? Maybe I was just imitating Mom as little girls do. After we got electricity and electric irons in the 1940s, I was eager to learn and Mom let me iron the hankies, pillowcases, and some linens. We have a photograph of granddaughter Rachel, at age two, nearly naked wearing a cowboy hat "ironing" on my toy ironing board. She didn't know what it was for at first, since most of us don't iron clothes anymore. Too bad, because ironing can be a time for reflection.

CHAPTER **16**

Heirloom Gardens

Tilling the garden those first promising days of spring got the soil ready for planting seed potatoes, the first crop to be planted in the right phase of the April moon. Old wives tale or not, we grew enough potatoes to last several families through the winter (or year). Potatoes have a remarkable fertility ratio. Every eye on a potato has the potential to start a new plant that produces 10 to 12 new potatoes under each hill. Each spring before planting, my parents brought a bucket of potatoes from storage in Nan's cave and I helped cut them in several chunks with an eye or sprout in each. Dad usually dug the four-inch deep holes and Mom and I followed, pushing each chunk firmly into the rich, black soil. I felt very useful, a trait my parents instilled in me well.

Before the potato sprouts poked out of the ground, Mom made sure the lettuce, radishes, peas and onion sets got planted. She laid out a straight line for digging rows using a string with sticks at the ends. Neighbors and club ladies often visited each other's gardens and straight, even rows symbolized skill in gardening.

I loved placing seeds in those rows and watching every day for seedlings to appear. As the ground warmed we planted carrots, string beans, and lima beans and made patches for watermelon, cucumber and cantaloupe vines. Later, cabbage and tomato plants completed the vegetable garden. Mom never liked to plant pumpkins and squash because they took over the garden with their fast-growing vines. They extended their long tendrils into the adjacent corn or oats fields.

Gardens required maintenance all summer to discourage weeds and insects. I had the distasteful job of picking potato bugs off plants and dropping them into my tin can of kerosene — probably a healthier method of insect control than chemical sprays of today.

Mom eventually bought seeds from Guerney's, a mail-order catalog. When did the custom of saving heirloom seeds end? Mom and both grandmothers harvested flower and vegetable seeds in the fall and used them for planting the following spring. When hybridized seeds with their colorful packets enticed gardeners with promises of greater yields and variety, the practice died out for most gardeners. Interestingly, old, hardy heirloom plants rarely developed wilt, mold or plant diseases.

Fresh organic vegetables from our garden graced our table all spring,

Waking to Mourning Doves

summer and fall. Canned produce lasted through the long winters. What a treat to open a jar of tart wild plums that we had harvested from our fence-line plum thickets. The same was true of the fruits that Mom purchased in lugs (crates) at the store in mid-summer. I helped preserve the peaches, cherries, pears, apricots and plums by canning them in Mason jars. We carefully packed the clean fresh fruit and then topped off the jar with a sugar and water mixture. Placing the jars in a canner or hot-water bath cooked and sealed the contents. For less acidic foods like vegetables and soups, we often used a pressure cooker. Canning in hot weather on a wood cook stove made sweat run in rivulets down our faces. When Mom got an electric stove, the canning task improved greatly. In the early 1950s, a deep-freeze made preserved corn, strawberries and raspberries much tastier.

As cucumbers ripened on the vines, we picked them every other day to make all kinds of pickles. Mom liked making sweet pickles and took great pride in their sweet, crisp taste. Only perfect two-inch cucumbers passed her rigid test. Days of changing from salt brine in crocks to crispen and a vinegar and sugar mixture transformed the cucumbers into pickles, which we then sealed with the heated brine.

I preferred the speed of preparing and the taste of dill pickles. Stuffing a sterilized jar with three- to four-inch cucumbers and fresh-picked dill topped with hot brine seemed simpler to me. I liked the salty taste. too. We made larger cucumbers into tangy icicle or bread-and-butter pickle slices. Watermelon rinds, crab apples and beets made good pickles, too.

Somehow we also found time to maintain a flower garden. Butterflies and bees darted from flower to flower all summer long in our colorful flower patches; we did not use any chemical pesticides in those days. Perennials and annuals provided a colorful display as tulips and lily of the valley gave way to iris, peonies and June roses. Later the orange tiger lilies, phlox, and daisies blended with the zinnias, cosmos, calliopsis, nasturtiums and gladiolas. Late-blooming asters, mums and marigolds lasted until the first October frost. Fresh-cut flowers interspersed with wildflowers growing in the ditches usually filled vases on our tables throughout the growing season, just as they have for most of my life.

Mom preserved every bit of produce on the farm. After I married, every year she gave our family boxes and boxes of canned pickles, fruit and tomatoes as well as frozen corn, strawberries, raspberries and chickens. And Dad rounded out our larder with a half of homegrown beef or pork every year. Food from the family farm was something they could give us that we truly appreciated.

CHAPTER 17
Funnel Clouds, Blizzards and Jackrabbits

July 31, 1949–Good birthday picnic at Union Co. Park. We had a tornado tonight- people were here a lot- took barn and ruined hog house and many trees down.

Tornadoes were always a possibility after sultry summer days. Our farm was hit twice. The first time was after my eleventh birthday party at Union County Park. Back home, Dad looked at the roiling greenish clouds and knew a storm was approaching. He climbed on top of the machine shed to nail a cover over the oat bin opening, where newly threshed grain had just been stored. The howling winds struck before he could make it to the house and he sat straddling a support post in the machine shed, holding on to the doors, which could blow out in the wind. Meanwhile, Mom and I were in the house. She was stuffing towels in the north kitchen window, which had blown out. I looked out the south dining room window and saw the hayrack dashed to bits against the silo. Then the barn roof started disintegrating. I figured it was time to head for the basement, but Mom wouldn't let me go there. I still can't figure out why we didn't seek shelter in the basement. Maybe Mom was worried about Dad. Winds let up, but it was the eye of the storm. We dashed out to see if Dad was OK, but in seconds, the winds came back stronger than ever. We all scrambled to the closest shelters, Dad to a car in the machine shed and Mom and me to the house. Then, almost as quickly, it was calm again. We all hugged and cried as we surveyed the damage. We were just thankful we were unharmed.

Entire farms were destroyed around us and possessions and debris were strewn around the fields. My Uncle George's barn blew down while he lay on top of Norman and Howard outside the barn in a hollow to protect them. No one was injured, but it was a frightening night as neighbors checked on each other and helped out as best they could.

August 3, 1949–The carpenters moved in last nite.

August 15, 1949–Fought with Dick and played with Joanne.

Disasters brought questionable fly-by-night carpenters to an area because there was so much reconstruction to be done. Dad hired one of those families.

Waking to Mourning Doves

They lived in a trailer house on our property for several months while repairing the barn roof and building a new chicken house. The family was very strange and wild. The children, Dick and Joanne, were rough, streetwise and about my age. We played together, but I didn't like them. They were hard on my toys. The parents had pornographic material in their trailer, which the children showed to anyone who acted interested. I was! Dick, Joanne and their mother lived with a rough character in the trailer, while the husband lived in our house, a very unusual arrangement for the times. We finally realized they were stealing chickens and Dad cursed and threatened them about calling the sheriff. They toed the line after that, but we breathed a sigh of relief when they left. Their shoddy construction techniques did not stand the test of time either.

In 1969, another tornado came and destroyed our barn. Neighbors helped my parents collect and rip apart the remains, which they burned or buried in the field east of the farm. One of the neighbors remembers my parents shouting at each other as Dad wanted to "get the hell out of there and sell the damn farm," while Mom tried to calm him down. He wanted to sell the farm again after his retirement at age 62, but Mom refused to leave because she loved the freedom of the farm.

> *June 25, 1951–Bad thunder and lightning storm and two inches of rain and hail.*

Hailstorms destroyed crops on a routine basis, but hail insurance occasioned a visit by the adjuster who gave cash value for crops lost. During a hailstorm, my grandmother held goose-down bed pillows against the windows to prevent breakage. I'm not sure why she did that because the windows cracked and got broken anyway. Sometimes we went out and gathered hailstones and made hand-cranked freezer ice cream after a storm. It was very discouraging for Dad and Grandpa to see their crops and hard work destroyed by hail. Farmers are so dependent on the weather: rainfall, windstorms, early or late frost, not to mention concerns about insects such as corn borers and grasshoppers.

> *January 26, 1950–It was another rootin, tootin cold school day.*

Winters in South Dakota seem more violent than where we live in Minnesota, maybe because the strong winds off the prairie blow even a few inches of snow into impassable drifts. School was often called off via the telephone party line and the fathers came to pick us up at school if the weather started getting bad. I never had to stay overnight at school, but some kids did.

March 7, 1950–We had an awful blizzard. Got home at 5:30.
Mom didn't get home. She stayed at Arends-novelty broke.

One time, Mom was at her Friendly-Hour Club and a blizzard raged so furiously that she and the other ladies couldn't get home. They had to sleep on the floor and use the chamber pot. I think they had a really fun time as I heard them reminisce and laugh about it in later years. They rarely got an evening with friends away from family responsibilities. That night Dad milked all the cows by himself and I was afraid to be alone in the house, so I fought my way to the barn in whiteout conditions. Luckily I made it, but it was dangerous and Dad scolded me. Dad fixed us popcorn and milk for supper, his only cooking skill other than great-tasting Denver egg sandwiches. In the middle of the night we heard a loud clanging downstairs and I wondered if intruders were invading our kitchen. We crept down the steep stairs to discover it was only the howling wind.

January 5, 1952–Got badly stuck in steep hill jack rabbit
hunting with Mom and Dad.

In the 1940s and '50s, Lincoln County had a bounty on jackrabbits, so my parents and I occasionally went out hunting at night. When Mom shone the spotlight on a jackrabbit, it stood up on its rear haunches, mesmerized, while Dad aimed and shot. That never seemed quite fair to the rabbit, in my opinion. One night we descended a steep hill in the car and couldn't get up the equally steep hill on the other side. I was afraid we would have to stay there all night. By shoveling out the snow, and pushing and stuffing army blankets and gunnysacks under the tires, we finally got unstuck after an hour's struggle. Mom and Dad shouted and grunted and pushed mightily, while behind the wheel I tried to gun the car to get out of there. My parents were never too eager to go again.

PART V: BRANCHING OUT

Erickson Christmas

Cousins

August & Edla Erickson

Ruth & Me

4H Float

New Accordion

CHAPTER **18**

Frozen Creeks and Drifting Snow – And Christmas!

South Dakota in winter is a world of white with beige weeds and crop remnants poking through the snow blanket. Endless horizons are bathed in blue and grey with fuchsia sunsets punctuated by ermine-tipped spruce trees. Plum thickets, ash and Chinese elm trees are shrouded in hoarfrost. Tumbleweeds impaled on barbed wire fences dot the sculptured marshmallow snow banks. Rainbow sundogs signal colder days ahead. Long icicles dripping and freezing from the eaves are temptations to snap off and have sword fights with, or lick like popsicles. Animal tracks are everywhere. Owls, mice, raccoons, deer and rabbits leave bloody fur traces of nocturnal meanderings and deadly interactions in the freshly fallen snow. House sparrows argue and chirp from their territorial headquarters in the barn and machine sheds.

On the drive to the farm in 2010, wind turbines like giant mixers churn the sky. Drainage ditches scar fields resembling fudge-striped cookies. The land is so flat you can see matchbook-size cars on roads a mile away across the open fields. As we drive, dense fog creeps as silently as Carl Sandburg's cat's paws, enveloping us in a suffocating, grey world. My family feared the frequent fog nearly as much as icy and snow-packed roads.

Viewing this landscape today evokes 1940s memories of childhood. In my mind's eye, I see patient kittens crouching in the snow with their sensitive paws carefully tucked under their dense winter coats. Mom and Dad emerge from the barn and navigate the snow banks with pails full of warm milk, and a conga line of a dozen cats trot along behind with fluffy tails reaching for the sky.

Dad says, "Why don't those goddamn worthless cats go hunt mice instead of waiting for handouts?" Dad swore a lot.

I think, "No, kittens are my favorite friends and they deserve the separated skim milk more than those feisty old pigs!"

I tried to sneak several cats into the house to warm them up, but they displayed poor manners in their search for food and promptly got thrown out by Mom. One favored housecat was allowed to stay inside to mollify me.

In my mind's eye, I am still a child of the '40s, eager to play outside with friends. Slatted red snow fences trap ten-foot banks of snow in our yard. I can't

Waking to Mourning Doves

wait for the neighbor boys to come over after their morning or after-school chores to excavate tunnels with me. Our moms bundle us up in snowsuits and thick woolen mittens and fortify us with chunky Pride-of-Iowa oatmeal cookies to stash in our pretend icebox at the tunnel entrance. Sometimes more neighbor kids join us as we build snow forts and houses with rooms made of firm blocks of snow.

An assortment of neighborhood cats and dogs follow us hissing and growling at each other while we holler and play. Maybe they're hoping for cookie crumbs or maybe they just like to romp and get as snow-covered as we do. Lying on our backs leaving impressions in the snow that look like angel bodies with wings leaves us covered from head to toe. To this day I am still tempted to flop down in new-fallen snow and make angels. Maybe the remnants of the child in us never leave.

Wind chills seem nonexistent as we are constantly on the move playing games like fox and geese, tag and keep-away. Folks might ask how we can live in that frozen, windswept tundra-like prairie of South Dakota, but I have always loved it, even more as I grow older.

Before we are ready to stop playing, Mom yells, "Come on in now. You're going to freeze your feet."

She would know. She froze her feet while watching folks ski on a hill in Canton when she was a teenager in the 1920s. Countless winter nights I watched her soak her feet in warm water and Epsom salts wincing in pain from the chilblains caused by frostbite. I felt bad for her and sat close by talking, hoping it would make her feel better. Sometimes I even filled a grey enamel basin with warm water and soaked my feet, too. Empathy develops early in an only child. We didn't have warm insulated boots, but somehow none of us kids got frozen feet, maybe because we rarely stood still.

Reluctantly, my friends and I tramp into the house and Mom sweeps the wet snow off our snow pants with her stiff bristle broom. She gives me a hug and says, "The hot cocoa is ready and I just made a batch of donuts."

We grab for handfuls of sugary donut holes as we sip marshmallow-topped hot chocolate from our Hopalong Cassidy cups. Gene Autry croons "Rudolph the Red-Nosed Reindeer" on our Philco radio console as we laugh and plan our next adventure. Sometimes I begged to have my friends stay for supper with us and Mom always relented. At seven PM the Lone Ranger program enthralls us as we cluster around the radio. We hear, "Hi ho Silver – the Lone Ranger rides again." His trusty sidekick, Tonto, was our first exposure to Native Americans. Although we lived in South Dakota with a substantial population of Indians, we never saw them because we never traveled far from home.

All too soon the party-line telephone rings —short, long, short — and my friends' parents tell them to walk home or that they'd be picked up soon. Paul and Kenneth lived just across the road, so they always walked home in the star-filled night.

> Mom writes: *Caryl would walk down to the creek to try and skate and there wasn't enough ice to learn. We often went on Nan's hill and coasted and once in a while on Jake Voegeli's hill. Sometimes Kenneth, Paul and Caryl made snow forts and houses and we brought food out to them.*

Sometimes frozen creeks beckoned us to slip on our ice skates and glide through the pasture bottoms. We dreamt of being Sonja Henie, the Norwegian skating champion, as we attempted long glides and circles. Clumps of dirt and weeds sticking up through the ice in the shallow places impeded our progress, but not our dreams. Mom and Dad gave me ice skates at age eight that still fit today. The first couple years I stuffed the toes with a sock to make them fit. How frugal is that!

Before we know it, the Christmas season is here and December with all its anticipation is upon us. For months my friends and I enjoy poring over the toy sections of the Montgomery Wards, Sears and Aldens catalogs, our wish lists growing longer day-by-day. I weigh the merits of each doll and choose a few favorites. Somehow, Mom manages to surprise me with the perfect doll each Christmas. Maybe not the one in the catalogs, but always just right. Mary, Caroline, Lily, Grace, Evonne, and Connie, my last doll at age 10, still reside in a cradle in our house. I wish they could remember the good times like I do.

Sometimes my grandmothers hand-stitched doll quilts for me from their overflowing scrap bags of fabrics. When clothing began to wear out, making quilts was the way to recycle them. Growing up in the Depression and during and after WWII rationing and scarcity of goods, I absorbed the frugality of my family and its unstated motto, "Waste not, want not." It certainly became my family's mantra. Yet we always had enough and I never yearned for more of anything.

Just after Thanksgiving we dug the boxes of Christmas decorations from deep in the attic storage. I couldn't wait to find my favorite ornament – a German ball-shaped Santa. Packed in layers of tissue my small hands searched for it every year. They still do. I feel connected to my mother and grandmother when that precious Santa is nestled in our balsam Christmas tree. I hope one of my grandchildren will treasure it as I do.

Mom and Dad climbed up on a shaky stepladder to fasten twisted strips of red and green crepe paper to the corners of each room. We fastened a

Waking to Mourning Doves

honeycomb foldout red bell to a light fixture in the center of the room. Sometimes we draped a few tinsel strands on the streamers. Whispers of draft from the wood-burning furnace registers gently nudged the streamers and tinsel. I found it magical to watch this quiet dance by the flickering light of our kerosene lamps.

Making Christmas decorations with Mom and my aunts was a much-loved lifelong tradition. Aunt Eva and I scoured the pastures and ditches gathering milkweed pods for decorating. We slathered the insides with red fingernail polish and dabbed the rough outside layers with gold and silver paint. With Mom and Aunt Hazel, we recycled tin-can lids into ornaments. Using tin snips, we cut 1/4-inch deep slashes and bent them in opposite directions. Mom got a few cuts doing the bending and wouldn't let me do it. In the center we glued a round Christmas card scene. We recycled greeting cards into gift tags, placemat collages, star shaped balls and made ornaments with toothpick edges as a frame. Every possible use of abundant spruce cones from our farm site trees adorned our houses, from tree shapes and wreaths to clear jars filled with cones, balls and sparkly lights after we got electricity in the '40s.

When the unrelenting South Dakota winds piled the snow in deep drifts on the road, we impatiently waited for the road maintenance machine to clear a path to town or school. Our neighbor George drove the huge, yellow-bladed machine, so we often had a route to town over the corrugated gravel roads before other neighbors.

I can almost hear Dad muttering, "Son of a bitch," as he struggled to put the chains on the tires of our 1938 Chevy. Sometimes we needed the extra traction to burst though the recurring drifts on the gravel roads and in our farmyard. A road could drift back shut an hour or two after the plow had cleared it.

Windswept prairies —an apt name for South Dakota – describe the 20- to 30-mile an hour winds that scoured the land and its occupants mercilessly. Crisp winds blowing soil eroded from fall-plowed fields created "snirt," a mixture of snow and dirt. The marbled effect of the snowdrifts reminds me of melting hot fudge sundaes. The fences trapped snow in the road ditches, which resembled slightly burned meringue scallops.

Beresford's water tower, festooned with hundreds of crimson lights, looked like a huge bell as we drove the three miles from our farm to town. Town folks had electricity long before we did and I loved seeing the bright red, green, and blue lights on houses and Christmas trees. Lonely stacks of Charlie Brown type spruce and pine trees are stacked by the K & K store. Priced at 50 cents to $2.00 each, my parents made a quick purchase. Selecting a Christmas tree in 30-below-zero wind chill was not unusual and made for haste.

Caryl Crozier

I remember Dad urging Mom and me to hurry up and do our shopping so we could get back home before the weather turned bad. Bruehler's Rexall Drug, Gambles, Ben Franklin and K & K stores were loaded with enticing toys and gift items. I liked the Evening in Paris and Blue Waltz cologne packages. Sometimes Mom bought hard ribbon-candy or chocolate-covered cherries.

The K & K department store, presided over by Marie Rasmussen in the fabric and clothing departments, provided most of our gift selections as well as most of our clothing. I loved it when Mom or Grandma selected a cut from a bolt of fabric on the shelves. Most of the time they bought it to sew clothing, but I imagined all kinds of wonderful uses: quilts and tablecloths for my dolls and toy dish sets or maybe craft projects that Mom learned at one of her clubs. Sometimes Mom made a food gift for the minister or a shut-in-neighbor and wrapped it bundle-style in a colorful piece of leftover fabric.

Racks of women's and children's clothing in the middle of the store across from the slips, undies, slacks and sweaters tempted us to rifle through them looking for a new Christmas or Easter dress. I still have my two favorite Christmas dresses. The first, a deep turquoise velvet jumper and the second, a taffeta dress with layers of light and dark blue ruffles, hang in my "vintage" clothing closet. The tactile thrill of feeling the soft velvet in my fingers still reminds me of newborn kittens and the security of being with family. A plastic pin of two rabbits adorned both outfits. I longed to have a white domestic rabbit as a child, but the pin was the closest I got. Each spring, Dad brought in a tiny cottontail bunny that he found while working in the field. After two tries of keeping them alive for a couple weeks, I decided to play with them a little while and have Dad take them back where he found them. Watching a small creature languish and die made me careful to observe wildlife, but not disturb it.

Fifty years later I spotted a white china rabbit in a Budapest, Hungary store window. Alas, the store didn't open till morning. I thought about that perfect memento of our trip all night. The next day we walked two miles back to the store to buy that rabbit, a long way from the K & K store in Beresford.

For our weekly Saturday trips to town, Mom and Dad boxed up crates of eggs to trade for groceries at the K&K store. The store gave us credit for the items we needed. Mom always compiled a short list. I liked to tag along and watch as the efficient clerk, Mary, reached for items on shelves behind the counter and plopped them in front of us. Customers were not allowed behind the counter and there were no rows of shelves to browse. Marshmallows, fruit, baking supplies and an occasional bag of licorice, plus Dad's favorite bologna, filled our bags. Candy slipped in my empty pocket by Mary enticed me to return time after time.

The meat market portion of the store held fresh meats along with cold meats and cheese to slice. A hefty female butcher deftly sliced the bologna or ham Mom selected and wrapped it in brown waxed paper tied with a string dangling from a roll near the ceiling. During the World War II years, 1941-1945, Mom carefully calculated which rations and blue and red chip tokens were needed for upcoming meals and entertaining. We ate well during those years because we had farm-raised meat, fruits and vegetables Mom had preserved along with eggs, chickens and milk. Not all people in Beresford were that fortunate.

Hans Solem, my friend Karen's dad, skied up the town alley to work at the Gambles store he owned. Karen told me she had seen dogs urinating on the wooden lutefisk barrels by the K&K store next door. Lutefisk — dry cod soaked in lye — is an acquired taste, but most Swedes and Norwegians love it. I am glad I didn't know about the dogs until recently, because that is where Grandma bought her lutefisk!

The most thrilling part of the shopping excursion was paying. Sitting high up in a corner of the store, one cashier handled all the transactions. A series of wires and bells connected her to the clerks in each department. They yanked a cord to get her attention, and she pulled the little black cash box up to her cubbyhole, calculated the value of the eggs we had brought in against the items we had selected, and sent back the change.

Friendly clerk Bob spent a lot of time spreading a green or red goop on the wooden floors as he swept and kept the store immaculate from all the winter traffic. He often helped carry groceries to the car and told a joke or two on the way. Dad loved to slap a slice of bologna between a couple slices of bread and chow down on the way home. Mom and I usually joined him.

Shopping at Mae Dewey's dress shop was a memorable experience, too. We usually looked at her selection of dresses and hats on trips to town. Her one-person dress shop contained racks of squished together new dresses from a dozen past seasons. A slight talcum-powder, peppery odor attacked our nostrils as we pushed open the front door of the shop. All seasons of purses, hats, handkerchiefs, jewelry and gloves crowded together in and on top of glass display cases. There was barely room to walk between overflowing drawers of slips, undies, nylons and garter belts, girdles, corsets and brassieres.

A child-size dressing room with a heavy curtain hung on wooden ring rods allowed privacy for trying on clothing, which Mae seemed to discourage. In fact, I am not sure she ever wanted to sell much of her collection because it never changed much that I could see. My friends and I rarely shopped there on our own because Mae scowled at girls unaccompanied by a purse-carrying mother. We occasionally went there as a dare and made a quick exit, saying, "We were just looking."

Sometimes during December Mae had an assistant, but I never saw a rush of customers. Both ladies seemed very old to me, but I liked their quiet, helpful demeanor. Mae was as short and chunky as her helper was tall and slim. They reminded me of the *Jack Sprat Could Eat No Fat* nursery rhyme!

When I got a new dress, I wore it to all holiday occasions: church and school Christmas programs, community concerts and many relative gatherings. If the dress still fit the next year, it made the same rounds. Sometimes, Mom let the hem down if I had grown taller, but I didn't like the line that always showed.

My favorite part of the shopping trip to town was stopping at one or two of my aunts' houses before driving home. Dad's sister, Aunt Eva, always welcomed me with a warm hug and seemed truly glad to see me. I adored her. All her friends called me "little Eva" because I looked so much like her. I failed to see the resemblance until I grew up, but by then she was gone. Ovarian cancer claimed her life at age 48.

Great Aunt Ida greeted us at her door with her apron covered with flour. Cookies and fresh-baked bread and cinnamon rolls were heaped on the counters, and we always got samples. Countless leaves from African violets sat in water on the windowsills and plant stands, promising blooms to come. Delicate varieties of violets bloomed in every possible nook and cranny. She willingly shared her green thumb talent with visitors. The violet plants and cuttings she gave us usually languished and died. I still have wood sorrel from her cottage gardens, a pleasantly invasive plant that pops up everywhere.

My diminutive great aunt Lily, who lived upstairs above the funeral home, gave visitors hot cider and frosted molasses cream cookies. JuJu, the name we nieces and nephews all called her, got the name from her granddaughter, Joyce, who couldn't say junior meaning her younger "junior grandmother." Lily loved the name because it referred to some spooky African spirit. Lily loved being different. Being a Unitarian and being cremated caused tongues to wag. I admired her rebellious personality.

AUNT LILY'S FROSTED MOLASSES CREAMS

Mix thoroughly; 1/4 cup shortening, 1/2 cup sugar, 1/2 cup molasses
Sift together : 2 cups flour, 1/2 teaspoon salt, 1/2 teaspoon ginger,
   1/2 teaspoon cinnamon
Stir into first mixture 1/2 cup water and 1 teaspoon soda
Mix all together. Drop on cookie sheet by teaspoon

Bake 8 minutes in a 350 degree oven
Frost with a powdered sugar frosting

Waking to Mourning Doves

Christmas preparations at my childhood home formed traditions that we still follow today: a flurry of cookie and nut-bread baking and mysterious packages hidden everywhere. Handwriting of cards and letters sent then with three-cent stamps and Christmas seals from the American Lung Association kept Mom busy many evenings. I loved trudging through the snow in the ditch to our big mailbox by the road to carefully place cards in the box and later get the mail. The rural mail carriers rarely failed to deliver mail and the Sioux Falls Argus Leader, the area newspaper, on our route number four. Stanley Fillingsness, our carrier, still remains a hero to me.

As the dark of December deepened and the nights fell to sub-zero temperatures, Mom or Dad put extra wood and coal in the basement furnace. Banking the stove just before bedtime kept residual heat through the long nights. My parents cut all the wood from nearby farm groves or dead trees in our own grove. Sometimes neighbors wanted a grove cleared for farming, and my parents were glad to get the wood. In the early years they used a buck saw or long saw to cut the tree down and then a gas-motor buzz saw to cut the wood into chunks. Dad then labored splitting the chunks with an axe and then Mom and I helped shove it down the chute placed in the basement window. The wood clunked and clattered down the tin chute and landed in the enclosed bin by the furnace. We kept wood on one side of the bin and coal on the other. Now, 60 years later, there is still wood and coal in the bin for emergencies, although the wood-burning stove was replaced with electric heat long ago.

I looked forward to weekends waking up to family breakfasts of fresh-squeezed orange juice and heart-shaped waffles made over the open grate in the wood cook stove. I didn't have to rush off to school and my parents slowed down a bit, too. Sometimes Mom cleaned off the stove's iron surface and poured pancake batter directly onto it. My mouth watered as the pancakes fluffed up. I felt real grown up when I got to flip them with the green-handled spatula — the same one I use today. A weekly batch of cottage cheese made from skimmed milk curdled on the back of the stove as we sat down to breakfast after my parents finished the outside chores.

On December weekends, we got into a frenzy of baking, decorating and gift-wrapping. Mom made magical ribbon bows and creative packages, primarily from white tissue paper and flat ribbon. I felt helpful when she let me take a scissor to curl the dangling ends of that ridged paper ribbon. I don't recall having Scotch tape in the '40s. We used paper seals that you lick and stick. I deliberated much too long over which colorful design to affix to each package —Santa, bells or snowmen. Mom usually humored my indecision.

Before the baking began, we cracked nutmeats from the shell. We always had a bowl heaped high with walnuts, hazelnuts and Brazil nuts with a silver nutcracker and picks nestling on top. Grandma Erickson had a huge black walnut tree from which we collected baskets of nuts in the fall. When they dried and the shell turned black, we cracked them with a hammer and extracted the unique tasting nutmeats for baking. Preparing nutmeats for baking in a small grinder with a glass bottom is one of my fondest memories. I loved putting the nuts in the chute, turning the small handle, and watching the chopped nuts pile up in the bowl. I think Mom let her granddaughters help when they were small, because that nutcracker bowl went in Michelle's "remember Grandma" box.

As ice formed in depressions in the ground or in containers outside, Dad took his axe and chopped a few pails full to make homemade freezer ice cream, our special winter treat. There are no words to describe the unique taste of that sweet mixture of cream, milk, eggs, sugar and vanilla. Any kid who has ever tasted it will never forget it. The mixture of raw eggs and unpasteurized milk might make folks apprehensive today, but the only thing that might have made us sick was eating too much of it.

The cream mixture, placed in a tin canister surrounded by ice and rock salt, became ice cream after turning the crank about a half hour. Anticipation grew as salt melted the ice and the crank became more difficult to turn . When Dad pulled the slatted beaters from the canister, we rushed to scrape off the best-ever vanilla ice cream. I had my favorite ruby red Depression glass sherbet dish ready for more. We made freezer ice cream all winter because ice, milk, eggs and sugar were always plentiful on our farm.

Nan often made what she called snow ice cream. After the first fresh snowfall, she gave me a large crock bowl to fill with clean white snow. She had cream, sugar and vanilla waiting for me to mix and magic happened as we stirred and tasted the first ice cream of winter. Soon fudge, divinity, peanut brittle, penuche, and cookies accompanied our ice cream.

A couple of weeks before Christmas, Mom popped humongous batches of popcorn on the old wood cook stove. She fired up the stove, dumped a handful of popcorn and a bit of grease in the cast iron skillet and plopped a lid on top. She shook the pan back and forth on the stove and the kernels began to pop. Soon, she emptied the fluffy white kernels into a big grey enamel dishpan and Dad and I rushed to fill our bowls. We all liked popcorn with milk and often made a supper of it. Sounds terrible, but I still think it is a treat. So what did we do with all the leftover popcorn? Popcorn balls, of course. Mom boiled up a syrup of sugar and water to the "soft ball" stage and poured it over the batch of popcorn balls. Then the fun began. We slathered our hands with butter and formed the sticky mass into softball size popcorn balls. As the syrup cools, the

Waking to Mourning Doves

balls stick together, so we worked fast. Next we wrapped the individual balls in waxed paper tied with a curly ribbon. I could barely wait to dig my teeth into one. Sometimes we made caramel corn with a slightly different recipe. Mom took these perfect popcorn balls to church or school auctions or sales as fundraisers. Hers usually sold first because her reputation preceded her.

> *December 18, 1949–Went to Eva's for dinner. Movie Red,*
> *Hot and Blue. Had our church program tonight. I was Mary*
> *and Bev was an angel for once.*

Church and rural school Christmas programs kept antsy children like me a bit nervous but excited all season long. I always wanted to be Mary in the church nativity pageant, but my blonde hair condemned me to a yearly angel role. Only once did I get to be Mary. Maybe my shy demeanor and an ability to memorize Bible lines typecast me into that unwanted Angel role. I can still recite, "Behold, I bring you tidings of great joy which shall be to all people."

A week before Christmas, Dad filled a pail with sand, added plenty of water, and then wedged our spindly balsam tree securely in place. We made decorative strings with popcorn and cranberries interspersed . Interlocking loops of red and green construction paper along with glass balls and silvery tinsel adorned our tree. On Christmas Eve, my parents lit real candles placed in the clip holders on the tree. We only let them burn for a short time. Dad stood by with a pail of water to douse the tree if a candle fire lit a branch. After we got electricity in the mid '40s we got colorful electric strings of lights. I longed to see the real candles glowing on our tree again. I still put candles in the clips on our tree, but we don't dare light them. We do light the old kerosene lamp, and nostalgia sweeps over me when it casts its meager light in our great room.

> *December 25, 1949–Ragnar, Eva, Nan and Grandma's were*
> *here for supper. I got vanity case, 5 view master reels, 7*
> *novelties and a good supper.*

We celebrated Christmas with both Dad's and Mom's sides of the family, alternating Christmas Eve and Christmas Day between families. With Nan, Grandpa, Aunt Eva and Uncle Ragnar, we had a traditional Christmas feast. In killing and butchering the Christmas goose, I hoped Mom would pick the cranky one that chased me. As Mom prepared other dishes, Dad sat in his easy chair crumbling home-baked white bread for dressing to stuff the goose. Candied sweet potatoes, mashed potatoes dotted with paprika and butter, other vegetables and pickles rounded out the meal. I never understood why

Caryl Crozier

all the dishes had to be washed and put away before we got to the presents. I helped so it would go faster.

White brocade tablecloths and the best china, silver and goblets made our table beautiful in my eyes. The Kinkner family loved music, and after opening gifts we always sang Christmas carols accompanied by Grandpa on violin, Nan on guitar and Eva on piano. Eventually they let me chord on the piano and I felt great pride being invited to join in. My dad and Eva sang glorious duets together, but Dad refused to sing in church despite Eva's pleading. Dad's voice equaled hers, and she was the beloved community and church soloist! I guess a basic shyness and insecurity on Dad's part kept him from public performance. Or maybe it just wasn't manly in his mind.

Traditions are often passed down on the female side of the family. We still have a Swedish emphasis in ours. Grandma Erickson observed a few traditions from her childhood in Normlosa, Osterjutland, Sweden. She placed a miniature church and snow scene on a mirror under her Christmas tree. Cotton batting resembled snow, while wax candles of angels, choristers and snowmen nestled there unburned. I have those very candles, still unburned, but antique now. Red cellophane wreaths cast a soft red welcoming light in her windows, just as they do in our home today.

> *December 24, 1949–We went to George's and I got sweater, bride doll, horse, slippers and when I got home I got a Midland watch.*

Christmas with the Erickson family alternated between Christmas Eve and day, and Aunt Alice, Mom, Grandma and Uncle George took turns hosting in later years. I liked it best at Grandma's house, because she made lutefisk and *ost kake*. Lutefisk, which is cod soaked in lye and then boiled and served with Swedish cream sauce, is an acquired taste. Most of the family hated it and eventually she supplemented it with the favored roast beef, mashed potatoes and gravy. Family members pot-lucked the rest. I tried serving lutefisk on Christmas Eve for our family, but Sherm smothered it with cranberry sauce to kill the taste. Michelle and Cherise took one bite with their noses plugged. Finally I gave up and made clam chowder or oyster stew. But my holiday still isn't complete unless we have lutefisk and lefse at a church dinner.

I loved hearing my aunts and uncles reciting their childhood table prayer in Swedish. Unfortunately, we cousins never learned it although Mom still recited it at age 96. I wish we had written it down or recorded it.

One silly rhyme that Mom taught me goes, *"My sufficiency is fully surrensified, more would be obnoxious to my superfluity."* It means, "I'm full."

Waking to Mourning Doves

After the women finished washing the mountain of dishes, scarcely disguised uncles or neighbors in Santa outfits distributed gifts. We always knew who they were but pretended we didn't. Seven young cousins quickly ripped the wrappings off our three gifts each: one from Santa, one from Grandma and one from whichever cousin who had drawn our name. Grandma always gave the nicest gifts. I still have a doll's tea set, xylophone and a small black suitcase for overnight visits to Grandma's house. Other more practical gifts like pajamas, slips, mittens and gloves reflected the frugal Depression years' mentality of our practical mothers.

When the gift exchange ended, plates of cookies and homemade freezer ice cream appeared. Aunt Hazel's chocolate chip pie, rice pudding or *ost kake* provided a rich smorgasbord.

We cousins played with new toys, sang Christmas carols and created short programs. We also giggled a lot. One year we put three-year-old Howard down Grandma's clothes chute going from the kitchen to the basement. Luckily he didn't get stuck and landed on a pile of clothes. After the hysterical concern and scolding from his mother, we never tried that again. We loved watching the Slinky toy slither down Grandma's stairs, maybe because it provided a place to escape the watchful eyes of our parents.

I wanted Christmas with my cousins to last forever, but too soon Dad warmed up the Chevy and we drove home trying not to get stuck in the ruts of snow on the dirt and gravel roads. After writing a short note in my diary, I drifted off to sleep feeling full, loved and contented. What more could a child wish for. By some standards we would be considered poor, but I know how rich our family was in what really matters.

Julebukking, a beloved Scandinavian custom, occurs during the twelve days of Christmas. Norwegian and Swedish families near Beresford donned costumes and went from house to house where neighbors receiving them attempted to identify who was under the disguises. The revelers walked right in, as people never locked their doors in Beresford. The men usually dressed as women and wore hats, and the ladies dressed in tattered men's clothing. Faces were covered with masks or nylon stockings. Sometimes a straw goat was thrown in the door as they entered. Julebukk is the Scandinavian word for Yule goat and is a holiday symbol of revelry as well as a popular Christmas decoration.

One time, a disguised group of friends entered our house at 10 p.m. and didn't say a word, a variation of Julebukking called "mumming." But the incident I most vividly recall is when a woman dressed in a long white men's union underwear suit stuffed with pillows marched up the stairs where Dad was already in bed. He was buck-naked and the adults howled with laughter as he tried to keep the sheets intact. I felt kind of sorry for him and was afraid he would start cursing at them. He didn't and they let him retain his dignity.

Once we guessed who our guests were, we dug through our old clothes and put on our own costumes and proceeded to the next house to repeat the process.

We always ended up at the home of the family that started the evening fun for a huge lunch. Sometimes there were at least 30 people, children included, who partied late into the night. Sometimes, the kids faded and went to sleep under the coats piled on the guest bed.

Our holiday vacation was over much too soon!

CHAPTER 19
4-H: Head, Heart, Hands, Health

In the 1940s and '50s, indoctrination to becoming a housewife began early for girls. We played with dolls, made play kitchens, prepared food and pretended to be nurses. Becoming a Home Economist harkens back to those early experiences and skills I learned in 4-H. Joining a 4-H club in 1949 only accentuated this process. My childhood games revolved around these activities, and I loved it.

4-H is the rural equivalent of Girl Scouts, administered by the US Agricultural Extension Service through land-grant colleges. Children ages ten to twenty were — and still are — educated in areas of productive farming, animal husbandry, and homemaking skills. Most importantly, we interacted with other kids and gained confidence in our own abilities.

October 5,1949–Went and joined 4-H at Thompson's.

I felt shy and frightened at my first 4-H meeting at a neighbor's home. Mom gave me a gentle shove to join the group of girls already gathered and then she retreated to the kitchen. As I joined the club, the girls recited the 1940s version of the pledge I came to know so well.

"I pledge my head to clearer thinking, my heart to greater loyalty, my hands to larger service and my health to better living, for my club, my community and my country, thus the name 4-H - head, heart, hands and health".

As the meeting progressed, my hands eventually quit shaking and the tension dissolved in the laughter of the group as our leader, Mae, cajoled, joked and made us all feel comfortable. Mae's rich sense of humor and creativity fostered a sense of teamwork that made us a tight-knit group, still friends today. By the time the first meeting ended, I felt excited that I had new friends. I especially liked Janet, with her long, thick blonde braids. Mae gave each of us twelve farmers' daughters a Home Life book, the required project of the year. Instructions for all kinds of activities sounded like fun: decorating ideas for my bedroom and craft projects that I knew Mom would enjoy too.

At the end of the meeting we gathered around the piano and sang songs like

Waltzing Matilda, Tell Me Why and *Red River Valley*. Through the years we always ended meetings with sing-alongs. Every year I looked forward to Christmas caroling for elderly or shut-in neighbors. Standing in the freshly fallen snow and watching their smiles were rewarding enough, but best of all, they always had candy and Scandinavian cookies for us.

Joining the Happy Homemakers 4-H Club had a large impact on my whole life. Little did I know when joining the club at Marion Thompson's home that experiences I would have would bolster my confidence, help shape my value system, and ultimately determine my career path as a Home Economist. The club usually averaged around a dozen neighborhood farm girls and sometimes a few from Bethesda Orphans Home. We met monthly at each other's homes and learned via demonstrations and health talks about our various yearly projects such as foods and nutrition, clothing, home life, handicrafts, gardening and horticulture. Mae Blumer was a dynamite leader for all the years I belonged. She knew how to inspire us to do our best. Most of all, her sense of humor made 4-H fun for everyone. Assistant leaders like Geri Bovill, Mildred Olbertson and my mother each had their own special talents and shared freely with all of us. Mom was a leader for ten years and I think she enjoyed it as much as I did. She had been in 4-H as a teenager and wanted to become a Home Economist, a fact that I did not know until much later in my life. She enabled me to do just that — to achieve her dream.

Each year we focused on one of the three major 4-H projects or elective activities: gardening, handicrafts or livestock. I never took an interest in grooming and showing cattle, pigs, chickens or rabbits at the county fair, but a few of our members did.

> *March, 1952–Marion came down and tried to figure out 4-H demonstration.*

> *April 2, 1952–Had 4-H here- those crazy Home kids- Mary and I had a demonstration, what a mess.*

Shortly after joining, I gave a Christmas centerpiece demonstration for my Home Life project. Piling a few colorful glass Christmas bulbs in spruce greens in Mom's American Fostoria bowl seemed simple, but I was a bundle of nerves preparing for it. That minor success built my confidence and may have planted a seed for a future teaching career. Some later demonstrations didn't feel as successful when we tried team demonstrations. I usually did better on my own.

> *April 2, 1950–George's, Grandma's, Harold Nelson's*

Waking to Mourning Doves

Elmer's, Eva's and Nan came to Ma's b'day- she got an electric mixer.

For my foods project for the county fair, I taped a checklist to the inside of our kitchen cupboard door and kept track of everything I made. . Baking powder biscuits, my culinary specialty, far outweighed the meat and vegetable entries on the chart. I loved baking, no question about it. Lining up flour, butter, sugar, milk, eggs and spices and then turning out delicacies that drew compliments spurred me on. In the 1940s, box mixes didn't exist; we made everything from scratch. Box mixes are quick to make, but never taste quite as good in my opinion. When Mom got a new electric Hamilton Beach mixer in 1950, we made every recipe in the booklet over and over. Spice cake became our favorite. I treasure that grease- and batter-stained booklet and use recipes from it to this day. I still have the reliable 70-year-old mixer and it works well. Appliances like old toasters and electric irons from that era seem to last forever. Now they are collectible antiques!

The South Dakota Lincoln County Fair Achievement Days in August is the time when 4-H members exhibit items made in their chosen projects. I started small by preparing a place setting of Mom's blue Modern Tone dishes and Art Deco style silverware placed on a white damask tablecloth accented with a cut-flower arrangement of zinnias and cosmos from our garden. I was sure it would win a first prize. The judge must not have found it quite as elegant as I did. My heart sank when she placed a red ribbon on my creation. A red ribbon is for second place, with blue for first place and white for third. A purple ribbon means your exhibit goes to the State Fair in Huron, South Dakota.

August 15, 1952–Got my first purple ribbon on sugar cookies at Achievement Days, Cleaned up at Canton; 1 purple ribbon, 2 blue, 5 red and 2 white.

In my second year in 4-H, I made my Grandma Erickson's recipe for sugar cookies. Mom taught me to roll the dough paper-thin on her old, tin-surfaced Hoosier Cabinet. Using Grandma's three-inch cookie cutter, I baked enough cookies to get six perfect specimens to exhibit at the county fair. I watched from a distance as the Extension Home Economist judge nibbled samples from plates and plates of cookies, deciding which deserved ribbons. When she put a blue sticker on my crisp cookies, I nearly burst with pride. When I returned later, my plate had a champion purple ribbon, meaning I would enter a batch in the State Fair. I earned many purple ribbons in succeeding years, but none as exciting as the first one.

June 6, 1952–Am in camp- Clarinda took us- on KP- Gail, Enolia, Mary and I- fun at talent nite and recreation-first time bunk bed and swimming.

The most astounding event of 4-H summer camp happened when I learned to float on my back in Lake Herman. Because of the polio epidemic in the 1940s and '50s, my parents wouldn't let me swim in the Beresford swimming pool. I wonder if they deemed swimming in a lake safer. South Dakota had very few lakes, but our 4-H camp hugged the shores of a small shallow lake near Madison. My friends and I spent every minute possible struggling to float and dog-paddle knowing it might be our only opportunity all summer. Sleeping in a ten-person cabin, camp activities and KP (kitchen duty) made the few days fly by too quickly. I enjoyed it a whole lot more as a kid than as an extension leader in 1958 and 1959. Sleeping on the top bunk bed supervising giggling girls who stayed up most of the night didn't seem a bit amusing.

August 15, 1951–We won first on our merry-go-round float.

July 2, 1951–Went to town to decorate float-it's the same as State Fair float.

Mom writes: *Caryl learned to sew on a singer treadle sewing machine until we bought an electric. She sewed quite well on it and sewed a lot. She was active in 4-H and we had many parties. We dressed up and went different places. We had floats in the parade, which meant time and again a lot of work. We made a train float, merry go round, Cinderella and had many work meetings. Some of the projects they did were Home life, clothing, foods and nutrition, home crafts and gardening. I was a 4-H leader 11 years and Mildred was too; Mrs. Anderson for a few years and Mae was leader for 12 years.*

As a group, we enjoyed making very creative floats for the annual August Achievement Days parades. We almost always won and then we took our float entry to the State Fair in Huron in September. Some of the themes I recall are: Cinderella (4-H Makes You a Princess), a merry-go-round, a train made from five wagons which Gail Bovill and I hand-pulled in three parades. We dressed in white skirts, blouses and caps as engineers. When the parades finished we looked and felt more like coal shovelers: sweaty, dirty, and tired. I was glad to put that float in the scrap heap.

Designing and making the floats took many hours of teamwork. My friends and I remember those times as our best experiences in 4-H. Mom often drove the car pulling the float, and her car was jammed with all the last-minute clothing and materials we used to make the float. We always wondered if we'd finish in time. When we won, Dad often hauled the trailer and float to the State Fair and drove in the parade. He grumbled about going at first, but I think he enjoyed it because he never said no. I guess he didn't think it was safe for Mom to pull a flatbed trailer behind the car the 100 miles to Huron.

The clothing project in my third year in 4-H started me on a lifelong passion. Mom and I basically learned how to sew together on her old, second-hand Singer treadle sewing machine. Although she had enjoyed 4-H as a teenager, she hadn't learned to sew. Her older sister, Hazel, and Grandma did the sewing for the Erickson family. Mom quilted but didn't sew clothing.

By the age of ten or eleven, I putzed around, sewing crude coverlets and clothes for my dolls, so the prospect of making a dress for myself didn't seem too formidable. I loved to pump that old treadle as fast as it would go and watch the stitches zoom down my fabric scraps. When Mom and Dad milked cows and did other outside chores, I made supper, usually featuring baking powder biscuits and fried potatoes, and then played with the sewing machine.

In 1953 I needed to get down to business and make a dress for the county fair for my clothing project. Mom and I paged through the Simplicity pattern book at the K & K general store in Beresford and selected a pattern featuring a full, four-gore skirt, fitted bodice with a Peter Pan collar, set-in cap sleeves and a peplum to go around the waist. I thought it was very fashionable and couldn't wait to get started.

My first rendition of the pattern in white eyelet fabric was deemed a success. Then, for the county fair exhibit, I wanted a pink and grey plaid fabric. Not a smart choice for a beginner like me, because plaids have to be matched. I got very frustrated having to rip out seams and try over and over again. Mom had endless patience as she coached and advised me. We didn't have a buttonhole maker on our treadle sewing machine, so she taught me to do painstaking, handmade buttonholes. I hated that part because my hand-sewing skills had much room for improvement. Finally, the dress had a final pressing and hung on the exhibit hanger.

The coveted blue ribbon seemed worth the effort as I modeled my creation in my first dress review. Actually, I thought I looked pretty cute in the dress and the judges must have thought so, too. Three purple ribbons followed in dress revue modeling competition. Dress Revue became my favorite activity. I made and modeled a garment in the style revue competing against other girls in divisions such as school, sport, tailored, dressy and formal. In my first big purple ribbon win, I wore a brown, pleated shirt-style dress, the second a wool school outfit of an aqua blouse with loop buttonholes and an aqua and black tweed skirt. My last entry, a brown tweed coat and slim green dress with hat, gloves, purse and matching shoes exceeded my wildest dreams. I won the state competition and earned a trip to National 4-H Club Congress in Chicago to model the outfit in a national style show. By then I knew sewing would be a huge part of my future, and it has been.

> Mom writes: *We went to Huron to the State Fair in 1956 to see Caryl and Margie Hill in the state dress review. Mildred Olbertson and I took Janet and Caryl up to be judges in food competition too. I went to see the girls in their 4 H outfits. Well, lo and behold, the head of it all (Kenny Ostroot) came and told me I had a winner in dress review. Caryl went on a train leaving Sioux Falls to go to National 4-H Club Congress in Chicago where she modeled her coat along with winners from other states.*

Winning a trip to National 4-H Club Congress in Chicago for being the best in a project is the ultimate goal of many 4-Hers. For me, I was excited for my first train ride, meeting new friends from all over the US and my first time in a big city. Being treated royally for a week whetted my appetite for more experiences and travel. The food, hotel service and cultural introductions were eye-openers for me. Most of us had our first taste of rare steak, Caesar salad and chocolate mousse in Chicago.

After several rehearsals, the dress revue participants put on a fashion show for the entire delegation. I felt terrified on the long runway, bathed in spotlights and trying to keep in step with my cute male escort. It was an unforgettable moment of glory. I hoped my hunky escort might ask me for a date or at least my address, but he didn't.

> *April 23,1951–Went to Lands Church to practice for Rural Life Sunday with the Thompson's.*

> *December 12,1952–Us 4-Hers went caroling in the Home bus to several places.*

The most enjoyable 4-H activities were those done with other clubs. My favorites were 4-H camp at Madison, Recognition event in November, folk dancing, statewide meetings at Brookings, State Fair, and Rural Life Sunday church services with the Pleasant Valley Livestock Club.

We celebrated Rural Life Sunday as the South Dakota countryside thawed and greened up after a long winter. Zion country church welcomed our two clubs, girls and boys, to conduct the entire service. It probably helped that the

Waking to Mourning Doves

4-H leaders and several members attended the church. Girls sat on one side and boys on the other — a dumb arrangement in my mind, since I had started getting interested in boys.

Thank goodness Mae never asked me to do the sermon. She knew my strengths and weaknesses. Until later in life, I cringed at public speaking. One year, my piano solo *"Nightfall in the Forest"* caused my Dad to exclaim, "I didn't realize you could play that well." Maybe accolades from other folks elicited this rare praise from Dad. Nan more than made up for Dad's lack of compliments. She bragged about me to anyone who would listen.

Farm kids helped harvest corn and prepare the farm and livestock for the winter. In November, a celebration of sorts rewarded club members at the Lincoln County Recognition Night. After leaders gave us awards in projects, it was time for what most of us came for, folk dancing. Everyone got matched up with a partner on the gym floor and the folk dances or square dancing began.

My favorite, the progressive Schottische dance, allowed me to meet and flirt with most of the boys on the floor. "Schottische to the left, schottische to the right, walk two three four, heel and a toe and around the ladies go, a heel and toe and on to the next." Meeting boys almost, but not quite, topped getting one or two pin awards a year in all the projects I ever did.

Because of 4-H experiences and a scholarship, in 1957 I transferred from Augustana College to South Dakota State (SDSU) in Brookings to major in Home Economics. While at SDSU, the 4-H club sponsored me as their entry in the Miss South Dakota Pageant. Meeting with judges for interviews, modeling the swimsuit, playing the piano for the talent competition (Rachmaninoff's Prelude Op.3 No. 2), and modeling a formal made me a bundle of nerves as I prepared. I didn't win, but it was a good experience.

Spending the summers of 1958 and 1959 as a summer Home Extension Agent in Chamberlain, Brule County, South Dakota began a wonderful exposure to work and life. I was exhilarated starting my first real job knowing it came with a large responsibility for supervising the women's extension clubs and the girl's 4-H programs in the county. Had I not gotten married in 1960, I would have returned there after graduation. Circumstances never allowed me to become an Extension Agent later, but I served on the Dakota County and State of Minnesota Board and Advisory Councils for extension in the 1970s and also helped daughters Michelle and Cherise with 4-H experiences.

4-H has helped shape my life in countless ways. I am sorry that state budget cutbacks in the twenty-first century, changing lifestyles and dwindling interest don't give every country and city girl the opportunities that I had.

CHAPTER **20**

Ode to Daisy Dewey

Grandma Erickson gave me my first musical instrument, a toy xylophone, for Christmas when I was four years old. My parents gave me a tiny toy piano that I plunked away on soon after. My aunts and grandmothers gave me an early introduction to music and most of all music appreciation in many forms: vocal and instrumental, recorded and live.

> Mom writes: *Caryl took piano lessons from Miss Dewey and sometimes I paid with egg and chickens. We had a piano down home and I don't know where we bought it. Hazel sold it to someone and it tipped out of the truck into the ditch and broke.*

Knix, knix, andante and allegro; these strange new words enhanced my vocabulary as I learned to play the piano from Daisy Dewey. *Gollywogs at Play*, my first recital piece, required a hand movement called knix. Patience personified, Miss Dewey supervised my delicate staccato hand actions crossing over each other, muttering "knix" to remind me. The graceful hand movements supposedly portrayed gollywogs at play. I thought gollywogs were tadpoles, but on my sheet music they resembled elves .

I faced each weekly session with trepidation wondering if my fingering and rhythm for the simple songs might elicit a word of approval from Miss Dewey. She coaxed and encouraged her cadre of 25 students to learn the basics of music. Some of us learned to love the piano.

Miss Dewey's Art Deco style older home in Beresford had honey-colored woodwork throughout. I loved walking in her front door viewing the seemingly endless winding wood staircase, barely containing the urge to dash upstairs to see her antique furniture and memorabilia. Once or twice she took me upstairs to let me see treasures in her bedroom. I felt very privileged. Daisy and her sister, Mae, who owned the dress shop in town, lived together in the cluttered house their parents bequeathed to them. Spinster sisters, tiny, round and jolly, they proudly displayed their patriotism and pride in their early American ancestry. I think their father, a Civil War hero, instilled a strong community spirit in them.

Heavenly odors of a casserole or beef roast wafting from her kitchen made my mouth water during my 4:30 after-school time slot. She often had cookies

Waking to Mourning Doves

or candy set out for us, but I longed to dig into that pot roast or chicken noodle casserole.

Daisy, a tad heavyset, always wore glasses that hung down from a chain. Sometimes she sat back and listened to me plunk out the tunes from the Wagner or John Thompson series of music books. However, when she put on those glasses and leaned forward and activated the metronome counter, I knew my lack of practice would result in her saying "Caryl, if you'd only practice and count."

> *December 5, 1949–I took piano lessons and it was dull and was Dewey ever crabby.*

Avoiding that annoying metronome became an incentive to practice at least a half hour a day. I also knew that the 50 cents per lesson stretched Mom's meager budget. She often paid Miss Dewey with her labors of garden produce, eggs, chickens or cream. Mom didn't have the privilege of having piano lessons as a child, so she made certain I had the opportunity, as she did with so many aspects of my life

> *February 18, 1950–Took ml [music lesson] got sheet music Johnson Rag and Charley My Boy.*

I longed to play the piano as well as my two favorite aunts, Hazel and Eva. Their interest and encouragement spurred me on. They had popular sheet music of the era like *Charmaine* and *I Want a Paper Doll to Call My Own*. I bought stacks of popular music from the '50s. My grandmother never had piano lessons, but played by ear for community dances and sing-alongs accompanying Grandpa on the fiddle. She loved listening to me practice and taught me to play simple songs by ear by age five. All my close relatives had upright pianos and phonographs, and their love of music rubbed off on me.

For seven years I dutifully practiced and trudged into Miss Dewey's home for my weekly lesson. When she pulled a new piece of sheet music from her stash, I felt like I'd just won the lottery. Bach, Beethoven and Brahams were okay, but who could resist songs entitled *Gollywogs at Play*, *Nightfall in the Forest* or *Meditation*: still some of my favorites.

> *June 18,1952–Played Nightfall in the Forest at piano recital.*

Each spring Miss Dewey's students presented a recital on stage at her Methodist Church. She required us to memorize our songs, and I remember sweaty palms and terror that I would forget the notes. She always reassured us that she had our pieces in her bag and would help us if we stumbled. We girls wore our best new Easter dresses for the recital and couldn't wait for the reward of cake, lemonade and praise when we giggled with relief that the whole ordeal was over with.

I never became the child prodigy my grandmother envisioned, but I enjoyed playing for vocal and chorus accompaniment at elementary and high school events. Playing duets with my friends LaVonne, Janet, Lois and Marcene for social events made practice worth it.

Our Congregational Church bought an electric organ in the '50s, and I practiced and taught myself to play well enough for Sunday School and church services. Sometimes when practicing alone in the quiet, cool sanctuary, I turned up the volume to make music reverberate from the rafters and imagined myself a renowned concert organist. A few sour notes would soon bring me back to reality.

Vocational-interest exams given on college entrance tests revealed that my interests most closely aligned with people who became musicians and music majors in college. I knew that I didn't possess enough talent for that profession, but as an avocation, it was perfect for me.

A preliminary 1958 Miss South Dakota contest had me in a panic regarding a talent selection. Back to Miss Dewey I went, even though I had stopped taking lessons several years before. She coached me through *Rachmaninoff's Prelude Op.3 No.2* so that I at least didn't embarrass myself in the competition. We both enjoyed the practice sessions and reminiscing. I even tolerated the dreaded metronome as we laughed about my childhood fears. Miss Dewey's legacy was a town full of girls and boys whom she inspired to appreciate music.

Now, in 2011, I have my grandmother's Segerstrom upright piano, a pump organ, and a Conn electric organ in our home as well as a beat-up organ at our Wisconsin cabin. Unfortunately, my arthritic fingers don't coordinate with my brain's desire to play, but I do remember and imagine myself playing in my prime.

Although playing the accordion seems hokey now, I thought my new twelve-bass accordion that my parents purchased for me in the seventh grade made me cool.

> Mom writes: *She had an accordion and went to Alcester for lessons. She went to different organizations and played and Ray took you to your lessons and I did too.*
>
> *December 1, 1950–Accordion guys came tonite and I got an accordion.*

An incursion of enterprising accordion salesmen made a huge profit selling accordions and giving brief lessons to Midwest children in the early '50s. We learned on our 12 bass accordions in group lessons, and soon the salesmen called on our parents displaying shiny new *120* bass accordions. (A "bass" is a button on an accordian.) The salesmen praised me for what a promising student I had become, so naturally, my parents bought the larger accordion I coveted.

> *February 21, 1951–I got my new accordion 120 bass of black and white.*

After more parents were sucked in by the sales pitch, and salesmen had saturated the area with accordions, they suddenly left town. There wasn't as much profit in the lessons. We then learned on our own or sold the new accordions at a loss. This reminds me of the popular play *The Music Man.*

> *December 13, 1951–Went to Guild and Marion and I sang a duet and I played the accordion also.*

> *February 17, 1952–Hertha and George's silver anniversary. I was waitress and played accordion.*

Thanks to Miss Dewey, I had a good background in piano, so learning the accordion seemed pretty easy. I practiced and eventually played for countless bridal showers and social club meetings. A few of us even formed an accordion band that played for dances, church suppers and other social events. The band folded [like an accordian!] after a couple of years due to flagging bookings, but we had fun and learned together. I remember playing South, In the Mood, Glowworm and Lady of Spain solo as well as in the band.

I still have that shiny, 120 bass accordion. It makes a wheezy, squawking sound and needs repair. Alas, no one is interested now.

Fascination with string instruments led me to take guitar lessons on my grandmother's steel-string guitar in the '70s. I learned well enough to do a couple methods of picking the strings and a few songs like *Take Me Home, Country Roads.* Unfortunately, guitar playing produces calluses on the fingertips. Teaching quilting, sewing and craft classes with calluses did not work, so I abandoned the guitar to have feeling return to my fingertips.

In the '80s I bought a dulcimer and zither, but never practiced enough to produce anything resembling music.

My only regret musically is that I didn't learn to play the fiddle like my grandfather. Maybe just as well. My memories of him applying rosin to his bow, grinning at me and launching into a lively tune still warms my heart.

PART VI: CLIMBING FENCES

Silver Lake School — Grades 1–8

Mom & Dad at Gothland School

14th Birthday Party

Cheerleaders

Slumber Parties

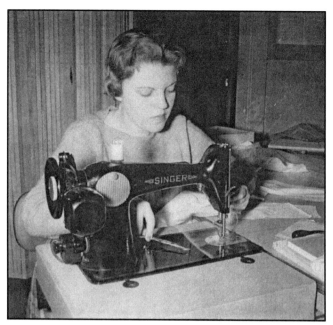

Home Economics

South Dakota State University

Caryl & Sherm
1957

CHAPTER 21

My One-Room Country School

My favorite painting depicts children bursting out of school at the end of the day, dashing for home across the prairie, lunch pails in hand. Harvey Dunn, the renowned rural-life artist from South Dakota, artistically interprets country schools in the painting, *Home From School.* I can visualize my dad in this painting and wonder if he felt as exhilarated as I did when the school day ended.

The print of *Home From School* we have hanging on our wall today closely resembles my school building and captures my father's era attending Silver Lake School District #59 in the NE quarter of section 28 of Pleasant Township northeast of Beresford from 1916–1924. The white clapboard siding and wooden shingled peak roof building had been serving students since the first Swiss settlers built it in 1885.

Things were pretty much the same when I attended from 1944–1952. It was still a one-room schoolhouse. The same recitation bench and wooden desks with the ink well in the front right corner served my classmates and me. Students' desks were arranged in five rows, with different sized desks in each row. Our teacher placed us usually by grade but sometimes based on a student's behavior the year before. The desks with their iron filigree frames were bolted to board bases so they could be moved. The desktops were occasionally refinished to remove initials carved in them, although with very limited success. Swivel-seated, lift-top desks eventually replaced the desks that Dad and I used. They were still there when the school closed in [1970]. I'm certain, too, that the brass school bell, front-wall blackboards, piano, roll-up maps, hanging globe, oak book cabinets, stern-looking pictures of Washington and Lincoln, well worn teacher's desk and flagpole remained in place long after the school was shuttered.

Rural one-room country schools were the frontier's answer to public education. County tax money funded one school in every township. Townships measured six-miles square: that's 36 square miles or 36 sections, and there was a road every mile. A section had four 160-acre quarter sections. Often there would be a family in each quarter section. During organizational meetings for new school districts, families selected one-acre building sites. Sometimes differences arose dealing with the distance children had to travel, so half-mile roads were sometimes established just for the siting of a schoolhouse to make the travel distances more fair.

The schoolhouses were for grades one through eight. One teacher instructed all eight grades in all subjects. Up to 30 students from within a three-mile radius of the school could attend; during my eight grades, our school averaged 16 students. At one time there were six in my grade, and four of us went through all eight grades and high school together.

Not many families moved in or out, so getting new kids in school was a really big deal. We were particularly excited when four families with two or three kids each moved to the district and expanded our classes. Two of the new guys, both named Jerry, were comedians and their pranks added spark and hilarity to our days. We missed them when their families left after a couple of years, moving on to another farm. Families who rented farms moved often, usually in March when farm leases typically expired. Fortunately, we owned our farm and I didn't have to move away from friends.

I had six different teachers during my eight years at Silver Lake Elementary School. Their training ran the gamut from a six-week summer course to a two-year teaching certificate to a four-year college degree. Some of the teachers boarded at a district member's home during the week because they did not have a permanent home nearby. My second and third grade teacher, Lida Swanson, was probably the best and most experienced teacher and laid the groundwork for my love of lifelong learning. Grace Hendrickson Lubbock, Elna Dann, Dorothy Young and Marie Muhlenkort were also excellent teachers. Dorothy invited students to stay overnight with her family of six brothers and sisters, and we loved seeing her in the role of big sister. My fifth grade teacher, whom I shall not name, was released at midyear because she couldn't control the older boys. Chaos ruled for several months with the boys scuffling on the floor during class and generally causing mass confusion. I felt sorry for her as she tried hard to gain control of the classroom, but being so young with just six weeks of training out of high school, she hadn't attained the maturity and experience to handle a room full of rowdies who tested her to the limit. She was replaced by Ardelle Thompson, a seasoned veteran, who had us shaped up and docile as lambs in one day. One look from her, and we behaved. We respected her and knew she wanted the best for us. She introduced us to the Hardy Boys mystery books, played ball with us and made learning fun with her creativity and enthusiasm. Mostly though, she taught us how to behave and treat others with respect.

Inspired by my mother's diary, I began keeping my own journal in fifth grade and continued until I was twenty-two years old. The entries were basic

Caryl Crozier

and simple in those days, but I have lifted a few from the earliest diary to document the mood of the seasons at country school.

December 3, 1951–I got so mad at dumb Dennis, he put my good sweater on top of the flagpole and it got greasy.

Sometimes kids were picked on for clothing they wore or for just being different. Nowadays we call it bullying. Luckily, I wasn't a prime target to be picked on, but when I was, a couple of older girls in my 4-H group fended off the would-be attackers. Sometimes a boy put a frog or something gross in my desk, but I knew it wasn't malicious and they only wanted me to act "girly" and scream. I did, which only egged them on. But truth be told, I liked the attention. Girls bullied by being snippy and exclusive, while boys acted more physical. The scuffling of the rowdy boys when I was in fifth grade rarely bothered the girls and we tried to remain aloof and do our school work. We just left the scene at recess and clustered in the old barn or grove and "hung out" before we called it that. We learned to fend for ourselves with all ages. One of the teachers put soap in a child's mouth if they said a bad word or misbehaved. Fortunately, the parents soon put a stop to that practice. By the time we were ten years old, we pretty much knew right from wrong and trusted that when we stood up for ourselves, the older kids or an adult would come to our aid.

Outdoor playground equipment at Silver Lake consisted of two wooden teeter-totters, a swing set, slide and basketball hoops north of the school and a ball diamond on the south. The road ditches had tall grasses and cattails and enough water to wade or skate depending on the season. Dad reminisced about playing the same outdoor games I did. It makes me smile to remember going from a never-win and last-chosen youngster to one of the big kids playing kitten ball (softball), Kick-the-Can, Fox-and-Geese, Hide and Seek and Jail around the flag pole. My personal favorites were Anti-I-Over and Pump- Pump- Pull-Away. My Iowa and Minnesota friends insist the game is called "Pom-Pom-Pull-Away," but we Beresford players knew it as "Pump-Pump," just like we knew "sloppy joes" were called "taverns."

Choosing sides for recess games had a distinct pecking order. The little first, second and third graders had fewer physical skills, so we expected to be selected last. As we grew older, the athletic kids who could run fast and throw and catch a ball better made the team quicker. I had none of those skills, but sometimes I was chosen a lot earlier than I deserved because the team captain liked me. Being chosen last hurt our pride, and most of us experienced it. I can't recall how team leaders were chosen. Maybe we took turns as I picked team members now and then. To decide who chose first, we threw a bat to the other captain who caught it vertically. The captains grasped the bat hand over hand till one reached the base of the bat, which determined the winner.

> *September 10, 1949–We played ball in school. I made a homerun, believe it or not.*

> *September 19, 1950–The Silver Lake Bombers played with Pleasant Hill – We beat 12 – 10. I made one score, 1 out and 3 times left on base.*

I became the designated softball pitcher in the upper grades, probably because catching a ball at the bases or infield was not my forte and the team had to put me somewhere. I threw a fairly accurate underhanded ball, but no curve balls or spinners. My team didn't expect me to strike anyone out, but once in a while I surprised them. I dreaded the exchange ball games with other schools and was afraid I'd be called "out." The snacks and meeting with other kids made up for the fear and sometimes I played okay.

In the Anti-I-Over game, the person with the strongest throwing arm threw the ball over the school building. If the other team caught the ball, they rushed around both ends of the school trying to catch as many of the opposing team members as possible till they got to the safe zone. Of course the opposing team tried to tag the good catchers and throwers and ignored kids like me. If one team ended up with the dregs like me who couldn't get the ball over the roof, we capitulated and declared the opposing team the winner.

We played Kick-the-Can during recess more than any other game. The "can" was usually a football, but in early days a tin can, thus the name. The unlucky person who is IT tried to keep anyone from kicking the ball away. Tagging someone before they kicked the ball put them in "prison." However, if the ball got kicked away, the prisoners were all freed. As the last stragglers lay in wait, the IT kid had to ferret them out of hiding places in the cob house, barn or cistern room and run a race to reach the can first. Mighty was the hero who freed the prisoners.

Most often we competed in games of softball, touch football or basketball. We took turns choosing games and the older kids pressured us to choose their favorites. I liked mind games and quizzes, but others preferred the physical games.

During the winter we spent our noon hours skating on the remnants of Silver Lake, pretending not to hear the school bell when the teacher rang it at 12:50 to signal us back to classes. Skating on pond ice didn't train us for the Olympics, but we learned the rudimentary skill of staying upright. We often shared a pair of skates with a friend, each wearing them about fifteen minutes while the other would run and slide as far as possible on the ice. My parents bought me skates for my third grade Christmas in a large enough size to last me a lifetime, which they did. Stuffing socks in the toes and wearing thick socks helped fill the gaps, but even lacing them tight didn't help wobbly ankles. After a deep snowfall, the boys shoveled open patches and paths on the small lake. At best, it was never very smooth. Aquatic plants and muddy bumps often protruded through the rippled surface. The ice cracked during the spring thaw, and we screamed in fear and delight if the surface buckled and a hole emerged or someone fell through. Since the deepest part barely covered our boots, no one worried about real danger. Reluctantly, we trudged back the one-fourth mile to school, many times with wet feet.

My father remembers the lake being much larger and deeper, and now in 2011, tile-drained cornfields have replaced the native prairie pasture and tiny shallow lake we loved.

Several deep creeks flowed through area farms and we often skated on them after school. Now those meandering creeks are tile-drained or dug out, resulting in straight ditches. Farmers don't want pond water on their land; passing it on to the farm downstream seems to be the goal.

> *January 14, 1949–Played bowling and cops and robbers at school. Also, Captain May I and Keepaway in the school hall because it was too cold to go out today.*

Like Silver Lake graduates before us, we liked to play Hide and Seek in the old barn that had been used to shelter horses kids rode to school. Very few rode horses to school when I attended, since fewer farms had a horse in the barn. I had a horse, but only rode her to school a couple times because she was slow and stubborn and liked to kick or bite people who got too close to her. The barn and the cob house, used to store wood and cobs for the basement furnace, provided places to hide either in or behind.

The outdoor toilets, one for boys and one for girls, were either hot and smelly or cold and breezy. Even so, it was a simple pleasure to raise the two fingers to get permission to go outside to the bathroom during school hours. We had finger codes to sharpen a pencil, get a drink, go to the toilet etc. I reveled in the quiet while walking to the toilet. In the spring, the meadowlarks sang, *"Kiss her. She's a pretty girl,"* earthy farm smells wafted across the fields, and I slowly meandered back to class savoring it all.

The outhouses always got tipped over on Halloween. The fathers arrived on November 1st, tipping them back up again amidst much laughter.

We all took turns doing chores: cleaning blackboards and erasers, flag ceremony, sweeping the schoolroom, entry and outdoor toilets, passing out

Waking to Mourning Doves

songbooks and library duty. I didn't like carrying water over the snow-banks from the cistern housed in a small room behind the school. We had no running water in the school building. We poured water over peoples' hands for washing. Conservation was not an insignificant consideration and we depended on rain run-off to fill our deep cistern. We had health inspection for good grooming and brushing teeth and received gold stars on a chart if we complied. I found a health book we used called *Spic and Span* at an antique store for $25, but I didn't buy it. Now I wish I had. I like the *Spic and Span* alliteration, and the 1940s illustrations seem quaint now.

> *March 21, 1951–What a blizzard, I didn't go to school. Pop went to pasture to get Ginger.*

Transportation during my father's school years was solely on horseback or horse and buggy. I usually got a ride to school in our '38 Chevy or cars driven by the neighbors with whom we took turns riding. As many as eight children rode in a car. Seatbelts were not required then. On snowy days, another adult went along to watch the edge of the road so we didn't drive into the ditch. Blizzards came up fast and furious on those windswept treeless prairies, but we always got home safely.

We didn't have a telephone at our school, so we were never sure if someone was going to pick us up at the end of the day. It was always exciting to get to the door after school to see who was there to give rides. We knew right away who had to walk home. The teacher sometimes stayed all night at school with children whose parents couldn't reach the school on drifted roads to get them. Getting back to school after a blizzard was a challenge when the township road grader didn't get the roads cleared quickly. We often had to go "the long way," two miles north, one west and two back south breaking through drifts. Dads got out to shovel snow away from the tires and pushed the car back onto the path when it slipped off the road tracks. We were lucky to have a car and hadn't heard of snow tires or 4-wheel drives.

Fresh, hard-packed snow made perfect conditions for building snow forts, huge blocks of snow piled igloo fashion by opposing teams into two sturdy fortifications. Of course, the fun was in the creation of the structures, which often took days. We had 15-minute morning and afternoon recess and one hour at noon to play. We couldn't wait to pull our snow pants and sturdy, three-buckle rubber boots on over our shoes and get outside. We had fierce snowball fights. When we got hit, we joined the other team in their fort. I wasn't a very good thrower, but I made mean snowballs. In South Dakota, the wind always blows, winter and summer. We hadn't heard of the wind-chill factor then, but somehow managed to avoid frostbite. Thermal wear and fancy Sorrel felt-lined boots were a long way off.

Long cotton stockings or two pairs of jeans and two pairs of socks were all the insulation we girls had under our snow pants. After outside recess, we all dashed in and clustered around the big heat register coming up from the furnace below. Steam rose when we put our soggy mittens on the register, making a smell not replicated since, but still lingering in my olfactories. I didn't mind white long stockings held up by a garter belt, but hated the ugly brown stockings and wore knee sox as often as Mom allowed. In the winter, girls usually wore a dress or skirt over jeans to school. We hung our headscarves, neck scarves, jackets and coveralls on our own coat hooks in the back entrance hall, boys on the right and girls on the left by the water cooler and hand-washing stand.

> *December 12, 1949–I've got mumps – goody, goody – ha ha – darn! Just on one side. Ma went to club & I was in bed in the downstairs bedroom.*

> *December 7, 1949–Mary has chicken pox, so has Leon so it's dull in school cuz Mary isn't here.*

> *December 1, 1950–Had the pukes last night so didn't go to school – accordion guys came tonight and I got a 12 base accordion. Nice.*

During my first years at school, we all drank from a common dipper, but after several bouts with colds, sore throats and childhood diseases, the school board got a Red Wing bubble cooler fountain. I avoided chicken pox until I was an adult, but caught measles, mumps and whooping cough at school. Two boys in the district had rheumatic fever and had to stay home for part of the school year. We were allowed to visit them if we washed our hands carefully after the visit.

> *February 8, 1950–I went to school and got down on the dumps with arithmetic. I had fun in town – hubba hubba, ding ding.*

> *November 16, 1950–We took tests, geography 92 1/2 B+. arithmetic 98 A, language 100 A, reading 90 A.*

I am sure the structure of the day remained the same for me as for my father a generation earlier and for the children of later generations. School began at nine a.m., though we'd often get there shortly after eight for preschool

Waking to Mourning Doves

playtime. For the first ten minutes, we had the flag ceremony and salutation outside and then came in and had singing, folk dancing or the teacher read a book for 15 minutes. We began the rotation of lessons for the day usually in this order: reading, arithmetic and finally penmanship at 11:45 with a noon lunch break. In the afternoon, history or geography, language, spelling and art once a week on Friday. Each class, when called, went to the recitation bench and had their 10-15 minute lesson, recitation, question period and assignment for the day. If appropriate, two classes like fifth and sixth or seventh and eighth were combined. Girls hugged one end of the bench and boys the other. I guess we were afraid of boy/girl germs! Every six weeks, standardized tests were sent out from the county. We dreaded them.

> *March 2, 1950–studied spelling words for the contest with Mary out in the hall. I can't get some of them.*

> *April 22, 1950–spelling contest, got fourth – Voegelis here for supper. Topsy had 4 kittens.*

My signature skill was spelling. I won the spelling contest all eight years at the local and four-district school levels. Twice I came in third at the county level at which I competed with 30 or 40 other district winners. I was happy to get at least an honorable mention (top five) the other six years. We spent weeks and weeks drilling and studying words at least an hour a day. That little blue book of first through eighth grade words has the cover torn off from hard use, but it has a treasured spot in our home library. Best of all, I got a new dress for the competition in Canton, the county seat. We all arrived wearing our new outfits, shy and laden with three or four newly sharpened pencils, a white soap eraser, and plenty of Kleenex or a clean handkerchief just in case there were tears. We met in the huge auditorium at the high school first and listened to Thelma B. Eidsness, the county school superintendent, whom we knew from her once-a-year visits to each school to observe for a day. Teachers called us by grades to the classrooms and we nervously chose a desk that was usually too big for us. I watched and wondered if anyone was more prepared than I. The teacher began by saying the word, using it in a sentence then repeating it again. We had at least 50 words, but the only word I can specifically remember getting wrong was "shepherd." Then came the long wait while tests were being corrected. We got acquainted with others from the county as we waited. I broke out in a cold sweat as winners were announced and names called. I was never the big winner, but I sure can spell yet and that's maybe the biggest win of all.

> *November 22, 1949–We just fiddled around in school – played*

Caryl Crozier

Grey Wolf and Kick the Can. I helped the little kids study reading in the hall.

The rural school system was like Montessori in that you are in the same room with all eight grades and all skill levels of students. We heard the same lessons for eight years and were bound to learn eventually. The constant commotion encouraged independent study and the ability to concentrate with high levels of activity around us, a good skill for life. The older students coached the younger ones and I often went out in the hall with my little band of readers or spellers from grades 1–4 and that may be why I eventually became a teacher. It is what I experienced early on and knew I could do well.

We had adequate textbooks, but our library was limited, consisting of a four-shelf metal cabinet with well-worn books, most of which I read several times. Fortunately, the county sent a traveling library to the school each month. It was a large box and I devoured those books, too. I loved the large Oxford dictionary on the wall stand. For fun at recess, we looked up words or found places on the well-worn pull-down maps or hanging globe, and then talked and dreamed of traveling to those exotic lands we learned about in geography, my favorite subject. Venice always seemed the most exotic destination to me, and gondolas and water were often depicted in my Friday artwork. My husband and I went there in 1983, and while it was exotic, it was not quite as wonderful as I had imagined.

Conformity rather than creativity seemed to be the hallmark at our school. The half hour allotted to art on Friday afternoons found us making posters from pre-printed designs from teacher's magazines. Not a lot of creativity there! Although we memorized great poetry, we were only called upon to create our own once a year when the county superintendent published a booklet of student poems and stories. When the time came to compose that poetry, I sat totally uninspired with a blank piece of paper on my desk for the half hour devoted to the task. Thank goodness my creative muse wasn't totally stifled in childhood because Mom and my grandmothers were quick to provide art materials and encouragement.

We practiced the dreaded Palmer Method of penmanship fifteen minutes a day. Although my eight laboriously earned penmanship pins residing in an old jewelry box give me pleasure, I remember the anguish of earning them. Ball point pens and pens that held ink or cartridges weren't available until I went to high school, so penmanship class required us to dip our scratchy pens in ink and practice the forms. Cards of those perfect forms placed above the blackboard were a constant reminder to me of my inadequacy in that area.

Rural schoolteachers worked hard to instill strong moral values in students. In addition, the Young Citizens League (YCL) met once a month in

Waking to Mourning Doves

our schools. Lyrics to the song are, *"Young citizens are we, leagued in a host whose watchwords are, youth courage loyalty. We march and we sing, our voices ring, young citizens are we."* Sounds like a WW II Nazi propaganda song, but we looked forward to the diversion of the meetings, elected officers and learned parliamentary procedures.

The phrase "under God" did not exist in the Pledge of Allegiance to the flag in the 1940s. A congressman from Michigan introduced it in 1954 under the Eisenhower administration and it became law. Religion in the schools didn't cause the heated debates we hear now. Mrs. Swanson enrolled us in a program of memorizing Bible verses with our parents' blessing. A pencil printed with Bible verses, the prize for memorizing John 3:16, enticed us to earn the next level prize of a small religious booklet.

I can still recite the verse, *"For God so loved the world that he gave his only begotten so that whosoever liveth and believeth in him shall not perish but have everlasting life."* A New Testament, which none of us earned, was the final reward. Prayer before lunch didn't do us any permanent harm either.

> *October 31, 1950–Had Halloween party in school Dennis and I were voted witch and ghost-had my black cat in school-went to town tonight- Mary, Lois and I trick or treated.*

We celebrated holidays in a big way in country schools, often with weeks of preparation. Halloween came first in the school year, and we used up all the orange and black construction paper and paints making posters and art projects to hang on the bulletin boards and windows. Best of all, though, was creating the horror chamber in the forbidding old basement furnace room. Students from the upper grades created it and took the younger students through it trying to frighten them. We stuck our hands into bowls of peeled grape "eyeballs," touched bones, sipped witches brew, saw dead men hanging from a rope or someone with a knife inserted in the chest with catsup blood running down. Flour was dumped on us and all sorts of chains, clanging and eerie screams and moans came out of the dark corners. When I was five years old, I was taken to school as a guest on Halloween and saw a boy with a knife and catsup blood on his chest. It was just too frightening and I ran sobbing out of the cellar like a shot. He had to come out of his fake trance, clean up and prove to me he was OK. The next year I was aware of the tricks, so it was fun.

> *October 28, 1948–The school had a roller skating party and I skated with guess who all the time.*

Grade school romances were innocent and foolish, but they seemed intense at the time. By interacting with other schools, 4-H events and frequent roller skating parties at the Canton Roller Rink, we had a wide range of acquaintances and crushes. Skating with a special boy for ladies choice or couples skate was the height of romance for us. One of the radio stations in Sioux Falls encouraged teens and pre-teens to call in or send requests for song dedications. We made up couples' names to be read on the air, including our own. Last fall at an American Association of University Women (AAUW) luncheon, I told a lady I was from Beresford.

She had lived in Sioux Falls at the same time and said, "Oh, I know Beresford. Those silly girls were always sending in boyfriend requests." When I said it was probably me, we had a good laugh.

Parents in the early '50s were pretty liberal in letting us drive cars at an early age, and South Dakota had no age limitations or permits required. When I was in seventh grade, a boy from town kept cruising by Silver Lake School at noon and after school, and I was flattered to learn he was trying to impress me. It is fun to laugh about these crushes at class reunions. At our 50th, I had my photo taken between my first and last boyfriends, the grade school beau and my husband.

> *December 22, 1948–We had our program at school tonight-*
> *I got a scrapbook, pins and jewel box. We had candy and*
> *chances.*

The Christmas program involved at least two months of preparation and was the best part of the school year. Our teacher chose three or four plays and gave each child parts to memorize. Props and costumes had to be gathered or made and we practiced until it was perfect. We sang several Christmas carols, some with actions. We practiced the songs daily and in later years I provided the piano accompaniment. The younger students had recitations or poems to recite. It always felt really special if the teacher chose you to help her operate the stage curtains, though in retrospect I suppose she tried to be fair to everyone.

> *December 4, 1951–Started on parent's gifts in school – fun in*
> *hall teaching little kids.*

We made Christmas gifts for our parents and grandparents. The older boys cut out items from plywood using old-fashioned band saws. Carved trivets, phone book holders, ornaments, wall plaques, scissor holders or garden row markers were sanded to get the wood smooth as velvet. We carefully applied decals and varnish. I sewed fancy pincushions with lace edgings for Mom and my grandmothers, who used them their entire lives. We were always thrilled and relieved when our parents thought the gifts we made were the best ever.

Waking to Mourning Doves

We looked forward to the day in mid-December when the fathers came to install the stage and curtains. The stage covered the front fourth of the room. From then on we could practice the whole program and organize props for our plays, recitations, and songs. The date of the Christmas program was carefully selected so that it didn't compete with dates from surrounding schools, since families often went to other school programs to see relatives' or friends' children perform.

Finally, after a solid week of dress rehearsals, the big night arrived. We put on our best dress-up clothes and arrived at the school, which was illuminated with kerosene lamplight. The lamps gave off a beautiful glow from the road as we approached, sometimes in falling snow. Would we remember our lines and recitations? Could we find the props we were responsible for getting on stage? Would the audience like our plays? Who would buy our lunch basket at the basket social? All these thoughts raced through our minds as seven p.m. and performance time approached. Amidst loud giggles, bedlam backstage and nervous looks at the program order, we got through the program and basked in all the compliments and applause from the audience.

Students drew names for gifts, but occasionally I received a surprise gift from a boy who had a crush on me. I still have a Blue Waltz perfume bottle and a jeweled pen given to me by my first beau. We liked each other until about sixth grade when we both discovered greener pastures meeting kids who went to town school.

We sold chances for a door prize and also had a "fish pond" with small prizes. Three fish casts for twenty-five cents allowed a fish line to be dropped over the stage curtain into a pool that caught a gift on our line. Gum, candy and tiny notepads attached by a volunteer mom produced a clamor as we eagerly waited our turn.

Mothers and daughters decorated food boxes and baskets for the basket social fundraiser with crepe paper ruffles and flowers in vivid hues. Somehow, the boys always knew whose basket was whose and bid accordingly. As a first grader, I was thrilled when Dennis and Leon, egged on by their fathers in a bidding war for my basket, hiked the price up to $5, a huge sum in 1944. I knew they both had a crush on me and the fathers all thought it was great fun to watch the bidding. As I recall, Leon won the bid and we sat in a corner eating lunch barely talking to each other. Other people enjoyed looking at us, though. Lunch usually consisted of fried chicken, home made bread and cupcakes or pie.

Toward the end of the evening, a loud commotion would occur outside and Santa (a faintly disguised school board member) would burst through the door and hand out bags of candy. Other than family Christmas celebrations, this was

Caryl Crozier

the most eagerly anticipated holiday event and one could savor the excitement for a long while. Best of all, a two-week vacation stretched ahead.

February 13, 1952–Worked on my valentine box, had fun – wrote valentines and letters to pen pals.

Valentine's Day each of us decorated a box in which others put valentines. We exchanged with everyone in school and often made our own valentines. I labored for hours with scraps of fabric, construction paper and paper doilies decorating my box. Mom helped me make crepe-paper ruffles on her treadle sewing machine to edge the box. Sometimes, friends and I made valentines, but we usually chose a packet of punch-out or penny valentines at the Ben Franklin variety store. We painstakingly selected a variety from the cards laid out in sorted trays. A valentine for the teacher or parents and grandparents might cost five cents. If we got a five-cent valentine from a boy, we knew he really liked us. We opened our valentine boxes the last hour of school and blushed as we read the verses if a special person's name appeared. Red Kool-Aid and heart-shaped sugar cookies ended the party.

Like all the other kids including our parents before us, we carried lunch pails to school. Most were the rounded-top black ones with a decal or decoration on the outside of the half circle top. Mine was plain. Some kids had a square bucket with a picture of a cowboy or movie star on the top or used the silver half-gallon Karo syrup cans. Most kids' lunch sandwiches were made from homemade white bread with peanut butter and jelly, cheese or cold meat. Mine were cold luncheon meat and cheese, or salmon with dill pickles, or ground roast beef, spam or chicken with mayonnaise and pickles that Mom carefully wrapped in waxed paper. Cling wrap had not been invented yet. It is a miracle none of us got sick from perishable food sitting for hours at room temperature. Mom always tucked in cupcakes, candy, pickles and potato chips, fruit and a pint thermos of cold milk. Sometimes the thermos was filled with hot Campbell's vegetable beef or chicken noodle soup. In the winter we brought potatoes to roast on a narrow ledge inside the wood-burning furnace. They were charred black on the outside, but nothing tasted better than that rich, fluffy inside slathered with butter and salt. A very boring noon game was guessing what kind of orange we brought, Sunkist or whatever. The others never seemed to tire of this simple game and I felt peer pressure to participate.

February 7, 1952–Mom brought hot lunch today – scallop potatoes. Also that day I brought my ice skates and went to the pond.

The mothers tried a "hot lunch program" and brought soup or hot dishes for us once a week. It must have been too much for the busy farm wives' schedules, as it was a short-lived practice. According to my childhood diary, my mother brought escalloped potatoes, goulash and vegetable beef soup. In the spring and fall we ate outside. The boys raced to get the favorite places to sit, but we girls either basked in the sun or by the cellar door on the south side of the school, or sought the shade of a small grove north of the school. We ate garden tomatoes with salt and fresh peaches and pears in the fall under those trees.

March 29, 1950–Gail's birthday. She got lots. I went around the north way to go to town with Thompsons. They didn't go so I walked home alone that whole mile.

March 27, 1951–Really trying to do makeup work in school. Folks went to a dance and I stayed with Marion and we talked about our beaus.

Spending time overnight or playing after school at friends' houses cemented our close relationships. I felt very comfortable at all the families' homes and often walked home with them after school. I loved walking "the north way" in the spring when the snow had melted enough to make wading pools in the ditches. Sloshing around in our boots and splashing icy water on each other made spring real after the endless winter. Flocks of honking geese pierced the silence and assured us of balmy days to come. I still have bursts of happiness seeing the V's of migrating geese in the spring.

April 1949–We had several tests today and I played ball. Dennis rode me home on his bike. Helped sow oats.

Many days, the neighbor kids and I walked home from school, a mile and a half for me the south way. In the fall we filled our dinner buckets with plums from thickets along the roadsides. If we were especially daring, we stole a crisp red apple from Swanson's tree by the road. They are the best apples I've ever had — cold, tart, and forbidden. Sometimes we rode our bikes to school, but most often I got a ride home on the handlebars of one of the bigger boy's bikes. In nice weather, all of us took a short cut across the fields, a three-quarter mile walk, climbing fences and trudging over corn and stubble fields or following the fence lines. We were often quite full of burrs when arriving home. We didn't walk across the fields when it was wet and muddy. I preferred walking on the road.

Most rural school kids helped with farm chores after school, milking cows, tending livestock and chickens or doing fieldwork. Mom liked to do animal chores and I hated them, so we worked out a deal where I made supper, helped clean house, pulled weeds or mowed the lawn. I liked driving the tractor and helping with fieldwork and learned early since I didn't have siblings.

As an only child, I envied classmates with siblings who could help with the farm chores. One time I told my friends that my mom was getting a tummy on her and I thought she might have a baby in there. We furtively looked at pictures of babies in a womb in Mom's medical book and tried to figure out the mysteries of life. The older boys at school taught us the F word and some misguided sex education, but living on a farm, we knew the facts of life early on. I learned a little song to the tune of *My Bonnie Lies Over the Ocean* soon after starting country school. "*My father lies over my mother, and that's how they got little me.*" So much for sex education!

While Mom and a neighbor dished up taverns, the Beresford name for sloppy joe hamburger meat, at a school program, Francis said, "I hear you're in the family way."

Mom almost dropped the plate of buns, gave me a scalding look, then laughed and said, "I think someone's been telling stories." I guess my parents thought one child was enough.

> *April 19, 1949–I studied spelling and we practiced on the harmonicas. We had our play tonight – Pioneers of 49. I helped Gail paint Indians and then I washed it off the kids.*

Rural schools competed against each other by putting on plays and skits at the Legion Hall in Beresford. Mrs. Thompson taught us all to play harmonicas and we dressed as cowboys and Indians and enacted a scene around a campfire. I don't remember the tune or plot now, but I still play *Country Gardens* and *Home Sweet Home* on my harmonica. Another year, Mrs. Dann developed a musical play based on *Shine On, Harvest Moon.* Paul and Marion sat in a swing while we serenaded them. I thanked my lucky stars not to be in that spotlight.

> *March 26, 1952–We didn't practice hardly at all and didn't know parts for the program.*
>
> *It was a flop. Teacher was late. We had fun behind the curtain.*
>
> *May 9, 1952–Mother's Day Program at school. Went over good. Ragnar came out tonight and we played canasta.*

My memories of spring and Mother's Day programs are vague, perhaps because they were ill-rehearsed flops. Since Mother's Day, final exams, yard cleanup and mid-May release from school occurred one after the other, these programs were quickly cobbled together. We invited mothers to come for cookies and coffee or Kool-Aid on a school day afternoon. We sang a few songs, read some mushy poems about Mother, gave them a homemade card and bouquets of wildflowers picked from the ditches. More often, we made big, garish, crepe-paper flowers. The moms brought any little ones not in school, so bedlam was almost guaranteed. The toddlers always spilled sticky Kool-Aid on the wood floor.

In the seventh and eighth grades, we took rigorous end-of-year exams in order to pass on to the next grade. The fear of flunking a grade induced us to pore over a few study guides supplied by the county. When we passed the eighth grade, a county ceremony was held in Canton, the county seat. I felt glamorous in a mint green organdy dress with huge pockets and a taffeta under-slip purchased for the occasion. As we clustered for a group photo, we knew our lives were changing.

> *May 18, 1951–Last day of school, Yippee! Had wiener roast and cleaned up the school house.*

A few days before the school year ended, we brought rakes and baskets to school to spruce up the grounds. The promise of a big bonfire and a wiener and marshmallow roast kept us busy during recess raking every inch of the school property. We tossed all the fallen branches and debris in the ditch along with end-of-the-year school papers. Each of us cut a willow stick from the thick growth in the wet ditches across the road and had the older boys whittle a sharp point on it for roasting wieners. After we cleaned out our desks on the last day of school, we exploded out of the building to set up our picnic and soon devoured as many hotdogs smothered in mustard, catsup and pickle relish as we could eat. My dad reminisced about this tradition and, like us, reveled in the sweet knowledge that the long slow summer stretched out before us. Truth was, I found out later, parents welcomed our homecoming more than we did because they truly wanted to spend time with us and have some extra help during the growing season.

> *May 20, 1951–Had our school picnic at Stuessi's grove and us girls had a game of ball. Lois, Mary & I won. Ate lots of ice cream.*

At the end of the school year, we had a school district picnic at Stuessi's grove, a deserted homestead a mile from school, with big trees and open pasture, woods, rock piles and a deserted house to explore. The giant trees are still there, and I never fail to drive by when we travel back to Beresford.

Boards were placed across sawhorses under the trees. Our moms spread vintage linens under massive bowls of hot dishes, fried chicken, escalloped potatoes, salads, pickles and pies. We always had a huge, insulated canvas bag with metal ice cream containers inside. We could have as many ice cream cones as we wanted throughout the day.

A fiercely competitive kitten ball game was played in the cow pasture and was the afternoon's featured entertainment. Dads, moms, grandparents and kids could all be on the teams. We had to be careful to avoid sitting or stepping on the cow pies. Some of us girls usually wandered off to explore the woods until worried mothers came to find us. At dusk, we said goodbye to friends, gobbled a last ice cream cone and made promises to see each other during summer vacation. We did, and the summers were never long or slow enough.

CHAPTER **22**
Beresford Watchdogs, '50s Era

September 2, 1952–First day of high school. Had 4 short classes and schedules this morn- tests at 1- am in one class of all boys- nice seating arrangement! Fun at noon.

Dazed confusion describes my first day of starting any school. Adjusting to new schedules, classmates and surroundings felt traumatic. Coming from a one-room country school of twelve students to a high school with four grades and two hundred students was no exception. The country kids came from a lot of one-room schools, while the big-school town kids had the advantage of recognizing already-formed friendships. Although I knew many classmates, the sheer volume of so many students in one large assembly hall was terrifying at first. Seated in alphabetical rows of about twenty to a row, I always ended up third or fourth from the front. On the first day of high school, we "freshies" gathered on the edges and halls near the assembly room and waited as the seniors, juniors, sophomores and finally our names were called. All the upper classmen stared at the new crop of freshmen as we meekly walked to our desks and tried to remain invisible. As freshmen, we felt self-conscious and the scum of the earth. I felt especially visible with the new braces on my teeth, a rare dental device in the 1950s. I entered high school rather shy, but knew I was smart enough to compete with the others. I also had some good friends.

Many country kids drove to school since bus service didn't begin until the 1960s in Beresford. I liked sharing a ride with long-time friend Lois all four years. I caught a ride with Lois and her brother the first two years and drove my little green 1949 Ford with the flashy white-sidewall tires the last two years. A couple of guys regularly hotwired my car and moved it around town and parked it in new locations to tease me, but usually helped me find it after school. I enjoyed the attention.

A typical school day began at nine a.m. with all the students seated in the large assembly hall. Teachers gave announcements and at 9:10 we shuffled to rooms throughout the two-story building for classes. When not in classes or activities, we returned to the assembly hall to complete our homework or lesson preparations. Only rarely did any of us take schoolwork home. We had more time for fun and relaxing than my grandchildren have with the ridiculously heavy homework loads today. Most of us who lived on farms helped with chores or fieldwork after school. Maybe that is why we had a light homework load.

We did not have a hot lunch program at school, so the country kids brought bag lunches and ate them together in the gym, or sat on the hall steps or in our cars. Mom made my school lunches if I didn't have time and I grabbed that brown paper bag full of nutritious sandwiches and fruit as I rushed out to meet the day. I ate the same kind of sandwiches day after day, year after year, the favorite being salmon or ground meat with dill pickles. Chunky homemade cookies and the sandwich of the day were carefully wrapped in waxed paper and tucked into the bottom of the bag. Grapes, apples and oranges or peaches and tomatoes in season provided variety and crunch. Now I wonder why raw vegetables seldom appeared then. Maybe it's because Mom always served overcooked vegetables at dinnertime.

Twelve years of sandwiches for lunch might seem boring, but it may have been better nutritionally than the junk food, French fries and sweets served in some school cafeterias today. We always had fruit, vegetables and protein along with the carbs and Cokes. We had a Coke machine at school, but no milk dispenser. We dumped a pack of Planters peanuts in the Coke bottle. How strange is that, but it tasted sweet and salty.

Kids who lived in town walked home for an hour lunch break, while my friends and I cruised the streets through town, either walking or riding in cars. After football or basketball games we ordered Cherry Cokes and French fries with ketchup at Mac's Cafe or Edna's. On the edge of town, Edna's was considered a wild and tacky place with a jukebox and a dirty, worn wooden floor where we could dance or watch the boys scuffle. Sock hops or other theme dances were often held after the games in the school gym or the Legion Hall.

November 19, 1952–GAA initiation-rolled peanuts and eggs with our noses across the gym floor.

Afternoon classes ended by four p.m., and we gathered back in the assembly hall for dismissal. In order to avoid chaos, the teachers had us exit row by row. The boys were more likely to have after-school sports activities than the girls, as we weren't allowed to have competitive sports. Only in the Girls Athletic Association (GAA) did we play sporadic intramural basketball or volleyball in addition to weekly physical education classes. My initiation rite into GAA was a race pushing a peanut across the gym floor with my nose, while a gaggle of boys watched. I wonder who thought up that cockeyed, demeaning idea! GAA basketball games were a nightmare of exhaustion and sweat for me, even though girls could only play half of the basketball court. We were not in condition like the boys were.

Waking to Mourning Doves

Before the 1970s, only boys had the opportunity for high school athletic competition. Women were considered too delicate to participate in any of the more rugged sports. I don't know if men who ruled thought our uterus would fall out or what! Then too, girls didn't want to appear sweaty and disheveled racing across a basketball court or soccer field. I always got red-faced and sweaty during active sports so it is just as well that side of me wasn't exposed very much. Girls didn't even have competitive golf or tennis, good lifelong sports for women. The state of Iowa allowed half-court girls' competitive basketball. The other 47 states chastised them. I think keeping women out of sports was a male gender domination ploy, as was the long battle for women's equal rights still going on today. Sports is one of the last all-male bastions to fall. Girls' sports news is rarely on the front page of a newspaper, but at least there are competitive sports for girls now.

In the 1950s, girls could be high school twirlers or cheerleaders, and could grow up to be teachers, secretaries, or nurses. Pretty limited. We were the last of that era and the vanguard for what our daughters and granddaughters could become.

In small schools like Beresford's, two hundred high school enrollment, students had the opportunity to dabble in a variety of activities and didn't have to be super good at any of them. My grandchildren have to train hard starting at a young age to be on a varsity team in their large suburban schools.

Girls had an unlimited number of school activities in which to participate other than sports. Some were volunteer and some were extracurricular. A favorite teacher, Minna Smith, was in charge of the school library at the back of the assembly hall, so I volunteered to be one of the librarians to check out books to other students and help maintain a file system. Browsing the shelves for books to read was great, as I had already exhausted the supply at Silver Lake School and the town library. Since we had very little homework, I spent many quiet evenings reading at home. An added benefit of library duty was that the guys were more interested in socializing and flirting with the female librarians when they loitered at the checkout window. That was fine with me.

Most girls joined Future Homemakers of America (FHA), which met monthly in the evenings. We held style shows, planned social activities and just "hung out." I enjoyed attending a state convention in Huron, South Dakota in my junior year. It was a big deal staying in a nice hotel and meeting girls from all over the state. Early on, we were programmed to be housewives.

In 1915, the Beresford Community built a state-of-the-art high school building for its rapidly expanding population. My parents, aunts and uncles and I all benefited from this investment in the future. Three generations of my extended family attended until it was demolished in the 1980s when a new school was built. Even the flowering crab trees that sheltered us as we burst out of school in mid-May fell to the bulldozers. I felt sad to see the school that held so many happy memories disintegrate into a pile of dusty bricks.

The high school my parents and I attended was a two-story building with a locker room and agriculture and vocational education room (industrial arts & shop) in the basement. The first-floor classrooms and the superintendent's office surrounded the two-story gym. Bleachers were set up in the wide halls in front of the classrooms for basketball games. The second floor above the gym housed the assembly hall, with over two hundred desks. The chemistry and physics labs, typing rooms, Home Economics department and restrooms completed the second-floor plan. A small teachers' lounge and storage rooms were in the front of the building up a few stairs on either side of the restrooms. My friends and I often met on those steps to eat our noon lunches, giggle and gossip.

My granddaughters say they want to know what the kids and activities were like in the '50s, so I will try to relate how I felt as a teenager. Since my diary entries focused primarily on my friends and activities, I will focus on them first. I don't think my life then was much different from theirs except for text messaging, Facebook and Twitter. Social media came way after my youth was spent. I cannot fathom what technology my future descendants will have, but I will tell you that we did quite well face to face. In fact, in my opinion, less information is better when dealing with peer group issues.

My biggest fear when starting high school was what kids would think of the braces on my teeth. Not to worry. I soon learned the advantages.

"I wonder what it feels like to kiss a girl who has braces on her teeth," were the thoughts of a few boys the fall of 1952 when I started high school.

Little did I know that my self-conscious smile provoked that kind of interest! Being only one of two girls in the whole school who had braces, I was prepared to be a social outcast. A mouthful of steel and rubber bands looked hideous to me. Much later, I learned that guys wanted to kiss me as an "experiment." What did it matter anyway, because kisses in those days were always close mouthed. I didn't even know what French kissing was then!

> *March 11, 1952–To Sioux Falls, got upper braces on my teeth- hurts- got new shoes and a slip.*

If Mom and Dad hadn't ponied up the $800, a lot of money in those days, for me to have braces, I probably would have spent my life as a shy, withdrawn person. By eighth grade, I always covered my mouth with my hand to hide my crooked teeth when speaking or laughing. My eyeteeth resembled fangs

Waking to Mourning Doves

and another tooth came in behind my lower teeth. Dr. Iverson took one look at my grotesquely aligned teeth and told my parents it would impact my life negatively if not corrected.

So, Dr. Iverson yanked out four molars, and the process of taking mud imprints and wrapping steel bands and wires around each tooth began. I gagged and choked when the orthodontist, Dr. Mehrens, jammed the imprint tray in my mouth. I wondered if all the discomfort would be worth it. He lined white, chalky imprints of patients' teeth on a little shelf, and he told me mine was one of the worst he had ever seen. Great! I didn't need that kind of distinction.

Every three weeks for two years, my parents drove me thirty-five miles to the Sioux Falls orthodontist to tighten the wires on my teeth. Eventually, it worked. After tightening the wire on my braces, it hurt to eat anything but soft food for a few days. Food stuck in my teeth and eating a caramel apple became impossible. Frequent brushing helped. I even carried a toothbrush to school.

> *January 27, 1954–made bread in Home Ec. Got braces off my teeth today-feels wonderful-4-H here tonight- Marcene visited.*

In 1954 the braces came off. My two front teeth appeared enormous and my toothy smile more noticeable than my braces. Some kids even said I looked better with the braces on. Oh well. One nice person said in my yearbook, "Caryl, with that dazzling smile you will go far." My daughters have teeth similar to mine and wore braces too. It was more common in the '70s. The two granddaughters had relatively straight teeth but wore braces to achieve perfection.

> *November 22, 1952–To dentist and running all over Sioux Falls shopping and got earrings, a slip and my first high heel shoes-dancing tonight with Johnsons for Verlyn's birthday.*

Shopping with Mom after dentist visits found us dashing from store to store: Fantles, Shrivers, and Baker's shoe store. I loved it and usually got a new outfit. Buying my first pair of clunky, black-suede high heels was a big deal. What on earth would my teenage granddaughters do with a full slip, though? I had a dozen or so in all colors, as it was a common birthday or Christmas gift. My cedar chest cradles a red full slip from the '50s that I can't bear to toss, and those first high heels are still in the original box.

Dad, Mom and I always bought Maid-Rite sandwiches before we drove home from the dentist. Maid-Rite was, and remains, a fast-food franchise specializing in sloppy joes, or "taverns" as they were known in Beresford. Just the word "Maid-Rite" still makes my mouth salivate. My taste buds still long for that earthy, distinctive taste that even Beresford's unique taverns can't match. If you have ever tasted a Maid-Rite, you know what I am talking about.

Equally as embarrassing as my braces, though not a major problem for me, teenage zits affected our self-image. My "monthly zit" always seemed to appear on the end of my nose or chin. Hot packs, frequent cleansing and Noxzema didn't reduce them any faster, but made me feel pro-active. Fortunately, my dry skin didn't harbor pockets of acne. Teens are persnickety and obsessed about physical appearances and I was no exception. I was somewhat repulsed by guys that had acne, especially those that didn't even seem to notice they had a problem. Our daughters battled zits and plastered on countless jars of Noxzema and skin potions. Granddaughters Rachel and Claire have blemish-free porcelain complexions. Or maybe they are more adept at applying make-up.

Church and Sunday school, for which I played piano or organ, and relative gatherings comprised my Sunday diary entries. Rarely did the three lines say more than, "Had fun in town," or " Karen and I had a good talk." The "secrets" are written in shorthand and my shorthand technique was so poor that I can't decipher it now. Oh well, some things are best left to the imagination of future readers!

Reflecting upon and writing about my high school years brings back moments that now seem like minor traumas and silliness. If descendants read my diary 100 years from now, they may think Grandma was a total "airhead," or maybe just a normal self-centered teenager on the road to independence with a few bumps and mistakes to still come my way. The diary entries are brief and usually reveal which boy I talked to or looked my way. Some entries document who I was hanging out with or our music and 4-H activities. Some entries describe our "cruisin' Saturday nights." Most entries capture snippets of time shared with my girlfriends

I had great girlfriends and I still consider them among my best friends. For me, there is something about high school friends that is very special. With them, I went through the angst of growing up and finding my way in the world. They supported me in the good and bad times, and even though I remember the stupid things I did, they selectively remember the good and fun times as being more important. These early friendships have sustained me and remain a support system through the years as we returned to Beresford often to visit parents and attend class reunions. We only had sixteen girls in a class of fifty-one. Lois, Marie, Darlene, Barb, LaVonne and Karen are seen most often, but reconnecting with Alice, Mary, Helen and Marcene G. at reunions

Waking to Mourning Doves

has been good too. Janet and Marcene K. attended a different school, but we had 4-H and dating ties and are still close. I could always rely on one of these friends to lend an ear or to accompany me when attending school events, sports activities, dances, movies, plays, shop, or just "cruise the streets" on a Saturday night in Beresford.

> *February 13, 1956–Solo practice- had Barb, Darlene, Rosamund, Joyce, Bonnie, Leona and Lois here for a slumber party-awake till 4:30 AM-slept on three mattresses-had a taffy pull, played cards, listened to Barb's stories, danced, made phone calls and made supper.*

Inviting my friends home for slumber parties was a blast. We put my mattress on the floor and four girls crowded together to sleep on it. Mom fixed a nice dinner for us and then we danced, played piano and sang, gave each other facials, hairdos and painted our fingernails and toenails. Sometimes we made popcorn and popcorn balls, fudge, divinity, or pulled taffy. Yes, we gossiped and giggled and talked about boys, too. We often stayed overnight with friends, but the larger slumber parties were the most fun. Boys sometimes knew locations of our slumber parties and sneaked through the yards by the houses and pounded on our bedroom windows, much to our screaming delight. Mom never let us invite them in, but we wanted to.

> *June 2, 1953— Karen here –we fooled around and then took the bus to Sioux Falls and saw "The House of Wax" in three dimension and "Salome" Fun!! Stayed with her tonight. Parents were upset.*

Karen, my good friend in eighth and ninth grades, moved to Sioux Falls in tenth grade. In ninth grade, we decided to take the Greyhound bus to Sioux Falls to see the movie *House of Wax*. We wore 3D glasses during that frightening movie followed by shopping, lunch, and another movie having no concern whatsoever that our parents didn't know where we were. We caught the bus home and arrived back in Beresford at 10 p.m., surprised at the fuss and concern our parents had endured. Maybe that is typical teen behavior.

I exhibited typical teenage thoughts: " Why would it matter what our parents' concerns are, as I am in my own little world trying to achieve independence and satisfy my own interests?"

As a mother and grandmother, that cycle has been repeated, but with a great deal more understanding on my part. I should have been grounded or punished in some way, but my parents were very lax in their discipline. All they expected was for me to be home by ten p.m. on school nights and eleven on weekends. I always told them where I was going and with whom. A small town was safe then, and everyone watched out for us. Usually someone who knew us observed everything. There were not many secrets.

February 19, 1953–Bad blizzard-fun fourth period- no religious ed-Howard, Jim and Irving came out tonight in the blizzard and Dad gave them heck cuz he thought I was going with them.

Boyfriends were a good part of my life, too. Having boys to play with at a young age raises the comfort level around the opposite sex. For me, it became an advantage in courtship as well as work situations. My granddaughter Claire had a similar experience. Claire's male friends were in day care and later in sports activities, while mine were an integral part of my daily life in South Dakota. Neighborhood boys and male cousins taught me the rough-and-tumble activities of boys. By the age of four, I intuitively knew how to make boys like me, how to act interested in them and their activities and even flirt a little if necessary. Maybe telling a couple boys I'd stick them in the oven and bake them wasn't a good approach, but who knows, maybe assertiveness had some appeal.

Romantic movies with Doris Day and Rock Hudson and musicals or dancing movies with Gene Kelly, Jane Powell, Cyd Charisse, Debbie Reynolds and Donald O'Conner thrilled the girls while the guys said they were too mushy. Encouraging the good guys in Westerns, munching popcorn, and surveying who was with whom in the audience spiced up our Saturday nights. Sometimes we drove to the nearby towns of Centerville, Canton or Alcester to see what was happening, but nearly every weekend found us cruising Beresford's Main Street on Saturday nights with girlfriends or on a date. We loved to "crack U's" endlessly, that is U-turns at both ends of Main Street. Sometimes, especially later in the evening, the only cars on the three-block loop would be high-schoolers in their decked out cars. We knew who was out in the country making out by who was missing in the loop. We could tell entire stories two lines at a time as our cars met and re-met on the loop. Seems to me like a bunch more fun than Twitter.

Teenage slang and fads spread like wildfire. A few choice phrases:
"Have a bird."
"Shit a fish."
"Spit tacks or shingle nails."
"Oh fart."
Not very ladylike, but we liked the naughtiness and it irritated our parents. My dad was profusely profane, but he didn't like to hear me swear.

September 8, 1952–That Antrim character-he's always turning around and asking me, "Do you love me?" He does that to all the girls.

Having a boyfriend in tow was never a problem. In high school, I dated a dozen or more guys, my attraction to them lasting for only a few months, and then it was time to move on to someone new. Unfortunately, I had no skill at extracting myself from a relationship and several times hard feelings were the result of my insensitivity, some existing to this day, in my estimation at least. For me, getting out of a relationship seemed much more difficult than getting into it. Reading my teenage diary fifty-five years later, I feel sad confronting my romantic callousness.

A few boyfriends helped me develop my criteria for evaluating men. My husband has many of the qualities I admired in early boyfriends: a sharp sense of humor, an eye for adventure, basic intelligence, honesty, athleticism, good communication skills and similar goals, values and upbringing.

Some high school romances were destined to last; mine weren't. Several of my friends married high school sweethearts and are still together after 50 years. I wasn't mature enough to know what I wanted at that age in a career or a life partner. I just knew I didn't want to be married and have a baby right away. Cuddling my friends' sweet little newborns didn't make me yearn for one of my own – yet.

Fitting in socially, including with the clothes we wore, was critical in the Fifties. We read *Seventeen* magazines as our fashion guide and spent hours shopping in Sioux Falls. I sewed most of my own skirts and dresses, but Mom helped me shop for nice sweaters and special dresses. Slacks or jeans were rarely worn, but I still have my high school jeans that I also wore on my honeymoon. Unfortunately, they no longer fit! There were some distinctive clothing fads of the '50s, like three-yard gathered or pleated skirts with three or four stiffly starched crinoline half slips underneath. We could barely walk through the aisles of desks at school. We wore poodle skirts, a neck scarf to match every outfit, saddle shoes and white bucks with rolled down anklets and rolled up jeans. Sometimes we fastened a dog collar on our socks. We could wear jeans only on Fridays, usually with a white blouse with rolled up sleeves and a neck scarf. Other days we wore skirts, sweaters and dresses. Classmate Alice wore a blue felt skirt that had a poodle appliqué that was the envy of all of us fashion-conscious girls.

February 29, 1952–Leap Year- Millie cut my hair and gave me a Lilt home permanent.

Having long, curly hair was "in" during the 1950s and with my straight hair, a Toni or Lilt home permanent gave it body. Tangled-frizzy-tight curls are a more accurate description and I detested the look after a home perm. Going to the beauty shop seemed a bit extravagant to my parents. Mom cut my hair and gave me home perms. Most nights I wound my hair in spit curls fastened with bobby pins or put prickly brush rollers in my hair. Getting comfortable sleeping on irritating brush rollers was impossible, but bearing the discomfort necessary in my mind.

Boys' fashions were as carefully scrutinized as the girls'. Crew cuts and greasy, slicked-back hair had to be carefully maintained. Plaid shirts, khakis, jeans, letter sweaters and jackets, loafers and t-shirts were popular. Out of school, some guys rolled a cigarette pack up in the sleeve of a t-shirt like James Dean. Boys smoked more than the girls in high school. I refrained. I didn't want to be considered wild and besides, it made bad breath. I detested kissing a guy that tasted like stale cigarettes. A few guys had motorcycles, leather jackets, cowboy boots or side-buckle engineer boots. Cars were the distinguishing possessions and status symbols for boys. Their cars ran the gamut from family clunkers and castoffs to two-tone exaggerated "fin" fenders on newer Plymouth, Ford and Chevrolet models. Fur dice, air fresheners, girls' garters, beads or other "trophies" hung from rear view mirrors. Cars didn't have center consoles and guys always wanted their dates to sit very close to them while driving. I thought that looked tacky, so I rarely scrunched up next to a boy.

May 1, 1953–Twirling tryouts, but I didn't make it. Darn!
Alice, Karen, Mary, Diana, Janet and Gwen did.

Girls tried out to be baton twirlers or cheerleaders at the end of our freshman year. I tried out for the twirling team, but fortunately, was not selected. To try out, the freshman girls strutted around the gym watched by the teachers who selected the winners. I found it highly embarrassing to march lifting my legs as high as I could and still try to look cute and not sweaty. The whole student body watched and the boys whistled and yelled catcalls. Was this sexual harassment? Maybe it would not be allowed in schools today.

May 20, 1955–Cheerleading tryouts- Bonnie, Leona, Dorene
and I made it- Good-Get to go to state 4-H Club Week!! Did
chores and rode Ginger tonight. Paul clipped her hooves.

I tried out and was selected for cheerleading all three remaining years. More than anything, that built my confidence and popularity, plus it was a good strength-building exercise. For the sophomore year we were junior cheerleaders for the football and basketball B teams. Our outfits ranged from corduroy slacks or full skirted dresses in purple and gold to hot wool outfits handed down through the years. They never fit quite right because they had been made for someone else. I kept my purple wool outfit and many years later had a rag rug made from it.

I enjoyed my sophomore and senior years of cheerleading because I was with close friends. During my sophomore year, Lavonne and Janice made cheerleading practices fun because our skill levels and interests were similar. In my senior year, LaVonne, Dorene and sweet giggly Leona and I had fun. As a junior, I was with three seniors and felt a bit out–of-place. We had tryouts each year, and the other three girls wanted a friend that they tried out with to win, but I got the most votes, so we had to work together as a team. They were all a little snooty, but it was good for me to learn to function outside my comfort level.

We led cheers at all the football and basketball games and caught rides with our parents, boyfriends or the school superintendent, Mr. Shennum, to games in other towns. The day of the games we led half- hour cheering sessions/pep rallies in the assembly hall. We took turns planning the yells we'd do. Teachers gave pep talks and students performed skits for added entertainment. I felt panicky the first few times that I did the planning, but it eventually became routine. As a basically shy person, it took some time to develop confidence. Now, people can't believe I considered myself introverted.

During the summer, cheerleaders met weekly at the Beresford City Park to practice actions and new yells and learn to synchronize with one another. Our skills at cartwheels, flips and somersaults were dismal, so our actions of arm and leg movements and high jumps had to suffice. We would never make it on the cheerleading squads in the 21st century.

Leading cheers for three years kept me physically fit with strong legs and thighs. Cheerleaders are typically thought of as airheads and are cute and flirty. Maybe that applied to me except for the airhead part, as being smart and getting good grades seemed more important. A couple of guys at Beresford's 125th town reunion told Sherm that I was a "fox" and not stuck up and spoiled like an only child. I think they were just trying to be nice!

Some hot summer evenings cheerleading practice and being with friends or an occasional date relieved the monotony of farm chores. Reading, piano, organ and accordion practice made the days go faster, too.

May 24, 1954–First day of teaching Bible school helping Mrs. Wheatley-fun-Town this afternoon with Nan- had cheerleading practice tonight- what a sweaty workout!

All four summers, teaching Vacation Bible School for a week at the

Congregational Church helped me form career ideas. Working with kids was exhilarating, and I knew I was a good teacher. Being in the cool church basement offered a relief from summer heat, as very few families had air conditioning at home. Sometimes I sewed or read in our basement in spite of the poor lighting and spider webs that hit me in the face as I walked down the stairs.

As a freshman, I wanted to participate in band, so I learned to play the tenor saxophone, primarily to please my dad, who liked the saxophone. Band members were required to play in the pep band at the games, and since I was a cheerleader I couldn't do both. Quitting band was difficult, but the choice became easier because of the instrument I chose. The tenor saxophone was cumbersome and too heavy for me to carry, much less play. Also, the band was kind of a ragtag group with a poor director. After we graduated in 1956, a new band director quickly provided the skill to make it the popular, first-class band it is today. Fortunately, our daughters and granddaughters have been members of remarkable school bands.

November 21, 1952–Had first accordion orchestra practice tonight at Darlene's- played lots of songs.

The fly-by-night accordion salesmen and their short-term teachers left dozens of local teenagers possessing accordions they rarely played. A few of us formed an accordion band, practiced together weekly and for a couple years, played for community events. We disbanded due to lack of interest, talent and bookings. Until college, I continued to play my accordion solo whenever people requested a program for bridal showers or club meetings. I also played in a few 4-H talent competitions. My costumed rendition of *Lady of Spain* got quite a few repeat requests.

Most of us were in both chorus and girls glee club during one of our free periods. We had seven-hour-long sessions or periods in a day at school; four were classes, usually one elective activity and one study hall and one hour for lunch. Harmonizing in chorus and glee club rehearsals every day gave us a break from classes. Concerts and trips to music competitions with other schools let us show off our skills and meet students from other schools. I accompanied soloists on piano and sang in a sextet as a second soprano. I scored high on music interest in college aptitude tests, but it seemed smarter to make it an avocation rather than a career. I lacked sufficient talent.

Homecoming Day activities were fun all four years. We spent many hours building floats, usually on the backs of pick-up trucks, flatbed trailers or hayracks. We stuffed endless boxes of napkins into chicken wire for a fluffy effect. I rode the freshman sponsored float, which featured an ugly black hat

Waking to Mourning Doves

with the slogan "Top Em." The other years, the cheerleaders walked or rode on the back of a convertible. In the 4th of July parades, we twirled huge flags marching behind the band. As usual, I hated being hot, sweaty and red-faced. July in South Dakota is often hot and humid, so I didn't look forward to the parades.

The night before the Homecoming football game, we built a huge bonfire on the empty lot behind the school, around which we performed yells and formed a snake dance that wound from the school grounds to Main Street. We ran screaming pep slogans like, "Beat 'em boys, beat 'em." Cheerleaders led and set the pace, but people at the ends were whipped around and sometimes fell and got hurt. Looking back, this resembles a pagan ritual. I later heard that my friend's dad, the school custodian, guarded the pile for the bonfire all night before the event. He didn't want a rival school lighting the fire.

> *September 19, 1953–Mom and I went to Sioux Falls and got my first formal-rose salmon strapless- also a blouse- saw Karen all afternoon- hoed tomatoes tonight.*

For Prom, Homecoming, Christmas and Valentine dances, most people had dates or if not, they didn't go or stay for the whole evening. Getting formals or new dresses for these dances was a highlight. I designed and sewed several of my dresses, but the most memorable formal was my salmon-colored net concoction from the ninth grade. I felt so glamorous in my first strapless formal, which barely stayed up. Clunky black suede high heels were a trial to walk in, much less dance in. We wore rhinestone necklaces, bracelets and clip earrings and applied a hint of makeup beyond the regular bright red lipstick. A floor-length lavender strapless formal was my sewing masterpiece for senior prom. By combining several commercial patterns I labored for days gathering yards and yards of scratchy lavender net, making row upon row of ruffles to adorn the bodice and long skirt of my frothy creation. Years later, granddaughters Rachel and Claire wore it in vintage fashion shows.

Junior and senior proms weren't quite as big a deal or as elaborate as today's teenagers' experience. My junior class decorated the banquet hall (Catholic church basement) with a Western theme. Crepe paper, Western artifacts and table decorations kept us busy creating scenarios many days after school. As sophomores, a few of us girls and guys were selected as waiters and waitresses for the banquet. For the pirate theme, we wore black toreador pants with long crimson sashes and white blouses.

For junior and senior proms, I had dates for the banquet and dance. Unfortunately, I was dating guys that were terrible dancers, so I don't have fond memories of the proms. In my junior year I double-dated with a girlfriend

Caryl Crozier

whose boyfriend asked another girl, so she was sad all evening and a "wet blanket" to be around. As a senior, three friends and I dated guys, whom they later married, and we all attended the dance together, but not the banquet. Guys that weren't in school couldn't attend the dinners. I remember being bored most of the evening and wishing I was somewhere else.

High school dances held at the Legion Hall or school gym could be very awkward. Most of the time we went without a date and the boys lined up on one side and the girls gathered in clumps on the other. None of us could dance very well and it was embarrassing if you were on the floor dancing and trying not to step on each other. But if you were a wallflower waiting for someone to ask for a dance, to sit alone was the ultimate horror. Then you made a quick trip to the rest room, checked out your coat pockets or joined another wallflower.

November 24, 1952–Dad was teaching me to dance-played volleyball in school. Joyce and I worked on samplers.

My parents were excellent dancers and Dad taught me the rudimentary steps. Unfortunately, the adolescent boys did more of a shuffle dance, which makes your legs tired and feel like rubber, so I never enjoyed dancing much until college and the jitterbug, twist and other dances became popular.

I participated in the all-school as well as junior and senior class plays. As a sophomore, I only had a small part in the play *Crazy, but Cute*, but rehearsals were fun and I felt encouraged to try again the next year. I was too shy to go out for debate and declamation, but the plays gave me confidence. It is strange I felt that reluctant after all the readings and music I provided at church and community events. Maybe it was competing and the need to think on my feet that held me back.

April 9, 1956–Got lead of Hannah in senior class play- hardest part- glad though- City government day- I was treasurer- tours, trials etc. 4-H tonight – gave demonstration at Renie's.

I have no memories of my junior class play other than the unruly wild rehearsals and our director, Mr. Dalen, who had no control over us whatsoever. Gathering vintage clothing and props for *The Hoosier Schoolmaster* was a senior year highlight. Minna Smith directed the senior play and ran it like a tight ship. She had enough confidence in me to give me the leading female role of Hannah, the bound (servant) girl, in the play. Memorizing a long part was much easier at age seventeen than memorizing or even remembering anything at age seventy.

Naturally, I took a lot of photos, which have kept the memories alive.

Waking to Mourning Doves

Nan was so proud of my leading role that she came and saw the play twice. She was the one person who encouraged my small-time public speaking, and I will always be grateful for her gentle prodding. Nerves about remembering my lines still appear in my dreams along with not knowing my class schedule or college building locations. Longtime fears never seem to dissipate.

November 21, 1952–Had 6 weeks tests. Got 100 in algebra.

Much to my surprise, high school general science and algebra became huge challenges to me scholastically. First of all, they placed me in a class of all boys in algebra. Teachers had mistaken my name for the boy's name Carl. As if that wasn't intimidating enough, the whole concept of algebra resembled gibberish to me, and I felt enough of a sense of panic to ask Minna Smith, my teacher, for help. I stayed after school and had her patient one-on-one help for several weeks, making her my favorite teacher of all time. My brain isn't math oriented, but she explained the concepts well enough for me to pass algebra and then geometry with surprising A grades. Maybe her help inspired me to tutor students later in life when I was a high school teacher in Cassville, Wisconsin. My dad quit high school when he couldn't pass advanced geometry and calculus, so I guess my fear was genetic. Our daughters are not math geniuses either, although they both mastered statistics and calculus. Mrs. Smith was a favorite teacher for many students and I always knew I could go to her for solid advice on any issue.

I earned my lowest grade ever in ninth grade general science. That shock shattered my confidence enough to avoid taking chemistry and physics in high school, a poor decision, since I had to compete in college with students who had a stronger background in science. How I ended up with a college minor in science is amazing, but I liked the biological sciences, which were required for a Bachelor of Science in Home Economics Education. Maybe my lack of interest in sciences was because the teachers in high school seemed a little "dorky," boring and disorganized.

Literature and grammar came far more easily. In college, I tested high enough to be exempt from grammar and placed in the advanced literature classes. Four years of high school English had obviously helped, although at the time Mrs. Finney's grammar class seemed incredibly repetitive and boring. When we went over homework in Mrs. Finney's class, I can't recall that her tone of voice or quiet demeanor varied from day to day.

Some teachers were memorable and others were not. Our history teacher, who was also the basketball coach, made a classic statement, "When Lincoln was assassinated, he was dead more or less." He used the "more or less" phrase in most of his sentences.

Caryl Crozier

Mr. Sweely taught government and bookkeeping classes and we all considered him a friend. One day in a bookkeeping class, he had us tell what we were thankful for. There were a lot of raw emotions that day. I expressed thanks to have survived childhood pneumonia and I wanted to know why and what my purpose in life would be. Mr. Sweely followed up privately with all of us to discuss any issues we had. He reassured me that I would find my purpose. He also tried to convince me again to join the debate team. Maybe he thought I was smart enough, but I was still too reluctant to try.

My Home Economics teachers were excellent and I enjoyed those classes the most. Undoubtedly that high school experience influenced my future profession. As a freshman, I made a turquoise corduroy skirt and vest for extra credit and my Home Economics teacher, Mrs. Guindon, used it as a good example in all of her classes. This planted another seed for my future career. I liked Mrs. Guindon because we had a connection. Her daughter married my uncle Ragnar's nephew, Bob, whom I had hero-worshipped since age two. I never forgot the windmill he built out of tinker toys for me. Mrs. Guindon knew a lot about me before I became her student. She gave me a lot of positive feedback for my sewing skills and had a wry sense of humor. Her habit of repeating, "Saaay girls," when she wanted our attention still makes us chuckle.

We had fun with our foods classes and preparing meals for teachers, and at the same time learned to be gracious hostesses. Once, Mom provided a large chicken (it must have been an old rooster) for us to cook, and it was definitely raw and tough when we served it. We had a lot to learn about timing and moist heat cookery! Our teacher gamely ate a piece and declared it delicious.

We stashed the jams, jellies, and pickles made in a food preservation unit in a little storeroom near the assembly hall. The four or five girls in our kitchen class units learned to work together quite well. In the fall, we studied foods and nutrition, and completed units like canning and food preservation, followed by bread, desserts, main dishes, meats, baking, etc. After Christmas, a clothing and sewing unit took forever to produce a finished product. I was accustomed to whipping out an outfit in a few days, but we shared a sewing machine with three other girls, and the projects spread out for months. We usually finished in time for a spring fashion show that mothers and the student body attended. I modeled three outfits, because we got extra credit for at-home projects.

My parents gave me a Brownie camera in third grade and my love of photography began. A flash camera upgrade in high school led to creative shots of friends, relatives and activities. Several of my photographs made their way into the Watchdog, our school yearbook. Slumber parties, Home Economics classes and class play rehearsals were my favorite subjects. Viewing the old black and white photo albums still makes me laugh out loud.

When television first came out in the late '40s, my family watched snowy, blurred scenes at Jay and Ida Gifford's home. On Saturday nights my friends and I stood on the street outside Messlers Radio, TV and Appliance store watching the Hit Parade Program. The ten most popular songs of the week were sung and it was a teenager's favorite program other than watching wrestling and baseball for the guys. The advertising sponsor was Lucky Strike cigarettes, whose ads tried to show us how cool it was to smoke.

When a family acquired a TV set, you could be certain a houseful of neighbors and friends would drop by nearly every night. In those days people didn't wait for invitations, they just "went calling" and showed up at the door unannounced. In June of 1953, my parents bought our first black and white RCA television set and it garnered a permanent place in our living room. Mom, gracious hostess that she was, kept busy serving sandwiches, cookies, cakes and beverages to our guests. As more families got their own TVs, the visitors were less frequent.

April 20, 1955–Had to clean trophy case in detention with Leona.

Superintendent Shennum was fun-loving and involved with the students. He loved to tease my friend Leona and me. One time he had us polish all the trophies in the case when we were on detention for some minor infraction. Well, it seemed minor at the time: it was for skipping a day of school and getting caught!

Each year, the senior class was allowed to declare a skip-day and they tried to sneak out of the building unseen. Word soon spread and someone hollered "Skip!" and we all rushed out of the building searching for a fun activity on this unexpected day of freedom. Usually, we just drove our cars around searching for something to do — maybe a trip to one of South Dakota's few lakes, nearby towns, the larger Sioux Falls or Newton Hills State Park. Our senior year, we five girls got our car stuck in deep, oozing mud on a dirt road south of our farm and had to get my Uncle George to pull us out with his tractor. He never let me forget that episode. I wonder how the District would handle the liability of skip-day these days?

In 1955, the school district built a new community auditorium for basketball games and school events as well as space for a cafeteria hot-lunch program. A hotly contested basketball game against a highly rated team, Hurley, added excitement to the opening event. Amid loud cheers and manic crowd excitement, our Beresford Watchdogs somehow pulled out a win.

Caryl Crozier

It was the most exhilarating game I ever led cheers for, and the guys were still talking about the win at our 50th class reunion, believe it or not. After this game, we circled Main Street with car horns blaring and celebrated at Edna's Cafe, where we danced, ate giant hamburgers, drank Cherry Cokes and idolized our basketball team: Paul, Dennis, Irving, Skip, Roger and Gary, most of whom I dated at one time or another. The sense of pride in our new building launched a winning season. We were also the first proud class to have our commencement graduation ceremony in the new auditorium in 1956.

Remodeling the high school to convert the old gym into several classrooms became necessary for expanding enrollment of post-war baby boomers after I graduated in 1956. In the 1980s, a new high school with an adjacent auditorium replaced the school I attended. Touring the old high school at one of our reunions brought back precious memories, both good and bittersweet. The elementary school playground now occupies the area.

Intelligence testing in our senior year prompted a summons to the superintendent's office. Mr. Shennum had never paid much attention to my scholastic pursuits and I apparently flew under the radar as being a star, even though my name was always on the honor roll. Counseling was unheard of in the 1950s; we never received career guidance. My score on the senior ACT intelligence tests was in the very high percentile range (as were my daughters' and granddaughters' in later years), so Mr. Shennum began encouraging me to take college prep classes. Too late, as I had avoided chemistry, physics, advanced math and Latin and I was a senior. Ultimately, I graduated fourth in a class of fifty-one and garnered a tuition scholarship to South Dakota State College, now called SDSU, a University. I could have worked a little harder in high school and college and maybe captured top honors, but having a full social life was more important to me at the time. Still, I managed to graduate from both high school and college with honors.

February 28, 1956—Started practice teaching and corrected arithmetic papers- third grade fun- had assembly meeting at noon- Ice Capades in Sioux City tonight.

I spent the latter part of my senior year in a teaching internship in the elementary school, observing and helping with a third grade class. My task consisted primarily of correcting a pile of arithmetic and language or reading papers, so I soon learned that teaching could be drudgery. However, working with the students was a joy when we actually had a chance to interact with them. My career goal to be a teacher seemed on target.

March 6, 1956–Was chosen FFA Chapter Sweetheart- quite thrilled.

March 22, 1956–FFA banquet tonight-Dennis stopped with a corsage and took me there and home again. Got jacket and had a swell time.

The high school Future Farmers of America (FFA) members selected me as their first chapter sweetheart in my senior year. I felt honored, as I always felt close to the members because of 4-H and my rural upbringing. Wearing the white jacket with the chapter sweetheart insignia was fun. This was a new idea in South Dakota. Escorted to the spring banquet by FFA president, Dennis, I was all gussied up in my lavender net formal, perhaps a bit overdressed for the occasion, but the corsage looked nice attached to my strapless gown. Wolf whistles pierced the silence as we entered the room. I remember ending the evening discussing the relative merits of my two current boy friends with Dennis, who was smart enough to resist giving advice. He was a good friend of both of them.

April 17, 1956–Bonnie asked me to be her maid of honor for her wedding- had sextet practice- discussed senior skip day- went to Marion T bridal shower.

Several of my friends got married shortly after high school graduation. Going to bridal showers and weddings let us gush over pots and pans and household goods. LaVonne asked me to be her maid of honor at her 1956 July wedding. I loved all the planning, showers, rehearsals and sewing my pink crystalette dress and hat. My friends and I hosted a shower for her and had her sit under an umbrella with long crepe paper streamers encircling her. We concocted a program of sappy sentimental poems and music that seemed sweet at the time, but are laughable now. We shed tears knowing that we would soon scatter and our relationships would change.

May 22, 1956–Graduation day at BHS-played a duet with LaVonne at commencement- 4th high honor student-cried as I came out- had a party at home and stayed out with friends getting home at 5 a.m.

LaVonne and I played piano duets — *Canadian Capers, Alice's Blue Gown, Tea for Two* and *The Lord's Prayer* —at our high school baccalaureate and commencement services. I felt overwhelmed with nostalgia for the carefree days I had spent with friends in high school. They were good years, sometimes uncertain and frustrating, but they gave me a foundation to make the exciting choices ahead.

Arriving home at five a.m. graduation night, after spending time with friends in Sioux Falls, I watched the sun rise over the fields and whispered a prayer for guidance. Age seventeen now seems extremely young to make life-changing decisions, but I knew my future meant leaving the security of Beresford and family. Sure enough, within a year, I met someone who became my life partner and made a decision for a fulfilling career, all by age eighteen. Life happened fast in those days.

I've never really left my small-town roots. Physically I did, of course, but not emotionally. Friends and family still support and sustain me, and that was never more evident than those last weeks we spent with Mom at the end of her life in 2009. I felt the entire town encircled me in its arms. Friendships there are truly life-long.

CHAPTER 23
Choices

The paradox of my college education is that I wanted to leave life on the farm, but it was the farm that financed my escape. I loved growing up in the country but knew I didn't want to spend my life tied down doing hard farm work and endless, repetitive chores. My parents couldn't be away from the farm for more than a few hours. The cattle, chickens and pigs needed constant attention. Maybe if I had developed an affinity for chicken chores (traditionally women's work on a farm), my life would have taken a different turn. Now 55 years later, I love staying at the farm for the freedom it provides. I have lived a rewarding life of freedom from being tied down, had every opportunity for education, travel, work and adventure. I can cherish and enjoy the leisurely days we spend on the farm now — we don't have to make a living on it working all the time.

Mom knew how much it meant to me to go to college. It had been an unfulfilled dream for her. Her father refused to send her to college saying she would just get married, which in those days meant becoming a fulltime homemaker. Forty years later, I learned Mom wanted to be a Home Economist like I became. She truly lived her dreams through me.

In spite of my limited exposure to the world, I felt ready for the new challenge of college, and deciding which college to attend seemed pretty simple in 1956. At that time, a girl's career choices were essentially limited to becoming a nurse, secretary or teacher. I wanted to major in Home Economics, but four more years of school seemed much too long when I could become an elementary teacher in South Dakota with just two years of college. Helping a third-grade teacher while a senior in high school cemented teaching as my career goal. I related well to the students, and teaching seemed fun and achievable.

After Mom convinced Dad that getting an education was vital to me, he agreed to sell some cattle each year to finance my college education. My Uncle Ragnar tried to convince my parents and me that I should attend Iowa State, but I chose Augustana in Sioux Falls, South Dakota instead. A few months into the Elementary Education program there I knew it was a misfit. An incident in a Teaching of Reading class drove it home for me: I couldn't print perfectly on the blackboard and got criticized for it by my instructor, who seemed to think perfect printing was more important than opening children's minds and curiosity. Besides, by then I knew elementary education wasn't what I really wanted. I realized that my true passion was for Home Economics.

> *September 9, 1956–Up at 9 a.m. packing and pressing. To Aunt Alice's for dinner and Augie this afternoon. Roommate Marcene and I on 4th floor- cute- no lights- supper bread, meat and tomatoes. Games etc. in gym.*

The college application process in the 1950s did not take long. I decided in late August to attend Augustana and began classes September 9, about a two-week process. Granted, I had visited other colleges: Yankton, South Dakota State College (now SDSU), the University of South Dakota, and three teachers colleges during the summer, but some friends were going to Augie, so I decided to go there too. I had been awarded a $300 scholarship to SDSU, which at that time was a significant amount. A year's tuition plus room and board cost about $700 in total there, and $1,000 at Augustana. Marcene and I were friends through double dating during high school, had similar activities and interests, so we decided to room together in an Augustana dormitory.

At Beresford High School, I achieved one of the highest academic records in the class of 51, so it was a rude awakening to have to study and compete with kids smarter than I. Lots of class valedictorians and homecoming queens attend small Lutheran liberal arts colleges. I eventually learned to study and develop good work habits after getting a few C's in tests. I hadn't taken physics, advanced math or chemistry in high school, so I struggled with a science class that included all three.

I rebelled against Augustana's focus on religion. It seemed forced at this Lutheran school: required chapel each day, dormitory devotions and a Christianity class didn't fit my liberal Congregational upbringing. Also, the girls that prayed publicly and acted devout were the ones sneaking down the fire escape at night, drinking booze and going to one of the Sioux Falls bars like Hernando's Hideaway on North Phillips Avenue. Hypocrisy was rampant and I saw it in the so-called campus leaders.

> *September 6, 1956–Won State Fair dress revue and got trip to 4-H Club Congress-really a thrill- finals this morning- judges so nice and Ima Crisman took pictures- bedroom exhibit blue ribbon- congratulated by so many people, on radio, TV, newspapers.*

> *November 23, 1956–Up at 9:30- mad rush getting things ready- finished rust dress- took train from SF for 4-H Club Congress in Chicago-dinner in pullman car.*

Waking to Mourning Doves

Several incidents happened in the fall of 1956 that helped me grow up and influence my educational and career decisions. I won the 4-H Dress Review at the State Fair , which qualified me to attend the National 4-H Club Congress in Chicago, where I was exposed to people and ideas from throughout the US. I learned there was more to life than what I had been exposed to in South Dakota — and I wanted it all. We 4-H participants rode and slept in a Pullman train getting to Chicago. We were wined and dined in luxury. For the first time I ate rare steak, Caesar salad and chocolate mousse.

October 7, 1956–Talking to Nan. She's much worse.

October 10, 1956–Dad called at 7:30 and said Nan passed away in the night. Wish I could have been home before- she didn't get my letter either.

As my diary noted, that October, my grandmother Nan died of congestive heart failure. The weekend before her death she and I talked about my future and her aspirations for me. They went beyond what my parents expected. I know they wanted me to marry a local farmer and stay nearby. Nan urged me to get as much education as possible and follow my dreams. I think Nan always regretted that they couldn't afford to send their daughter, Eva, to college. Eva dated a local lawyer, but his mother ended that relationship because she wanted a college-educated woman for her son. This rankled Nan most of her life, and she wanted more for me.

By then I was working harder in college and pretty confident in myself. Aunt Lillian Jackson counseled me to find a partner who was my intellectual equal and not just "settle." It was expected that girls would marry before age 21 in this era. I had grown tired of the local guys I had been dating and none of the Augie guys were much better. I can barely recall the ones named in my diary.

September 25, 1956–Carie, Ann, Lil and I to cheerleading tryouts, but didn't make it. Supper at the Huddle.

I naïvely thought I could become a cheerleader and sing in the choir, two of my favorite activities in high school. I didn't make the cut when I tried out for those activities at Augie. The Sioux Falls girls from the larger high schools had the edge on me. I liked campus life at Augie, and I loved American History, Children's Literature and advanced English. Being exempted from grammar by testing put me in an advanced class. I had great girlfriends, Bev, Marcene, Barb and several in my dormitory and classes that I have lost touch with.

The college deans did not allow us to go home on weekends at first and we adhered to rigid dorm hours and rules by being in our rooms at 10 p.m. for bed check and devotions. After all the freedom I experienced in high school, this felt much too restrictive. I have no idea what I would have done with more freedom, though. I was pretty intent on studying and had no desire to go home every weekend. Maybe I just wasn't used to rules.

College clothing fashions consisted of mid-calf skirts, wool sweaters and dresses, rarely slacks. I wore leotards to keep my legs warm, fur-lined boots and a heavy navy pea coat for long walks across the bitter-cold campus. We usually ate in the school cafeteria. I missed Mom's good gravy and roast beef. Sometimes we snacked and hung out in the "Huddle," the social spot on campus. It was usually crowded with the popular upper classmen, so we were on the fringes socially. I never felt that I fit in at Augie, even though I tried.

Campus activities such as going to football and basketball games, plays, folk dancing and parties were fun. My friends and I enjoyed movies, church and various activities in Sioux Falls. Since I didn't drink or smoke, the bars had no appeal and I was pretty conservative, close to being prissy, something I don't regret to this day.

My roommate, Marcene, had major surgery soon after we started school. By the second semester, our parents met with the Dean to discuss the possibility of us living off-campus. The stairs to the fourth floor of the dormitory and the tight restrictions were too much for Marcene, so I agreed to move too. Her parents, who were devout Lutherans, had forbidden a relationship she had with a Catholic boy she was in love with and it affected her whole life. For a Protestant and Catholic to date and marry pre-1960 could be compared to a Christian marrying a Muslim today. Such harsh prejudices and suspicion ruined lives and was centuries in building. Caucasians marrying blacks was even more forbidden. These restrictions have now faded in some parts of the US population, but most parents still prefer that their children marry within their faith and value systems.

After Christmas 1956, we moved to 2415 S. Norton in a basement apartment with a shared bathroom and a hot plate and small refrigerator for cooking facilities — not exactly luxury living. The other two roommates, Anita and Bernie, became friends quickly. Our landlady from Hungary was always in a panic over many members of her family still under Communist rule there. The revolution in Hungary occurred during the year we lived there and she cried a lot, told us her family stories and watched over us like a protective housemother. She chastised Anita's boyfriend for selling Marcene and me Lustre Craft stainless steel pots and pans for $200 with $12 monthly payments. Ironically, it turned out to be a good buy: I use them daily, 50 years later.

Lois, my long-time Beresford childhood friend, lived in Sioux Falls attending Nettleton Business College, while babysitting for a family in exchange for room and board. We spent a lot of time together giggling and talking about everything, just as we had in high school. She continued to be my closest confidant as we both adjusted to new lives. A true best friend to this day in 2011.

> *March 15, 1957–More work on term paper and science study. Ed Crozier down (State grad) and another guy-he's nice- asked me for date (I was so goofy) went to science help class- dry- late studying.*

January and February were uneventful. The bitterly cold north wind hit us much harder as we faced it for several blocks trudging through the snow to reach campus. While studying Shakespeare in a lit class, we were analyzing the "Ides of March," when a life-changing event occurred for me on March 15, 1957. Ed Crozier (called Sherm by his family) and I met purely by chance when he came to Sioux Falls to take a pre-induction physical prior to being considered for drafting into the army. He came along with a fellow inductee to our apartment to visit my roommate, Anita. I was washing dishes in the bathroom sink because we didn't have a kitchen. At first, I didn't pay much attention to Anita's visitors, but Sherm plopped down on the stairs and didn't seem anxious to leave. He was wearing a long beige trenchcoat and said he had a degree in wildlife management, which sounded pretty exotic to me. I didn't know guys who wore trench coats, much less college graduates. After a little bantering back and forth, we were immediately attracted to each other. He seemed more mature, interesting and adventurous than the local boys, so I readily agreed to a first date if his new friend and another girl, Beth, went along. He said in his memoir that I had a good personality, seemed smart and was attractive. I learned later that he also preferred blonds like me.

The next night Sherm and his friend drove 60 miles in a blizzard to see us. We saw a Judy Holliday movie. Sherm laughed in strange places and kept leaving to go to the bathroom. Nerves, he said later. After the movie we got stuck in the snow-covered hills of the Minnehaha Country Club. I stuck my head out the window to watch the guys trying to push the car out while Beth drove. Sherm walked over and brushed my cheek with a cold kiss as the blowing snow coated my face and hair. I probably fell in love at that moment.

The blizzard was still raging as I prepared for our second date, and I was certain he wouldn't come. As I stood on the bed by our only basement window in my sexiest, cinnamon-brown Pendleton wool dress, he came slogging by in the snowdrifts. Not wanting to act too eager, I hoped he hadn't seen me, but he had. According to my diary, we got into some rather deep discussions about families, religion, future hopes and dreams on those first dates. I wasn't sure about him then, but I was intrigued.

There seemed to be enough chemistry there for a couple more dates before he left for the beginning of his career with the US Fish and Wildlife Service at Crab Orchard Wildlife Refuge in Illinois. We wrote frequent letters for a month until he came back home when he was drafted for two years of Army duty.

When Sherm called to tell me he was coming back from Illinois and wanted to see me, he pretended to be my Norwegian pen pal. About this time I'd been writing to a Norwegian guy from Trondheim, who planned to arrive in Omaha, Nebraska by bus the first part of April. He wanted to come and visit me. Sponsored by the Mormon Church, he was headed to Utah. When I asked my parents for permission to have him visit, Dad went ballistic and said he didn't want any dumb foreigner around. What would people think?! I didn't agree with that philosophy, but the boy seemed a bit weird, so I never wrote back to him explaining why it wouldn't work out. I know he was looking for an American wife to get US citizenship. I still feel sad for being so rude.

In late April of 1957, Sherm returned from Crab Orchard National Wildlife Refuge in southern Illinois after being there only a month before getting drafted. We had only eight days to see each other before his induction into the Army. I scrambled to finish sewing a grey spring coat and lavender dress for Easter and his return. He took me home to Beresford where he met my parents. About all I remember about that visit was looking at baby chicks in the brooder house and realizing that Sherm and my Dad had no chemistry whatsoever between them. They barely spoke and didn't try to engage each other in conversation. They didn't seem to have much in common. Prophetic, as that continued until Dad's death. I guess no man is good enough for a daughter, and Dad fully expected me to marry a local farmer and not move on to a different life so far away from Beresford. I think Mom understood that I had already moved on.

> *April 7, 1957–Ed came and got me and we went to Jasper to his place for the weekend- met parents, Candy and Grandpa-hunting gophers (16) to quarry for a picnic, bonfire and canoeing- said he loved me on lake- went home – studying on divan- I like him.*

A few days after Sherm met my parents, we went to Jasper, Minnesota, so I could meet his family. Our relationship seemed to be moving fast. I felt nervous because meeting a boyfriend's parents was a new experience for me. I wanted to make a good impression.

Waking to Mourning Doves

I changed my mind several times about going, but my roommates said, "Go for it."

Fortunately, I had a lot of self-confidence, but not in the outdoor activities like canoeing that I knew we'd do. Sherm had been a canoe guide for a summer in the Boundary Waters canoe area in northern Minnesota. Growing up on the prairies of South Dakota I had barely been in a boat except for fishing a few times with Uncle Ragnar, an expert fisherman, originally from Norway. What to wear? I didn't have any fashionable outdoor clothing, just jeans and shirts, so Marcene and I made a hurried trip to Fantles Department store in downtown Sioux Falls and I bought a light green jacket, pedal pushers, a matching striped shirt and grey tennis shoes, which I later thought were ugly.

All too soon Friday arrived and we were on our way to Jasper, approaching the town from the west. Sherm thought it was more impressive from that direction. Later I preferred coming from the south. The highway curves down a hill exposing Jasper rock and native pasture as you approach the grain elevators and the lumberyard with the big grey-and-black "Jasper Yards" painted across the whole building.

Sherm had spoken highly to me about his family, but I had not expected to like them as much as I did. They were welcoming and gracious. As we pulled in the driveway of their new rambler on North Sherman Street, his mother, Ella, met us at the car with a pitcher of homemade lemonade. Twelve-year-old Candy stood beside her mother peering expectantly into the car window. I felt at ease. His father, also named Ed, and Grandpa Crozier were a bit more reserved, but pleasant to be around. I liked the whole family and the weekend went well.

Sherm showed me around Jasper, including a visit to the abandoned east quarry, where he used to swim, and the south quarry, where he worked for one summer as a laborer. The first afternoon we went hunting gophers, of all things, and Sherm shot 16 of them using his dad's 22-caliber rifle. I guess he was demonstrating his shooting skills, but since I had grade-school experience with drowning out gophers and bashing them with a baseball bat, that didn't seem so unusual. Farmers in that era had ongoing battles with gophers burrowing in fields and ruining crops. Minnesota's nickname is the "Gopher State."

That first evening we had a picnic at Split Rock Creek State Park, then known as the Ihlen Dam, which was built by the Work Projects Administration (WPA) during the Depression. The park was a favorite Crozier picnic site, and Ella packed a wiener roast meal for us. Then came the nervously anticipated canoe ride. During the summer that Sherm had been a canoe guide, he purchased an old, canvas-covered wooden canoe for $25. I had never been in a canoe in my life, but somehow I got in without tipping it over and making a fool of myself. It was wobbly and tipsy, but I quickly learned that if I sat very still, Sherm's sure J

Caryl Crozier

strokes with the paddle propelled us forward without the wobbling. Thankfully I wasn't invited to paddle that night as I was getting my "sea legs."

As a beautiful prairie sunset descended upon the lake, he told me he was falling in love with me, this being our fifth real date. Fifty years later we have very different memories of that moment. He thought it was a warm, fall evening and I know it was a very cool April evening. I was shivering in my inadequate outdoor clothes and too demure to say anything, maybe because of my reserved Swedish upbringing. Warm it wasn't, as my teeth were chattering, but I tried to act outdoorsy and tough! My diary reads, " I like him." Well, that was a good start, but I wasn't ready to express my feelings to him yet.

April 28, 1957–Went to Methodist Church with Sherm, Ella, Ed and Candy-went bird watching by a creek- telling about when we were kids-piano, sewing, cheerleading. Canoeing with Candy and Judy- had chicken dinner- Candy is going to write to me.

The next morning we went to the Jasper Methodist Church where I got the once-over from the congregation. Sherm says he liked showing the hometown folks that he had a girlfriend, and a very attractive one at that. He hadn't paraded any girls around Jasper before, as he had not dated much. In the afternoon we walked along one of Sherm's favorite haunts, the creek, and went bird watching.

Ella fixed her legendary fried chicken dinner after church. It was crispy perfection! Years later, I can't eat chicken with the skin on, much less fried in butter. Her homemade whole-wheat bread from his grandmother's German recipe is a specialty we still make and enjoy. Potato salad, dark bread and cold cuts for supper is a tradition we shared for years.

That afternoon we walked along Split Rock Creek, just a block north of the Crozier home. I heard tales of Sherm growing up somewhat unrestrained with very little parental supervision in this town of 800 residents. We also loaded the canoe on top of the car and canoed again on the Ihlen Dam Lake. Candy and her friend Judy begged to ride along and spent the afternoon splashing and shouting along the shore. This time I was confident enough to try paddling this relic craft. The canvas-covered canoe, then about 30 years old, leaked a little bit. Now 55 years later, it resides behind the woodshed, a sentimental reminder of our youth.

That weekend was probably the seed that solidified the start of a relationship, but it lay dormant for two years while Sherm served in Texas and Germany. We wrote letters, but we were free to date others. In total we'd had around 30 dates by the time he left for Germany in the fall of 1957.

April 30, 1957–Sherm in SF- goes to army tomorrow-had malt at drugstore and talked 6-10PM at McKennan Park-took a realistic view of us, school, army, Europe etc.

On Sherm's last evening before leaving for Ft. Hood, Texas, where he would take his infantry training and begin his two years with the Army, my diary says we had a realistic talk about school, the Army and travel to Europe. I am not sure we were on the same page, as he wanted to get engaged. He also said he thought it was stupid for me to be thinking of Home Economics. Maybe he thought I might meet too many other guys at SDSU, since the ratio was five guys to one girl. He also wanted the status of dating an "Augie girl," as they had the reputation of being the prettiest in the state. Apparently, there was an argument. I didn't write for two weeks and he apologized in one of his first letters, saying he had jumped to conclusions.

In a subsequent letter, Sherm enclosed a ring. But it was no ordinary ring – it was actually an ID band for geese – and Sherm explained it signified that we were "engaged to be engaged." The description is similar to a banding record note he'd make when banding a wild bird:

Outstanding species banded, pretty blonde, co-ed with local name of Caryl Kinkner, from now on to be my special project – band # 508-39521, banded June 19, 1957, Sioux Falls, SD.

I might be the only recorded human being with a goose band!

Inside the band there was a scratched inscription "MBLO," meaning "my banded loved one." Sort of corny, but romantic, I guess. Yet, in 2008 he didn't recall that we had any commitment at that time. Apparently his memory is not as good as mine. We agreed that we were both free to date while he did his time in the Army. I still had a lot of growing up do, so that was best for me.

I was dating other guys during this time. One boy had been a good friend and playmate since I was three years old and more like a brother to me. He was a great guy, but deserved someone more suitable than me for the life he envisioned. Luckily he found her and we remained friends.

According to my diary, I was still mildly interested in a Beresford High School senior athlete. He was fun, but not someone I wanted to build a lasting relationship with. I continued to date him occasionally for the next several years and he was a good friend. About this time too, I also dated a guy named LeRoy, whom I recall as very good-looking. In my 50-year-old memory, I thought we dated only a few times, but my diary says otherwise. It lasted several months until my boredom must have set in.

April 12, 1957–Polio vaccine declared good.

Caryl Crozier

Growing up during the polio epidemic in South Dakota made my parents very cautious about letting me be in crowds or swim at the municipal swimming pool. Consequently, I did not know how to swim. But when the first polio vaccination shots became available, our parents were more at ease about us swimming in crowded pools, and I enrolled in a swim class at the Sioux Falls YMCA the winter of 1957. Many of my new friends couldn't swim either, so we jumped on city buses three times a week and slowly learned to have more skill in the water. I already knew how to float on my back, and eventually passed the intermediate test – and what a test it was. We had to dive fully clothed into the deep end, remove our outer garments, and tread water for five minutes. It was terrifying, but we all did it.

Getting an A in an Introduction to Literature class in June 1957 proved I had learned better study skills. We were required to do a term paper using note cards, footnotes and extensive library research. High school had not prepared me for that. I labored for hours in the library researching *The McGuffey Readers*. My parents gave me a portable, red Royal typewriter for Christmas 1956, which I used in college and into the 1970s and 1980s to prepare adult education papers and long-term-care research papers. Packrat that I am, the typewriter is still in my possession.

I think my parents began to detect a change in my life outlook, because at the end of May, my dad sold my horse, Ginger, for $90 along with my saddle and bridle. Although I hadn't ridden her that year, I was very upset and emotional that they sold her without telling me. She died a year later, so maybe it was good she helped finance my education.

The summer of 1957 was a time for reflection about my future. I had honed my study skills, getting A's in classes. I talked to a counselor who advised me to take sociology, psychology and literature in summer school, which I did, and I got A's in all of them. Studying for two months in that dismal basement apartment wasn't great, but I took breaks going swimming nearly every day with Bev, Lois, and other girlfriends.

Changes were in the air all around me. Marcene was not planning to finish her education and Barb decided to get married. I explored moving back on the Augie campus, but it filled me with dread because I knew it wasn't what I wanted. I still dreamt of a Home Economics career. On August fifth, after moving out of the apartment, Mom and Dad drove me to SDSU in Brookings to talk to Home Economics Dean Hettler about a transfer. It seemed feasible, and my scholarship could be reinstated, so the decision was made to transfer to SDSU in September and follow my dream.

Chapter 24
Following My Dream

August 1957 flew by as I got into my usual sewing frenzy, getting exhibits ready for Lincoln County 4-H Achievement Days and fashioning a few clothes for college. I made a navy wool dress with a short jacket, which eventually earned me a blue ribbon the State Fair. I also sewed a flattering grey wool skirt and jacket.

A photograph of me in front of the SDSU Development Hall dormitory in the grey suit prompted cousin Jan's male business college teacher to say, "She looks pretty well developed to me." Yes, I had grown up!

Our Happy Homemakers 4-H Club float placed first in the county parade again, so that meant a quick trip to the State Fair two days before registration began at SDSU in Brookings. We loaded the car with clothes and items I needed for college and headed for Huron. Dad drove and pulled the float in the parade. We stayed for the evening to watch my friend Janet place in the top five in the evening dress review, after which we drove two hours to Brookings. Naturally, we didn't have a reservation and the motels were all full. At midnight, we stopped at a rooming house where the lady took pity on us and let us sleep on a couple of sofas and a roll-away. That's when I learned to always plan ahead and take charge when traveling with my parents, a lesson well learned as we made a dozen trips together in later years.

The next morning I rushed to the dorm and discovered I didn't have a roommate yet, so I left a note in the room of a fellow transfer Home Ec student asking her to wait for me to go to a student event. She did. I had never felt so alone and frightened. I went to my room and cried when Mom and Dad left. Dad said Mom cried all the way home to Beresford.

Being a transfer student wasn't as easy as I had anticipated. I felt that we were treated as second-class citizens. Because of a dormitory room shortage, the freshmen and sophomore girls were placed in two traditional halls, Wecota and Wenona. The junior and senior girls and transfer students were relegated to the old cement-block Development Hall. Sherm lived there when it was a boy's dormitory when it was first built in 1954. The building was pretty marginal then, too. As a consequence, we transfer students didn't see much of our sophomore classmates. We took introductory Home Ec classes with the freshman girls. I lived at Development Hall two years then spent my senior year in the new Waneta Hall. It was closer to the main campus, and we seniors had classes, student teaching and Home Management house together.

Registration week found me in a blur of tests, tours, mixers and dances and finding my way around. As a relative stranger, I was forced to mix, unlike at Augie, where I had a ready-made social circle. That turned out to be a blessing as I made new friends quickly. My worried parents drove to Brookings the next weekend to see how I was doing. They left reassured that I was adapting just fine.

My assigned roommate, Doris, finally arrived. She was already a graduate and working as an Extension Home Economist coming back for a quarter of graduate classes. She had a car, was fun and I liked her. My new friends, Boots and Jo and I spent a lot of social time with her. Jo had transferred from Augie to major in Home Ec, too. I met Karlene, another Lutheran liberal arts transfer from Wartburg College in Iowa. She became my roommate and best friend the last two years in college.

In the second quarter Boots, Jo and I shared a room. Sometimes living with three in a room caused tension. Boots never seemed happy when Jo and I were on dates. Boots had a great collection of jazz records and we listened to them on my record player along with my Mantovani and Broadway recordings. Exercise to tone our bodies took some unusual forms. Propelling ourselves forward on our butts up and down the halls looked pretty stupid, but many of us thought it made svelte behinds and broke up cellulite.

My fall classes began with chemistry, psychology, design, clothing, speech and physical education. Chemistry was difficult, but Professors Ma and Pa Grebs nursed me through it and I got a B by some miracle. Speech was a bit intimidating, but good for me.

My favorite cousins, Norman and Lanney, were enrolled at SDSU and I enjoyed spending time with them my sophomore and junior years. They had cars and provided rides home and moral support if necessary. A good friend, Charles, from high school was also there, so I had a good male support system.

Sherm was home on leave from the Army from October 18th to November 5th, and we saw each other nearly every day and spent time in Jasper and Beresford at our parents' homes. We also visited John and Ruth Carlson at Waubay National Wildlife Refuge in South Dakota so I could see what living on a wildlife refuge would be like. They could have been a poster family for living that life. I was favorably impressed. After we were married, we only lived on a rural wildlife refuge for nine months in North Dakota, but it would have been fine if we had spent more time in the "boonies."

Waking to Mourning Doves

Fall is hunting season and I was introduced to Sherm's life-long hobby. Ella once said after we were married, "Well, that's his whole life."

"Well not quite," I replied. "He has a family, too."

We went pheasant and duck hunting a few times, enjoying the fall colors at Newton Hills State Park in South Dakota. The photograph of Sherm standing by a gnarled oak tree sat on my desk for the next three years. The fall of 2009, Mom, Sherm and I revisited the site for a noon picnic lunch and saw that same tree fifty years later, pretty much unchanged, but we've changed considerably.

When Sherm left, I felt we had a pretty firm commitment, but we were not engaged. Ella said she was glad he had someone to write to. And write we did, a letter or more per week for one and a half years. I wanted him to meet my German pen pal, Marianne, and he made an initial contact, but said he was afraid to take the confusing European trains to her city. Ella thought meeting Marianne was a bad idea, as she feared he could stray. I think she decided I was to be her future daughter-in-law. I was the kind of girl that you took home to meet the parents and maybe she recognized that. In the next year and a half I made several weekend visits to Jasper and kept connected with the Croziers.

So, as life and school went on, I became enmeshed in studying, school activities and eventually dating others. I didn't let other relationships with young men become very serious and always said I was somewhat committed to someone in the military service. In many ways that provided a handy way out of stale dating relationships.

Joining a few activities like chorus, Home Ec Club, 4-H, Kappa Delta Pi (Honorary Education Sorority) and Phi U (Home Ec Sorority) made campus life fun. In the spring of 1958, I was a finalist for the Ag School Queen, one of the many excuses to have queens and beauty contests. That competition proved to be humiliating when eight of us girls were asked to come to the Livestock Pavilion where the Ag Club met. That was also where cattle, hogs and sheep were judged. They asked us to stand in the front of the room and then turn around. I guess they wanted to judge our backsides. We felt like a herd of Herefords and went out the door fuming. They didn't ask questions, barely talked to us and acted like immature jerks.

May 5, 1958—Beauty contest interviews and tea with judges- preliminaries in ballroom, bathing suits, talent and formal- a wonderful experience. I was eliminated but didn't feel at all bad.

The same group asked me to represent them in the Miss SDSU beauty pageant, which was a preliminary competition for the Miss South Dakota contest. People said I was a dead ringer for Marilyn Monroe. Sherm did too. I was blonde and had the same measurements. I didn't like the comparison because I thought she was a slut. A bathing suit, evening gown and talent portion to the contest took some preparation. Miss Dewey, my Beresford piano teacher, helped me perfect a piano solo by Rachmaninoff and I bought a flattering black one-piece bathing suit.

I wore high heels with the swimsuit, which prompted my roommate Boots to say, "You don't look half bad." Not a huge endorsement! I survived the interview, teas, and talent portions, but eventually was defeated by the girl that became Miss South Dakota that year.

> *May 1, 1958–Had the big organic chemistry test. God, I hate that course.*

The chemise dress style had come into vogue and I purchased a light brown chemise to wear for the judge's interview. A chemise is not flattering, of course, and my figure was my best asset, which the dress certainly didn't accentuate. A current boyfriend, Les, tried to forbid me to buy and wear a chemise. I purchased and wore it mainly to spite him. I have never taken well to any man telling me what to do. However, he was an OK guy and an invaluable help in my passing organic chemistry that spring quarter. He helped me study and understand the concepts. He also escorted me to Home Ec social functions and college dances without complaining.

> *February 17, 1958–Nearly blew up the garbage disposal by putting in prune pits- Colburn all excited. I also burned a pan.*

> *March 5, 1958–luncheon menu cucumber red cabbage salad, cheese souffle, Norwegian prune whip.*

The foods, clothing and design classes were a welcome relief from the Augustana Elementary Education curriculum, and it all just felt right. We wore ugly white uniforms and hairnets for the long laboratory classes. With a kitchen partner, usually Jo, we experimented with all kinds of cooking and baking techniques. I loved it! Sometimes we planned and served meals to faculty guests in our food labs. Once I accidentally threw some prune pits into the garbage disposal and our instructor, Miss Colburn, had a hissy fit. Several times, I practiced meals and what I considered elegant serving styles when visiting the Croziers in Jasper. They put up with it and humored me. Obviously, I was trying to make a good impression on them. They especially liked a rolled stuffed fish recipe, which I used for many years thereafter.

By the end of my sophomore year, I felt content that I had found my life's work and had made the right decisions. Now I needed a summer job. Going back to Beresford and helping on the farm didn't hold much appeal. I wanted adventure.

CHAPTER **25**

Missouri River Summers

May 12, 1958–Got my extension job.

Little did I know that having Aunt Lily as my great aunt would provide the opportunity for securing a summer job as an Extension Home Economist. Rather late in the spring of 1958, I heard that some Home Economics students were being hired as Summer Extension Agents and were already assigned to South Dakota counties. I rushed to get my application in to Nell McLaughlin, the State 4-H Extension Supervisor. In talking to her, I found out she was a friend of my Aunt Lily.

She said, "Oh, I'm so sorry, Caryl. The positions are filled, but there is a possibility we could create a position for you in Brule County at Chamberlain. The current agent is pregnant and maybe can't finish the summer. Her baby is due in August, so you could work together."

I knew that Nell wanted to help her friend's niece and she recognized me from my 4-H involvement. I also said I had a car and would have to explain later to my parents that I would be needing the family's old 1949 Ford. Nell worked her magic and I accepted the Extension job. Mom and Dad were not pleased at first, to say the least, but I was determined to accept the job for the experience. Working in Extension was my career goal and I knew this job was perfect for me.

June 15, 1958–Here I am in Chamberlain. This is a wonderful set-up.

Well, surprise! When I reported for work in June, Ann had a one-week-old baby. She tried to pass off her eight-pound baby boy as premature, but everyone knew she "had to get married," a social stigma at the time. She invited me to her home the first morning I reported to work. She served banana cake (still a favorite recipe) and told me I would be in charge of a cherry pie-baking contest that afternoon. She had also arranged for me to judge an evening talent show called Share the Fun that same week, plus meeting with a couple of 4-H club members to help them prepare county fair demonstrations. Nothing like throwing me into the fire without any training! Fortunately, the county had several capable volunteer club leaders who provided guidance when needed, and I was familiar with all the projects and had enough skills to keep my head above water most of the time. Ann also provided support whenever I asked. I was relieved to know she was only a phone call away.

ANN'S BANANA CAKE RECIPE

2 cups flour	1/2 cup shortening
1 teaspoon soda	1 & 1/2 cups sugar
1/8 teaspoon salt	2 eggs
1/2 cup sour milk or buttermilk	1 cup (3-4) mashed ripe bananas
1/2 cup walnuts	1 teaspoon vanilla

Cream shortening and sugar, add eggs and beat. Mix in mashed bananas and vanilla. Add dry ingredients and beat. Sprinkle 2 Tablespoons flour over nuts. Add flour and milk alternately. Fold in nuts. Bake in 9x11 greased pan or 9 inch square pan in 350 degree oven for 45 minutes.

Ann found me an upstairs room at a private home and since my friend Karlene was working at a cafe in Chamberlain for the summer, we decided to share the room at the Yates' home. In two cars, my parents, Aunt Hazel, Uncle Clarence and I drove the one hundred miles to Chamberlain and were pleased to learn that the landlady was a sister of the Lincoln County Rural School Superintendent, Thelma Eidsness. Mrs. Yates had already checked me out with her sister, so she went along with my parents' pleas to help me if necessary. Dad also went to the local Standard service station to talk about servicing my car. I am sure Mom cried most of the way home on that journey too, as she did every time they left me or visited us after we were married.

Chamberlain is a little town of about 2,000 on the east bank of the Missouri River. It is considered the transition point between eastern and western South Dakota. Farmers lived on the east side and cowboys lived and worked in the range country west of the river. Brule County, on the east side of the river, had its share of range cattle and a few cowboys, but corn and other crops dominated. Chamberlain was quiet during the week, but Friday and Saturday nights brought a clash of cultures with Native Americans celebrating with their weekly paychecks and West River cowboys with their Stetson hats, cowboy boots, western gear and even an occasional horse tied up outside the saloons. The farmer/ranchers east of the river were less flamboyant, but a little alcohol and high spirits often caused conflict spilling onto the streets downtown. It was a street we avoided on those nights. On Monday morning, when I went to work at the county courthouse and administrative building, a group of women and children waited beneath my office outside the jail to take their men home

Waking to Mourning Doves

after they'd been put in the slammer after Saturday night brawls. All of this would be repeated the following week.

Working with the 4-H Clubs comprised a sixteen-hour a day job. In addition to working an eight-hour day in the office or at meetings, I visited 4-H Clubs all over the county at least three evenings a week. Driving the dark country gravel roads at night worried my parents, but I felt safe. Families included me in their activities throughout the county, and I never got bored. Even livestock auctions were fun, and riding horses once again felt great. Taking twenty-five 4-H members to camp and teaching a class in outdoor cookery was one of my first big activities. I prepared diligently. I knew zilch about cooking over a campfire, but the coffee-can beef stew, s'mores and foil-wrapped dinners were a success, more so with the mothers than the kids.

I had partial responsibility for the adult extension clubs the first summer because Ann helped when she could. The second summer I was totally in charge when presenting lessons and workshops. Women brought their pressure cookers to my office to be pressure tested. I was terrified of the whole process and avoided it whenever possible. I won't use a pressure cooker to this day. The old fear of it blowing up prevails.

Each summer the state 4-H Extension staff conducted a week of leadership training for active 4-H members at SDSU. My friend Janet and I, along with others from Lincoln County, had attended two training sessions while in high school, accompanied by adult leaders. Being the adult leader from Brule County put a whole new perspective on that week. Although it was fun to compare ideas and programs with the other summer Extension Agents, my job was to keep track of the girls under my supervision. I failed! The second night, three of the girls left the dormitory using the fire escape as a means of egress. I found them missing at the 11 p.m. bed check. I frantically called Melvin, the Brule County Agent, and we called the police. Searching for them was nearly impossible and the police didn't consider it an emergency. We were up all night drinking strong coffee and fretting. Finally, at 5:30 a.m., I checked their rooms again and someone had let them back into the dorm after they had spent the night in a park with some Brookings boys. Although I felt angry at them, I wanted to hug them in relief. Of course, we informed their parents and imposed stiff restrictions on further 4-H activities that summer. We didn't take a group to Brookings the following year. One girl, the cherry pie baking champion and the bread baking demonstration winner, was allowed to go to the State Fair only if accompanied by her mother. I am glad she was not denied that privilege to show off her many talents.

On summer weekends in the Chamberlain area, Karlene and I and other friends enjoyed wedding dances or shindigs at barn-like halls. Getting hot

Caryl Crozier

and sweaty dancing the polka in non-air conditioned buildings was the norm. In the process of trying to shed a couple of boyfriends, I met the local nine-man football team hero from Plankinton at a dance. He also attended SDSU. He became an on again, off again boyfriend for a couple of years. I wasn't interested in making any serious commitments until Sherm came home from the Army so I could see if there really was something there. This jock was somewhat OK with that arrangement. He was a good dancer, smart, perceptive, an athlete and part of the Air Force ROTC officer clique. He definitely fit the description of a "hunk." He and most guys at SDSU didn't have cars, so dates consisted of studying at the library, campus dances, social and athletic events or coffee at the Jungle, the school cafeteria. I didn't drink or smoke, so I never considered going to the bars. I loved the Friday night sock-hops held in the Union Ballroom. That is where most of my friends hung out.

The first summer, my room was only a block from the United Church of Christ where I went nearly every Sunday. Reverend Koehler, formerly my favorite minister in Beresford, served that church. We always dressed up for church and wouldn't be seen without a hat and gloves. Karlene usually worked evenings. This meant that I ate alone at Al's Oasis west of the river or at the local cafe where I also had lunch alone. We didn't have cooking privileges at the Yates', but we could make toast for breakfast.

My SDSU roommate, Jo, got married in August of 1958, so Karlene and I decided to room together our junior year. We had become good friends and were quite compatible. Karlene was from Kimball in Brule County, and I spent some weekends with her and her five brothers at their family farm. Telling my former roommate, Boots, my plan caused great disappointment for her and she left SDSU to attend Northern State at Aberdeen, SD.

By the end of the summer of 1958 my confidence level was high and Brule County wanted me back the following summer and after graduation. Had I not gotten married, I would have gone back to Chamberlain as an Extension Home Economist on a permanent basis and lived a very different life.

At the end of the 1958-59 school year, I had a couple of days to prepare for another summer in Chamberlain with my little green Ford. The apartment I shared with three teachers seemed spacious and luxurious in spite of the suffocating cigarette smoke from their chain smoking. Fortunately, two of them left after two weeks and I could cope with Shirley's smoking. In fact, I smoked a few cigarettes myself that summer, but quit when Sherm said he wouldn't marry me if I smoked. I guess that was a proposal of sorts!

Hitting the ground running my second summer as an Extension Agent is an understatement. The second day on the job, I judged a "Share the Fun" contest in Wessington Springs with the Healy's, an active 4-H family, and

Waking to Mourning Doves

things never slowed down all summer. I had much more responsibility than the year before. If not working with the local 4-H clubs day and night I was judging in other counties. My diary contains many blank pages from that busy summer.

I took a commercial flight in a clunky two-propeller plane to Dubuque, Iowa to visit Sherm over July 4th for four days. I wore my new pink plaid dress and felt quite sophisticated until the plane hit a bump and I spilled coffee down the whole front of my dress. So much for that false sense of pride!

The week got better, though. After visiting Cassville, Wisconsin where Sherm lived, the Dickyville Grotto, Potosi, local schools, the surrounding river bluffs, Nelson Dewey State Park and the Mississippi River, I thought I wouldn't mind living there. I found the areas where he worked in the bottomland sloughs, lakes and secluded island sandbars fascinating. Well, maybe the company had something to do with that! The weekend visit sealed our fate. We decided to get married a year later and I told my parents my plans when I got home.

The remainder of the summer was a whirlwind of work and a few dates with some leftover boyfriends. It was a varied summer learning to fish, water skiing on the Missouri River, conducting copper craft workshops for adult extension clubs and helping to mastermind Achievement Days for 4-H.

In mid-August, I joined Sherm in Jasper and met his sister, Maxine, and her husband, Jake. We did the usual Crozier thing, having picnics at the Ihlen Dam and visiting the rock quarry. Maxine demonstrated her crow call, which I thought was a little weird. No one can make the screeching call as well as she can. She and Jake both had a great sense of humor and I liked them and knew I could fit into the Crozier family.

In addition to writing a weekly newspaper column in Chamberlain, I also did a few radio shows providing household hints, recipes and 4-H news. When played back, I hated listening to my nervous giggle during the first two broadcasts. Fortunately, I improved fairly quickly and sounded slightly more intelligent. In August I narrated and was Mistress of Ceremonies for a Hawaiian theme 4-H dress review. I gussied up in a grass skirt, with a lei around my neck and laced flowers in my hair. I didn't mind the wolf calls!

That evening, I made what I knew would be a final public appearance as the Brule County Home Extension Agent, a poignant time for me. Someone said, "That sounded like a farewell speech." It was.

August 29, 1959 was my last day of work in Chamberlain. My parents picked me up in their new Nash Rambler for a seven-day trip to the Black Hills of South Dakota. We did the full tour — Mount Rushmore, Custer State Park, the Needles, the Spearfish Passion Play, Deadwood, the Homestake Gold

Caryl Crozier

Mine — and then came home via Pierre and the nearby Indian reservations. My parents proved to be fun to travel with and Dad even rode a chairlift with me at Harney Peak, when Mom refused. I enjoyed traveling with them numerous times after I got married.

CHAPTER **26**

Contusions and Crutches

Ringing in the new year of 1958 in the emergency room of a hospital was not my plan.

> *December 30, 1958–Clark, Gerald and Lloyal all called for a NY date and turned them down as I promised Gary. Damn!*

> *December 31, 1958–Accident- torn tendons in my foot plus stiffness, sore muscles and a locked jaw.*

News Year's Eve of 1958 became a disaster when I was in a car accident as a result of a poor decision on my part. Four different guys asked me for a date that evening and I went with the first one who asked, thinking that was the proper or courteous thing to do. My date told me that we were going to a dance in Beresford. After getting in the car and before I could object or control the situation, we were driving through thick fog to Sioux City to pick up the driver's brother. The two guys were drinking whiskey and tried to force me to drink too, which I refused to do. Consequently, I had already decided to leave them at the bus station where we were picking up the other fellow. I planned to call my Uncle Ragnar who lived in Sioux City to ask him to come and get me. Unfortunately, before we got to Sioux City, we crashed into a car that was stopped in the fog on the highway. Bob, the driver, somehow ended up in front of me before we crashed, and he got a deep cut on his leg from the gearshift. I had time to brace my foot on the floor before we crashed, so didn't get flung forward. My date's head went through the windshield. He was pretty badly cut up and bleeding. The guys quickly threw the whiskey bottle into the Missouri River before the police arrived to take us to Methodist Hospital – a fortuitous location for me because Ragnar's wife, Wave, was the Director of Nursing there.

I called Ragnar and they rushed to the hospital. Wave knew just what to do to get me x-rayed and seen by a physician. The doctors found nothing broken, but I had torn tendons in my foot with severe contusions. I spent the night at Ragnar and Wave's house thinking I was in pretty good shape. Their rum eggnog might have helped! They took me to the hospital the next morning because the pain in my leg had become unbearable. My jaw was locked for a couple of days, so I consumed a lot of milkshakes and couldn't talk much.

My leg was bruised from toe to thigh and totally wrapped, so I remained in the hospital a few days. I hobbled around on crutches for two weeks.

Youthful experiences like this can come back to haunt you later in life. This horrible experience was bad enough when I was 20, but at age 65, the old injury led to knee replacements, and the tendons in my injured ankle are still weak.

January 12, 1959–Got back to classes and got tired of explaining what happened.

January 15, 1959–10 degrees below zero, so I hired a taxi to take me to class at the Ag building

When I returned to college after the Christmas break, I had a difficult time getting to class on crutches. Sometimes I took a taxi. Dad gave me money and insisted that I do that. Negotiating snow, ice and long flights of stairs about did me in.

January 20, 1959–Got bandages off and my leg and foot is cracked and blistered and black- a mess.

My accident garnered a lot of sympathy from boyfriends that spring quarter. Juggling several of them, they sometimes saw each other coming and going. With one of them, I worked on a campaign to elect his friend as the president of the student body. He had great friends and family near Beresford, all of whom I met. Both of us frequently had family celebrations on weekends in the Beresford area, and we attended them together when we were at our parents' homes for the weekend. He was the personification of nice, and not bad looking either! I think my parents hoped our relationship would become serious and that I would spend my life on a farm near Beresford. Not to be!

My junior year of college before and after the accident went smoothly. Karlene and I became roommates at Development Hall, and I had more classes related to my chosen field. Chemistry was behind me and even Bacteriology, Economics and Educational Psychology didn't seem so bad. Speech was tolerable. My instructor encouraged me to take public speaking. I had gained confidence in that area having done it all summer as an Extension Agent.

Sewing classes were always my strong point and I looked forward to Flat Pattern lab sessions with Miss Rosenberger, my favorite teacher. We took body measurements and made a pattern from scratch. I designed a basic dolman long-sleeved, fully lined black wool dress. I was very proud of that dress and it looked good on me. In Tailoring class, I designed and sewed a turquoise skirt, and coat with matching blouse and lining. I wore that outfit

Waking to Mourning Doves

for many years and knew the color flattered my blonde hair. Those, and a few other special garments, still have a home in my cedar chest.

Seven to eight hours in classes, plus three-hour sewing and foods labs, didn't leave much time for studying or a social life. I was exhausted by the end of the day. I got elected dorm vice president and counselor and also took an active role on the board of Westminster Pilgrim Fellowship (WPF), chairing a committee now and then. I joined Kappa Delta Pi, an educational sorority, and continued with chorus and Home Economics Club. By the end of the year, I was initiated into Phi Upsilon Omicron, an honorary Home Ec sorority.

Weekends always included going to dances, church and maybe a movie, library or coffee dates. My friends liked to eat Nick's hamburgers smothered in onions or chicken-fried steak at Mike's downtown. Pure grease, but it tasted great and both cafes were always packed with college kids. We usually ate healthier food on campus. Karlene and I always got up to trudge to the Jungle cafeteria for a good breakfast.

Many students were given the opportunity to work part-time on campus. For two years I answered phones at the dorm as a receptionist. "Doing bells," it was called. I had also saved a bit of money from the summer job, so I could help pay tuition.

> *June 10, 1958–Candy and I had a steak fry at Newton Hills- Mother-Daughter tea at church- everyone wondered who Candy was and she announced that I was to marry her brother.*

I continued to write to Sherm while he spent 18 months in Germany. I visited his parents several weekends. Sherm's 13-year old sister Candy liked to visit me in Beresford and took her role in her brother's courtship process seriously! Candy and I had a steak fry at Newton Hills State Park, and she loved exploring the farm and giggling with my mother. Much to my surprise, she announced at a mother-daughter banquet in Beresford that I planned to marry her brother. It was not certain to me at that point, but it was to her!

In December Sherm sent me a Voigtlander 35 mm camera and a navy wool sweater. I think that time he also sent a Wedgwood cup, Hummel figurines and a beer stein at my request. Prices at the Army Post Exchange (PX) were quite reasonable.

Spring classes kept me pretty busy. I liked the biological sciences much better than the physical sciences and graduated with a minor in science, just short of a double major. Some nights I studied until 3:30 a.m. and woke up at 5:30 a.m. to study again before big tests. End-of-term exams usually fell on the same two, stressful days.

Family Health, Children's Clothing, Tailoring and Foods and Nutrition classes were pretty intense. Our daughters, Michelle and Cherise, and grandchildren, Rachel, Claire and Nate, eventually wore outfits I had made in Children's Clothing. Michelle wore a blue-check smocked dress for a 1961 Christmas card photo and a yellow embroidered eyelet dress for her February 1962 baptism. The boy's blue suit jacket and short pants were on reserve for all family pregnancies. I had to search for it when Nate was on the way. He wore the outfit in a 2007 fashion show.

Sherm left Germany by troopship on April 8, 1959 and arrived in Brookings April 23, a long anticipated reunion. We shared experiences from the past year and a half and decided chemistry still existed between us. We continued to see each other as much as possible until he left for a new job as the Refuge Manager of the Cassville, Wisconsin District of the Upper Mississippi River Wildlife and Fish Refuge on May 31.

I distinctly recall an April 24th dinner date at the Ihlen, Minnesota Glass House supper club. I wore a flattering turquoise dress and black patent heels. Sherm thought I looked like some of the sophisticated European women he had seen in Paris, London and Rome. He seemed shocked and said, "Wow!" when I walked into the room. Yes, I had grown up.

CHAPTER 27

Mapping My Future

Before school started in the fall, Sherm, Ella and I drove to Cassville to spend the week at his rustic river cabin on Jack Oak Slough south of town. We were quite interested in being alone, so didn't include Ella in all of our activities. I know she got very lonely being our chaperone, but understood. One time, we returned to find her in tears. On all of my visits to Cassville, I stayed at the local game warden's house or had a chaperone along.

On one day of that visit, we drove to Dubuque, Iowa to explore the town, or so I thought. As we headed into a jewelry store, I realized Sherm had another agenda. He later said he wanted to make sure I didn't continue dating others my senior year. We chose a diamond solitaire ring in a platinum band. Short on cash, Sherm bought the ring on the installment plan. Until he paid in full, the jewelry store refused to let him take it. I calculated he would slip the ring on my finger at Christmas.

Karlene and I moved into the new Waneta Hall as roommates the fall of our senior year. What an improvement over the decrepit old Development Hall. A few days after school started, I got my usual fall tonsillitis episode. In my childhood, most kids had their tonsils removed. I was so terrified that my parents never forced me to have the surgery. My leg and ankle had healed from the accident, but walking around campus and other forms of exercise made my foot hurt. The pain and swelling went on for years. Dad let me take the car to college, so that was a welcome relief from walking everywhere on my painful foot.

Courses in Experimental Cookery, Marriage, Comparative Religion, Housing and Methods of Teaching Clothing had me immersed in time-consuming lab classes once again. I didn't go to Beresford very often that fall and winter and needed a place to relax away from school. My Aunt Alice and cousin Verlyn lived in Brookings near campus, where Alice taught elementary school. I went to her home often during my senior year. She was an excellent cook and insisted on feeding me the moment I got in the door.

I rode the slow, rumbling train across Minnesota and Iowa several times that year to visit Sherm in Cassville and interview for a teaching job there. Alice drove me to the train station and often picked me up in the middle of the night upon my return. She usually slung on a coat over her pajamas and roared down to the depot. She drove fast whether it was in the town or country.

Sherm drove to Brookings on October 13th. After attending my friend Alice's wedding, he gave me the engagement ring at the old farmstead on the south 80 acres. My parents weren't too happy. Dad thought I'd quit school and get married, his fear from the beginning of my college education. I guess he didn't want his money wasted. But that wasn't about to happen – not after all the work I'd put in!

Sherm and I spent some nice fall days together planning our future. Parting was difficult, so on the spur of the moment, I rode back to Cassville with him driving all night to get there. He made an early morning visit to the Post Office to pick up his pay check, which he used to purchase an airplane ticket for me to fly from Dubuque, Iowa to Sioux Falls via Kansas City. I had parked my car at the Sioux Falls airport before we left South Dakota the night before. It was a flying trip in more ways than one. Then Sherm went on the river to do some wildlife law enforcement work after no sleep and driving all night.

Sherm and I made several rather risky trips that year to be together, mostly on icy roads.

In November, he drove for twelve hours on icy roads to get to Jasper. He drove home again at Christmas and Candy and her friend, Kathy, rode with us back to Cassville as chaperones. They were delighted when we kept sending them off to the movie theater. The girls and I took the train back to Tracy, Minnesota in a blizzard where Sherm's father, none too happily, picked us up.

At the end of January 1960, I went to Minneapolis where Sherm was attending a wildlife conference at the Curtis Hotel. We rented separate rooms so "it would look right." We must have thought his work cohorts would notice and care! He had attended graduate school in Minneapolis and wanted to show me around. I was not too impressed with the long walk to Augies, a rather disgusting bar. Italian food at the now closed D'Napolis Cafe, a Minneapolis tradition, was OK. We did a lot of walking on cold snowy streets, attended Hennepin Avenue Methodist Church and visited the Minneapolis Institute of Arts. I loved the big city and all its sights and sounds and hoped we could one day live there. Luckily it happened in 1966.

February 14, 1960–Cooked a beaver dinner and went to church.

I took the train to Cassville to meet Sherm in February, and we cooked a beaver at his shack on Jack Oak Slough. The local game warden had given him the confiscated animal, although we can't remember why. Many years later, friends told us we smelled really badly of beaver when we arrived at church. Smothering it in catsup and onions didn't improve the taste, either.

Waking to Mourning Doves

I stopped in Winona, Minnesota on a layover on this trip and went to visit Sherm's supervisors. I asked them about his prospects for the future and they must have been amazed at my audacity. I am too, thinking back. The report was good.

Taking the Child Development classes and working and observing at the pre-school nursery school made me wonder if choosing an education major was a mistake. I loved the kids and their interactions, but I knew finding a job in education was much easier in some of the remote areas in which I thought we'd live. I studied diligently my senior year, determined to keep my grade point high enough to graduate with honors.

In February, I taught my first adult education class for our foods labs course and enjoyed it a lot. Maybe that's one reason I chose to teach adult education for twelve years later in life. Wives of students attended the classes on campus and their enthusiasm made it fun, even if it meant a lot of preparation for me. I remember using a recipe that needed red pimento. I removed the pimento from stuffed olives, a frugal technique that I had learned from Mom, and the ladies thought it was hilarious.

March 16, 1960–Interview with Mr. Downer after taking the train to Cassville.

March 28, 1960–Signed and sent contract to Cassville.

In March of 1960, I had an interview with the high school principal in Cassville in mid-March and signed a teaching contract a week later. It seemed surreal, as I was just starting my student teaching internship at Howard, South Dakota. Who knew if I could even be successful in teaching students. It felt like the school board at Cassville was taking a big chance on me. The interview consisted of a few questions from Mr. Downer, after which he sent me to a car body shop owned by a school board member. This guy exchanged a few pleasantries with me and by the end of the conversation, I knew he thought I had already been hired. Strange! A few days after I returned to college, a contract came in the mail, and I signed and returned it. I can't remember actually being offered the job. A brand new school was nearing completion, and apparently they didn't want to offer the current Home Economics teacher the job. She must have been terribly hurt by the board action. Later, we learned that her classes had a very low enrollment and students told me she was not a very good teacher. Maybe the school board had high hopes now for the use of three rooms for Home Ec in the new school with a young teacher.

To get a degree in education from SDSU, we had to complete a six-week teaching internship. Now I had to prove my mettle in student teaching. Karlene and I were assigned to do ours in Howard, under a rather inexperienced teacher. We later learned she didn't like us very much. We shared an upstairs cubbyhole in the home of two sweet older unmarried sisters. They didn't communicate with us much except for a welcome tea, a couple of nights of watching television with them and a farewell in-house picnic.

> *March 23, 1960–my first day of teaching at Howard and I love it – got rapport with the kids teaching freshman clothing and sophomore foods.*

By April 26, being with a class of teenagers was pure pleasure and others told me the students liked me too. My main skills were enthusiasm and a sense of humor, as students of all ages have told me throughout my career. Preparing lessons and tests and then checking and grading papers meant a lot of evening work. I understand how teachers have 60-hour a week jobs. Teaching clothing is a little easier, as it is primarily done in lab sessions. A teacher's main job is wandering around giving encouragement and ripping out seams if the students want you to. Foods and Nutrition, Child Development and Finance took much more preparation and organization to make it interesting to teenagers. At the time, we didn't require as much homework as our grandchildren have now, which seems excessive to me. Kids need time to dream, explore ideas and be outdoors having fun with friends and family. Growing up in the computer age is certainly different from my childhood.

> *April 7, 1960–Moved into the Home Management House.*

The last course required for my Bachelors degree at SDSU was four weeks in the Home Management House. The college maintained two houses to teach us how to manage a household, one on campus for six girls and the other in a suburban three-bedroom home for four girls. I lived in the off-campus house, a typical suburban ranch style tract home with a fenced-in backyard resembling several we later lived in the first years of marriage. I recall a wall of books in one bedroom, an idea we later copied in our home. Cora, our instructor, was an adventurous lady who had lived for a while in India and traveled extensively. She collected beautiful Marghab linens and was instrumental in building an outstanding collection now in the SDSU Art Gallery. She encouraged our interest in travel and the world, and we felt that our house had a lot more fun than the stuffy one on campus.

I was excited about my upcoming marriage, but our instructor and one of the students were divorcées, so they weren't too impressed by my plans. Karlene was still my roommate and excited about a job teaching in California as well as planning a post-graduation trip to Europe.

Each week we were given different jobs as cook, hostess, housekeeper and laundress, shopper and planner. The cooking week was the most challenging. We planned elaborate entertainments and dinners. One morning I hit upon a Scandinavian brunch theme and made ebelskivers, a time-consuming endeavor. Decorations and table settings followed the theme. I served fresh strawberries in 7 UP in stemmed goblets, but can't recall the remainder of the menu. We still make ebelskivers at our home on Christmas morning, now a long-standing tradition.

> *May 7 & 8, 1960–Sherm missed the train and flew home- one day here and gone the next.*

The month of May flew by with wedding planning, sewing and coursework. Finally graduation day, June 6, arrived. My parents and the Croziers attended graduation ceremonies in the Sylvan outdoor theater while Sherm fulfilled his military obligation at a two-week Army Reserve session at Camp McCoy in Wisconsin. After saying goodbye to friends, I felt ready to start my new life.

> *June 6, 1960–I am a college graduate with the whole world to go out and face. I am glad Sherm will be there to hold my hand. I will miss my friends.*

PART VII: NAVIGATING THE RIVERS OF CHANGE

June 24, 1960

First Home — Cassville, WI

Michelle — North Dakota, 1961–1963

Cherise, Michelle & Me — 1966

Michelle, Cherise & Maize — 1970

Croziers & Kinkners — 1978

CHAPTER 28

Just Keep Paddling

"Don't look back, just keep paddling!" were the words of encouragement shouted by my new husband on the last leg of our honeymoon camping trip as we paddled a canoe across a Canadian wilderness lake through a heavy rainstorm, high winds and waves. In looking back, that is pretty good advice for all of life, as was "Love many, trust few, always paddle your own canoe," an entry our neighbor, Hertha, wrote in my pre-teen autograph book.

Weddings in the 1950s and 1960s were far simpler than today's lavish celebrations. Beginning only a few months before the planned June 24 wedding date, we talked with the minister, booked the church and arranged the other details. The receptions in my hometown consisted of fancy sandwiches and cake served in the church basement. Only the Catholics had wedding dances at the Veterans of Foreign Wars (VFW) and that seemed a bit scandalous to the staid Lutherans and Swedish Evangelicals I grew up with.

Friends and family hosted bridal showers in homes and churches and sent formal invitations, unlike the small town practice of today where announcements are put in the local newspapers inviting anyone to come who cares to. Often, women's feelings got hurt if they weren't invited to a shower. Bridal registers at the major department stores are used today, but in my 1960s era, brides received what could be purchased in the local stores, as well as wonderful sets of hand-embroidered or crocheted linens and dishtowels. The dishtowels had Sunday through Saturday embroidered with a housewife's task for the day outlined in cute animals or kitchen objects. Monday was washday, Tuesday ironing, Wednesday shopping, Thursday sewing and mending, Friday cleaning, Saturday baking and Sunday church. So goes the 1950s and '60s expectation of the perfect little wife. It describes my life for the first few years of marriage. A few women worked outside the home awhile before children were born, but in my circles, having a full-time career was frowned upon.

After our engagement in October 1959, I tried on a few wedding dresses at Fantle's bridal department in Sioux Falls. Later, while walking through the fabric department, I spotted a silk organza appliqué leaf design fabric, which I couldn't resist. After paging through the sewing patterns and bridal magazines, Mom and I returned later and purchased yards of this cloud-like fabric for me to sew. Maybe not a smart decision, since my senior year was hectic enough

Waking to Mourning Doves

without adding this task. But what the heck, I was a skilled seamstress and it seemed appropriate to sew a dress for one of the most important days of my life. My basic personality has always been to take on more than I can handle, so I decided to sew all the bridesmaid dresses for Jo, Janice and Candy. I also sewed six ruffled waitress aprons and my entire trousseau including a going away suit with skirt, jacket, pants and blouse, and a white lace and batiste peignoir set.

Throughout the winter and spring of 1960, I completed all the sewing projects on weekends with help from Mom. By April, my dress was nearly completed except for loop buttonholes and covered buttons down the entire back. With all the other details to work out such as wedding invitations, guest lists, flowers, wedding gift registers, plus student teaching and the home management house course at college, I gave in and hired a lady in Sioux Falls to make the buttonholes.

It is the custom for brides to choose the colors to be reflected in the bridesmaid dresses. For some reason, I wanted an all-white wedding, maybe because it seemed more unconventional than the salmon, turquoise and mint green that most brides were choosing then.

I used yards and yards of white organza, making the mid-calf taffeta-lined dresses that I designed for the bridesmaids by combining several commercial patterns. Candy, only 14 at the time, needed a pattern to flatter her smaller frame, and the pattern also needed to enhance Jo and Janice's fuller figures. A challenge, but the bridesmaids looked good with their matching hair bows and daisy bouquets. The dresses each cost $12 and there was enough fabric left over to make the six three-layer ruffled waitress aprons.

I wrote the dress descriptions that appeared in the Beresford newspaper: "The bride was gowned in silk organza over satin. The bodice was fashioned with a scoop neckline and short shirred sleeves. The bouffant skirt featured a chapel train with embroidered organza appliqué. Her illusion fingertip veil was secured to a cap of seed pearls and silk organza. She carried a cascade arrangement of white gardenias. The bridesmaids were attired in white silk organza and carried colonial bouquets of white daisies."

I wanted our wedding to be classy and different from what people were used to seeing and in some ways, I went overboard. My biggest regret in retrospect was in not liking the frothy, ruffled dress Mom selected for herself and brought home on approval. I thought it made her look like a cupcake, and a few days later I went shopping with her to select a slim. navy blue dress that flattered every slim inch of her. I know she had a very simple red dress to be married in, and this choice may have been a substitute for the fancy dress she never had. With maturity (mine) comes understanding, so I made sure she had gorgeous dresses of her own choice for our daughter's weddings.

It still bothers me that although I had already asked Uncle Ragnar and his wife, Wave, to be dining-room hosts, my family influenced me to ask Mom's brother George and his wife Dorcas to do that task. I knew it would hurt Ragnar and Wave's feelings and although I felt closer to them, I acquiesced anyway.

Mom's friend Clara Peterson made our all-white wedding cake and it truly was a tasty work of art. The bride's family usually made the food for the reception, so instead of having it catered, Mom, Aunt Hazel, Matron-of Honor, Jo and I frantically made fancy little rolled and stacked sandwiches with a variety of fillings the morning of the wedding. We made cookies ahead of time and froze them. We also set up all the chairs and decorated the church aisle, pews and basement the afternoon before the 7:30 p.m. nuptials.

Our wedding invitation, as classic and simple as I could find, did not include enclosed RSVP cards, as no one bothered to reply anyway. They just came, invited or not. Our Beresford Congregational Church was small, but everyone got in and there was enough food. The black-tuxedo-clad ushers, Verlyn and Stan, set up extra chairs for people and also filled the choir loft.

In late spring of 1960, Sherm moved into an empty apartment on Main Street in Cassville, Wisconsin, where he was employed. Since the river shack he had lived in came furnished, we decided to order furniture right away so he could settle our new home before the wedding. I had just completed a housing and design course and knew that Early American furniture would blend well with a few old pieces and accessories from my grandmother's home. We shopped in Sioux Falls and decided on the Provincetown maple line, which Sherm ordered and had delivered from Prairie du Chein, a larger town upriver from Cassville. A round kitchen table, four captains chairs, hutch, sofa, chair, end tables, coffee table, harvest bench, bed, dresser and chest of drawers were delivered to his bachelor pad and were waiting when we arrived in Cassville in July. The furniture was good quality and is still being used today.

In addition to selecting furniture, Mom and I chose dishes, crystal and linen, which were registered at Akers, a specialty shop in Sioux Falls. The Maria White Rosenthal china, Merry-Go-Round Franciscan wear, Boda Swedish crystal and Wallace Rosepoint sterling would still be my choice, although we've added stacks of other dishes, crystal, silver and linen over the years.

Beresford's two drug stores sold Fostoria glass, so we received many pieces of Century Fostoria, my pattern, and novelty colored pieces, which are very collectable now. I think Mom enjoyed all the selecting and shopping, as

Waking to Mourning Doves

her wedding in the 1930s Depression years had virtually no celebrations or preparations like ours.

June 1 was my last day of college, and I soon got caught up in a whirlwind of shower and wedding preparations.

My parents would have preferred for us to marry in August so I could spend the last summer with them, but we wanted time to relax and get settled in our new home before my fall teaching schedule began. Long blissful summer days on the Mississippi River beckoned also.

Blood tests were required to get a marriage license, so with growing dread I went to Dr. Nutter in Beresford. He was hopelessly inadequate at finding a vein; after nine tries, he got some blood from the top of my foot. That fiasco has given me a lifelong terror of having blood drawn. I seem to have "slippery veins" and some of the more capable nurses miss and get frustrated.

Brides had trousseaus in the 1960s, which just meant clothing to take on a honeymoon. I recently found my old list of clothing items; it looks like it must have been my summer wardrobe. There were five Bermuda shorts, two slacks, two toreador pants, one pair of shorts, nine blouses, nine sport dresses and nine dressy dresses, eight slips and three nighties. I got busy and sewed a few outfits before the wedding. My trousseau list included three dresses, a black and white checked three-piece going away suit, jeans, Bermudas and three blouses.

The round of bridal showers began right after graduation. I wore my favorite new dress, a blue linen wrap-front with a white collar on June third in Sherm's hometown of Jasper, Minnesota. The shower hostesses designed a gadget corsage that included a cherry pitter, strawberry hucker and fluted pie pastry cutter, a creative idea, and I am still using those utensils 50 years later. During my thank-you speech, I thanked Ella for Sherm. That pleased the lady friends of the Crozier family and earned me points!

A typical bridal shower in the Fifties included a short program of music or readings followed by the bride, both mothers and an attendant opening gifts for all to see and compare to who gave what. Practical gifts of bowls, utensils, linens, electrical appliances and kitchen items made a high pile on the gift table. Since I had given countless readings, piano and accordion solos at showers, it was nice to be the recipient for a change. My aunts hosted a shower on June 10 in the church basement, and it was packed with friends and neighbors.

Package bows kept in a bundle were used as the practice bridal bouquet at the wedding rehearsal. Mom kept my net bag of bows for 50 years in my former bedroom closet at her farmhouse. I still can't bear to throw it out!

On June 14, Janet and her mother, Mildred, hosted a china-themed shower

Caryl Crozier

with my 4-H club friends. Lois and LaVonne hosted a linen shower with high school friends. Hertha and Delores held a kitchen shower June 15, at which groups made fun scrapbooks of my life. It felt great to have the support from friends and neighbors as I started my new life.

Seventeen days after graduation didn't allow much time for me to finalize all the wedding details, bridal showers and trousseau sewing. Since Sherm was working in Wisconsin, I had to book a motel in Sioux Falls, rent a U-haul, order flowers, pose for a bridal portrait, get a blood test and marriage license, finish the sewing projects, write shower thank-you notes, get thank-you gifts, plan the reception menu and organize the setup at church. Somehow, it was all finished by the time Sherm arrived June 21 after spending the preceding two weeks in training as an Army Reservist at Camp McCoy in Wisconsin. He had a six-year commitment as an Army draftee: two years active duty, two years active reserve that included two weeks of summer training, and then two more years without any summer camp duty.

The three days before the June 24th wedding were better, as Sherm was there to give moral and physical support. We picked up the groomsmen's black tuxedos in Sioux City, got the marriage license in the county seat in Canton, met with the minister to go over the ceremony, purchased the last-minute gifts, set up the chair and table arrangements in the church basement, and decorated and held the rehearsal. Ella, Maxine and Georgia Thompson hosted the groom's dinner of salads, hot dishes, cookies and bars at the church after the rehearsal.

The wedding flowers cost $62.73, which seems ridiculously cheap today, but incomes were far less then. My teaching salary was $4300 per year, one of the highest for the SDSU graduates in my field, and Sherm's annual federal salary was $3800 per year at the time.

My gardenia bridal cascade cost $15 with a removable corsage to wear with the going- away suit. The bridesmaids each had $4 colonial bouquets of white daisies. The mother corsages were $3.50 white roses. Aster corsages were worn by Betty Grow, organist; Joyce Tornberg, soloist; Lois Norling, guest book; Dorcas Erickson, dining room hostess; and Maxine Jacobsons and Ruth Hansen, coffee servers. The ushers and groomsmen had white carnations and white asters for a total of $10.

> *June 9, 1960–Joyce's soprano voice is breathtakingly beautiful in a silent church.*

The music at our wedding is not memorable to me now, but I intended it to be different. Most brides chose *I Love You Truly* or *Always*, which were popular at the time. Instead of the familiar strains of Lohengren's *Here Comes* the *Bride* and the common recessional, the minister's wife, Betty Lou, helped me select Henry Purcell's *Trumpet Voluntary in D Major* as the processional along with John Gross's hymn tune called *Praise, My Soul, the King of Heaven.* The recessional was *Psalm XIX* by Benedetti Marcello. Joyce sang *Panis Angelicas.* Reverend Grow sang *The Lord's Prayer.*

> *June 24, 1960–Became Mrs. Crozier at last at the Congregational Church at 7:30 PM. The happiest day of my life – so far.*

The wedding day dawned sunny and beautiful, but I didn't have time to take much notice as Hazel, Mom, Jo and I were making fancy sandwiches, pressing clothes, making floral arrangements, decorating the church and unwrapping a few gifts people had brought to the house. The custom then was to have someone else open the gifts at the church and put them on display for all to see and compare what others gave. My pregnant friends, Leona, Marcene, and Marie, along with college friend Muriel, hurriedly opened ours before the wedding, but I requested they not put the names with the gifts. Unheard of and it frustrated the guests, so many folks later went to Mom's house where she had it all set up with names on the gifts.

On the day of the wedding, the Croziers came to my parent's farmhouse at 4:30 p.m. and lingered a long time. Mom and Dad, of course, acted like the perfect hosts and entertained them and looked at gifts, while I was getting frantic knowing my folks had to milk 12 cows and do all the chores and then take a bath and get dressed in an hour and a half. They made it with five minutes to spare for the 7:30 p.m. wedding time, so I lost the opportunity to have Mom help me dress in my bridal gown, those special mother-daughter moments that I later shared with our daughters. Jo was helpful, but it was not the same. Maxine and Ella fussed with Candy in the cramped dressing room in the parsonage, as she was pretty excited. Of course, my parents should have hired someone else to milk the cows, but everyone was coming to the wedding and didn't want to. As a result, I was on pins and needles and afraid we would have to delay the wedding.

As Dad walked me down the short aisle, I breathed a sigh of relief that we'd put it all together on time! As the processional began, I'd asked for the guests to remain seated, another break in custom. I still smile looking at the photo Oscar Graverson took of Dad and me, with the guests looking startled in the background.

The double-ring ceremony performed by Reverend Roger Grow included a touching homily, but I can't remember a word he said. We should have written and memorized our own vows, but we chose traditional except for the "obey" part. Having communion was a different touch, too. I am not sure why we chose to do that, since neither of us is very religious.

The altar stage of the church became crowded when my dress with hoop skirt took up the space of three people and if I got too close to someone, it flipped up in a strange way. The bridesmaids wore layers of crinolines too, so the four of us full-skirted gals nearly pushed the groomsmen off the altar.

We still remember it as a beautiful and meaningful service. After hugs and congratulations from our guests after the ceremony, the photographer took over and photos of the bridal party were painstakingly arranged. The guests downstairs waited and waited and waited. It became an even longer wait than usual because one of Sherm's rude Army buddies called in the middle of the photography session and they talked for a half-hour. Just what could be that urgent, I'll never know and I get upset thinking about it 50 years later. The caller was a self-centered jerk in my opinion, and Sherm should have refused or shortened the call.

The photographs were very important, as the local newspapers published wedding photos and write-ups. Like obituaries, the style of writing was very distinctive of the era. Our wedding article described the clothing worn and went into great detail as to who did what at the ceremony and reception.

Finally, we made our way to the reception, but the guests were about ready to call it a night and we didn't get to talk to many. Nowadays, the wedding photographers take pictures before the wedding, but in those days it was considered bad luck if the groom saw the bride before the ceremony. How stupid is that?! We barely had time to grab a couple of sandwiches and cut the cake. We quickly looked at the gifts and Sherm pocketed the money, about $50 total which for some strange reason irritated my dad. Granted, we didn't have much money, but Dad got the mistaken notion that Sherm was greedy.

We changed into our going-away clothes, and the crowd prepared to throw rice at us. Since the custom in Beresford was for the local young male friends to steal the bride, we handcuffed ourselves together before we came out of the church. We ran to groomsman Ray Hart's waiting car that would transport us to the Linden Hills Motel in Sioux Falls where Sherm had left his car. The crowd decorated my parent's car thinking we would drive it, and later Mom and Dad drove it up and down Main Street with the usual hoopla reserved for the bridal party. After a two-mile, dangerously fast car chase up Highway 77, when the locals in one car seemingly tried to force us off the road, Ray stopped the car and chewed them out. They shouted "Soreheads!" at us and sped away, not the way I wanted the evening to end, but it was all in fun.

Brides in the '60s wore dresses, hats, gloves and high heels as going-away

Waking to Mourning Doves

outfits, complete with a corsage. Since we were going on a Boundary Waters canoe camping trip, the jeans and Bermudas and swimsuit were necessities. For the camping trip, the white lace and batiste peignoir set I designed wasn't appropriate, so I had black leotards and a coverall nightshirt, which matched one I had made and sent to Sherm in 1958 in Germany. I am sure he never wore his, but half the photos of me taken on the canoe trip are in the red print nightshirt, leotards and yes, the ugly grey tennis shoes from 1957. Well, Sherm said the nights would be cold up north, but with our new zip-together sleeping bags, that wasn't an issue. Blue jeans from high school, a pulled down sailor hat and Sherm's grey Irish sweater and a couple blouses completed my ensemble. Since we had to backpack everything across portages, I packed sparingly. Although we did go swimming, the swimsuit was useless, as we never saw another human for five days.

The morning of June 25th dawned and at last we were married and in the same bed. I devoured breakfast and then went and got my long blonde hair cut off. I wanted long hair for the wedding, but not for a canoe voyage. After a quick stop in Jasper to see Sherm's family, we began our honeymoon trip to the North Shore via St. Cloud and a celebration lobster dinner.

Both Sundays while we were on our honeymoon, we attended a local church service, a Baptist church in St. Cloud and a fieldstone Episcopal Church near Grand Marais, Minnesota. The congregants were very friendly and when asked to introduce ourselves, everyone figured out we were newlyweds.

Driving along Minnesota's north shore of Lake Superior on our way to the Gunflint Trail, we stopped at some of the places we still enjoy: Two Harbors ore docks, smoked ciscoes eaten on the rocky shoreline, Gooseberry Falls and Split Rock Lighthouse, and even the same quaint restaurant in Grand Marais. One habit we picked up on the trip was stopping at a few antique shops. In Detroit Lakes, we spent $15 of our wedding gift money on an antique oak cased clock that chimed the hour. It has kept perfect time as a soft backdrop to our lives and has always been a comforting reminder of time passing. The other habit learned was stopping the car on a dime and backing up on the highway to pick roadside flowers, an activity not always appreciated by the driver! The daisies and lupines still bloom in profusion along those highways.

June 29, 1960–Started from Gunflint Lodge on our canoe trip
– beautiful – my first camping experience is quite pleasant.

The canoe trip, heightened by all the new experiences, was unlike anything I had done before. I had never been camping in my life and I faced it with trepidation.

Years later, while doing a book review of Eric Severeid's classic, *Canoeing*

Caryl Crozier

with the Cree, I compared his 1934 to our 1960 honeymoon trip. By reading my gushy diary entries and then describing the actual conditions, my friends thought it was a comedy routine. Well, in some ways it was.

When we arrived at the outfitter's headquarters, we met Janet, the woman for whom Sherm had worked as a canoe guide the summer of 1956. She gave me the once-over, guessed we were on our honeymoon and observed, "Well, she looks sturdy." Sturdy! That's hardly the image I wanted to project on my honeymoon. At 5'2" and 115 pounds I would have preferred a more flattering adjective.

Sturdiness, though, became a virtue as we packed supplies for a four-day canoe trip in heavy Duluth packs. Lightweight camping gear and freeze-dried foods were unheard of then. One of the pictures shows me hunched over carrying a full pack filled with canned food, cooking utensils, and even an axe handle sticking out. We had to cut firewood to cook our meals. It felt like my pack weighed at least a hundred pounds!

On the Gunflint Trail, we paddled down the Granite River going from lake to lake, where the river flows though fast-flowing rapids between lakes requiring portages. That means carrying the canoe and all the camping gear over rocky, vegetation-tangled trails. Stumbling behind Sherm as he carried a backpack plus the heavy canoe on his shoulders, I didn't want to act like a wimp.

Finally, after paddling and portaging all that first day, we reached our island destination. By this time, I was comfortable in a canoe, but hadn't expected to paddle and portage like an old-time voyageur. But what the heck, I was "sturdy" and determined to prove it. Tucked in our double sleeping bags the first night lived up to the first glowing diary entry.

> *June 30, 1960–Sherm should have been a Home Economics major as he is a good cook. Thunder, hail and rain couldn't disturb us in our cozy tent.*

Sherm demonstrated his skills cooking a variety of meals over campfires. The food was better than I expected. He chopped wood, did all the cooking and clean-up. We used an open-air toilet, which consisted of a stick you sat on that was nailed between two trees. We covered leavings with dirt and leaves.

About midnight on our first night on the island, all hell broke loose, as what seemed like the storm of the century ripped across the lake and our vulnerable island campsite. Strong winds, hail, sharp lightening that seemed much too close, branches falling and torrents of rain pounded our "cozy" tent on the highest point on our little island. I was terrified, but we lived to see another day dawn bright and sunny. Sherm had dug drainage trenches around

Waking to Mourning Doves

the tent, so nothing got wet. There are a couple of pictures we took the next morning that make us look like we had been on a week-long bender. In the pictures there is an odd light around my head that my friends were convinced was a halo, as they thought I was a saint for putting up with all this on my honeymoon. We heard later that many of the other campers returned to the base camp (Gunflint Lodge where the outfitter was located) after the storm, but we stayed out for two more days and enjoyed perfect weather. Exploring the lakes and woods and skinny-dipping was fun and I hated to see it end.

> *June 1, 1960–Caught some fish and spent the afternoon getting the fish line untangled in a shallow place – our last night here has been perfect.*

> *July 2, 1960–Rowed back in the rain - I hated to leave although it felt good to be in a luxurious motel again.*

We paddled back a long distance toward the base camp in a deluge of wind and rain. Going across Gunflint Lake, Sherm kept hollering "Just paddle!" over the rage of the storm. By that time, I finally began to wonder just what kind of life I had gotten into. Prophetic, as many of our later camping, canoeing, and backpacking adventures have been trials of endurance. The most extreme was a 12-day rafting trip on the wild Colorado River through the Grand Canyon. When our daughters got old enough to survive the rigors of hiking and backpacking and accompany Sherm, I was happy to see them off and retreat to a comfy B & B. We experienced many great camping experiences as a family, which are elaborated on in the travel chapter.

The best part of that last stormy day on the canoe trip ended in an all-white, immaculately clean motel room just north of Grand Marais, where we spent the first night. In Bemidji, we spent two nights in a housekeeping cabin with a huge fireplace, also memorable. We had shelter over our heads, but I had to start doing the cooking. My first cooking effort was a breakfast in which I displayed my culinary skills serving pancakes that were raw in the center and fried eggs with broken yokes.

It didn't help when Sherm voiced his opinion of my cooking by dumping his plate of food in the garbage can saying, " I thought you were a Home Economics major." I didn't take offense, as it really was bad and I can't remember if we just abandoned the idea of breakfast or ate out.

> *July 5, 1960–Stopped at Lake Itasca and then went on to Jasper. End of a wonderful trip and the beginning of our new life.*

In the course of one year, I had graduated from college, got married, moved to Cassville, Wisconsin to live with Sherm, taught 9-12 Home Economics and 9th Grade English, became pregnant with and gave birth to our first child, then moved again to Jamestown, North Dakota. Had I known the changes ahead in that eventful year, maybe I'd have just taken a long nap!

Our family treated us to a luxury 50th anniversary package at Gunflint Lodge in 2011. Having a cottage with a hot tub and sauna, a boat with a motor and complimentary meals and massage was a sharp contrast to our honeymoon.

CHAPTER **29**
You'll Be a Cute Mama

One of my senior Home Economics students wrote in my school yearbook, "You'll be a cute mama." Those were the very last words I expected to come true my first year of marriage and teaching. Little did I know that the cavernous black leather purse I bought the summer of 1960 for a trip to Europe would become a diaper bag! My first year of marriage, teaching and becoming a new mother are experiences I remember as if they happened yesterday.

Now, nearly 51 years have passed since our arrival in Cassville, Wisconsin where Sherm got a job managing a district of the Upper Mississippi River National Fish and Wildlife Refuge. I felt overwhelmed entering this new phase of my life.

Why on earth should I feel anxious? I had just completed 16 years of school, engineered a wedding and paddled like a voyageur on our honeymoon. After Mom, Ella and Sherm reupholstered Nan's old platform rocker in Beresford, we packed a small U-Haul trailer with wedding gifts and a few pieces of cast-off furniture, and our new life began.

> *July 8, 1960–Drove to our new home in Cassville. I was sort*
> *of afraid at first. Saginagaw (many puddles) enjoyed the trip.*
> *Love the new furniture.*

At the last moment before leaving home, I must have felt a need for security and familiarity. We chose a female calico kitten from the neighbor's menagerie to accompany us to Cassville. Sherm must have loved me a lot to go along with that, because he hates cats! Saginagaw, later renamed Poo, became an ill-mannered cat that vexed Sherm in every way she could.

I had visited Cassville several times during our engagement, but this arrival felt totally different. Now I had to make it as a wife and teacher.

As Sherm carried me across the threshold of our Main Street upstairs apartment in Cassville, I reached around to turn on the light switch and a stiff furry creature startled my fingertips.

"Awk," I screamed as Sherm unceremoniously set me down to pluck the decaying creature out of the light switch. A bat in our house! Horrors! Chasing live bats with a tennis racket became a frequent activity during our first year of marriage in our apartment located just a block from the river. Bats are not all bad, as the rich bottomlands of the nearby Mississippi river produce hordes

Caryl Crozier

of insects hatched daily and at night marauding bats hold them somewhat under control. Nevertheless. I am still squeamish when a bat whishes by my face.

Upon regaining my dignity after the bat encounter, I was thrilled to see the Provincetown maple furniture we had selected. Sherm had had it delivered and in place for my arrival. We went in debt $1,000, 1/8 of our combined salaries, for a bedroom, living room and a kitchen set. Those were good purchases: we still use that furniture every day.

We settled in quickly, and Cassville is still one of my favorite places in the US. This quaint little river town has just five streets squeezed between the high river bluff and the river itself. It is a very old town that was established early on in Wisconsin history because of its proximity to the river. It became the first capital of Wisconsin. At the time we lived there, some people still made their livelihood off the river by commercial fishing and working on barges that haul products back and forth between Minneapolis and New Orleans. Some could be called true river rats.

July 21, 1960–Have been going on river to help Sherm with duck brood counts and banding them early mornings and late at night.

The summer of 1960 we plied the backwaters of the Mississippi River by boat, enjoying a combination of Sherm's work activities like banding wood ducks and spending long days on the river lolling on the sandbars. Life was good. We made new friends and welcomed visits from our parents. We entertained Smiley Meyer, a farmer and fur trapper who lived in a coulee north of town, as our first dinner guest.

My lifelong passion of seeking and identifying wildflowers began. Flowers grew abundantly in Nelson Dewey State Park on the river bluffs north of town and the river bottomlands. We enjoyed sunny days, wildflower identification book in hand, with a goal of learning the names of every flower we found. We even started a small garden and found a building site near the park. An old letter from Smiley contained an offer to buy the land for us. We didn't take him up on it, but I wish we had. Cassville has become a popular vacation destination with Stonefield Village and the river.

I revamped the lean-to porch of the apartment into a work area to prepare lesson plans and ideas for my first year of teaching Home Economics to grades 9-12 in the Cassville High School. A sense of panic set in by mid-August, when I realized the nearness of my approaching teaching debut. In addition to Home Economics classes, the principal of the school assigned me two classes of freshman English. In smaller school systems in a town of 1,000 inhabitants,

Waking to Mourning Doves

teachers wore several hats. I hadn't taken an English grammar class since high school, so I was a bit rusty.

The school was brand new, so in late summer I was responsible not only for textbook purchases, but for equipping the sewing room with the latest sewing machines and outfitting four kitchen units for teaching foods and nutrition. During the school year, I served as staff advisor to the junior class, supervised the school lunch program, chaperoned school dances and sold tickets at ball games. A pretty busy schedule.

> *August 26, 1960–In service training began- met the teachers,*
> *a motley crew! Some are really odd.*

Coming up with a hook to attract student enrollment for elective Home Economics classes happened by accident. A two-week unit in floral arrangement and design happened when several ladies offered me access to flowers from their gardens. Starting my junior/senior class with a pastime I loved piqued the interest of several students who enrolled when they noticed the enthusiasm of others.

> *August 31, 1960–more girls keep joining my classes- four*
> *today- taught all day at last and enjoyed it.*

Glamelias, a camellia-like flower formed from a gladiola stalk, prompted one student, Janet, to remark. "I didn't know we would do fun things like this in Home Ec. It's not just cooking and sewing."

Fifty years later, Janet wrote:

> *You were the first Home Ec teacher who really taught the*
> *things we needed to know and have used over the years. You*
> *taught us how to arrange flowers and how to make a glamelia*
> *from a stalk of glad blossoms. We cut around each section*
> *of a pineapple sticking toothpicks in it to use as an edible*
> *centerpiece at the Luau we had in Home Ec. And...because of*
> *you, I've always felt confident that if I ever had to deliver an*
> *unexpected baby at some time during my life, I would have*
> *known how, because you covered that also. So, yes...you have*
> *come to mind many many times over the years. And, yes...*
> *you made a difference in my life, for which I'm very grateful.*
> *Thank you.*

After two grueling weeks of preparation and teaching five classes of 20–25 students, I thought retiring sounded like paradise. In spite of planning a trip to Europe in the summer of 1961, we became somewhat lax in birth control.

By October, teaching seemed manageable and the students stimulated me to try new ideas. But it was stimulation from an entirely different source that caused me to add a new unit to the curriculum: A "rabbit test" (a urine indicator of pregnancy) proved positive and my lesson plans did a total reversal. Suddenly, a child development unit emerged, which in retrospect proved timely, as several students were pregnant too. Teaching birth control in a predominantly Catholic community did not prove controversial, nor did it catch on. It was too late anyhow for several of us.

Circumstances soon dictated a reduction in plans for foods classes, as I barfed at the mere thought of food in the morning.

A quip in the school newspaper was silly, but true. Sometimes we did stop in a pretty spot north of Cassville and smooch. "Wanted by five juniors and a sophomore...a parking place that Mr. And Mrs. Crozier haven't as yet discovered. It's embarrassing to park beside your teacher!!!!"

Meanwhile, at home, my morning sickness episodes became more dramatic and miracle of miracles, when I'd mention feeling sick, Sherm ran to the bathroom and threw up on several occasions. Talk about empathy! Unfortunately, that's all the further his involvement went as my waistline expanded rapidly. In December, Sherm lent me his black suede vest and I instigated a new fashion trend in Cassville. The students suspected, but weren't sure why my vest wardrobe emerged, but by the end of 1960, no doubt remained. I appeared the rest of the year in my two-piece smock outfits.

One student quipped, "Oh, we knew you were pregnant since last November." Well, so much for trying to keep secrets from observant students. Maybe they heard me throwing up in the kitchen area before classes began.

Sometimes women in my era were not allowed to teach while pregnant. I informed the principal of the high school before I was showing, but he had no qualms about my continuing. Maternity fashions had not developed much since the "hide it" attitude of my mother's generation. Slacks were forbidden for teaching, so I made skirts with a hole cut out to fit my expanding belly. A variety of voluminous smock tops covered the hole, but I know the students had a full view of the gap when I stretched to write on the blackboard. Those stretchy inserts were not available until my second pregnancy in 1964. I only made one dress for my maternity wardrobe. Why I didn't sew more than one dress I'll never know.

Aside from the incidents mentioned, being pregnant barely affected my first year of teaching, but my presence in the school did prompt some changes. Teachers gathered in the smoke-filled teacher's lounge, and the male teachers expected me, as the Home Ec teacher, to make coffee and clean the cups and coffeemaker each day. Since I detested smoke and didn't drink coffee and never used the lounge unless required, I refused. They were shocked. Being a

Waking to Mourning Doves

servant wasn't in my playbook! The only other female teacher acquiesced and fulfilled the traditional role. My campaign against smoking and second-hand smoke had begun. I like to think Michelle listened to this passion while in the womb and made it hers in the 21st Century as she worked on her career and PhD on anti-smoking issues.

I loved teaching, and my students inspired me every day. Keeping ahead of the English grammar portion sometimes required a quick session with the senior English teacher, but I muddled through. One student asked me why diagramming sentences with parts of speech was important. I can't recall my answer, but we kept scratching on the blackboard.

Since I enjoyed nursery school classes and labs at college, my senior students and I planned a two-week morning day school for community kids less than five years of age. We set up a variety of play stations and educational experiences for the children, and the whole school got interested and drawn into our experimental project. Parents wanted it to continue for the remainder of the school year, but we had to move on.

Sometimes all the new challenges of my first year of marriage and career overwhelmed me, but in the end being together energized Sherm and me in countless ways. He distinguished himself in his career, and I realized my goal of becoming a successful teacher.

Both of us joined in the life of the community. Sherm wrote a weekly newspaper column and led a Boy Scout troop. I joined a bridge club and a teachers' wives social group. We were active in the Methodist Church and attended social gatherings. I remember thinking if only Sherm made $10,000 a year we would be rich and I could be a stay-at-home mom. We made a little over $8000 in combined salaries in 1960 – just enough to cover basic expenses .

Poo, our kitten, grew into a feline with no manners whatsoever. While we worked, she had the total run of the house. Her favorite napping spots were in the middle of the table, on Sherm's chest between his book and face, or wrapped around our heads at night. Awful! Sometimes we threw her out of the bed, but she jumped right back. We did not have a door to close to our bedroom. She whined if we shut her in the bathroom, so we just gave up. Poo perched on the arms of our captain's chairs and tried to grab food from our fork while we ate. In the spring she came in heat and to avoid the loud caterwauling of tomcats on our outside porch and her weird behavior, we just opened the window and let her come and go. What were we thinking! We certainly knew about the birds and bees by this time. Of course, she got pregnant and became an amazing hunter. She caught frogs, mice and once a

Caryl Crozier

brilliant red cardinal. I think we both secretly hoped she would wander off, but she continued bringing her catches back to our apartment to devour.

Much to Poo's dismay, Bart Foster, a wildlife employee, gave us a Golden Retriever puppy the fall of 1960. Poo hissed and scratched and arched her back at him, but he seemed to love her in spite of her crankiness. Sherm built an outdoor kennel for Torg, so we didn't have two pets in the house. After that year, we never had pets in the house again. I swear we find Poo's cat hair after 50 years!

The year passed quickly and I was eager to meet the new life inside me. The baby's first flutterings felt like butterfly wings brushing my skin. Later, the legs and elbows felt more like a gentle jackhammer! I loved to rest my arm on my belly while teaching, knowing that my baby was listening and maybe learning too.

We bought a few items for a layette: gowns, receiving blankets and booties. Doctors didn't perform ultrasounds, so we didn't know the sex of the baby. I wanted a girl so I could call her Michelle Ann, but we had Scott Edward in mind just in case. Fortunately, my Home Ec students turned a Hawaiian banquet we prepared for their mothers into a surprise baby shower for me. They inundated me with things pink: dresses, gowns, blankets and booties and said they hoped I'd get my little girl. I never doubted that we would.

Our baby was due on the last day of school. Good timing. Right on cue, the labor pains began that evening and we excitedly timed the intervals and drove to the hospital in Dubuque, Iowa, 30 miles away. Shortly after the nurses got me prepped and the doctor arrived, the pains stopped. Nurses suggested we go to a movie and relax and see what would happen. We saw *101 Dalmatians*. The song *Cruella de Vil* saturated my brain through three days of false labor after we went back home.

In the midst of this entire false labor trauma, Poo gave birth to four kittens. She had gotten outside a couple of months before and apparently became promiscuous. She made her nest in Sherm's sock drawer and jumped out and squalled as each kitten was born. I watched in fascination and horror.

Soon after Poo was contentedly nursing her kittens, four days now since my labor pains had first occurred, I knew we needed to head for the hospital again. Doctor David was in Lancaster, Wisconsin delivering another baby, so we decided to go there. The nurses were shocked to find me already prepped. Mostly, I was embarrassed that the birth was taking so long. Now I know that is normal for a first baby. I snarfed down a dish of canned peaches in the delivery room because I told them I was hungry. I asked for a milk shake too, but didn't get it. Meanwhile, Sherm waited patiently in the very public family room while several men arrived, became fathers and then left for home again.

Waking to Mourning Doves

I am sure the wait seemed as endless for him as it did for me. I know he read all the magazines in the waiting room several times!

Men weren't allowed in hospital birthing rooms in the '60s. How dumb is that? Finally, the nurse showed Sherm a little bundle wrapped in pink. Yes, Michelle Ann had arrived and she was perfection in our eyes. She tells us she is glad she was born in Wisconsin and not Iowa. I don't think she controlled my false labor, but maybe! I guess we are a Midwest family. Sherm was born in Minnesota, Cherise in Illinois, Michelle in Wisconsin and I in South Dakota.

We stayed in the hospital over a week, so different from the 24-hour turn-around now. Nurses asked my age and were surprised I was almost 22. They thought I was 16. No one thinks I look six years younger than my age now.

Sherm was offered a job delineating potholes (wetlands) in Jamestown, North Dakota while I was in the hospital. We quickly accepted because it was a substantial promotion. After a quick visit from Mom and Dad, we packed and left Cassville two weeks after Michelle arrived, a scenario I would not care to repeat.

CHAPTER **30**

Mothers and Daughters

A relationship between a mother and daughter is a slippery slope. Not until a daughter has her own daughter can she understand the dynamics of that relationship. Most mothers want their child to be independent, but feel surprised and frustrated when the daughter embarks on that treacherous road away from Mom. In a heartbeat, Mom goes from friend to foe. I was totally unprepared for this transition.

As an only child, I had a close, almost psychic relationship with my mother. We had an uncanny connection in our adult lives whereby we could sense from a distance when the other was in trouble. For example, Mom was fretting all night in 1972 when Sherm and I were returning from Hawaii on a plane threatened by a bomb scare. I know she felt my emotions telepathically just as I often felt hers. Even though she's gone now, I feel her comforting presence in my life.

I learned how to be a mother from Mom. She gave me the foundation for everything I am today. To me, it meant support, encouragement and involvement in a daughter's activities. Mom provided that by making certain I had every opportunity possible in school, 4-H and social activities. She was a 4-H leader for 11 years and sat by my side as we learned sewing and many new skills together. I tried to do the same to teach my daughters and granddaughters.

Although I gave her grief in many ways, I confided in her and we didn't argue. Eventually, I did what she feared the most: I moved away from Beresford. To put this in perspective, her mother left Sweden at age 18 and never saw her mother again. This wrenching of a relationship must have influenced Grandma to try to keep her daughters close by for a lifetime. She succeeded. I know my parents wanted me to marry a local boy and continue the pattern. My template took a different turn, but like Mom and Grandma, I wanted my daughters to live nearby too. Although we had opportunities to move to advance Sherm's career, we elected to stay in the Twin Cities hoping our daughters would grow to love the area and remain somewhere in the Midwest. Michelle and Scott moved to Atlanta, but Cherise, Bill and the grandchildren live only four miles away. We are blessed.

Through the generations, mothers feel the wonder of cuddling a newborn to our breast as they nurse, a sensation no mother will forget. I felt prepared

Waking to Mourning Doves

emotionally and educationally bringing Michelle home, but having been an only child, I lacked practical skills. Sherm taught me how to fold a diaper. His little sister, Candy, was born when he was twelve years old, so he knew more about caring for an infant than I did. Thanks to Sherm and the Dr Spock book, I muddled through.

Coping with a lack of sleep, piles of cloth diapers to rinse, wash and fold seemed simple after the intensity of teaching, which I gave up to become a full-time mom. I luxuriated in the free time and marveled at each milestone of Michelle's growth: holding her head up, rolling over, sitting up and crawling. Her first real smile was breathtaking. I often sat in the nursery watching her sleep. Rocking a baby to sleep is pleasant, but not always a wise practice. The moment we would put her in the crib, she would wake up shrieking until we rocked her again. Finally we decided to let her cry it out. It was awful. She stood up clutching the crib rail snot-nosed and red-faced with tears dribbling onto her jammies. We learned to cuddle and rock Michelle at other times and never got into the rocking routine with our second daughter.

Unlike today, our babies were started on rice and oatmeal cereals at six weeks with Gerber or Heinz vegetables, fruit and juices soon to follow. Grandson Nate, born in 2006, had only breast milk and formula for six months.

Hanging cloth diapers on the clothesline in sunny, breezy North Dakota and Quincy, Illinois never seemed like a chore. Hearing the birds sing, watching my red dahlias bloom and having an occasional chat with a neighbor made it enjoyable. Michelle played in the sandbox or picked dozens of dandelion bouquets for me as I worked. Our dog, Torg, kept a watchful eye on us from his corner of the yard if he wasn't straining to escape to pursue a bitch in heat.

After surviving a nine-month winter at North Dakota's Tewaukon National Wildlife Refuge, we moved to Quincy in 1963. Cherise joined our family June 15, 1964. She was an amazingly contented baby. I think she knew we all adored her. Church volunteers in the nursery told us they argued over who would hold our beautiful baby. She weighed almost nine pounds at birth and came home from the hospital hungry. With her healthy appetite, she was a chunk at a year old.

My friend Betty, said, " Homely babies often turn out to be gorgeous girls."

I didn't know whether to be insulted or encouraged, but the ugly ducking stage didn't last long. Betty's prediction came true.

Our daughters wrote their first life memories in books for our 40th anniversary.

Michelle writes: My first memory is of being with Grandma Ella in the hospital parking lot. Mom held Cherise up to the window and that's the first time I saw my sister. This was in the days when kids couldn't go inside hospitals. I also remember the smell of paint from that time. Grandma and Dad painted the kitchen yellow while Mom was in the hospital. Another memory from Quincy was getting bit on the finger by the horse in the backyard. I can clearly picture sticking my finger through the fence. Mom, Cherise and I took long walks in matching yellow outfits.

Cherise writes: *My earliest memories are from Bloomington. I remember getting into Mom's powder, and Mom ironing and watching soap operas. I knew all the commercials and songs from WAYL. I liked watching Batman and that was how Mom and Dad helped me measure time- two more batman's till we get to Grandma and Grandpa's. I also measured time by a colored "Ford" piece on the dash by the glove box. We had hamsters under the pump organ and yellow carpet. We had little painted and snapping turtles that we kept in a clear plastic tray. They died and dried up in the sun. I remember bumping down the stairs and sitting under a desk playing with blocks while Mom taught classes in the basement. I cut and pasted at a summer Bible class and thought my last name was Kinkner.*

I loved having two real-life dolls in my life. I spent every minute reading, pretending and playing with them. Luckily, I got to do it again with two granddaughters, Claire and Rachel. Sadly, none of them remember those years under age three, but I do. I like to think I had an impact on their intelligence and values.

The experts say classical music helps brain development and they all had my favorite "long hair" music playing in the background. Michelle and Cherise listened to my old 33-rpm record player and Magnavox stereo player. Granddaughers Rachel and Claire used a DVD player and now we all have iPods. I wonder how my great grandchildren will hear music.

From the time I started to sew in the late 1940s through 2005, my sewing area always had five or six projects in various stages of completion. Flimsy tissue patterns, piles of cotton, blends and knit fabrics cluttered every surface. Although I taught all the girls to sew and made clothing for them, it did not become the passion for them that dominated my life. Rachel spent hours draping fabrics around herself and sorting through my piles of fabric, buttons and laces. Maybe it planted a seed to become the graphic designer she hopes

Waking to Mourning Doves

to be. I know sorting through my grandmother's scrap bags of fabric had an impact on me.

I taught Claire and Rachel how to sew by helping them make fifteen matching bibs and burp cloths and a couple of simple receiving blankets before Nate was born. They whizzed along on my sewing machine like they had been doing it for years. Later Rachel made a layered skirt and to my horror she chose a difficult Burda pattern to make a dress. She learned all the basics of set-in sleeves, zippers and darts and did a great job. I think she will never wear the dress though, like so many first major sewing projects.

Michelle and Cherise have expressed interest in my "take" on their childhoods. If they ever want to discover it in great detail, it is available. I frequently described the girls' activities in letters to Mom. She kept all my weekly letters to her from 1956 to 2009, the year of her death. My letters are boxed in chronological order as are hers to me from 1978. I miss that weekly exchange of letters. Those times come alive again when I select a few to read. The art of letter writing is disappearing with e-mail, texting, Twitter and Facebook. My grandchildren will never see a weekly account of their growing years other than my letters to Mom until 2009.

I had the luxury of being a stay-at-home Mom during our daughters' school years, as our income was more than adequate. Eventually, I taught adult education classes and did some substitute teaching, but in their early years I wanted to be home and involved in the girls' activities.

By using some quotes from our daughters, a glimpse of their childhood is revealed.

> Michelle writes: *Mom made quite an effort for our birthdays. We always had nice parties with the neighbor kids. Mom made cakes shaped like animals. We had great dogs growing up. The first was Maize/ The best times were when she had puppies. They were so cute. We'd play with them constantly dressing them in doll clothes. Dad built a plywood structure in the basement that we decorated with our drawings. The puppies sold for a lot of money at the time. Mom and Dad were serious about breeding our dog with champion lines. I got blamed when Maize got pregnant by Shep, an icky neighborhood dog. When I was mad at Mom and Dad, I'd go sit in the dog kennel and the dogs would make me feel better.*

> Cherise writes: *We spent time at the Kinkner's farm in SD. I will never forget the smell walking into their house and the*

Caryl Crozier

polka dot linoleum floor. Grandma had cinnamon rolls and lots of sweets we didn't get at home.

Michelle writes: *We spent lots of time in the trough in the cow-yard singing and dancing for the cows. They would stare at us and moo. I was quite skilled at mooing back. Grandpa called the cows with a "come bossie" or an abbreviated "c'boss, c'boss.*

There were lots and lots of cats at the farm and they were never taken to a vet. Their eyes were often drippy with yellow stuff. The highlight was finding litters of kittens. Grandma served a plate of cookies at breakfast. She made me mounds bars and I'd eat too much and throw up.

I led Girl Scout and Brownie troops and was a 4-H projects leader in art and sewing. The girls and I learned arts and crafts projects together and they helped me teach children's classes in art. Coordinating transportation to dancing and piano lessons, play dates and all their school activities and sports kept us on the go. As a family, we enjoyed many outdoor pursuits including cross-country skiing, boating, hiking, camping, gardening and travel to name a few.

Michelle writes: *Mom provided guidance throughout all these experiences- which seems like a lot of effort in retrospect.*

Cherise remembers: *The smell and sound of the mimeograph machine that Mom used to prepare for her classes, riding Dad as a horse and sliding down his legs like a slide; he held my wrists in one hand and ankles in the other and threw me onto a bed, Shakeys pizza with the big black furniture, player piano and being able to watch them make pizza through the window, my green and blue polka dot dress and coat, big furry white hats when they started building our house, canoe rides with Dad going quickly and quietly like Indians, making Christmas cookies; candy canes, chocolate wreaths, painted sugar cookies sometimes with a life saver in them, krumkake, rosettes and kringle, stocking stuffers with the Croziers, Barbie dolls and Holly Hobby, 4-H demonstrations and exhibits, demonstrating applehead dolls, hayrides and 4-H talent show, failed Dorothy Hamill haircut, golfing with grandparents, boxes of baby chicks, mud pies and mulberries, houseboat on Rainy Lake, Children's*

Waking to Mourning Doves

and Guthrie Theaters, piano and flute lessons, pep and marching bands and trips.

Michelle and Cherise were both A students and on varsity cross-country ski teams. Both earned letter jackets. One time Cherise called us tearfully asking to be picked up because she came in last at a ski meet.

She wrote: *Mom and Dad's words of wisdom- there will always be someone better and worse than you, a good but hard lesson.*

We were proud of their scholastic and sports awards. We looked forward to parent teacher conferences because teachers always heaped on praise. Turtle sundaes at Bridgeman's may not have been the best reward for good grades, but it was our way to celebrate.

Our parents lived 200 miles from Minneapolis. Visits were frequent and our daughters experienced farm and small town life and a showering of love from both sets of grandparents, who were close friends.

Mom and Ella were the best grandmothers ever and took their roles seriously. They showered Michelle and Cherise with love. They wrote letters, sewed cute dresses and were always available to help out, sometimes for weeks at a time. Ella even took a bus to our home in Quincy and helped Sherm paint most of the rooms in our new house when Cherise was born. She helped with the moving, too, while Cherise and I remained in the hospital. When she visited us, she always offered to clean my oven, a job I hated. I was fortunate to have a terrific mother-in-law.

If our daughters perceived that I was doing something wrong, like forcing them to take swimming lessons, they wrote to their grandmothers for help. Wisely, Mom and Ella abstained from advice to them that conflicted with our goals for the girls.

I can say without a doubt, I loved being a mom. Still do. Sure, there were frustrating days and many, many things I should have done differently. We had our ups and downs and arguments, some due to my PMS, which wasn't understood at the time. Mostly, though, I took on the role of disciplinarian in our family because Sherm and his family avoided conflict and mine didn't. I like to say what I think (often without thinking) and clear the air. That didn't always work, especially in our daughters' teenage years.

We got through the turbulent times, hopefully with minimal damage. I am immensely proud of the strong, independent women our daughters have become.

CHAPTER 31

Country Calico

"Country Calico by Caryl Crozier," a phrase I coined for teaching quilting classes, became my trademark. I like alliteration a lot! The path of arts and crafts activities that led to twelve years of teaching adults was a familiar one to housewives of the 1960s and '70s. Although most women didn't delve into this type of creative activity as heavily as I did, it was an era when women had leisure time, being stay-at-home moms, before the majority of women joined the work force.

My high school teaching career ended in 1961 when Michelle was born, and a new career began: being a full time mom. After seventeen years of attending and teaching school, the unstructured time seemed like paradise. Michelle was a good baby and I had time to try new leisure pursuits. Knitting was first on my agenda, and surprisingly, Sherm was my first teacher. He learned to knit using the pick method during World War II, when school children knit six-by-six inch squares to make bed covers for wounded military personnel. Thousands of children contributed to making quilt-blankets for the soldiers.

With her thick brown hair and big blue eyes, I knew Michelle looked good in red, so I knitted (not purled) and completed the sweater by the time Michelle could sit up by herself. Then I tackled a bigger project, a beige stockinet stitch (knit a row, purl a row) wool sweater for Sherm. The project seemed endless, but it was something I could do while Michelle napped or crawled around on the cold floors of our house in Jamestown, North Dakota. By Christmas 1961 it was finished, and my newfound confidence led me to knit sweaters with more difficult patterns for everyone in the family.

The first challenging sweater for me was a pattern I admired in McCall's Needlework and Crafts magazine. My goal to finish in time to take it on our first big trip to the western US nearly ended in a total disaster. When I had only one half of a sleeve left to knit on this deep olive-green masterpiece, I ran out of yarn. I quickly sent for more yarn, but it wasn't a perfect match. I finished and proudly wore the sweater on our trip, but learned a lesson about buying ample yarn in a dye lot. I still love wearing that sweater.

When we moved to Quincy, Illinois in the summer of 1963, I spent hours knitting but felt ready to learn some new skills. The local YMCA sponsored sewing classes and also offered a nursery school setting for Michelle. I enrolled in two sessions of millinery classes and learned to make frames from buckram to cover either with fabric or plaited straw. Many hats, still in the attic, are used for style shows and teas now and then. In the spring of 1964, a large-brimmed, white linen and straw hat creation balanced my eight-months pregnant shape. In one of my favorite photos, Michelle stood by me wearing a pink fabric- and lace-brimmed hat to match a dress and pouch purse that I made for her.

I made new friends taking the millinery class, and Michelle had playmates in the nursery school. At age two and a half, Michelle was shy and rarely talked to other kids in her nursery school. The last day of the class, her teacher called me in for a conference to inform me that she thought Michelle was retarded. What a downer. I knew that wasn't so, and I've often thought I would like to throw Michelle's summa cum laude degrees and PhD in this woman's face. That same day, I was presented with a much more serious issue: Cherise had positioned herself for a breech birth and didn't seem inclined to move. Dr. Lamburtes pushed on my stomach to reposition her and succeeded.

During the two years we lived in Quincy, I continued to knit and sew and design hats. As a result, I was asked to coordinate a home-sewing fashion show at Vermont Street Methodist Church. We also attended the Unitarian Church, and both churches gave us baby showers for Cherise. We eventually joined the Methodist Church, as we wanted the girls to be raised in a more mainstream church. Now we're all back where I was raised, a liberal Congregational Church.

Several friends admired my knit creations and wanted to learn, so I conducted weekly teaching sessions, marking the beginning of almost 15 years of teaching adults. As I learned to do new things, people kept asking me to teach — so I did.

Teaching adults gave me incredible positive feedback. They were enthusiastic, eager to learn and were there because they wanted to be. Furthermore, I had the skills and enthusiasm to connect and — as they said — inspire. A class never went by that people didn't tell me how wonderful it was, a great ego builder, something that rarely happens in other fields.

When we moved to Bloomington, Minnesota in 1965, I joined a garden club and met Marlene, someone who loved taking hobby classes as much as I did. For a while we could have been cloned, as we looked so much alike it was bizarre. We had the same interests: gardening, sewing and learning every new skill we could. Living in a larger city presented a wide variety of choices in new classes. I took dozens of classes, mostly in new crafts such as decoupage, pressed flower pictures, tole painting, calligraphy, loom weaving, board art, stitchery and scrimshaw. Eventually, my new skills led to my participation in art shows to sell what I'd created, then to the inevitable start of teaching classes for acquaintances who wanted to learn the skills.

The first classes I taught in our home at 171 Maplewood Drive in Bloomington were knitting and decoupage. Several ladies came and worked on projects while Cherise sat nearby looking at her books or putting puzzles together, her favorite activities at ages two and three. The ladies all thought she was so intelligent to do so well at puzzles. She had good language skills, too. Teaching allowed me an outlet, and I could still be home with the girls.

A new sewing fad became the rage in 1967, and I joined the rush of ladies learning to sew lingerie. Whoever dreamed you could sew your own tricot panties, half-slips, peignoir sets, bras, girdles and even swimsuits?! It seemed everyone wanted to learn this new phenomenon and before I knew it, friends and neighbors asked me to teach them, and my three-year teaching marathon began.

In downtown Minneapolis, the Munsingwear Company had a remnant room where we purchased tricot by the pound or yard. They were manufacturing high quality lingerie as well as knit items such as t-shirts and golf shirts. Bins of fabric left from the manufacturing process enticed thousands of home sewers to dig through the tangled assortment of very inexpensive, but high quality remnants.

When the harried clerks measured a yard of the 102-inch wide nylon tricot fabric hung on bolts, you always got at least one and a half yards for your $2. They didn't have the time or inclination for accuracy. I dragged Michelle and Cherise along on Munsingwear trips to buy a carload of fabric, lace and elastic. Sometimes I put tricot, lace and elastic together in kits for sale to students, primarily for the Beresford people when I held classes there. Mom had a little business going for a while, but we never intended for it to be a store. Years later when cleaning out her house, I found a suitcase full of fabric, elastic, and a red plastic purse with change for her sales. I think Mom enjoyed her business venture as well as sewing gifts of lingerie.

Teaching a lingerie class in Beresford ultimately resulted in the purchase of a new Bernina sewing machine in 1969. I had purchased a beige Singer model with my Home Economics teacher discount soon after we were married in 1960, but when Dad carried that sewing machine out to the garage to load it into the car, he accidentally backed over it, dragging the tension knob and face of the machine over rough gravel. Needless to say, it didn't work for me to do my usual demonstrations on. Fortunately, I had samples of every stage of construction to bring along. Dad felt terrible about it and paid to have it repaired, but it never functioned well, so I purchased my dream sewing machine – a Bernina, which I still have.

Waking to Mourning Doves

The Bloomington neighbors didn't complain about the cars lined up on the streets to take my classes, but they must have found it irritating. I'd always had a coffee klatch relationship with them and they tolerated it.

Most of the ladies were considerate while in our home for classes. At first I allowed them to smoke, as that was the social etiquette of the time. The last straw came when one lady flipped her ashes on our gold carpet. I plunked an ashtray by her and announced there would be no smoking in my classes from now on. I am sure she felt embarrassed, but she kept coming to the remaining eight sessions.

My students brought rolls of brown paper and copied patterns for the garments I taught. I chuckle every time I remember my friend Jan J, 8 ½ months pregnant, on her hands and knees on the floor tracing around patterns. Her belly almost touched the floor!

Several demonstration lingerie items always hung on the basement walls for display, so I suppose it must have looked like a bordello to the young telephone repairman who came one afternoon to do some repair. I went downstairs to show him the problem phone and he started coming on to me, maybe thinking the lingerie all over was an enticement. When I realized what was happening, I quickly explained that I was teaching classes in sewing lingerie and he did a quick retreat from that pursuit!

I sewed lingerie for gifts to family and friends. I made Sherm's mother a bright red peignoir set which she loved wearing. She always said if there was a fire at her house, she'd hurry and put the peignoir robe on so the firemen and everyone could admire it. Mom's response was quite different. She never wore hers, as her tendency was to save everything "for good." I designed it in 1969 and I found it hanging in the back of her closet in 2007 unworn. A friend modeled it in a vintage fashion show. Now I look at some of those garments I made and am amazed at how well done they are, something I no longer have the dexterity to do.

After building our new home in Burnsville, Minnesota in 1970, it took a few months to decorate the house and become integrated into the local community. The first order of business for me was placing my sewing machine in front of a large window with a spectacular view of the pond. Time flew as I spent some of the happiest times of my life gazing out the window as the seasons changed. In the spring, the robins nested outside the window and we looked right into their nest. Summer rains drenched the woods, and I loved sewing with the windows open listening to the rain and smelling the freshness. Fall colors were intense with the variety of oak, basswood, birch, cottonwood and ironwood trees in our back yard. Sometimes flocks of wood ducks descended on the lawn to harvest the acorns as Maize and Caper watched from their outside kennel. Winter snows made a perfect backdrop for the colorful cardinals, purple finches, woodpeckers, blue jays, nuthatches, gold finches, and chickadees outside my panoramic window.

My sewing room always resembled a disaster area with patterns, fabrics and sewing notions and paraphernalia strewn about. I created best in what appeared to others as chaos, with multiple projects going on at once. I liked the adage that creative people never have neat workspaces.

Since I had been one of Michelle's Brownie Girl Scout leaders in Bloomington, I continued as an assistant in her new troop at Orchard Lake Elementary School in nearby Lakeville. Then I led a troops of girls by myself the next few years, mostly girls from our neighborhood. They were a great bunch of girls, and we had fun doing craft projects as well as exploring the Burnsville parks and natural areas. One project they especially remember was picking cucumbers from my garden and making dill pickles. An easy task, but one they'd never experienced. The girls were into earning merit badges, and Michelle earned a whole sash full.

We made several visits to the Faribault State Hospital to visit severely retarded older men. We were told they were the group most in need of visitors. Sometimes some of the girls' mothers went along to drive; they were hesitant, while the girls jumped right in and related to the residents with ease. We also visited nursing homes with the same results. I hoped the girls were learning empathy for people with disabilities.

Michelle and Cherise joined the Sky Blazers 4-H Club, and eventually the leader recruited me as an assistant leader to work primarily in arts and crafts and sewing projects. This eventually led to my training with the University of Minnesota Extension staff learning new skills at the workshops and retreats they presented. I didn't it realize then, but this trained me for classes I would later teach in adult education at the General Mills Betty Crocker Creative Learning Center in Edina and in community education programs for the next ten years of my life.

Board art was the first adult education class I taught in our Burnsville home. The technique was to wet strips or chunks of newspaper with wallpaper paste and make three-dimensional shapes of fruit and vegetables to stick on a board. Celery, strawberries, grape clusters, carrots and baskets with strawberries or flowers rose from the newspaper goop. The plaques dried and were covered with gesso, acrylic paint, varnished, antiqued with black walnut oil stain and varnished again. Boards were weathered scraps of plywood or pine left over from building our house. The Jasper lumberyard, scene of many of Sherm's boyhood adventures, was also a good source of scrap lumber. My father-in-law, Ed, was always helpful in finding wood treasures to work with.

Waking to Mourning Doves

About the same time, I learned tole painting with oils, so now I had an excess of board art, tole painting and decoupage, which I began selling at art shows: mostly sidewalk events sponsored by various communities. Sherm built me a wire display frame of turkey wire and pine boards, and when he was available he helped me set up the display at shopping centers such as the Burnsville and Southdale Malls, the Uptown Art Fair, Murphy's Landing in Shakopee, other street fairs and the Dakota County Fair. He also helped distress (make them look old) and sand off the edges of 16 X 20 decoupage we sold for $15 each. We thought it was a big deal when we sold a $15 picture! Michelle and Cherise often went along to help, and they sold some of their own craft creations: quilled snowflakes, Christmas decorations and paraffin-covered soap. Dried wild flowers/weed bouquets also sold well, as did hollowed out brown eggs nestled in wisps of straw in antique frying pans or baskets.

Sometimes I shared a booth with friends: Sharon and her beautiful watercolors and oil paintings, Lee with her brass rubbings and Jan with her paintings or board art. Mostly, we worked hard lugging heavy boxes around and setting up the display tables for endless hours of selling (or not). We worked the art show circuit for four years. One time the girls got bored and swung on the station wagon car door and broke it. Interest was waning for all of us, and it was time to move on to something new.

Teaching classes in our home was not something I wanted to continue, as the layout wasn't as conducive as at the Bloomington house and I grew tired of the hassle of setting up and cleaning up. Adult community education started coming into its own, so I began teaching decoupage in Lakeville adult programs, which eventually led to offering other craft classes in Apple Valley and Burnsville. Most of these classes were offered at night when Michelle and Cherise were home, so I began to explore other options. Edina closed an elementary school, which then became available for community education day classes. Burnsville got in the act, too, and started using churches for day classes.

About this time, the Betty Crocker Creative Learning Center was established and offered daytime classes. After a brief interview they signed me on, and I started teaching there several days a week until it closed in 1979 when the Control Data Corporation bought it to slowly convert it to a computer education center.

Teaching during the day was a good vocation for me, as it allowed me to be home when the girls got home from school and spend the evening with the family. Coming up with new ideas for classes could be exhilarating, but also time-consuming. Reading letters that I wrote to Mom during the 1970s, I couldn't believe all the projects I worked on.

Caryl Crozier

Just as I had made samples for lingerie classes, I found myself at the beginning of the latest fad, women learning to quilt. Under my Country Calico umbrella, I introduced spin-off classes such as Calico Purse and Tote Bags, Patchwork Purses, Quilts and Other Comforts, Holiday Wreaths, Christmas Stockings, Strawberry Patch, Old Fashioned Dolls, Christmas in July, Placemats, Calico Chickens and Wall Hangings. Students learned the basic quilting techniques of patchwork, appliqué and trapunto by doing small items, which gave them confidence to attempt more complicated projects. The highlight of nearly every class I ever taught was "show and tell." By sharing what they'd created, the ladies inspired one another and me and we all worked a little harder on the next project. By their pride in their own work, they deemed me wonderful too.

In the 1970s, the popular television miniseries "Roots" made researching family history popular, and we began doing some genealogy research ourselves. Because of my interest in my Swedish heritage, I learned to make Swedish straw and wood curl ornaments, which I ended up teaching along with Scandinavian Crafts and Customs and Swedish Christmas trees.

I enjoyed teaching a macramé mini-class in which the students made a plant hanger in one session. That led to other fiber art classes such as coiled basketry and circle weaving. Control Data sent me to Bermuda for a week in the late 1970s to teach those classes to the wives of their best salespeople. Sherm went along and it was a fun vacation as well as a bit of role reversal —pride on my part to be the spouse taking the other on a business trip. The ladies chose my classes over bonsai, the other course, much to the consternation of the meeting planners who had shipped so many expensive bonsai plants to Bermuda. Finally, they forced the ladies to take the bonsai, and I added extra classes so they could do both.

I learned various weaving, puppet and craft techniques in Extension workshops, which I relabeled in a class called Crafts for Kids ages six through twelve. Michelle and Cherise helped me teach the workshop class at the Creative Learning Center. We had puppet shows, lots of circle frame weaving and various methods of printmaking. Some of it turned into greeting card workshops for Christmas and Valentine cards for adults, in which we did instant batik, linoleum block printing, ammonia paper printing, brass rubbing and vegetable styrofoam printing.

Sculpture with natural materials led to apple-head, dough, soft sculpture and cornhusk doll classes. When you peel and sculpt an exaggerated face on an apple, it will dry into a wizened face in a few weeks. By adding padding and clothing to a wire body, delightful apple-head personalities emerge. Our daughters sometimes used the ideas for 4-H or school demonstrations.

The Bloomington schools hired me to do in-service classes titled Expressive Arts Workshops for teachers working with students four through eighteen. The five main topics were puppets, sculpture, weaving, fibers and print processes. I came up with the term "happy accidents" — a surprise effect as a result of the fun of creating that began each session to get everyone in a creative mood. Materials used included inks, sand, crayons, seeds, smoke, plaster, paper and paint. I can't recall just what we did, but this icebreaker required no talent. So many students are reluctant and say they aren't creative. This took the pressure off.

Wildflower identification and propagation and pressed-flower pictures became a favorite pastime for me, so naturally I ended up teaching wildflower workshops, which included pressed-flower pictures, potpourri, parchment stationery and sometimes quilting wildflower designs. We put together a wildflower photography slide series and I taught identification and cultivation, too.

Teaching quilling (the art of curling strips of paper to make snowflakes and other tree ornaments), cards and embellishments landed me a small feature in a Christmas Redbook article. I learned to do quilled snowflakes from a lady in Jasper, Minnesota, and it became one of my most popular classes.

Michelle made and sold many quilled white snowflakes at art shows. We hung them on windowpane dividers and on Christmas trees and gave them as gifts. Mom enjoyed quilling and made floral pictures as well as cards and ornaments. Her Friendly Hour Club often did projects I'd shown her, and I used some of their creative ideas, too.

During those years features of me appeared in many newspaper articles like "Quilting Is Tradition For Local Folk Artist," "Creativity Spills From Her Fingertips," "Family Oriented Program Cited by 4-H Leader," "Preserving the Past in Burnsville," "Resident Starts Business Based on Every Day Hobby," and "Folk Artist Vocation Bridges Past and Future."

I enjoyed the publicity and someone said, "Your name is becoming as familiar as Betty Crocker, the General Mills icon."

These were happy and stimulating years for me and certainly the most fun and satisfying job I ever had, but after 12 years of intensity and creativity, I was ready for change and something that earned more money, as well as job security.

In the 1970s, I did some substitute teaching in the Bloomington School system and turned down an offer of a Home Economics position, because I didn't want full-time work while the girls were still at home. Besides, teaching 7–12th grade students was more of a grind and not as rewarding as working with adults who were there because they wanted to be.

Creating original designs, an integral part of teaching my Country Calico classes, presented a new opportunity. Tea cozies, appliance covers, purses, tennis racket covers, and placemat patterns were given freely to my students. A strawberry placemat and potholder pattern was the most popular one. A student said she'd like to go into business with me marketing my designs. She had strengths that I lacked, so we agreed to give it a go. First, I needed to design more patterns and then we looked for ways to expand. I spent hours designing patterns for fruit placemats including an apple and a pear, in addition to the strawberry placemat which I refined. They came in four sizes —dinner, luncheon, potholder and coaster. During this time, my "partner" contributed nothing and never found time to help or meet with me. The only time we met was the night of Michelle's swimming award banquet, an event I still regret missing, but it opened my eyes. She was only interested in counting the money she thought we'd make, but was not willing to expend any capital dollars or help with designs or ideas for marketing. Some partner!

After an hour of discussion, we parted ways and I decided to go ahead on my own and market the patterns in fabric stores and by mail order. My Home Economist friends were willing to critique the patterns and instructions and participate in my amateur attempts at market research. I hired a professional photographer for the pattern photos. My friend, Sharon. developed my "Fence Post" logo. Having 1000 patterns printed along with photo brochures was a risk, but worth a try.

I met with distributors and placed ads in Decorating and Craft magazines. Soon my patterns were in 50 stores throughout a six-state area. I had a thriving mail order business and needed a second printing. I hurriedly designed more patterns: lemon/lime, orange/blueberry, a Christmas bell and tree and then just a potholder-only set. By now my market needed expansion, so when we were on a trip to Florida with our daughters, I stopped and ripped the fabric-store pages out of the local telephone books to get addresses. The Internet had not been invented yet! The girls still chide me for this as teenagers are wont to do, but those addresses resulted in expanding pattern sales.

Pattern sales went well for a while, but it wasn't much fun for me dashing to the post office and handling the bookkeeping aspect. I also sewed and sold samples for store floor-displays to market the patterns. Fortunately, sales reached a saturation point and began to wane as I lost interest in the whole project. I much preferred the interaction and inspiration from teaching. Many patterns were sold in my classes, but I ended up with boxes of pattern inventories and probably never cleared more than a few thousand dollars.

All in all, it was a good experience and in some ways prepared me for a career I'd never even dreamed of – becoming a long-term care facility administrator.

CHAPTER **32**

Wood Ticks, Woodcock and Wildflowers

I am happiest when planning and executing changes in my surroundings. This compulsion to remodel and redecorate goes back as far as I can remember.

Maybe it all started in early childhood making mud pie playhouses. Or maybe I liked getting friends' compliments when I plastered my walls with movie star pictures and had strange collectables like rocks and feathers cluttering the room.

Mom always got into a frenzy of spring and fall housecleaning, which usually meant a fresh coat of paint or new wallpaper. Coal furnaces that stain the walls necessitated this ritual. She let me help select the wallpaper, paint colors and furnishings for these projects, but I never wanted to help with the actual work of applying it.

My parents remodeled a house when I was 13, and I assisted the carpenters and family by fetching tools or supplies. I struggled with the laborious job of stripping old paint and varnish off the wide oak woodwork that I wanted for my room. Mom helped me, but the smelly task is probably why they replaced the vintage woodwork with cheap pine.

I learned decorating basics in my Home Life Project in 4-H and sewed or refinished furniture projects for my room. Hot pink, grey and black were popular colors in the '50s. I made a bedspread, curtains, pillows and a dressing table skirt for a 4-H project. I still can't bear to throw that bedspread away. It gathers dust in our attic.

In college, our dorm rooms got a new look with new bedspreads and posters every year. I remember the bedspreads as being dull, beige and plaid with a hint of kelly green. Apparently, my Home Economics major requiring creative art, sewing and interior design classes didn't make our dorm rooms very zippy!

After getting married, I delighted in making all kinds of changes in every house we lived in. Fortunately, Sherm is handy with a paintbrush and applying wallpaper and shares my redecorating passion. While living in Jamestown, North Dakota, we repainted the entire rental house, inside and out. Despite our efforts, that ramshackle house never looked very good. The floors were built on a slab and ice cold in the winter.

In Quincy, Illinois while I was in the hospital for the birth of our second daughter, Sherm and his mother moved all our furnishings from the house we

Caryl Crozier

were renting to a house we purchased at 17 Ruby Court. They painted all the rooms, unpacked boxes and arranged the furniture before we brought Cherise home from the hospital in June of 1964. I didn't have to lift a finger. Ella had fresh caramel rolls and a bouquet of daisies on the table. What a gift! Had we been a little smarter, we would have known that by law we wouldn't have had to leave our rental house that was being sold until Cherise was three months old.

Although we had enough furniture early in our marriage, I got interested in collecting antiques. Old family furniture usually had thick layers of ugly beige or institutional green paint or cracked varnish. I've refinished over 50 chairs, chests and wooden antiques in my lifetime, everything from laundry tub benches to Hoosier cabinets. One might call it an obsession. It was!

I could barely wait to start revamping the ranch style house we bought at 171 Maplewood Drive in Bloomington, Minnesota when we moved from Illinois in 1965. Sherm grew up playing in a lumberyard in Jasper, Minnesota, so he had some carpentry skills and enough nerve to start a basement rec room project. Determined to make it unique, we confiscated a cattle fence on my parents' farm that had been made of old boards from Grandpa Kinkner's barn. Dad thought we were crazy, but he allowed us to tear down the fence. My parents had salvaged some batten boards when Grandpa's barn was torn down so we used them, too. Sherm scrubbed the caked manure off the boards with a steel brush and let them dry in the sun in our back yard. When a red streak of infection went up his arm, I wondered if the effort was worth it. Thank goodness for antibiotics. The Bloomington neighbors watched with growing curiosity as the lawn disappeared under old boards.

Using rustic barn board was an original idea with us, although it became popular soon after. The barn board wainscoting combined with wallboard, wallpaper and a muted red paneling on the opposite wall looked great. We had leftover barn board that we eventually used for space above the kitchen fireplace mantle and basement wainscoting in our Burnsville house built in 1970. It is a nostalgic daily reminder of my family roots in South Dakota.

In the 1960s, stores like Hardware Hank and Rudy Boschwitz's Plywood Minnesota catered to the do-it-yourself crowd. We hauled supplies every weekend and finished the project quickly. Sherm even installed a Franklin wood-burning stove on a brick hearth he built in the corner of the basement family room. Getting the insulated steel chimney through a first floor closet and the roof of the house was a tricky job. As a finishing touch, he built a cedar closet under the basement stairs to utilize every inch of space in that basement. Our daughters had their own playroom, toy storage and benches. I was so proud of that basement and to think we had done it all ourselves! It was a perfect venue for big parties and teaching lingerie and decoupage classes.

Waking to Mourning Doves

Once we finished a project, we always started to look for another. While boating on Crystal Lake in Burnsville in 1968, our dog ran off from the beach on the west end of the lake. Sherm searched for Maize and found her on a beautiful parcel of wooded land on the southwest corner of the lake. The girls and I followed and before we knew it, we owned that piece of land and built our dream home there. We borrowed money from Sherm's aunt and uncle, but soon paid it back. Our parents tried to talk us out of building on our wooded slope, but we persevered. I guess parents often wonder about their offsprings' wisdom in matters of money.

After a year of deliberating over house plans we decided on a classic two-story, four-bedroom colonial house like we had seen in New England. We hired Jerry Spande, a local contractor, and enjoyed the hours of negotiations and building. For $41,000 we felt we had created a masterpiece by the time we moved into it in 1970. Cherise had just finished kindergarten and Michelle third grade. It seemed a good time to move and we have never regretted it. I used to have nightmares about having to leave this house. Not unfounded, because Sherm turned down a few job offers to move to Washington, DC that involved good promotions and opportunities for even further career advancement.

The girls and I strongly objected to any move and said, "Why should we move just so you can get a higher number (job grade level)?"

We didn't move and I intend to live here the rest of my life.

While building the house, we had picnics and wiener roasts on the property and in the partially finished house. As the construction progressed, we marveled at the magical views of the woods and lake. We couldn't wait to move in. The springtime woods were carpeted with rue anemone, bloodroot, meadow rue, ferns and showy clumps of yellow moccasin flowers. I knew we had found paradise. Spending hours in the woods was pure bliss. The girls made trails and spent days outside exploring our new environment.

I must admit that during the construction we had numerous run-ins and frustrations with the builder and carpenters, but eventually we worked it all out. I am glad now for the experience, because I learned to be assertive with construction teams and contractors, a skill I used later in my job as a nursing home administrator.

When we concluded the project I said, " If a marriage can survive the stress of building a house, it can weather anything."

While an administrator at four nursing homes from 1983 to 1993, I was heavily involved in remodeling and redecorating projects at all of them. Thank goodness I was comfortable with confrontation. In fact, I rather enjoyed bossing men and contractors around!

Caryl Crozier

In the mid 1970s the girls and I got tired of being alone on fall weekends when Sherm was off hunting woodcock and grouse in Pine County, Minnesota. After a lengthy search we bought the Enders 190-acre wild land farm north of Markville. The property had a ramshackle house that we expended a huge amount of energy remodeling.

> Michelle writes: *In all honesty, my memories of the farm are not all pleasant. This was an old farm my parents purchased for hunting. It was in Pine County- which is fairly poor and has tons of bugs. My best memories are walks through the woods on Dad's trails- especially getting to the dirt/gravel road a mile back into the woods, spending time by the creek on the other side of the road, playing Flinch (which is a rather slow game), and pretending we were murdered. There was also some kind of festival in Markville that wasn't too bad. There was no warm water and no indoor toilet. The early years mainly involved labor. Other memories are picking woodticks off the dogs (they had hundreds), the dogs getting attacked by porcupines, and Dad's hunting friends who brought good food. In the fall, we gathered pinecones to sell at art fairs. We gathered dried weeds too. The fall colors were spectacular some years.*

Cherise said her memories involve bloodsucking parasites, gutbusters and DQ shakes at Hinckley, and Duxbury hamburgers and pie.

Our daughters hated the farm and I can't say I blamed them. Wood ticks, woodcock and wild flowers didn't appeal to them as much as they did to Sherm and me! In the spring it was almost worth getting 23–30 wood ticks on our clothing to see the carpet of trillium, wild ginger and emerging ferns in the woods. Sherm had five miles of walking trails bulldozed through the woods for hunting and dug a few ponds. Maintaining the trails each fall with a handheld brush cutter was a major task. Eventually, Sherm bought an old 1950s Ford tractor which helped ease the task, but it required a lot of mechanical maintenance, which he is not skilled at.

> Sherm writes (in his *Dream Hunter* memoir): *We cleaned the old farmhouse as best we could, scraped old wallpaper off some walls, repainted and put up curtains and pictures. It became quite comfortable and was a good restoration of a 1920s farm home, complete with old family furniture from*

our home and that of our parents. By the fall of 1975, it was rustically comfortable.

We sanded the wood floors. They were quite nice except where some fuel oil had soaked a spot on the kitchen floor. A few boards in the kitchen floor had buckled an inch or so higher than the rest of the floor, due to the extreme changes in temperature. One day, while Caryl and the girls were at church in Markville, I took the chain saw and made a cut through the floor to create some expansion room, then stomped on the buckled boards until they flattened out. It was a bit crude, but it worked. Only if you looked close could you see where I had cut. That bit of skilled carpentry became a family legend.

I loved walking the trails we built beside the old stone fences. The original owner cleared stones off the three open fields to farm and as a result left a poignant monument to his efforts. Brush and trees soon hid his labor.

The following quote from *Dream Hunter* captures the mood of the farm's beauty.

The spring of the year at Enders Farm could be pleasant, but you had to time it right — like a warm spring day when the last of the snow was melting but before the insects had emerged. It was easy to walk about, but rubber boots were always needed, for the farm was generally low land and poorly drained. Any bit of rain would leave puddles, which was great for some wildlife like woodcock.

The springtime evenings were particularly pleasant. The chorus of singing frogs was nearly loud enough to keep us awake when we went to bed, even after a hard day's work. A special treat was the courting dance of the male woodcock. On quiet evenings we would walk to the edge of the lawn and look over the hayfield into the western sky. The dark masses of the aspen trees would mark the far edge of the field. If we were lucky we would hear the "peent" of the male woodcock coming from the center of the field opening.

We were always thrilled with this wild sound of spring. Along with the vocal " peent" there would be a whistling of wings, as the male woodcock would spiral up into the darker sky, eventually disappearing, then the tiny wingtip euphony would come downward to earth. Those aerial mating dances always made me feel optimistic about having more good days in the coming days of fall hunting. I suppose the nearby female woodcock must have been optimistic as well.

Equally satisfying were the rolling drumbeats of the male ruffed grouse that could be heard scattered around the land on warm spring days. The rhythmic drum of the male grouse rapidly flapping his wings on a drumming log would rise slowly to a crescendo then fall to just a faint beat then silence. Somewhere in the back of the farm "Old Thumper" was calling to a prospective lover.

Still later in the night, usually when we were lying in bed thinking about the day's events, coyotes would begin their nightly melodies. Their yelping seemed primitive and mysterious, Their nightly entertainments were the only evidence that they were sharing the farm with us; we never saw them there. It was then that I would remember that the singing frogs, the dancing woodcock, the drumming grouse, and the yelping coyotes were ancient sounds that had been there long before we arrived, or for that matter, before any man had lived there. I also knew that these were inherent patterns of behavior that are part of the continuous cycle of life that perpetuates these wonderful citizens of the woods.

Our family enjoyed cross-country skiing in the winter and made several winter trips to the farm to ski the trails. Crusty snow allowed us to glide through the woods with speed, but only after we had taken turns sluggishly breaking trail. One New Years Eve, our friends, the Jacobson family, joined us at the farm. It was our first and last celebration of that sort — we didn't like having to use the outdoor toilet in weather below zero!

Sometimes the ghost of John Enders spooked us. Another quote from Sherm's memoir follows.

According to his relatives and nearby neighbors, John had a mail-order bride who lived with him only a short time. There were different versions of what had happened to her early in the marriage. According to his niece, who had inherited the place, John's wife had been hit by a train in Duluth and killed. The neighborhood version was that after her mother

Waking to Mourning Doves

came to visit her and saw the conditions she was living in, the mother took her back home.

With his wife gone, John lived most of his life on this farm as a single man, but he longed for a woman. In his attic we found newspaper and magazine clippings of women who all looked more or less similar. Amazingly, they also looked somewhat like Caryl. That similarity was one of the reasons we always thought during those first years that John Enders' spirit was with us. There were some weird happenings in the old house. Several times while we were fixing the place up in the first year or two, Caryl would need things like a safety pin or a comb, and then almost by magic the items would be found lying nearby. It was almost as if he were helping her. Then there were times when lights would come on at night in the bedroom he had died in. I suppose there were logical reasons for all of these. We preferred to think John's ghost was there and he was keeping a helpful eye out for us as if he wanted our family to be there, taking care of the place and enjoying it. After a while we no longer felt his presence. His spirit evidently had left. Maybe he felt comfortable that we were good caretakers.

By 1989, after our daughters were married, the farmhouse was nearly uninhabitable, so we had to make a decision to abandon or remodel it. Being the impractical people that we are, we remodeled. Naturally, it became a growing project that eventually required replacement of the rotting floor beams under the old house. We hired a firm to lift the house up, which in turn made the construction of a new foundation and partial basement seem practical. New electrical wiring, plumbing and a septic system followed. The finished project sure beat the cold-water faucet and outdoor biff. A wall of windows in the new porch faced south and provided hours of warm cozy comfort. I couldn't wait to get to the old farm on weekends and shed the stress of my nursing home administrator job. Tree frogs provided a soft lullaby as we fell asleep instantly in our cocoon sleeping bags on the new porch.

In 1990, we decided to look once again for lake property. We knew our daughters didn't like the north woods farm, but thought they and their new husbands might visit us in a lake home. We reluctantly put the farm up for sale and found a cabin and small acreage we liked on the Minong Flowage in Wisconsin only 30 miles from the farm. The half log red house resembles a Swedish stuga like we had seen in Sweden. I decorated it with a Swedish theme

Caryl Crozier

using Carl Larson prints along with Swedish Dala painting and rosemaling. The cabin is on the wild Totogatic River with access to the 1600-acre lake of the Minong Flowage. The woods are filled with ferns, little pink lady slippers and an abundance of other wild flowers. Upstream, the bay is a sea of wild rice that the local Native Americans harvest in the fall. I love listening to the steady rhythm of their paddles as they bat the rice into their canoes. We rejoice in the solitude of the little-used wild river catching bass and northerns. Our classic Boston Whaler is just right for navigating the twists and turns of the small river. Boating, fishing, hunting and entertaining at the cabin occupy many summer and fall hours in our retirement.

Maybe we bought the cabin because we wanted another remodeling project! We did remodel the kitchen with new cupboards and redid the bathroom and floors throughout the house. We liked the honey-colored knotty pine walls and ceiling, so this wasn't a huge renovation. We cleared one of the other four lots to build a new cabin, but common sense prevailed and we used the money to put a new addition on our Burnsville house that will allow us to live on one floor in our old age. We don't regret the decision and enjoy the spacious sun-lit comfort of our home in the woods in Burnsville.

In 1996 after we both retired, we added the 18x24 two-story addition with a full walkout basement to the original house. Living in a house during remodeling is ten times worse than building a new house. Luckily, I could escape during the day to the Barnes home while providing day care for Rachel and Claire, but Sherm lived in the chaos 24/7. I am sure the workers didn't appreciate the close surveillance. We felt it was needed. We survived that too and are spending our retirement years in a house with a spectacular 22-window view of the surrounding woods and lake. It feels more like being in the northern woods than it does at our Wisconsin lake cabin. Gazing out the windows into a beautiful natural area seeing birds and wildlife makes each day a new adventure.

Sometimes I think I should have pursued a career as an interior decorator, but maybe I did just that!

PART VIII: SHIFTING GEARS

Long Term Care — 1980–1993

Grand Canyon & Daughters

CHAPTER **33**

Do You Know Ed Crozier?

My long-term-care career began as a direct result of personal health issues and ended with some exhilarating as well as stressful work experiences. Becoming an administrator of a long-term care facility had certainly not been my career goal. Circumstances fell into place, and I found myself in a position a direct opposite of my interests and prior experiences.

Our daughters were reaching college age, and I wanted a job that provided steady income without capital outlay and uncertain sales. Also, many friends were getting divorced and all of a sudden women were expected to have a career, a total turn-around from those first carefree days of our marriage and starting a family. I wanted to be financially independent. Women like me were now expected to be super moms and have a career, too. So, the search and interview process began. The competition was difficult, as I had been in what some considered a "hobby job" all those years, and I lacked management skills to start a high-level job. And so began my start on the lower rung in long-term care (LTC).

Why did I leave a teaching job I loved? Primarily because Control Data was phasing out the adult education program at the Creative Learning Center and installing computer-based education. I had been teaching there two or three days a week for twelve years and then filling in some days and evenings in community education in Edina, Bloomington, Burnsville, and Lakeville. I knew I had to make a change.

I interviewed for several jobs and usually came in second. One rejection came because of animosity from Scott County Commissioners who were upset that my husband was concerned about a bridge to be built across the Minnesota Valley National Wildlife Refuge.

One of their first questions in my interview was, "Do you know Ed Crozier?"

I stated, "Yes, I sleep with him every night." Their illegal question and my answer, which probably sounded impertinent, essentially ended that interview!

For another job, the interviewer was an animal rights activist opposed to Ed and his staff sharp-shooting an overpopulation of deer on the refuge. He asked the same question and I gave the same answer. I knew he considered the interview over at that point.

Waking to Mourning Doves

I simply wasn't qualified for some jobs that I applied for. Although I learned from going through the interview process, it took me several months to work up the courage to apply for another job. Rejection is not easy for me.

The summer of 1979, I took my parents on a trip to Colorado. Mom was sick some of the time and I didn't know what was wrong. When we got back home, I learned that she was stalling until October for her cancer policy's six-month waiting period to be over before going to the doctor. She surmised that she had cancer and wanted better insurance. She ended up having colon cancer surgery October 5th of that year. I got substitute teachers or cancelled my classes and went to South Dakota to help. While there, I felt sharp pains in my abdomen and three weeks later had surgery myself. During my recuperation period, I started to rethink my career plans and felt that I should find a job that was steadier and paid more. Michelle had enrolled at Gustavus Adolphus College in St. Peter, Minnesota that fall and I wanted to help finance her education.

In the late spring of 1980, I resumed teaching some adult education classes after a trip to Washington, D.C. as a representative to lobby Minnesota state senators and representatives to appropriate money for the Extension Service, which was beginning to have severe financial issues as a result of cutbacks. The need for rural education, for which the Extension Service was founded, was changing. Probably I was lucky to not get the job I interviewed for in Scott County. Extension staff work day and night with no extra duty or overtime pay. It would have been a physically exhausting job.

I checked the want ads and inquired about a few positions. Kay, a Taylor and Eng representative, hired me to demonstrate wok cooking in department stores and specialty culinary shops for $25 an hour, high pay at the time. I loved trying all the new techniques using a wok and the food was delicious. However, I spent dozens of unpaid hours trying recipes and preparing for the demonstrations. I didn't like lugging a bag of heavy equipment to each location. Although enjoyable, it did not have the career status I sought.

I answered one ad to be a Therapeutic Recreation assistant at Ebenezer Long Term Care facility in Burnsville. The young woman who interviewed me said she wanted to hire me on the spot, but had to check with her boss. The facility was in the process of making budget cuts, which I came to know all too well, so they didn't fill the position. I felt let down once again.

The young woman from Ebenezer and I kept in touch. That fall we car-pooled to a class (Multi-disciplinary Perspectives on Aging) at the University of Minnesota. She was part of a Finnish dance group and they performed at the family Christmas party I helped organize at the Bloomington facility. We kept in touch through the years and sometimes had lunch together at fall

Caryl Crozier

conventions. She always lamented the fact that she wasn't allowed to hire me and was impressed that a couple of years later I became an Administrator. She was probably the reason I decided to look into another LTC position. She was creative and intelligent: two characteristics I'd never associated with nursing home staff up to that point. I soon learned differently, working with many dedicated creative, sharp people in my 13-year career in long term care. Unfortunately, there were a few who gave me major stress, a couple of supervisors and maintenance men in particular.

Shortly after the Ebenezer interview, I was hired by the Gold Medallion Company to be the half-time Coordinator of Volunteer Services (CVS) at the Bloomington Maple Manor LTC facility.

In April 1980, I found myself sitting in the dining room at Bloomington Maple Manor waiting for my boss to arrive. As I sat there, I became more and more uncomfortable and somewhat nauseated by the surroundings. Not one staff person greeted me and the residents all seemed very debilitated. Finally, I approached a table and sat down by a resident named Ida and we started to talk. In that brief ten minutes, I discovered what I like best about LTC – the elderly residents with whom I could easily communicate. They reminded me of my grandparents.

Soon, Muriel, my new boss, came and showed me to the basement office I would share with the Activity Director and her chain-smoking assistant, Mitzi. I abhorred cigarette smoke and I quickly looked at the personnel policies, which said smoking was not allowed in offices, only the break room just down the hall.

I mentioned my concerns to the Staff Development nurse who was giving me a facility orientation. She gave me a strange look and said, "Talk to Muriel."

After enduring four hours of chain smoking in my new office, I marched into Muriel's office at the end of the day and said, "You have my resignation if you don't enforce the personnel policies and end the smoking in my office."

Since a powerful person at the corporate office had hired me (Carol, who later hired me as her assistant), Muriel wasn't about to screw up and let me go. She knew she was on tenuous ground herself and was fired a few months later.

Anyway, Mitzi stopped smoking in the office and resigned not long after that. I felt a little bad about it, but I was a heroine to some of the other staff who hated smoke. They were afraid to speak up since the administrative staff all smoked in their offices and now had to stop that practice because of me.

The anti-smoking crusade never ended for me. At Weldwood Health Care Center, I shared an office with the Staff Development and Infection Control

Waking to Mourning Doves

nurses who didn't smoke. However, the staff wanted to smoke while in the room getting training. I objected strongly and prevailed. Most of the nurses and the Administrator smoked, as did the residents. I avoided the blue haze as much as possible. At Crystal Lake, where I was an Assistant Administrator in Training, I refused to share an office with the Administrator who smoked. That didn't endear me to her either.

When I became the Administrator at Ambassador Health Care Center, the residents had a small smoking area and the staff could only use the break room. That seemed more sensible to me.

At Inver Grove Care Center, I was appalled that residents were smoking right by other residents using oxygen tanks. That is asking for an explosion and serious injury. I quickly set aside a small private room area where residents could smoke with staff supervision. Even staff that smoked hated the haze in that room! After several months, we no longer allowed residents to smoke anywhere and didn't admit residents who did. I made the entire building smoke free, which was before hospitals and other public places enforced policies like that. Staff complained, of course, but liked me well enough to live with it and adapted to catching a smoke "out back" away from the view of residents and families. We built a small shelter with walls and roof, planted flowers, added a table and chairs and tried to make it as comfortable as possible.

Working at the Bloomington facility was a positive experience. Several staff said the whole atmosphere changed after I arrived because I brought in a lot of new youth and adult volunteers .We worked with the Activity staff, involving the residents in all kinds of simple craft projects. I was teaching again, and the residents loved it.

Rather quickly, I caught the attention of Earl, editor of the Gold Standard (the monthly company newsletter). The following titles reflect stories he wrote about me:

CVS Juggles Many Roles, Apparel Problem Solved at Bloomington, Volunteers Make Colorful New Bibs, Volunteer Coordinator Draws on Friendship Network, Volunteers Undergo Instant Aging, Adaptive Clothing Workshop, Special Patients Prompt Special Care, Administrator in Training. He must have been desperate for human-interest stories. I liked the publicity, though!

Getting to know nursing homes as a family member and an administrator has given me a sympathetic insight into the trauma of placing a loved one in a facility. I know that nursing homes are not the "hell-holes" that some people dread. In my experience, long-term care staff can make residents' last years enjoyable and often better than living alone. Good nutrition, health

Caryl Crozier

care, mental stimulation and hugs from staff help. Most employees that I have worked with had caregiver personalities and did their best.

We couldn't have hoped for better care than my mother received during her four years at Bethesda Nursing home in Beresford, South Dakota. Small town facilities have a strong tie with the community and a feeling of home and familiarity. Mom knew many people in the facility, both staff and residents, and had nieces and children of her friends who worked there. As family, we knew how to advocate for and accept the care she received.

CHAPTER **34**
And He Had No Feet

My family never understood my melancholy mood on Christmas Eve when I came home from work in a nursing home. I am not sure I did entirely, either.

Since families of many residents never visited, we accepted donated gifts for them. One Christmas was especially poignant. A resident opened a package and it was a pair of socks. The look on his face told it all. He had no feet! Another man always wrapped up one of his old shirts so there would be at least one package for him. We usually did this distribution on Christmas Eve morning and then I went home and tried to get into the spirit of Christmas. Seeing these people so alone and forgotten made me sad.

For many years my family and I invited a lonely person to our home for Christmas and other holidays. We enjoyed hosting Elroy, a barely off the street person, who adopted me when I chaired an Adopt-a-Grandparent program in the inner city through our Community Action Council. We couldn't make up for all the lonely people in the world, but we hoped it would inspire compassion in our daughters.

After nearly a year at Bloomington Maple Manor, I wanted a full time job. I told Carol, my boss, that I was searching for other work. She suggested that I work half time at the corporate office as her assistant and half time at Weldwood, a Gold Medallion-owned facility in Golden Valley to start a volunteer program there. I accepted even though it was a long commute of 25 miles on crowded freeway driving.

Weldwood had 88 residents including many mentally ill and behavior problem patients. Staff thought of themselves as surrogate family members, since many residents' families had literally abandoned them. As a result, it was a caring community of staff and I thoroughly enjoyed the team spirit. Joyce, the administrator, had been there since 1973; she set the tone and did a fine job. She chain smoked, but I liked her anyway. She threw parties for us at her home, a practice I later adopted for both residents and staff. I know she wasn't sure about my beginning cadre of unpredictable teen-age volunteers. We had a few rough spots, but some of these young volunteers did very well and convinced their parents to volunteer. The residents loved those kids and the energy they exuded. Weldwood had never had an active volunteer program, but within a year I had it going strong with 100 capable volunteers, a miracle in the staff's eyes.

Caryl Crozier

I expanded into all sorts of areas in my two years there. We had monthly meetings of the Volunteer Coordinators from all the Gold Medallion facilities. Carol had me write a book, *Information Guide to Volunteer Resources in the Twin Cities*. It was a huge project and we were planning to publish and market it, but fate stepped in. Gold Medallion sold the whole company to an "upstart" group called Good Neighbor and my life would never be the same after that. I wanted to be a recognized author, but it didn't happen.

At Weldwood, I also had the detested job of taking orders from and shopping for the residents. Anyone who knows me is aware that balancing a checkbook or keeping track of expenses down to the penny is a totally foreign concept. I drove the two bookkeepers wild, as they needed to post each expense to the respective resident's account. I was usually a few cents off and they made me struggle to find the problem and gave me a bad time. However, when I became Administrator at Ambassador, they both sucked up to me and wanted a job there. I have a long memory, though.

The best part of that shopping duty was working with the residents, especially Richard. Confined to a wheelchair, he couldn't talk or write legibly and drooled excessively. Several times a week he wheeled himself to my office and with a pen and paper scribbled his indecipherable order. By guessing his gestures and nodding, I could figure it out: candy, pencils and paper and sometimes a harmonica when his got too slobbery to function anymore. A big smile from him or a hand reaching out to touch mine made my day. He liked to just sit and watch me do paperwork or whatever. When he passed away months later, attending his funeral was difficult. A few family members attended, but none of us had ever seen them visit him at Weldwood. I choked back tears giving a short eulogy.

Weldwood had many residents that had been institutionalized most of their lives. Some were fairly young and mobile. I remember one lady who wore extremely heavy makeup and ordered more every week. She hallucinated about seeing snakes in her room. Another lady had been a figure skater and for some reason, ordered a box of matches each week. She smoked, but staff never allowed residents to light their own cigarettes with matches. I never purchased the matches, but when I got a volunteer to do the resident shopping, she bought the matches without realizing the danger. Staff found over a dozen boxes in the resident's drawer before we corrected the problem. She could have lit the whole place up in flames.

While at Weldwood, I conducted an "instant aging" workshop for volunteers. Jan, the Staff Development Coordinator, and I designed a program to introduce volunteers to the kinds of sensory deprivation and impaired mobility that Weldwood residents experienced daily. Volunteers placed

Waking to Mourning Doves

soybeans in their shoes to mimic corns and calluses, taped thumbs to fingers to impair dexterity and endured wraps that immobilized their arms. Sensory deprivation devices like cotton in the ears, field-cut glasses, blindfolds and nose clamps made them relieved to end the experience of instant aging. They told us that our hoped-for result of making them more empathetic worked.

Volunteers helped me start a large garden project for resident participation. At a minimum, residents could use the hose to spray the plants and be outside in the fresh air. The ground was incredibly fertile there and residents enjoyed harvesting the produce. We built raised wheelchair gardens in which residents nurtured lettuce and some flowers.

Seeing a need for adaptive clothing for our residents, I put together a workshop for families and staff from eight facilities. It was well attended, and resources and patterns were shown. I designed bibs, wheelchair wrap skirts, catheter bag covers and wheelchair saddlebags, and recruited volunteers to sew them. I researched other adaptive clothing ideas and asked a businesswoman to present her line of adaptive clothing to purchase. My sewing background came in handy in many ways and I gave some thought to starting a business in this realm.

I felt good being active in Twin Cities networks of volunteer director organizations and became chairperson of the Minnesota Association of Health Care Facilities (MAHCF) Volunteer Services Task Force. Joining Directors of Volunteers in Agencies (DOVIA) allowed me to help with some workshops patterned after some I had developed. I also met a bevy of nice women!

In the early summer, many facilities hold volunteer recognition events. By the second summer at Weldwood, I had a large, active volunteer group, so we decided to celebrate in a big way. We had a dinner for volunteers and a popular piano entertainer/humorist. It was crowded and really fun.

Jill, the social worker, said she told the other staff, "We won't have Caryl very long. She is too good." I don't know about the good, but it was prophetic.

The following spring, when I came back from a family vacation backpacking in the Four Corners area in Utah, the company had been sold to Good Neighbor Corporation. Carol had been laid off and half of my job was gone, too. Not good news! I knew that I had to move fast. I immediately went to the new corporate office after "Black Friday" when so many lost their jobs and knocked on the door of the second in command, Allen. After 45 minutes, he offered to send me back to the University of Minnesota to obtain my Long Term Care Administrator's License and pay me full time while doing it. I am still not sure how it all happened, but I was pretty good at self-promotion and enthusiastic. Maybe it was because Allen was an Iowa farm boy and I can talk

Caryl Crozier

pigs, agriculture and rural schools with first-hand knowledge. This time my farm background paid off and Allen became my mentor and always helped me over any rough spots until he left the company. More than anything, the new company needed trained administrators.

In the spring of 1982, I started classes in LTC administration at the University of Minnesota. That fall, I was assigned to Ambassador Health Care Center for seventeen weeks as Good Neighbor's first Administrator in Training. I spent a week with each department manager and gained invaluable training from staff. One and a half years later, I became the administrator there, so knew the staff and routines well.

While in training, I continued my volunteer coordinator job at Weldwood, attended classes, read countless books and wrote papers. I averaged about four to five hours of sleep at night. Luckily, our daughters were in college by this time. I don't think I could have coped with teenagers' problems nor my feelings of guilt for not spending time with them. Sherm was just as absorbed as I was in his job as the first refuge manager at Minnesota Valley National Wildlife Refuge. Maybe these were good times, but I would not care to repeat them.

In 1983, I completed the required 300-hour internship at Augustana Care Center in downtown Minneapolis. Here too, I spent a week with each department manager learning how his/her department operated, even working double shifts, changing beds and resident diapers. I was their first intern ever, so they went out of their way to help me, even refurbishing an office space for me. I did research and wrote a paper on a new concept, Respite Care, which is now widely practiced.

After completing this arduous internship while still taking classes and writing papers, I took the dreaded state boards in May. I managed to pass with what would be considered a B+ in school – high 80s. As a reward to myself, we took our first trip to Europe in June of 1983. I read the travel brochures on the way to the airport and on the flight to Bergen, Norway. Much to my dismay, we were seated near smokers. They were allowed to light up and smoke anywhere. Imagine my delight upon landing in clean, fresh Norway, still the most beautiful place in the world to me.

When we returned from Europe, I worked another month as the Volunteer Coordinator at Weldwood and trained my replacement. Good Neighbor had offered me the Assistant Administrator position at Crystal Lake Health Care Center in Robbinsdale, an even longer commute. When I started at Crystal Lake, the company was doing an employee satisfaction survey and I was put in charge of tabulating the results. To my horror, the reviews were coming back with scathing attacks on the Administrator and I had to be the one to break the news. Staff told me that Ruth was the type of person who ignores the

Waking to Mourning Doves

message and destroys the messenger. Fortunately, the Director of Nursing was fed up and leaving, so she put her negative evaluation under Ruth's door to save my hide and career. I shall be forever grateful. Several department heads had issues working with Ruth. I reluctantly became their sounding board and tried with my limited power to steer Ruth into more acceptable methods of operation. A slippery slope!

The regional supervisor, Dave, felt that I had the needed maturity to handle the survey and I wrote it up in the most positive manner possible. After that, Dave asked me to work with him during that year on various other projects. We established the concept of administering a couple of small home-care units: six residents to a house staffed with a nurse and several assistants. I wrote up all the policies and procedures, but it never totally proved to be a financial winner. It was ahead of its time, for now it's a popular arrangement. To my knowledge we were the first to experiment with it.

CHAPTER 35

You Are the Geranium

In the spring of 1984, I was asked to "volunteer" to be the Administrator at Horizon West, a facility for the mentally ill and handicapped near the inner city of Minneapolis. Good Neighbor was helping with management issues for a few months because the facility had received a devastating Health Department survey. I had been there a few times as a consultant to jump-start the volunteer program, but going there full time even for a few months as an administrator was a frightening prospect. The Administrator had been fired and the place was a mess, although I soon learned they had a staff of excellent department managers.

Most of the staff was black and lived in the near north side and were very street smart. Three of the department managers were also black. Well, I had zero experience in working with a black staff, much less very young mentally ill, sexually active residents. My first day on the job I got a call from the child day care center across the street saying two of our male residents were having oral sex where the children could see them. My immediate thought at the time was to retreat to my safe home in the suburbs, but with help from three wonderful nursing department managers, we arranged for the men, one of whom was from a different facility, to have private in-house visits for their pursuits. No problems from them after that.

Another young woman prostituted herself for a hamburger at a nearby Burger King. Staff had to walk a fine line to let younger residents have some freedom versus not allowing them to come to any harm. Later, she did run off and a policeman found her wandering the streets in a Wisconsin town and arranged for her return. Every day I feared I would lose my license for some infraction like this, but luck was with me.

One of the residents, a huge, mentally challenged white man named Donald, took a shine to me and followed me everywhere. There were three floors in the building and I had to walk the stairwell or use the elevator. I was always aware of who was behind me, but more than once Donald snuck up behind me and pounced putting his hand on my shoulders. He thought we were friends. I guess we were.

Quite by accident, it seemed, the staff began to like me. I knew how important it was to leave my door open and eat lunch with the staff. I managed by wandering around talking to staff and residents. I made at least three

Waking to Mourning Doves

rounds on all three floors daily and greeted each resident, learned names and somehow managed to act unafraid. Working with an all-black staff was an eye opener and I grew to love their openness. If I did something they didn't like they told me about it. If I did something they liked, they hugged me. Talk about culture shock for me.

I started taking the staff person of the month out to lunch. The third month, staff selected the mother of the dietary manager. She was reluctant to go, so I invited her daughter to go, also. It turned out the mother had never eaten in a restaurant before, much less with a white woman. Again my farm background was a conversation lifesaver. Her experience growing up in the South and picking cotton and working in the fields was something I could relate to. We talked about a mutual love of food and music, too.

From the start, the Dietary Manager supported me and that was fortunate. She was the unspoken leader of the facility and her husband was the Maintenance supervisor. I knew her influence kept me safe. The next administrator didn't get along well with the staff, and her car tires were slashed. She said I was a hard act to follow, but I know she had a closed-door policy, which simply didn't work at Horizon West. She also accused the staff of bringing in roaches. That comment raised their ire. I hired an exterminator to do roach control, but I sure didn't accuse staff of bringing them in!

A month or so into the assignment, Mary, the Director of Nursing, told me the story of the geranium. "A geranium was placed in a room and people started cleaning up around it and improving things. Eventually, the whole building was cared for and improved." She told me I was that geranium.

We had to do a major cleanup and renovation to prepare for the next Health Department survey. I had to coordinate those chores as well as get the charting and resident care improved so we wouldn't be cited for the same things again. I made one big mistake, which I thought was helping. I had a cleaning service come in and help for a few days to catch up. This hurt the pride of the housekeeping staff and they quickly told me about it. I had the sense to apologize and took the whole housekeeping staff to lunch at Market Barbecue and told them how much I appreciated them. After that they really dove in and worked. The floors were so shiny you could see your reflection.

Eventually, the health department returned for the follow-up survey, and the results were good. This meant my consulting job was ending and I would be leaving. The staff begged me to stay on a permanent basis. I did interview with the owner who was also the assistant maintenance man. He said he was afraid in the beginning that I wouldn't be tough enough to do the job. He said he changed his mind at one department meeting when he was trying to override one of my decisions. I told him in no uncertain terms that I was in charge and

Caryl Crozier

he shut up, probably out of shock. In the interview with him, I named an exorbitant salary and he said he couldn't meet that. Actually, I didn't want to leave Good Neighbor, so that was fine. Most of the strong Horizon West department managers left after I did. They could see things sliding downhill again. Several found jobs with Good Neighbor and did well.

About a month after I left Horizon West, the Good Neighbor Company offered me the administrative position at Ambassador Health Care Center in New Hope. The company had just fired the administrator. In some ways, it is easier coming in after a fired employee, because anything I did, staff viewed as positive. After several months at Horizon West, I had culture shock being in the more reserved all-white facility. I had grown accustomed to the spontaneity of a diverse staff. When we went to a movie in Burnsville, I felt uncomfortable with all the white people around me. I missed the staff that I had enjoyed so much.

CHAPTER **36**

PR in a Pressure Cooker

Ginger, a gentle Yellow Labrador Retriever, arrived at Ambassador Health Care Center in New Hope, Minnesota a year before I arrived there as the new administrator in 1984. She had been adopted from the Humane Society as a result of positive interaction between residents and pets that had periodically been brought in. The Humane Society staff had chosen a dog that was gentle, attention-loving, intelligent and calm around large groups of people. She could be outdoors in the winter, but lounged indoors most of the time. Fortunately, she was big enough to avoid being stepped on. She wandered around spreading joy visiting from room to room or curling up at someone's feet in the lobby. Residents who seldom responded to humans opened up as Ginger approached. Her presence made Ambassador feel more like a real home. This became my own philosophy and the major goal in my career as an administrator. Trying to promote a feeling of family between residents and staff is something I learned at Weldwood Care Center and as I've so often heard, "It starts at the top."

My style of "management by wandering around" made Ginger and me quite compatible in our respective roles. Her preferred home was under my desk, so when she finished her rounds she snuggled up for a nap at my feet. She shed clumps and wads of hair from her thick coat. I've never liked dogs in the house, so this was a big change.

Dogs are said to be stress relievers and I certainly needed that at Ambassador. The facility had the reputation of being a career breaker for past administrators. There were many reasons for this, not necessarily the administrator's fault. It became a huge challenge for me, also.

The 120-bed facility in New Hope is in close proximity to other facilities that are huge and popular, St. Theresa's and Northridge. The other nearby smaller facilities, Colonial Acres and Weldwood, also drew from the same client base. The biggest drawback at Ambassador was that it only had rooms that housed three residents. Most families wanted a private or at least a two–bed room. As a result, census (filled beds) was always low, which meant less revenue for operating the facility and less profit for the owners. Owner profit was to become a huge deal at Good Neighbor as I eventually learned.

When offering me the job, the corporate office said I could earn specific bonuses of $1,000, $2,000 and $5,000 to fill the beds. I started the job with naïve optimism thinking that the goal could be reached. Despite a very aggressive marketing program, extensive remodeling and community outreach, those goals were never reached under my tenure. Full census was reached many years later, when Ambassador downsized to 80-some beds (two residents per bedroom) and built a large rehabilitation addition.

Since I had previously spent 17 weeks at Ambassador as an Administrator in Training, I was very familiar with the staff and residents and their mode of operation. As a result, I hit the ground running and kept it up for my two-year stay there. It became an all-consuming job for me and much of the time I just spun my wheels, since we still had heavy local competition and those unpopular three-bed rooms.

Inheriting another administrator's staff never worked out quite as well as managers I hired myself, but I tried hard to improve things. My immediate supervisor, Linda, was a joy to work with. She was a proponent of positive reinforcement and didn't micro-manage. She worked hard at making resources available to me and then let me make the decisions to implement. I worked well in that kind of environment since my management style is democratic, also. Although that is my natural leadership style, which is not so different from good teaching practices, Linda taught me by example that it really works. In a subsequent job at Inver Grove Care Center, I had two autocratic supervisors who micro-managed and just couldn't get comfortable with my participatory ways with my staff. I liked to hire good people, give them the resources and support they needed and let them excel. I also liked to involve staff in decision-making as much as possible. It works, and it baffles me that so many managers don't figure that out.

One of those micro-managers said, " Caryl, I will give you credit for one thing, you sure do know how to hire good people." Well, duh, it is how you manage them that is part of the process too, but I never got recognition from those two supervisors for that.

My first new hire was a Volunteer Coordinator, Jill, who had a strong background in journalism. Her creativity, outgoing personality, enthusiasm and ideas were just what we needed. She designed a prize-winning brochure for Ambassador using the new style of "incomplete sentences." Some folks at the corporate office thought it was terrible and didn't want us to print it. I ignored them. They ate crow when the Minnesota Association of Heath Care Facilities (MAHCF) gave it their top award. Jill became part of our outreach team and made a good impression wherever she went.

My first impression of Ambassador's exterior was that it looked tired and run down. One of the first projects for which I requested funding was an exterior face-lift, which included planting shrubs and flowers and installing

Waking to Mourning Doves

new glass doors in the gloomy entrance. Since it was fall, that planting project happened quickly, and we also resurfaced the crumbly parking lot. (Corporate was a little desperate to do anything to fill those vacant beds.) Since I'd just had experience with extensive renovation at Horizon West, as well as building our home in Burnsville, I felt at ease working with contractors. The corporate office had consultants to help us, both in renovation projects and decorating. We installed a gas fireplace and redid the dining room floors and window treatments. Eventually we selected new wall coverings, paint and pictures for the halls and new draperies for the resident rooms. The facility looked good.

I loved making all those improvements and felt a great sense of accomplishment. But now that we looked good, we had to get down to the nitty gritty of filling those beds. By this time, the corporate office had a two-person public relations team to consult with us. We drew up a game plan of community outreach, mostly implemented by the Director of Nursing, the Social Services Director and me. Part of the process of getting residents referred to our facility was to get referrals from the hospital social workers. We held several luncheons and dinners at the facility to get them there to see our new look and become familiar with our services. One or all of us called on hospital social workers and eventually most of them accepted our invitations for lunch or dinner. I recall one outdoor luncheon where the yellow bees outnumbered the social workers twenty to one.

We did outreach in other ways, too. I attended Chamber of Commerce meetings and cultivated relationships with the two political representatives from our area, Ember Riechgot Junge and Ann Rest. They came to many family social events at the facility knowing it was good publicity for them, too. Ember was even the mistress of ceremonies and sang at the family Halloween party. She was an invaluable contact at the legislature for me at a later date.

We continued to brainstorm ideas with the corporate public relations team and became known as the company Public Relations experts. I later learned that the PR team really didn't want to take Ambassador on as their first project. They felt it was doomed to failure because of the three-bed rooms and local competition. Alas, they were right in some ways, and the corporate office of Good Neighbor finally realized they had to take a drastic step to help us.

We began meeting with an architect in the fall of 1984 to design a huge new addition of 40 beds and new offices that would give us all two-bed rooms. We worked with the company Director of Development, Richard, who had a lot of grandiose ideas. He had a positive can-do attitude and I was excited to think this might actually happen. By April of 1985, the plans were complete and we began searching for contractors. Sherm and I decided to take another European trip in May of 1985. Shortly before we left, our team had a

Caryl Crozier

celebratory dinner upon completion of the plans. I left the USA in a euphoric mood that upon return we would commence with building the dream. What a shock it was to learn that the state legislature had passed a moratorium on new building projects in nursing homes because of state reimbursement costs. In other words, the state would end up eventually paying for those costs in their medical reimbursements to nursing homes, and state budgets were tight.

I was crestfallen and it was the start of a discouraging year for me. My boss, Linda, and I met with Senator Reichgot Junge who said she would start working on getting the moratorium changed. I met with her several times, and several years later the legislature did allow projects like this, but it was too late for our Ambassador addition. Good Neighbor's President said years later that it was my initial persistence that started the ball rolling at the legislature. He called me tenacious. That was a nice compliment, but the legislative changes came too late to build my dream facility.

Well, now in the summer of 1985, it was back to the hard-core reality that Good Neighbor's corporate office couldn't help us. We would sink or swim on our own. Meanwhile, I learned a hard lesson in hiring a staff person who proved incapable of doing the job. I had failed to ask more probing questions and to thoroughly check backgrounds and references. After a few months and countless performance goals never reached, I had to fire him. I learned my lesson and my interview skills improved immeasurably after that. I never left a stone unturned in checking references and became a much better judge of character.

Shortly thereafter, the housekeeping/laundry supervisor had a heart attack and had to resign. I hired her replacement, as well as a new dietary director and nursing supervisor. I hired good people, but it was a lot of turnover and stress in a short time.

Meanwhile, my mother-in-law was dying of cancer. In August, before Ella died, Michelle and Scott visited Ella on her August 22nd birthday. The following weekend Cherise took Bill to Jasper, Minnesota to meet her. I was glad she knew the girls had found good men. She died in September of liver cancer and Ed, her husband, was very ill and virtually collapsed. Sherm and his sister, Candy, found him a home in Colonial Acres Care Center, near Ambassador.

Just before Ella's funeral, Michelle and I had to euthanize our Golden Retriever, Caper, since Sherm was out of town. She too had liver cancer. Saying goodbye at the vet's office was a heart-wrenching experience. I wished Sherm could have ended it for her in our woods like he did for Caper's mother, Maize.

My father passed out at Ella's funeral, and I urged him to see a doctor

Waking to Mourning Doves

right away. He did see a local doctor, but was given too strong a medication to bring his blood pressure down safely and a massive stroke resulted within weeks in October. My RN cousin, Corrine, later told me that that doctor had more patients in the cemetery than in the town. She urged me to complain to the South Dakota medical board, but I didn't. Dad was hospitalized for weeks of rehab and then lived at home for ten more years. After the stroke, his personality changed, making him bitter and difficult for Mom to handle. So, in the course of two months, we had virtually lost three parents to death or serious illness.

In the fall of 1985, it became business as usual at Ambasssador. My new hires were fine, but there was the underlying current of, "We will never fill the beds to reach full census." Since most of the corporate office personnel were ten to twenty years younger than I, their understanding about the loss of our parents was zilch, and only Linda seemed to empathize with my sense of loss over all the issues of 1985. She often told me how perceptive I was and told me I was one of the up-and-coming stars in the company. She thought I would be considered to be the administrator of Northridge, our huge competitor that Good Neighbor was in the process of buying. As it turned out, Good Neighbor spent $4 million trying to purchase Northridge, the deal fell through, and the company lost the $4 million. Our facilities became responsible for making up for that loss, although the owners never told us that directly.

The Good Neighbor owners hired a think-tank operator, Bob, from Washington, D. C. Bob came on like gangbusters and everyone was somewhat terrified of him, since he represented the owners. He made major changes and improvements, which resulted in more profit for the owners of the company, the president of the company being one of them. Now I know the ultimate goal for Bob was to build up the facilities and sell them at a huge profit for the owners. That is exactly what happened a few years later when Good Samaritan purchased Good Neighbor in 1990. I think Good Sam may have been unpleasantly surprised that the facilities weren't quite as profitable as they looked on paper. They ended up selling four facilities and downsizing Ambassador to 80-some beds to eliminate the triple bedrooms and added a rehabilitation wing.

We had a few minor crises at Ambassador that year, the most memorable being an outbreak of scabies, which are a tiny flea-like insect that can invade and multiply very quickly. That requires a major purge, which means taking down drapes, stripping beds and sending all the residents' clothing to a commercial laundry. We did it by sections to eliminate cross-contamination. Staff working on cleanup and stripping were not allowed to have contact with other staff and residents. After the rooms were stripped, we had them fumigated. Of course, this meant moving residents to areas that had been cleaned up.

I was part of the five-day cleanup team and never worked so hard physically in my life. Every day when I got home, I had to strip naked in the garage, put my clothes in a bag to be laundered immediately in a special soap and then shower and shampoo with another strong soap. The residents all had to be bathed in the same manner, and we couldn't allow visitors to enter. After two days, the commercial laundry starting asking questions. Apparently our laundry staff neglected to mention the problem. The commercial laundry needed to take the same precautions and weren't pleased. They got a lot of money from us, but may have felt it wasn't worth it. We managed to purge the pests and probably emerged with a greater sense of teamwork than before. Staff expressed amazement that I pitched in and physically worked just as hard as they did on the dirtiest of jobs.

Another crisis occurred when a nearby business owner claimed that half our parking lot covered his land. He demanded a huge price, so I called our new superman, Bob, to handle it. He deftly put the owner in his pocket by flattering him and then negotiated a fair price for the land. That's when I started to appreciate Bob's skills.

A few weeks later a duplex right next to Ambassador came up for sale and I called Bob again knowing that someday Ambassador would need that land for expansion. He bought it. I rented out the apartments, which became a major headache, because the downstairs soon flooded in a heavy rainstorm even though it was on high ground. We had to put drain tile in and do a big basement renovation. In the long run it was a good investment because they did use it for expansion, but it was a headache for me.

There were ten duplexes on the same street as the nursing home. My dream was to buy them and have a continuum of care with assisted living. It was not to be, as Good Neighbor was then in the selling mode, which Bob engineered.

That same summer of 1986, Sherm and I took a twelve-day rafting trip down the Grand Canyon in four-person rubber rafts. It was a wild trip and not the quiet relaxing break that I needed. When we returned, I was battered and almost disoriented. The sound and clamor of civilization bothered me after spending twelve days feeling a oneness with time and the universe – a profound religious experience I can't adequately describe.

On the trip I wrote in my journal:

> *I feel a oneness with time, nature and all eternity during this whitewater rafting trip for 12 days down the Colorado River in the Grand Canyon. The first night I slept in a tent with my*

*feet out the door flap. Subsequent nights it seemed a sacrilege
to not be a part of nature and the universe under the canopy
of stars. Generations of people have come and gone. I feel
such an indescribable feeling of peace and timelessness; a
profound spiritual experience I can't find words to explain.
It is a wonderful feeling that all is well with me and the
world and the whole order of things. Senses are sharpened;
smell, hearing, taste and yes, fear of the rapids that we face
tomorrow. Animals sniff us in the night and we see tracks not
there the previous evening- catlike in size. At least the red
ants aren't nocturnal in case we bedded down on them.*

Upon returning to work, the Medical Director took one look at my swollen, nicked-up legs and said, "Go home. Caryl, take a diuretic and sleep a couple of days."

Good advice. On the trip we had all taken salt tablets and most of us ended up with swollen legs. I guess it was to combat salt lost while sweating, but it was unnecessary.

In September 1986, my father-in-law died and my father wasn't doing well with his drastic personality change. It seemed like too many changes too fast, and I couldn't see that I could ever improve the census problems at Ambassador. Luckily, Good Neighbor threw me a lifeline and asked if I would like to transfer to Inver Grove Care Center, which was closer to home and had no census issues. Their administrator was transferring and it had always been a pattern to move administrators every two to three years. With some regrets, I accepted the offer despite the fact that I had vowed to stay at Ambassador until we got a new addition that would fix the census problem. I knew that was not to be, so in November 1986 I began my seven-year stay at Inver Grove. The residents at Ambassador gave me a ceramic owl as a going-away gift, which has become the favorite family stocking-stuffer gag gift. It is kitschy.

Before embarking on my new challenge at Inver Grove, Sherm and I enjoyed a quick trip to New Orleans and cruised the lower Mississippi River on the Delta Queen steamboat. The cruise entertainment and food had a Cajun theme, and the riverside plantations we visited were decorated for Christmas. I came back refreshed and ready to start anew.

CHAPTER 37
From Good to Great Neighbor

Transferring to Inver Grove was truly a breath of fresh air for me, as I no longer had that "census" chain around my neck. I went home relaxed and happy almost every day. The 66-bed facility enjoyed a reputation for good care with a family atmosphere. Located on South Robert Street near Highway 494, there were no major competitors in the immediate area. It was the facility of choice, a big change from Ambassador. Many staff members had been there for years, providing a stable environment. Wayne was my first supervisor there, and his management style was similar to that of Linda, my supervisor at Ambassador. They both went on to high-level jobs after the parent company, Good Neighbor, sold the facilities to Good Samaritan. Both Wayne and Linda were top-notch supervisors.

After the fast pace at Ambassador, it was difficult for me to slow down. The first couple of months I felt compelled to "make improvements." Since redecorating and renovations had become my specialty, I pushed corporate for the dollars to give Inver Grove an updated look. I loved redecorating and knew it could make a difference. The corporate office agreed and assigned Design Dimensions, the corporate designers, to coordinate the effort. We started by installing new wall coverings and pictures, plus carpet in the hallways, lobby, break room and offices. They gave us some choices, and I asked all levels of staff and some residents for their opinions on what they preferred. I knew from previous renovations how disruptive it was. With staff buy-in, they would feel it was their project, too.

So, as that got underway, I started looking for something else to improve and hit upon the idea of updating the personnel policies, a boring but needed job. Staff worked hard to meet my goal of finishing one section every week, but finally one RN who was the Assistant Director of Nursing said, "You can slow down, Caryl. This isn't Ambassador."

I readily took her advice and we were all happier for it. It took several months to finish those policies. and we had a lot of laughs over my frenetic start.

That open communication continued all seven years of my tenure at Inver Grove. It made for a pleasant work environment. Staff knew I was approachable and would listen to and act on their concerns. In fact, my open-door policy may have been too open, as someone — staff, family and residents — was

Waking to Mourning Doves

always dropping in to chat or give ideas. . I finally realized my job description could be summed up in one word: "interruptions."

Six months into the job, the Director of Nursing decided to move on to a higher paying job and I hired Mary, a capable, fun-loving Assistant Director from a nearby facility. When I interviewed her I told her that we were going to tear up the old carpet in the lobby and dining area and install new. She joked for years that she never thought that "we" would be the department heads in jeans doing the manual labor of ripping it out. We did it to save our limited budget from Good Neighbor.

I felt very proud when my new dietary supervisor implemented a hot-food cart program, which offered residents a choice of several entrees served to them at their tables. It seemed much less institutional than having a tray plopped in front of them.

Our family parties and dinners were exceptional because of her expertise. The corporate office brought people they wanted to impress to Inver Grove for meals and observation.

Hiring good staff is not always easy, but I lucked out often. I am grateful we had a really outstanding team at Inver Grove and I was happy to be part of it. We had several team-building exercises. One of the events I enjoyed the most was a retreat to our Pine County farm to plan how to become a "Great Neighbor," a new corporate goal. The first evening we explored the farm after having a couple margaritas. We had a hilarious time and it felt more like a group of friends having fun than a work meeting. Yes, I know, the alcohol helped! In retrospect, I am lucky there were no accidents. Our wildest activity was observing the twilight woodcocks' "peenting" flights while sipping wine. The next morning we got down to planning and strategizing successful ventures that cemented team sprit and helped us reach our Great Neighbor goals.

Countless meetings are a major part of administration. Monthly meetings of five or six administrators under one supervisor were all-day affairs. The exchange of ideas was good, but it always resulted in a stack of new work for us. Sometimes, we had rewards like golfing, boating or going to a lake cabin. The lunches were always a treat, and the supervisors tried to reward us as much as possible. Groups consisted mostly of men; women were always in the minority.

Several times a year, all of the administrators met for a full day and listened to corporate directives. New programs and policies were in constant flux, and we often broke into small groups for discussion and input. I never felt a close connection to the majority of administrators. I thought many of them acted phony at these meetings with their constant posturing. I did enjoy several of the women though, and a few of the men.

I dreaded the yearly three-day company retreat for administrators. The one I recall most notably was in northwest Wisconsin at Minnesuing, the retreat of millionaire Curt Carlson, who started the Gold Bond Stamp Company. It was a beautiful spot not far from where we now own a cabin on the Minong flowage. By this time, Bob, the new miracle man, was in full power and in charge. In retrospect, I know that the owners hired him to generate a huge profit, as well as improve the operation of the care centers. The owners' goal was to make the company look profitable to prospective buyers. Bob knew he had to get buy-in from the facility administrators to make it work. Most of us were altruistic enough to want to make the care centers better for our residents and staff; otherwise, I don't think we'd have continued in this field of low pay and high stress. So, the company leaders manipulated us into coming up with strategies and goals to become a "Great Neighbor." We thought the ideas were ours, and we fell for it hook, line and sinker. We were all challenged to become Great Neighbor homes. When we met the criteria, we were rewarded with a party and each staff member received a cheap watch that said Great Neighbor on the face.

I sound cynical, but in actuality we did make some improvements in the care centers, and it did promote teamwork as we worked to reach these goals. Cost-cutting was a big part of it, but better resident care and staff appreciation were even larger for us at Inver Grove. We reached Great Neighbor status in about a year.

Then, the rumors started to fly that the company was for sale. Secret negotiations had been going on for a few years. In 1991, the company was sold to Good Samaritan, headquartered in Sioux Falls, South Dakota. All the administrators were interviewed and we all kept our jobs. My interviewer was a charming woman who was a fellow Philanthropic Educational Organization (PEO) member. I knew after a couple minutes that she approved of me. PEO is a sisterhood, and there is instant rapport with a fellow PEO. I lucked out!

Good Samaritan is a large, nation-wide non-profit corporation that started in rural North Dakota. It had a philosophy that "In Christ's Love Everyone Is Someone," which I agreed with. We had to incorporate prayer and devotions into daily activities as well as use some of their policies and procedures.

In 1991, I began to entertain thoughts of retirement when Cherise announced that she was pregnant. Unfortunately, her good news ended in a miscarriage, which was a difficult time for all of us. I swore that if we ever were lucky enough to have a grandchild I would resign from my job to provide day care. For the next two years it was painful to see staff members having babies.

When we learned that granddaughter Rachel was on the way in 1993,

Waking to Mourning Doves

I began to plan my exit. So as not to jinx anything, I didn't tell staff until Cherise was in labor. Of course, they guessed right away that I'd be leaving, which is exactly why I waited so long. I wasn't certain that it would be a permanent retirement, though. I asked Wayne, my supervisor, for a "grand-maternity leave" to take care of Rachel during the school year when Cherise went back to work.

Surprisingly, he agreed and when I asked why, he said, "Because of the sincerity of the request."

Pam, a former volunteer coordinator and a friend, came to fill in for me as administrator. I left work on a Friday at the end of August 1993. On Monday morning Rachel arrived at 6:30 a.m. ready to be fed, bathed and clothed. After the first day I knew I'd never return to work full-time again. This started six of the best years of my life, caring first for Rachel and then, two years later, granddaughter Claire joined us.

During my nine-month semi-retirement, Good Samaritan kept me on the payroll for the few days a month when I attended meetings or worked with Pam at Inver Grove. After a few months of this, I told Wayne that I wouldn't be coming back full time because Sherm had plans to retire in 1994. He then asked me if I'd like to be kept on a retainer and do some Health Department inspections that the company had been hired to do as consultants. They also needed occasional fill-in administrators when someone left a facility. I readily said, "Yes." I missed the contact with residents and staff.

I filled in as administrator for two weeks at Bloomington Care Center where I had started fourteen years before. It felt great to be back where my journey began. A few of the same staff were still there. By this time, Sherm was retired and available to help take care of Rachel. I started work at two p.m. for an eight-hour shift at Nicollet Care Center. For two months I worked these unusual hours so that I could care for Rachel during the day. The Corporate office bent over backwards in helping me make it work. A few times I took Rachel with me to visit for an hour. I loved showing her off and had her photos plastered all over my bulletin board. Talk about a proud grandma!

Later, I was asked to do in-depth interviews of staff at several rural facilities that Good Sam was consulting with. Staff opened up readily to a grey-haired grandma type, so that worked well. I was good at asking the right questions.

Good Samaritan, the new owner, disassembled the large corporate staff at the old Good Neighbor headquarters. Many found jobs elsewhere, as did my boss, Wayne. He tried to convince Good Sam officials to send me to other states as an interviewer and troubleshooter, but Good Sam preferred to use their own staff from Sioux Falls. Now my employment in long-term care was finally finished, although they called me several times to see if I would be an interim administrator at other facilities. I always declined because taking care of Rachel and Claire was too enjoyable to give up.

I kept my Administrator's license current, and some old work associates who had started a consulting firm called Pathways asked if I'd like to do some work for them, either in administration or as a Health Department-type inspector/consultant. By this time Rachel and Claire were in school and at Pat's Day-Care, so I agreed. Four 12-hour days in Wisconsin Rapids writing recommendations and looking for problems was a grind; I did not enjoy it.

I did the same work a few weeks later in Superior, Wisconsin. But my career came to an abrupt halt in September 2000 when my mother suffered a massive stroke and I went to South Dakota to help with her recuperation. After that, I didn't feel free to accept the several interim administration jobs they asked me about, as we never knew when Mom would need us. I wanted to be available, so a year later I let my hard-earned long-term-care license lapse.

All in all, I had a satisfying career; stressful for sure, but I proved to myself that I could manage a large, multi-million dollar business with hundreds of employees and be a totally independent woman. In my era the working woman had gone from scorn for leaving the hearth and home to the expectation of being "Super Mom." Being "just a housewife" was no longer an esteemed vocation. Getting back into the workplace after years of absence was a huge mountain for women to climb, including me. "Displaced homemaker" became a common term as we tried to re-enter the workplace.

To some, my twelve years of teaching adult education and substitute teaching in the local schools before my career as an administrator was viewed more as a hobby than a real career, but in many respects, I was always in the work force.

As my mother-in-law said, "You really don't have to work, Caryl."

I suppose she thought people in her small town would think Sherm couldn't support a wife. Well, I did have to work, for my own self-esteem if nothing else. It was common knowledge when I was a volunteer coordinator and administrator that work wasn't a financial necessity for me. A couple of my supervisors thought it was great that I worked because I wanted to. A two-person income wasn't as necessary twenty years ago as it is for families now. However, my hard-earned income helped put our daughters though college and masters degree programs, remodel homes, purchase lake property, and enjoy extensive travel after we retired. It was a cushion that benefited the whole family.

PART IX: BEYOND OCEANS

Ancestral Home — Sweden

Vacations
1980s

Expanded Family
With Scott & Bill

CHAPTER **38**

Horsey Rocks to Houseboats

Early in our marriage we developed an overall life philosophy of doing things we wanted to do at the first opportunity rather than wait. We had seen or heard of too many couples that put off travel and other leisure pursuits until they had more money, were older with more time, retired or waited until kids were on their own. Then all of a sudden it was too late, usually due to poor health. Several years after we were married, I developed an autoimmune disorder that under certain conditions could have been fatal. Consequently, I decided to take advantage of all opportunities, particularly travel, whenever they arose regardless of whether it was the most appropriate time of our lives.

The reader may find a description of our family travelogue akin to viewing 400 travel slides! Nevertheless, this memoir is written for our descendants. I know many of our friends experienced similar travels and frustrations and can relate. They may enjoy the tales. Travel in the first year of our marriage found us loading the old 1953 Ford sedan with Poo, the cat, Torg, the puppy, and driving the narrow, concrete curbed US Highway 18 across Iowa for Christmas of 1960. Torg sat on my lap as I tried to keep warm in our unheated car while Poo pouted on the back window ledge alone. She and Torg never did reach a friendly truce.

Mom had my favorite homemade vegetable beef soup waiting as we tried to thaw out from our frigid trip. Even cardboard placed in front of the radiator hadn't helped warm the car. Since morning sickness no longer restricted my appetite, I enjoyed Mom and Ella's comfort foods. I must have gained at least eight pounds enjoying fried chicken, gravy, Christmas cookies, and homemade bread. A blank baby-photograph book given to parents announced our surprise. They were shocked, but pleased. Participating in Crozier and Kinkner holiday celebrations all of the years of their lives through 2008 comprised our Christmas holiday travel, usually across wind-swept, snow-packed roads.

We took short driving trips in all the areas where we lived, exploring rivers, lakes, parks, wildflowers, historic sights and museums. The North Dakota Badlands National Park seemed achievable for our first family camping trip while living in Jamestown, North Dakota in 1962. Michelle's diaper pail, high chair and crib, along with Torg's food and all our gear filled every inch of our

Waking to Mourning Doves

new Ford Falcon. Sherm's skillful packing has been a necessity throughout the years.

I usually planned a new wardrobe before a trip. For heading west, I packed my bulky, olive-green hand-knitted wool sweater, Bermuda shorts, knee sox and jeans. My wardrobe was complete for cooler September weather. Or so I thought. Long underwear and down coats would have been more appropriate!

In late August of 1962, we dropped off 18-month-old Michelle at my parents' in Beresford and headed west, camping in Yellowstone and the Teton mountains in Wyoming, and Glacier National Park in northwestern Montana. Waking up to snow on our tent in Glacier resulted in a luxurious, snowbound sojourn in a motel for a few days. That suited me just fine, as my first bear encounter had occurred the day before in a Glacier Park campsite. As I sat down to eat spicy chili cooked on our camp stove, Sherm muttered an "oh" and I turned around to face a large black bear only a few feet away between me at the picnic table and the tent. He must have smelled our chili and been as hungry as we were.

I panicked and thought, "Oh my God, I'm going to get mauled here and now."

Sherm clanged on pots and pans and scared the bear off, but I retreated to the safety of the car to eat my chili.

Years of up-close and personal encounters with animals while camping made me nearly impervious to critter surprises. While listening to a campfire talk in the '70s in Yellowstone with our daughters, a mouse crawled up my pant leg. Without uttering a sound, I grabbed and eased him down my leg to fling him into the nearby woods.

Experiencing the misty rainforest and Olympic Peninsula, Pacific Ocean and the Seattle World's Fair reinforced my vow to travel as much as possible. I never missed many opportunities. On our return to Jamestown, we picked up Michelle from my parents and Mom later told me she didn't want to let her go. Michelle and Mom formed a strong bond that lasted 48 years until Mom's death in 2009.

When our girls were too young for long camping trips, our moms seemed happy to provide childcare. In the spring of 1965, Sherm and I loaded our spiffy new yellow Buick Skylark and headed northeast. The bug for travel had bitten me hard and I loved the short respite from childcare. I had long blonde hair and a new wardrobe and felt very chic and adventurous. We camped all the way to Acadia National Park in Maine and then down the coast to Boston and New York City. Growing up on the prairie hadn't prepared me for the overwhelming clamor and crushing hordes of humanity in the big eastern cities. I loved the skyscrapers, riding subways, seeing a Broadway play starring Sammy Davis Jr., Greenwich Village, ethnic foods and neighborhoods. I tried to imagine how my ancestors felt viewing the Statue of Liberty. I tried to keep the wind from blowing my dress over my head as we peered out from the top of Miss Liberty's crown. After a stopover visit to Washington D.C., we were ready to head home, lonesome for Michelle and Cherise.

By 1965, when Michelle was four and Cherise about 18 months, we decided they were old enough to take long camping trips with us. We headed for Colorado and the mountains. The girls remember playing and sleeping in Erma Egger's huge porch in Littleton, Colorado; driving up Pikes Peak in the snow, ice and fog; and the North Pole Santaland where they touched an icy pole as they sat and petted a tame deer. [reindeer?]

In the campgrounds the girls rode "horsey rocks" (their name for large boulders that served as pretend horses), explored nature, and complained about the camp food: usually oatmeal for breakfast, soup for lunch and something "icky" for supper cooked on our camp stove. Eating out was a treat they rarely experienced. Generally they traveled well, slept soundly and entertained each other and us. Cherise saw the Mesa Verde ruins perched on Sherm's shoulders, and Michelle held my hand as we climbed and explored kivas. We rode the old train from Durango to Silverton. Sherm rode on the gangway between the cars and inhaled a lot of engine smoke in the process. His subsequent vomiting is the part of the trip that the girls remember most.

I always sewed the girls and myself new wardrobes before we traveled. They weren't impressed with the fashions looking back years later. On the long drive to Colorado, we chose a name for our soon-to-be-acquired Golden Retriever puppy. As we sped by endless cornfields, "Maize" seemed like the perfect name.

My parents usually visited us in the fall before the corn harvest and enjoyed trips in Minnesota. The fall of 1967, I packed enough food in a cooler to last five days and we all piled into the Buick to see the North Shore of Lake Superior. I think the girls, ages three and six, enjoyed sitting on grandparents' laps and staying at North Shore cabins that dotted the spectacular and then-uncrowded shoreline. Cherise busied herself collecting rocks, a lifelong passion. My parents marveled at the sights and displayed their unabashed enthusiasm for travel. In later years I drove them on trips to Yellowstone, Rocky Mountain National Park, the Grand Canyon, Michigan, Wisconsin and Minnesota, often while Sherm and the girls went backpacking in the mountains or on canoe trips into wilderness areas.

As our penchant for travel and camping grew, we realized we needed a larger vehicle. We purchased a green Ford station wagon that held all of our gear as we drove around Lake Superior. It was a gas-guzzler, but with gas at less than 29 cents a gallon, we didn't obsess about good gas mileage. The long drive consisted of tall trees, endless boring roads and rocky shorelines. It was not my favorite trip after I had seen the big cities back east. Sherm taught the girls to skip rocks across the water. They still liked finding horsey rocks and playing with Barbie dolls on their back-seat stage.

When they asked, "How much longer?" over and over, we replied by saying." Two or three Batmans" — a half hour of TV time they understood.

Sherm built a mint-green plywood cupboard that fit in the back of the station wagon. We lowered the tailgate of the car so it acted as a counter and pulled out the stove and cook kit from the cupboard to prepare a meal. It functioned as a miniature kitchen. The large umbrella tent and other camping gear were piled high in a rooftop storage box.

Our trips often coincided with Sherm's work assignment as a planner with the National Wildlife Refuge System. Our daughters visited more states by the time they were eight and five than I had seen by age 20.

In 1969 we bought a used pop-up tent trailer and headed to the East Coast where Sherm had a work assignment at Chincoteague, Virginia. The girls were thrilled to see Peanuts, the colt of the *Misty of Chincoteague* series of non-fiction books we'd read. My fondest memory is watching the girls in their first ocean encounter. Sherm walked into the surf clutching their hands as they giggled and screamed in delight. Gentle waves brushed their red, white and blue homemade knit sun suits. As larger waves rolled in, they coaxed their dad to go out deeper. When a huge wave reached them, they ran back to shore sputtering and screaming that they'd almost drowned.

We gathered shells on the isolated wildlife beaches not normally visited by the public and went fishing in the ocean bays. We caught a few blowfish, a strange little fish that inflates its prickly body so predators can't swallow it.

The girls were a bit young to absorb the rich history of Williamsburg and Washington, D. C. Their highlight was finding ladybugs and playing leapfrog on the lawn by the Archives building. At Williamsburg they liked the Welsh rarebit lunch at a pub and buying souvenirs. We were saving money to build our dream house, so I went in grocery stores with only two dollars to provide meals for the day. It felt like poverty.

One night a powerful rainstorm approached our campsite as we were returning to our tent trailer. We cowered in the car as trees bent toward us and hail, wind, rain and branches pummeled our camper trailer. It was the first time the girls were up close and personal with a violent storm.

Driving the corduroy gravel ALCAN Highway in 1971 into the Yukon and Northwest Territories surpassed my wildest dreams. As a child listening to Sky King and his Yukon adventures, I had fantasized about experiencing the far north. Now, here we were, driving for six days approaching Fairbanks, Alaska. The profusion of fireweed, endless purple mountains, and frontier towns almost made up for the choking road dust and gigantic trucks spewing rocks at our windshield. It was like a demolition derby. We kept the windows rolled up in our non-air conditioned car to keep out dust. We had 90,000 miles on our green Ford and were prepared to abandon it beside the road as many others had done before us.

Michelle and Cherise, eight and five, gave up asking, "How much further?" as we drove 600 miles a day. Occupied with Barbies and books, they became resigned travelers and didn't complain — much.

They sang, "We can see the mountains, (pine trees, Eskimos, beaches) ya, ya, ya, ya, ya," with every new vista.

The Eskimo Olympics exposed us to a culture we tried to absorb. We bought books, Eskimo-made ivory and seal-fur dolls, scrimshaw walrus teeth, baleen, ivory, cottonwood and soapstone carvings — worth a small fortune 40 years later. A bag of fur scraps provided the most fun for Barbie and Eskimo doll interactions. A child's Eskimo cookbook provided hours of Barbie entertainment.

While Sherm and his planning team flew with some US Fish and Wildlife personnel to the North Slope to exotic locales like Shishmaref, Nome, Point Barrow, Prudhoe Bay and Kodiak Island, the girls and I explored Anchorage and the Kenai Peninsula. I bought a seal coat with a wolf ruff hood for $75 at a church mission sale. Little did I know that the natives used the urine method to process hides. Phew! I never thought it smelled bad, but barking dogs chased me down the street whenever I wore it. Maybe it was the wolf ruff hood.

> Michelle writes: *Even though I was in elementary school, I can still picture many of the sites- fireweed, totem poles, dead bear in the road, taking the car on the ferries, gigantic cabbage, Russian Orthodox churches etc. Mom bought a seal fur coat that stunk. I wore a sweater at the beach and we had to run from the tide. I remember a strip club near the hotel.*

> Cherise writes: *Smoke from fires and dust from the highway were always with us as we traveled in our green station wagon with the green plywood food box and camped in the big green tent. We saw Musk oxen. We got fur scraps for our Barbies so they could be go-go girls. Mom wanted to eat whale blubber.*

Waking to Mourning Doves

On our way home through British Columbia and Banff and Jasper National Parks, we laid our sleeping bags out in a field minus the tent and woke up surrounded by prairie chickens. That Alaska adventure remains our most memorable family trip.

A spring trip to Aransas, Texas on the Gulf Coast introduced us to the roadside carpets of bluebonnets and Indian paintbrush. Camping with a symphony of mating cardinal songs was magical. We ate fresh steamed shrimp and huevos rancheros every chance we got. It sure beat camp chow. We girls wore hip-hugger pants with bell-bottoms and macramé belts.

Armadillos, alligators, javelinas and wild boar fascinated the girls. We got blistering sunburns on Gulf Coast beaches near Galveston; mine was through a lacey midriff swimsuit. Who knew a speckled tummy burn could be so painful?!

A side trip to New Orleans exposed the girls to pralines, beignets and the seamy nightlife on Bourbon Street,

I heard a passerby comment, "I sure wouldn't take my little girls here at night."

In Memphis, we pulled into a campsite in the dark and woke up in the middle of a garish gypsy camp. A slum also surrounded the campsite. Maybe the torrential rain kept us safe.

We dropped Sherm's parents in Oklahoma City one March in the mid-'70s to visit the Jacobsons, after which we headed west to New Mexico and the Grand Canyon. We expected sunny, warm weather but encountered snow on the canyon rim. This lent an unexpected beauty to cactus and desert scenes. I preferred the Grand Canyon etched in snow to the 100 degree temps in later visits. On our drive home from Oklahoma City, I had a bout of food poisoning with frequent stops at wayside rest rooms. I was extremely sick and nauseated, but we drove on despite my pleas to stop at an emergency room. Ella tried her best to help me, but the Crozier men were hell-bent to get home. The journey ended when we got to Beresford and my parents realized how sick I was. That trip introduced my now infamous statement, "Anything south of Lakeville (MN) is not worth visiting." Never again would I be such a wuss while traveling.

Since the girls traveled well, we decided to take a month-long trip west in 1978 to the national parks and monuments: Yellowstone, Grand Teton, Bryce, Zion, Yosemite, Muir Woods and Redwood. In Los Angeles, we visited Disneyworld, Knotts Berry Farm and Universal Studios. Fog shrouded us on Highway 101 up the coast to Hearst Castle. I insisted on stopping at all the California mission churches.

The girls began their perennial complaint of never getting to the beach early enough. They delighted in drawing ugly pictures of parents. After we left Las Vegas they wrote a song about parental neglect, which they remembered and sang at Michelle and Scott's groom's dinner.

Utah is a rocky land, and it has a lot of sand. It even has a mighty view, but I'd rather look at Timbuktu.

The food is scrummy yummy too, ham sandwiches all day through, peanut butter raiseny goo, to spread on our celery-ooh!

It has a river here and there, but the water isn't all quite there.

We get a fourth a can of pop, but that's not enough to make us hop.

Although it isn't Minnesota, it certainly fills its beauty quota. Although it's a simple place, it seems to have a certain grace.

On a later trip to Florida, Charleston, Savannah and Hilton Head, South Carolina, Sherm and I checked off our visit to every state in the US. We drove into Alabama so our teenage girls could take a photo of us standing in the red soil of our last state to visit. Like most teenagers, they thought everything we did was stupid. The only time they weren't scowling and complaining is when they clung to us while we were observing college kids on spring break on Daytona Beach. The wild scene cured them of ever wanting to go on a college spring break. I think they were horrified with the alcohol, loud music, sexual fervor, fur-lined tents and souped-up cars. I know I was.

I dug up a couple of Spring Beauty and Dutchman's Breeches plants on our way home. They thrived and our Burnsville woods floor is covered with this ephemeral reminder of spring.

We often included a little family history research in our travels, which completely bored our daughters. Cherise at times was provoked to sarcasm.

Cherise writes: *Got up at 5:45 and left by 6:15. Ate old rolls and seedy oranges for breakfast. Drove to Genoa, Illinois, to trace roots, looked at graveyards- North Kingston to our dismay no relative's graves were found. We drove into Genoa, ate the second box of cookies, looked and drove around, wasted time, looked and took pictures of church and depot*

and schoolhouse. Mom enjoyed it. It was a special morn.
Father and daughters didn't feel the same.

Camping allowed us a mode of travel we could afford. Our big tent, army cots, sleeping bags and screened dining tent were more enjoyable to us than a motel. We loved the outdoors. Wilderness campsites were OK until the girls decided they needed to shower and shampoo every morning. Many campgrounds have showers, but overall they don't lend themselves to glamour.

In our early years of camping, we always left gear unattended in the camp. That trust ended when all our gear except the old umbrella tent was stolen near Wichita Wildlife Refuge. There was an Army base nearby. We felt violated, but things worked out OK when the insurance covered a whole set of lightweight gear including compact, down sleeping bags.

We spent a lot of time as a family on canoe trips in Minnesota and Wisconsin and boating in our Boston Whaler on the Mississippi and Minnesota rivers. Most of these outings were wonderful. An overnight canoe trip on the St Croix River brought our usual woes, rain and mosquitoes. Even worse, Michelle and I had to man a canoe alone over rocks, rapids and sand bars. Cherise sat like a princess in Sherm's canoe eating snacks while Michelle and I struggled to keep moving forward. Maize gazed on us with pity. The last half-mile, we just tied a rope to Sherm's canoe and let him pull us paddling by himself.

When lightweight backpacking equipment hit the market, we completed outfitting the family in 1977. I thought it would be 100% better than shouldering a Duluth pack as I did on our honeymoon. Oh boy, was I wrong! Sherm thought we should test the gear on a short hike and overnight near McGregor, Minnesota. After what felt like ten miles of stumbling over rocks, tree roots and weeds, we reached the campsite. Hordes of mosquitoes hovered and dove as we set up pup tents and ate a hasty meal. Scratching and swatting through the night, I rejoiced when dawn arrived. We hastily broke camp and headed out. I set a record for speed dressed in my raincoat with the tablecloth wound around my head. Did I mention it was 90 degrees and humid?

Sherm and the girls had some good backpacking trips. Michelle and Sherm hiked the 61 miles of Isle Royale. Michelle neglected to break in her new Red Wing boots in advance, so her boots still have blood and blister stains. Cherise and I rode the mail-boat around Isle Royale, stayed in motels and visited Canada.

Michelle writes: *Dad made a big effort to spend time with us outdoors. His most valiant effort was hiking Isle Royale*

Caryl Crozier

with me. Unfortunately, I had new boots that caused horrible blisters- the juice leaked through the leather. We would arrive in camp in the afternoon and I would just sit. Hiking was an endurance test which may have helped me earn a doctorate. We would walk 25 minutes with a five-minute break. Getting started was the hardest because the pain would be fresh. One day a moose walked through our camp. The boat ride out was rough. People were seasick and throwing up over the side of the boat.

Another time, they all hiked 57 miles in the Bighorn Mountains and took photos of beautiful floral meadows. I was a little jealous of that. Sherm lost ten pounds and his face shriveled.

Cherise writes: *The Bighorn trip was great. We hiked up to Florence Pass and felt a real sense of accomplishment. We swam in mountain lakes and found out trash bags worked better than Gore-tex.*

They also took a canoe trip in the Boundary Waters and gained weight eating too much gorp. They were probably relieved I wasn't along. I took Mom and Dad on trips while my family had their outdoor adventures. Dad had a satchel of money he enjoyed spending, so we ate well and stayed in nice motels. Their enthusiasm and wonder were infectious. It was great spending time alone with parents as an adult.

Four years later, the family talked me into a backpacking trip to the slick-rock desert country in the Four Corners area in Utah. Predictably, I might have enjoyed a root canal more. The desert had no mosquitoes, lakes, trees or snakes, just sun and spectacular cactus flowers. Unfortunately, lightning and downpours forced us to cower under rocky ledges and take shelter in caves. Hiking required balancing on slanted. slick rock and climbing or descending long ladders wearing a heavy backpack. Yes, I complained. Sometimes Sherm, Michelle and Cherise just walked on, and I had to climb or be deserted.

The first night out, the girls' tent leaked, so Sherm had to pull out their ground cloth to drape over the tent. Dinner was awful too; an inedible freeze-dried tuna-a-la-king. Freeze dried food was in its infancy then. We took a few bites sheltered in a dark musty cave and ended up burying the foul mixture. Thank God we had plenty of crackers, cheese, raisins and granola bars.

After two brutal backpacking trips with family, I decided to just take my parents on vacation while Sherm and the girls ate gorp and battled mosquitoes. Michelle, Cherise, Bill, Rachel, Claire and Sherm (age 70 at the time) went backpacking in the Beartooth Mountains in Montana in 2004. I had the good

Waking to Mourning Doves

sense to stay in a comfy Philanthropic Educational Organization (PEO) B&B in Red Lodge. I don't think Rachel and Claire complained as much as I did!

For the last nuclear family trip, we rented a houseboat on Rainy Lake on the Canadian border. With minimal training, we launched the boat, went a half-mile and ran aground on a sandbar. Sherm struggled and pulled us off using the small attached motorboat. That evening, our anchor rope broke when we threw it out near an island. We knew we were in big trouble without an anchor. Michelle was a certified lifeguard, so we tied a rope to her ankle for safety and she dove deep to retrieve the anchor. It frightens me to think of it today. The remainder of our last family adventure went well other than enduring strong winds and sunburns.

Since the girls have gotten married, we have all taken some great family vacations together: St George Island (Florida), Lake Meade (Arizona), California, Europe and several canoe trips.

CHAPTER **39**

Was Great-Great Grandma a Polygamist?

Great great Grandmother Lucinda Lower's stern portrait hung on the wall at the foot of my grandmother Kinkner's bed. Every night that I stayed with her, she told me tales of Lucinda's life on the Wisconsin frontier: stories of how she clutched her babies near her while big old panthers prowled the surrounding woods and prairies. I coaxed Nan, a consummate storyteller, to tell the most exciting tales to me night after night as I snuggled up next to her in the dark, crowded bedroom. Sometimes I pulled the heavy wool comforter over my head for protection from the scary parts.

Nan whispered with mounting suspense, "Grandma heard the big old panther on the roof and saw his huge yellow eyes looking down the chimney. She grabbed a kettle of boiling water and threw it up the chimney. The startled panther jumped away howling in pain."

Now how could she throw boiling water up and not get burned! Nan had a tendency to embellish stories to regale a child. She added details of the life she knew as a child growing up in Raymond, Wisconsin near her Grandma Lower.

My other favorite story is about Lucinda's husband, Leander, returning from butchering a steer at a neighbor's farm. As he walked through the woods in the deepening darkness, a hungry wolf followed him. Leander cut off chunks of the fresh liver he was carrying and threw them to the wolf. By the time he reached his cabin, he threw the last piece of liver to the wolf as he bolted inside into his children's waiting arms.

Pretty exciting stuff to a five-year-old like me who had only experienced tame farm animals. I heard a few coyotes howling every night, but panthers and wolves? No way!

My grandmothers and great aunts all delighted in telling ancestor stories. I listened and absorbed the stories although they are only dim memories now. Thanks to these women, my interest in recording family history became a lifelong pursuit and the reason for writing seven family history books and this memoir.

As to whether Great Great Grandmother Lower was a polygamist: yes, indeed she was in her teenage years. Family legend states she married a man, trekked to Utah, found out he was a polygamist and returned home with her two sons, William and Rufus. The truth lies somewhere in between. I researched her life via census records and found an 1890 Roberts Missionary

Waking to Mourning Doves

Journal written by a member of the Utah Fillmore family about a visit to Lucinda in Raymond, Wisconsin.

Lucinda Fillmore was the youngest of ten children born in Bennington, Wyoming County, New York in 1834. The family lived close to Mormon founder Joseph Smith. Several of her siblings and parents converted to the Mormon faith prior to coming to the Racine, Wisconsin area in 1843. They practiced Smith's teaching, spoke in tongues and engaged in healing, and two of her brothers were preachers in the church. One brother was sealed in the temple in Nauvoo, Illinois. After Smith was killed in Nauvoo in 1844, a Mr. Strang, a self-professed leader of the Latter Day Saints Church (LDS), lived near the Fillmores in Wisconsin and evidently continued the Mormon influence on the family. Polygamy was an accepted practice in the Mormon Church at the time, and the Fillmore families were devout Mormons. Due to the extreme prejudice against the Mormons, the Fillmores publicly attended the Baptist Church.

In 1846, Lucinda's sister Martha married Alvus Patterson just after her 16th birthday. In 1849, Lucinda, then 15, also bore a child with Alvus. Obviously, the Pattersons were practicing polygamy in the 1840s and Lucinda was the "second wife" at the very young age of 14. It was not legal, but it was practiced anyway. It is upsetting to me that her parents did not protect her from this practice, but they probably condoned it. In 1857, the Pattersons moved to Rice County in Minnesota to escape the prejudice against the Mormons. They made the trek to Utah in 1860, eventually becoming church missionaries in Arizona.

The entire Fillmore family except for the oldest brother, Newton, and Lucinda and her two children joined the huge Mormon migration to Utah. Newton helped Lucinda raise her two little boys until she married Leander, a jovial, blustery widower who lost his wife and four children in the 1854 cholera epidemic. Lucinda, age 21, and Leander, 46, had four children. The first two, Albert and Clarissa, my great-grandmother, were named after the children Leander lost, a common practice at the time. Leander was an outspoken opponent of the Mormon Church and called them "the damn Mormons," as did many of the residents of Racine County.

This family story and hundreds of others were further researched, documented and compiled during our intensive genealogy effort from 1990 to 2001. Beginning in 1970, I had collected and recorded oral histories and information from older relatives and had them identify old family photos. The Mormon connection and their family-history libraries have been invaluable in our research. Michelle and Cherise helped with the painstaking process of reading microfiche census rolls at the Latter Day Saints libraries in the 1970s. Now the research can be done more easily online using Ancestry.com.

My Dutch ancestors settled in New Amsterdam and Albany in 1630. My ninth-generation great grandmother, Anneke Jans, was said in family lore to be the daughter of Prince William of Orange. Research indicates she was his illegitimate granddaughter by one of his four known mistresses. But, blood is blood and this is not folklore. The eleven-generation descendant records kept by my family were accurate in that line.

An early history of America is chronicled in our ancestors' settlement westward. They followed the edge of the frontier. One even "carried the chains" (meaning he was a surveyor) for Daniel Boone into Kentucky.

Old family photographs of Sherm's maternal great grandfather with guns and fishing rods was enticing enough to get him interested in tracing his roots. On the Crozier side, "We trod the bogs" — a single phrase, passed down through generations, was the only family information available about the origin of that side of the family. At least that is all Sherm's father was ever told or could relate to us as to where the Croziers lived before they came to America. Although there was a hint of Ireland or Scotland attached to that phrase, it was not enough to start a genealogy search.

So, like all of our genealogy searches, we followed family lines moving backward in time. We traced the Crozier line from Minnesota to Iowa, then to Illinois and finally to Washington County, New York where it began with a John Crozier, Sr. who first bought land in 1770, the first official record of the Crozier lineage in America.

Sherm's and my ancestors have many connections in northern Europe and later in America. Our Scottish ancestors belonged to warring clans, the Scotts and Armstrongs. Family immigrants from the same area in Germany came across the ocean on the same boat on their way to Pennsylvania. Some of our ancestors were patriots who fought in the Revolutionary War and are buried in the same counties in New York. Earlier immigrants, the Fillmores and Croziers, settled in Washington County, New York. Our ancestors populated the east coast from Cape Cod, to New York, to Cape May, New Jersey to Pennsylvania and Virginia.

As our family history research progressed, we hired professional genealogists and collected information throughout the US, the east coast, Kentucky, Indiana, Iowa, Illinois, Wisconsin, Minnesota and South Dakota. We found the Church of the Latter Day Saints (LDS) Family History Center in Salt Lake City and the Regional Historical Library in Madison, Wisconsin the most helpful. It took many years to fill in the blanks on all of the lines we researched. Unlike some family histories, we followed all the female lines as far back as we could, too.

All of this information (over 7,000 individuals with documentation of events, facts and notes on each) has been recorded in a computerized database using Reunion, the family history software for our Macintosh computer. We

Waking to Mourning Doves

also used it to generate the different parts of the books such as the stories about individuals in the family.

As a result of our passion about family history, we used all the information we had collected to produce seven books of between 300 and 600 pages each. The books contain information that has been collected over the past 20 years through visits with family members, researching family records, browsing through courthouse records, libraries, history centers and on-site visits in America and countries in Northern Europe from which our ancestors emigrated.

Using our great grandparents as the starting point, we recorded ancestors back as far as the information could be readily found. Then we collected information coming forward on all the descendants of our great grandparents plus the descendants of their siblings. We contacted each family of which we were aware for information, family stories and photographs. Some responded in varying degrees, some not at all. One branch of Sherm's family that was already well documented historically by others was not very cooperative regarding descendants, so we did not prepare a book for that branch of the family, hence seven instead of eight books.

Each book has two parts, a Family History Report that includes information on the ancestors and descendants of our great grandparents, and an Appendix that includes additional information about the family. The books vary in size, with the largest over 600 pages with 450 photographs. They are bound in three-ring binders so that they may be modified or added to, hopefully serving as tools for maintaining a continuous family history. At first, we intended to give the books only to our immediate family, but we decided to share them with the extended family and cousins. A limited supply of each book was printed and provided at cost to descendants of our grandparents and their siblings.

We had numerous adventures as we unraveled the secrets and family connections in musty courthouse basements, overgrown graveyards, and county history centers and libraries in the US. We followed the footsteps of ancestors as they migrated from Sweden, Czechoslovakia, Holland, Wales, England, Scotland, Germany and Ireland to America. We learned of hardships on the journeys westward. Adventurous people seeking new frontiers and lives, they eventually settled in the heartland of the US where we now live. Their determination, sacrifice and hard work to have a better life for their children is the American dream and we are living it.

Not surprisingly, after landing in America, some early in the country's history, my ancestors and Sherm's moved westward through the decades, unknowingly following each other until Sherm and I finally met in South Dakota in 1957.

PART X: SANDWICH GENERATION

Cherise, Claire, Nate, Rachel & Bill

Michelle & Scott

Mom & Dad

Friendly Hour Club — 2006

CHAPTER **40**

A Void in My Heart

My good friend Jan Chorzempa told me, when our first grandchild, Rachel, was born in 1993, "She will fill a void in your heart that you didn't know was empty." How right she was. I think most grandparents would agree.

In a 1993 journal I wrote, "Bill and the nurse carried this wet little bundle of nakedness out in the hall to weigh her. Her bottom end was toward me, so that is what I saw first.

Bill said, "Meet Rachel Catherine." My heart melted immediately as she looked around at me and her new world.

Later in the day, a note posted on the Inver Grove Care Center bulletin board read:

> *5-10-93- Caryl Crozier had a Granddaughter – Rachel – born 5-10-93 at 2:18 PM – 20 1/2" long 9# 1/1/2 lbs. Congrats Caryl*

My staff correctly believed my tenure at Inver Grove would end soon. When Sherm decided to retire in 1994, I didn't care to return to work. Spending time with Rachel was just precious time I wanted to savor for a bit longer.

Mom and I were both ecstatic about Rachel's arrival and got into a frenzy of creating nine baby quilts. We must have worn ourselves out, because the second granddaughter, Claire, was two years old before she got one that Mom and I made together. My knitting needles produced more booties and sweaters than Rachel could ever wear.

> Cherise writes: *Mom and Dad volunteered to do daycare for Rachel. I'd change Rachel, bundle her up and drive down to Burnsville. Mom would dress and bathe her and give me a detailed review of Rachel's day when I picked her up. Having daily contact with Mom and Dad again was nice- especially when we could focus on delightful Rachel.*

The days taking care of three-month-old Rachel after Cherise returned to work were pure joy. I look back on those days as some of the happiest of my life. I couldn't believe how beautiful she was. I loved it when people exclaimed over her distinctive auburn hair and big brown eyes. Still do.

Waking to Mourning Doves

A friend gushed, "If they needed a model for a doll baby, she'd be the one."

My journal entries describe long lazy days sitting in the sunshine on the living room floor with Rachel playing with toys, reading and listening to music. I was fascinated with her every move and mood. I have reels of video and stacks of photos to prove it! Journaling about Rachel's progress physically and mentally fill many pages. The emotion in the writing carries me back to those days she will never remember. On her 18th birthday in 2011, I gave her the journal so she will know how much she has always been loved.

We learned Claire was on the way a few days before my dad died in 1995 as a result of a fall and broken hip and an aortic aneurism a week later. I am glad Dad knew another grandchild was coming soon. There is that hope for your own immortality tied up in grandchildren.

When Claire Elisabeth arrived Dec 1. 1995, the happiness doubled. Having two little girls to care for was like déjà vu remembering our daughters' early childhoods.

When Claire was first born, Rachel didn't like it when I cuddled Claire. She knew she had to share her parents but wasn't so sure it was necessary to share Nana and Papa.

She pouted, saying, "You're *my* Nana," and didn't want to share me with Claire.

The long walks pushing the stroller, reading books and playing simple games with Rachel and Claire gave my retirement years purpose. Sherm retired in 1994 and together we felt privileged to know our grandchildren as few grandparents do. We could have all the fun, and the parents could do the worrying.

Claire was a good baby, loveable and easy to take care of. She rarely cried or fussed and put herself to sleep sucking her thumb and picking holes in her "blankies" which I continually repaired. She loved soft, fuzzy toys. She was and is a touchy-feely tactile person. She loved to crawl up on our laps and sprawl out on us. Always a bright ray of sunshine quick to show her adoration for people, she is perceptive and can sense when someone needs comfort and hugs.

Claire was talkative from the time she babbled. Words burst out of her in sentences and complete thoughts rather than random words. Having an older sister and family that read to her helped.

Her father, Bill, used to sing, "Daisy, Daisy, give me your answer do." She shocked everyone by spitting out that whole sentence when she was one and a half years old.

Before she was two, she dragged a nude doll around by one leg saying," Me baby Jesus' momma. Hard work all the time."

Caryl Crozier

Both girls ate well and preferred string beans to chocolate chip cookies. How strange is that! It ended when the Barnes chocolate/sweet addiction took over. When asked her favorite food Rachel answered, "Sweets."

In 1996, during their daytime stays at our house, Rachel, Claire and I watched transfixed as the huge basswood tree crashed to the ground to make space for the great room addition to our house. We spent hours looking out the dining room window at bulldozers ripping up the turf, foundations being dug and lumber hauled in while the great room began to take shape. After Christmas that year the carpenters started tearing the interior of our house apart, so I spent the days taking care of the girls at the Barnes home.

After the remodeling was complete, we came back to our house and the girls had twice as much play space. They loved the antiques on the downstairs shelves and served us make-believe meals and played store with the cash register. They liked puzzles, blocks, drawing, painting, Play-Doh and the sandbox. Claire liked to get her hands in messy substances like finger-paints, clay and mud. She still does and is the family's best whole-wheat bread kneader.

I felt bereft when the girls started going to Pat's Day Care in 1999. They needed new experiences and exposure to what we couldn't provide: friends their age. Although Papa spent time playing Barbies under the table with the girls and we gave them 99% of our attention, they needed more variety. Also, after six years of providing day care, Sherm and I were ready for more freedom to travel and socialize with friends. We had done the majority of our seven family history book writing and publishing, remodeled the house and redid the yard, gardens and brick paths while the girls were with us from 1993 to 1999.

I imagine we had something to do with fostering Rachel and Claire's vivid imaginations in their play and artwork. Both are now budding artists with their own creative styles. They excel in school and are in Advanced Placement classes and the A honor rolls. Faithful grandparents that we are, we attend band concerts, cross-country ski and track meets, soccer games, scholar award ceremonies and every activity the girls are in. Claire had a ball in her hands from the time she was a baby, so soccer seems a natural for her. Since we live only four miles apart, we can help out with babysitting and transportation when needed.

Years of ballet lessons gave Rachel and Claire athletic grace with strong bodies. I got goose bumps watching them perform in recitals and the Nutcracker performances. Seeing Rachel en pointe in her ballet shoes was surreal. How could someone with that poise and grace be my granddaughter!

In October 2005, Cherise called and asked if we were sitting down. At

Waking to Mourning Doves

age 42, she announced with tearful emotion in her voice, "I'm pregnant." We were thrilled!

The pregnancy couldn't have come at a better time for me. During 2005 I had both knees replaced and the onset of an autoimmune disease that severely limited my mobility and strength. I felt weak and discouraged, but the thought of a new grandchild gave me hope. We also decided to get a French Brittany puppy and the words "baby puppy baby puppy" reverberated in my mind day and night.

The puppy, Patch, joined our family in December and chewed his way through most of our upholstered furniture. At times exasperating, he gave me something else to think about. Sometimes the thoughts were not kind because I have never liked having dogs in the house. I think Patch enjoys his life in the outside kennel watching the squirrels and birds. He lives for daily walks with Sherm in the woods and for hunting trips in the fall. Actually, he hunts every day, usually finding something disgusting to roll in. His role in keeping Sherm healthy is well worth it.

When grandson Nate was on the way, Cherise pleaded, "Mom, don't knit any more blue sweaters, we already have six of them!"

On June 26, 2006 Nate entered our lives becoming the first boy in the nuclear family after Sherm. At midnight, Rachel, Claire, Sherm and I hovered in the waiting room at Fairview Southdale Hospital predicting Nate's weight, hair color and length. When the nurse called us, we rushed to see Bill carry cheesy little Nate into the hall to be weighed.

The nurse told Cherise, "There are three ladies out there taking a lot of pictures."

Rachel, a budding artist and writer, wrote her rendition of Nate's birth and his impact on the family.

> Rachel writes: *I remember the very day I learned the importance of my role as a big sister. Up until age thirteen, all memories seem to mix together and swirl around like pebbles being pushed about by waves of the ocean. I spent time with my little sister, Claire, every day. When we were little, we would play imaginary games and go on "big adventures" outside. Every new bug and tree we found would create a daring quest or journey. We turned every simple object into something fantastic.*
>
> *Claire would yell across our backyard, "Look at this! (Holding up a stick) It's my wand!" Not wanting to be outdone, I'd*

quickly find one for myself, and respond, "Hey I have one too!"

Our games would continue like this creating forts and spending hours exploring around the lake in our backyard as well. We pretended to be princesses, and explorers, and animals, and time travelers. We would play "house", and Barbies, and Play Mobil, and loved spending every possible second with each other. Of course there was the occasional argument or fight, but we couldn't stay mad at each other for very long. We have always been inseparable, and I never really thought of her as a little sister or someone I need to take care of or have responsibility for. No matter how bossy, silly, or flat-out weirdly I behaved, Claire remained simply a friend and playmate to me. The stereotypical "big sister role" never really affected my life. As playmates, the two-year difference never mattered.

But changes came in our household when my mom announced there would be a new member in our family. I remember when she first told us we needed to talk when Dad got home: I knew that very second what it could be about. Somehow, I just knew. Looking back now it seems ridiculous, but I was a little upset and confused. How could she do this to me? What would people think? I managed to hold it all in and act surprised when she told us, but this would undoubtedly change my life forever.

My life transformed the first time I held Nate in the hospital, and looked at his tiny little hands and feet, and know that perfect couldn't describe him, and that I would never stop loving him. Claire and I took turns holding him and commenting on every little movement. We were shocked by the softness of his skin, just like a caterpillar's.

We were thrilled to watch him change every day: the first time he crawled, first bite of food, first steps, and first mumble, jumble of words, each more exciting than the last. He caused a huge change in our lives, but undoubtedly for the better. With him, I began to realize what being a big sister was all about. Claire and I gained new responsibilities in our role as big sisters. We had to baby-sit him, change his diapers, read books to him, and play with him every day. We still spend as much time as possible with each other, but it's different now with Nate in our lives.

Having responsibility for him has made us much more mature and understanding. Nothing in this world means more to me than spending time with my siblings. Nate has created an even stronger family connection, and constant entertainment. Sometimes Claire and I will be fighting with our parents, and Nate will run into the room with his pants off singing, "Hey hey you you I don't like your girlfriend... clueless about the meaning of those lyrics and we all just start laughing, the argument completely forgotten. Other times, while working on homework in my room, stressed out of my mind, and ready to breakdown, he will come in, wearing my high heels, carrying potatoes or some strange object with him, and it can turn my whole day around.

Nate, a non-stop talker, has shown us how different little boys are. There isn't a button to punch or a nook and cranny to explore that escapes his attention. Mechanical, inquisitive and social, he has benefited from Pat's excellent day care as well as his two big sisters who dote on him.

Claire, 15, recently confirmed at Plymouth Congregational Church in 2011, wrote her statement of faith, which echoes our family beliefs.

I feel that the Holy Spirit is a what rather than a who, a feeling that comes over you when you are truly happy, whether that feeling is warmth on a snowy Minnesota day or the pride in creating something beautiful. I nurture my spirituality by doing what makes me happy. Usually I do this by expressing myself with art. I can feel this spirit when I witness something beautiful and am able to capture it on my camera, when I take a picture it's like I'm holding onto that moment. Whether it is the simplicity of architectural line or the complexity of the earth and all her creatures being able to show others the beauty that I see in everyday life makes me happy. I also nurture my spirituality by spending time with friends and family. I need that feeling of connection and compassion. Whenever I am doing something I love or am

*with the people who love me I can feel the Holy Spirit inside
me because to me it is simply happiness.*

We are proud grandparents as we watch all three grandchildren grow, experiment and mature. The girls are strikingly attractive with their auburn and strawberry blonde hair. They dress like fashion mavens in their own distinctive style. Nate's style is developing. We are certain it will be awesome! His first printed message to me was, "I Love You Nana, Nate." What more is there to say!

CHAPTER **41**

Hollywood Comes to the Farm

"Quiet on the set, rolling, slate, scene 4, take 2. Action!"

These are words I thought I would never hear on my parent's farm. But here I was, seated by a dusty cob pile frosted with raccoon poop in the pole barn playing the role of my grandmother in a film about Mom's Friendly Hour Club. I watched in disbelief as Tara Samuel, playing my aunt, rolled in the dried cow dung to get her bib overalls and denim shirt soiled. Is this what Hollywood actresses must do to get in character! Deborah LaVine, the talented director, uttered words of encouragement as I made my shaky film debut. Beads of sweat broke out on my neck and forehead from nerves and the stifling 95-degree July heat. Thank goodness I was wearing a feed-sack apron to wipe off the sweat. The cameras started rolling to film the simulated 1930s scene. Action!

How did this all begin? Aunt Hazel's story captured the hearts of the director and producer after seeing our nephew Tom Jacobson's play about the Friendly Hour Club in Hollywood in 2008. They brought a crew to Beresford to film on location, and the resulting 22-minute short *Prairie Sonata* is now making the rounds of film festivals to garner financial support to make it into a full-length feature. It has already been chosen winner in the 2011 Moondance Film Festival in Boulder, Colorado.

One afternoon in 1934, near Beresford, South Dakota, several young women met to start a friends group that lasted for 70 years. Imagine their astonishment if they could have seen Hollywood come to Beresford to film their lives.

A quote from the Sioux Falls Argus Leader newspaper tells the story:

> *Once the old house where Elvera Kinkner lived for decades couldn't contain the laughter that bubbled up during meetings of the Friendly Hour Club. It wafted out the windows, floating away on soft summer breezes, was flattened by fierce winter winds. First it was young women laughing as they shared stories of dating Beresford-area bachelors or adjusting to married life. Then, the laughter came from new mothers, then middle-aged matrons and finally silver-haired senior*

citizens. Eventually, the laughter ended. The Friendly Hour Club disbanded in 2007. But the Friendly Hour Club met again, through the words of playwright Tom Jacobson.

In the early years, there may have been a dozen small children underfoot who are now senior citizens themselves. The women were a support group for each other and exchanged many ideas for cooking, sewing, needlework projects, child care and farm issues. They celebrated birthdays, anniversaries and holidays and had secret pals to whom they gave gifts and greetings for every holiday and special occasion. The ladies decided to change the Go-Pher-Fun club name to the Friendly Hour Club in 1942. Because of gas and food rationing, the group did not meet regularly from 1942–45 during the World War II years, but became active again after the war.

Later, they celebrated their children's graduations, weddings and grandchildren along with their 50th and 60th wedding anniversaries.

January 8, 1952–Mom had Friendly Hour Club. I ate six taverns. Had plenty of dishes to do.

The club met on the first Tuesday afternoon of each month and the hostess always served a tasty lunch. Many times the group voted to have just one thing for lunch, but it never lasted. They liked the hot dish or salad, rolls, pickles and dessert along with candy and nuts. Mom often made pineapple cookies when she entertained.

PINEAPPLE DROP COOKIES

1 1/2 cups sugar
1 cup butter
2 eggs
1 small can crushed pineapple
3 & 1/2 cups flour
1 teaspoon soda
A pinch of salt

Makes 5 dozen cookies- Drop by teaspoonfuls on cookie sheet and bake 15 minutes at 375 degrees.
May frost with a powdered sugar frosting

A brief business meeting was held followed by sewing or craft projects, fancywork or contests and games. Most of the ladies brought knitting,

Waking to Mourning Doves

crocheting or embroidery projects. At one time members fined each other a nickel if they didn't bring fancywork along to work on. They collected dues of ten to twenty-five cents at each meeting. The treasury averaged around $15 through the years and once it got as high as $44. Each year the group gave most of their earnings to charities and held fund-raisers for community projects. Best of all, they exchanged ideas, got caught up on all the local news and provided support for each other. Most of the ladies were farm wives, so they had to head for home in time for chores.

As soon as we daughters were old enough, we got caught up in preparations for club meetings. Often it meant washing walls and curtains, scrubbing floors and vacuuming furniture. In the summer, I mowed the lawn and weeded the flower and vegetable gardens to help. Mom thought it important to have the yard in perfect shape. I preferred winter meetings! All the ladies got out their best linens and china and spent days experimenting on new recipes to serve. I thought it was silly to put that much work and thought into a club meeting. Now I do the same thing, but hire a cleaning lady!

During the school year, we children got picked up at Silver Lake, Gothland, or Pleasant Hill schools to go to club for lunch, which usually became our supper. We were always ravenous. Fortunately, the hostess provided enough food for at least twelve children plus the pre-schoolers already there. Nobody got babysitters for club. We kids always tagged along.

Mom liked her active social life, belonging to the Get-To-Gether, Sew and So, Congregational Circle and Guild groups. Maybe that is why I too am in so many social groups: Philanthropic Educational Organization (PEO), American Association of University Women (AAUW), Daughters of the American Revolution (DAR), Home Economics groups, antique, book, stitchery and garden clubs. I am just patterning Mom.

Would my first written description of the Friendly Hour Club pass the muster of a writers' group? Absolutely not. But would I change a single word of that small kernel of writing that exploded into an experience and exposure beyond the club ladies wildest dreams? Of course not.

Lifelong friendships are a rare thing in our mobile society. These ladies have had the good fortune to have shared life's experiences and have supported one another throughout their entire lives.

Years before I comprehended the difference between the passive and active voices in writing, I stumbled upon a way to reach the hearts and souls of my mother's friends, her support group for over 70 years through the ups and downs of her life.

Thanks to Mom's friends I got my tiptoe start in creative writing. Although we had written seven family history books that included personal stories and photos, the full impact of validating life's personal experiences hadn't sunk into my psyche yet.

In the spring of 2005, the six remaining members of the club met at my mother's apartment accompanied by daughters who now had to help their mothers prepare the required "tasty lunch," set the table with the "company" dishes and provide other logistical support. The protocol of roll call, paying the 25-cent monthly dues and reviewing old and new business never varied.

Watching these now frail 80- and 90-year-old ladies keep their traditions alive, something touched my heart. Holding back an unexpected rush of tears, I impulsively asked if they would like to help me write a history of their club.

The idea hit a responsive chord and they instantly started reminiscing to tell me what should be included in their history. The daughters quickly caught the enthusiasm and chimed in.

Jotting down notes as laughter and stories filled the room, I realized how important this unexpected project could become. Energized, the meeting went long beyond the usual five p.m. departure. Mom and her friends lived their lives without much recognition and suddenly the idea of telling their story seemed exciting.

Little did I know then that this would become a life-changing event for me, too. Recovering from knee replacement surgery earlier in 2005 and facing an autoimmune disorder that severely limited my mobility, my focus changed to something I could do — writing. By realizing my own mortality, empathy for Mom and her friends' desire to tell their story emerged.

Upon returning home from Beresford, I e-mailed our family Yahoo group about the meeting. Sherm's nephew, playwright Tom Jacobson, sent back his usual one-liner, "Sounds like a play to me."

I replied, "Are you serious?" and the collaboration began.

Over the next few months I met with the ladies again and they endorsed what they wanted in the brief history. Names of members and community service emerged as the most important.

Clearing out 60 years of accumulation in Mom's house led to the discovery of a collection of brown spiral notebooks containing the minutes of the Friendly Hour Club from 1954 through 2006. The 1934 to 1953 notebooks eluded me until 2009, when we cleaned out an old deep-freeze that Mom used to store and protect old blankets and quilts from mice and moths. I found the early history of the club tucked in between the layers of flannel sheets and wool blankets.

We reviewed my draft history at Mom's 93rd birthday celebration in 2006, and I surprised the members and their daughters with a summary of the minutes of each club year. The best surprise, though, brought a reaction of mild shock and delight when they learned of Tom's play entitled *The Friendly Hour*. My summary of the minutes and stories about the club and community formed the nucleus of a poignant fictional play chronicling 70 years of the club. Tom's creative writing skills provided enough drama and sensitivity to the women's characters to result in the production in a North Hollywood theater the fall of 2008.

Attending the premiere with family members brought tears of joy as we watched the lives of these strong South Dakota women being celebrated in Tom's award-winning play.

Just a year later, as my mother's health declined, we learned that a Hollywood director and producer were interested in making the play into a movie. When Sherm, Michelle and I told Mom about the movie plans, she shook her head and tears rolled down her cheeks. A perfect ending for a well-lived life. She left this world two weeks later.

Nine months after Mom's death, a seven-member Hollywood film crew arrived in Beresford to film the 1930s portion of the film to make a "short" to be shown at film festivals to garner support for a full-length feature movie. Using Mom's house, clothing and props along with other Beresford homes and locations made the scenes vivid. Playing my grandmother, I even got into the act.

We all look forward to completing the film in Beresford in the near future.

> *Deborah writes: PRAIRIE SONATA is an award winning short film telling the story of friendship, love and loss in rural 1930's South Dakota. The film, shot on location with the support of the Beresford, South Dakota community providing authentic props and costumes, tells the story of Wava, a spinster carrying the torch for her best friend's husband. A tragedy causes a rupture in the friendship, leaving a void in both women's lives and disrupts the social order of the small community. PRAIRIE SONATA is a lushly visual, quiet and poetic homage to the intrepid women who helped forge the American heartland.*

CHAPTER **42**
Goodbye to Dad and Mom

Final goodbyes to parents are difficult. After Sherm's parents died in the 1980s, we stopped at their empty house in Jasper on the way to visit my parents. An embroidered picture on their wall always brought me peace.

I heard a bird sing in the dark of December, a wondrous thing and sweet to remember.

Now hanging on our wall at the cabin, it says to me that even on the darkest, most difficult days, there is joy in the world and the spirit of loved ones will always be with us.

Dad had a massive stroke a month after my mother-in-law's funeral and his whole personality changed. It was shocking to all of us. When younger, Dad doted on our daughters and thought they were perfect. He loved to tease and play games with them, particularly the game of Aggravation. He'd drive many miles to pick up the girls and me to visit them in South Dakota. He liked to buy things for his granddaughters or slip them twenty-dollar bills. Despite his despair over how he looked after his stroke, he attended their weddings in 1987 and 1988 and later great granddaughter Rachel's baptism in 1993.

Dad was vain and worried about how he looked. He dyed his hair when it turned white and hated living in a crippled body. He didn't want to be around people the last ten years of his life and he was difficult for Mom to care for. He needed medication on a sustained basis. His depression was a factor and his behavior became worse when Mom didn't consistently give him his medicine. If he leveled out and seemed okay she didn't think he needed the anti-depressants anymore, so she quit giving them to him. Then he would sink to a new low and act mean to everyone. Mom hid knives, matches, guns and car keys for fear that he'd have an anxiety spell. He needed his medications on a sustained basis. After an outburst he became contrite, affectionate and asked for forgiveness from Mom. Somehow she endured this for ten years and remained her steady, calm self outwardly, but she shed many tears in private.

Like a cat with nine lives, Mom was a survivor and conquered health issues that normally put people six feet under. Her Swedish genes, healthful living, exercise through hard work and optimism helped.

A burst appendix in 1964 caused peritonitis and a miracle recovery. Two-year-old Michelle and I took the train across Iowa to be at her side. Cherise

Waking to Mourning Doves

nestled inside me; I was six months pregnant at the time. We stayed a few weeks and Hazel, Dad and I did our first major cleanout of the basement burning old papers, magazines, and clothing. We burned stacks of comic books that would be worth a small fortune today. Now, in 2011, cleaning out that basement is still a major project. The 1930s era Depression mentality of keeping everything is one I can understand, although my hang-up is keeping nostalgic items.

In 1979 while accompanying Mom and Dad on a trip to Yellowstone, Colorado, and the mountains, Mom was somewhat restrained and ill. She had been having bowel problems and suspected cancer, but waited to see a doctor for six months until her cancer insurance policy kicked in. Dr. Bucy discovered a growth in Mom's colon, which turned out to be colon cancer. Surgery on Oct 5, 1979 resulted in having a colostomy for the rest of her life.

It was 30 years later on that date that Mom died. We will always be grateful to Dr. Bucy from Beresford, the daughter of church friends, who gave the diagnoses that saved her life. Chemo and radiation were not necessary and periodic checks showed no recurrence of cancer until Sept. 2009 when pancreatic and liver cancer took her life at age 96.

Dad's stroke left him unable to use the chain saw, so Mom, at age 75, decided that she would cut up some brush. When she leaned down, so did the buzzing chain saw and the top of her foot got a deep, bleeding gash. She and Dad helped each other into the house and he called Wayne, a friend, for help saying only that it was Ray, so of course Wayne went to the wrong house thinking it was another Ray. After an hour of putting the injured foot in water and Mom finishing bread baking, Wayne showed up and called the ambulance, which rushed her to the hospital. Why my parents didn't call 911 for help I'll never know.

At midnight, Dad somehow figured out how to call me to tell me what happened. It was clear he was sun-downing and frantic. I called their neighbor Laura, who went to our house and watched over Dad that night and drove him to the hospital the next day. He ended up in the hospital himself. I flew to Sioux Falls the next morning and found Dad restrained to a bed and frantic to get to Mom's side. He'd been combative with the nurses so they sedated and restrained him. All he wanted was to be taken to Mom to see if she was okay. I wheeled him to her room and he was calm again so that I could take him home and stay a few days while Mom recovered. Needless to say, I confiscated that chain saw and locked it in neighbor Laura's shed. A month later I drove to Beresford after a meeting in Redwood Falls, Minnesota, arriving in South Dakota a day earlier than expected. As I entered the porch the first thing I saw was a second saw which Mom intended to use, but keep hidden from me. I had a hissy fit and locked that one in Laura's shed too. I chewed out the dealer who had sold it to them. Finally the chainsaw era came to an end (I think).

At age 81, Mom had hip replacement surgery. I did some research to find the best doctor and stayed with her during surgery. Meanwhile, Dad was in the Viborg Hospital having therapy and care because I couldn't handle caring for both of them at the same time. Every day during two and a half weeks of Mom's rehab, I visited them both and Dad's attitude was as sweet as pie. We brought Mom back to our home for a few weeks. After taking her back to the farm, Dad insisted on going back home and despite our objection, Mom brought him to the farm.

Seven weeks after Mom's surgery, we went to South Dakota and found Mom on her hands and knees pulling weeds in her bountiful garden.

She stated, "The weeds are getting too big to wait for you to help." Obviously there was no way to restrain her work drive.

A year later, when she was climbing a tall ladder and tearing down an old chicken house board by board, we decided to take action and bulldoze and burn the two old chicken houses, hog house and machine shed. I hated to see these buildings that held so many childhood memories go, but at the time it was necessary for my parents' safety. Mom was endangering herself tearing them down and Dad, when in a depression state, threatened to burn them down while he was still inside.

Through the years we made flying rescue trips by car and plane to help. From 1985 to 2009, every vacation we made was tinged by, "What if we need to go to South Dakota to help?" Trip cancellation insurance became a necessity.

Cherise and Rachel were visiting my parents in South Dakota when Dad fell and broke his hip in 1995. Cherise helped out those first days as we rushed home from an Elderhostel trip to North Carolina. I called the hospital staff often, but was dismayed when they decided to let a couple of flunky doctors practice hip replacement on him at midnight.

I am sure their attitude was, " Well, he is old and disposable, so let's let these new guys get a little practice."

When we arrived home to spend a few days with him, he was bitter and belligerent and didn't want to see us. I removed Mom from the room when he was ranting and raving and that made him even angrier. After arranging for nursing home placement in Sioux Falls, Sherm and I flew to Orlando, Florida to meet Sherm's sister, Maxine and husband, Jake for a week in a Good Samaritan Company home I'd reserved. Upon arrival Max met us at the car and said my Dad had died.

Waking to Mourning Doves

True to Sioux Valley Hospital tradition with our family, the doctors botched the operation and his groin area and private parts became horribly swollen. When one of the doctors squeezed his testicles, he had an aortic aneurism and muttered an "oh" and died. Despite a do not resuscitate order, a code blue was begun and the team tried to resuscitate him for 45 minutes. Fortunately, niece Sarah heard the call and spent those frantic moments with Mom and got help for her.

After staying awake all night, we flew home, a very difficult time. His death and planning his funeral were so different from Mom's. I felt almost detached from him, as, unlike Mom, he clearly didn't want me around. I guess he knew I didn't take anger and bad words from him like Mom did and I walked away. Maybe I could and should have handled his illness with more empathy but I didn't know how. The stroke was a disease that changed him so dramatically.

After Dad's death, Mom lived alone on the farm for five years, planted her huge garden, socialized, became her brother Clarence's caregiver and spent long visits with us accompanied by Kitty, the stray kitten that wandered up her cement sidewalk to the farmhouse and became her beloved companion. I was thankful that Mom had Kitty's companionship.

Mom seemed to thrive and relax those five years. She felt free of the stress of taking care of Dad and kept busy sewing, quilting and doing crafts with her Friendly Hour Club. She loved being outside gardening, mowing the lawn, pulling weeds and tending vast flower gardens. Sherm and I tried to help her with gardening when we visited, but after a few minutes of hoeing, we'd sit down panting while she kept on for another half hour. Her little short handled hoe dispatched weeds in a flash and her endurance was amazing. That strong heart from years of hard physical work just never wanted to stop. Even after she took her last breath in the fall of 2009 her heart was still beating.

In September 1999, a lung embolism put Mom in the hospital again and she miraculously survived and was put on coumadin for six months. The doctor feared that she might fall and bleed at the farm, so he took her off coumadin, which resulted in a massive stroke in September of 2000. A mistake on his part, but she became his miracle patient and lived another nine years, but not on the farm she loved. After spending nearly a month with her in recovery rehab, I helped admit her to the Bethesda Nursing Home in Beresford, where she spent three months in rehab before moving to an independent living apartment at the Bethesda Inn for the next four years.

Although her speech aphasia resulted in using the wrong words, making some folks think she was confused, they were good years. She spent three months out of each of them visiting us and enjoying fishing at the cabin.

Meanwhile her kitty (Kitty) lived with us for a year and a half until we found her a good home with Brett in Richfield.

By the fall of 2005, Mom had developed paranoia of fearing that men were trying to shoot her. This led her to leave the apartment and move into the Bethesda Nursing Home where she remained for four more years. She continued frequent visits to our home in Burnsville and we visited her about every six weeks. Mom enjoyed the art classes which drew out her artistic talents. Later we made greeting cards using 20 of her quilting and art creations.

Mom's four years at Bethesda had many ups and downs, but we knew she was getting good care. She and her brother Clarence suffered hallucinations during urinary tract infections. Bachelor Clarence thought the room was full of beautiful women all wanting to have sex with him. Mom feared men in the room would rape or shoot her. I prefer Clarence's paranoia!

We will always be thankful to the Bethesda staff for their care and compassion during her last days in 2009. We were glad we could spend the last three weeks of her life at her bedside and that her grandchildren and friends had meaningful last visits with her.

At her funeral in October of 2009, Cherise wrote and Michelle collaborated on the following tribute.

Tribute to Grandma

At first when I thought about talking to you about Grandma I was a little nervous, because although she was a wonderful grandma, we never had the kind of relationship in which we would sit down and talk for hours about values or our dreams or politics or even current events. It seems like our time together was always busy with something and maybe neither of us had the kind of personality to get into deep discussions. But the more I thought about it, the more I realized that I do really know what was important to Grandma and what her values were. As I look back on my 45 years of memories of my grandma, what stands out are her commitment to family and friends, her hard work and always being busy, her talents, and how richly and fully she lived her life.

Through the eyes of a little girl growing up in the suburbs of Minneapolis, visiting Grandma and Grandpa on the farm was a fascinating world apart and Grandma always made those visits special for us. She took her role of Grandma seriously.

Waking to Mourning Doves

She entertained us, spoiled us and shared parts of her daily life with us. Her purse was never without Blackjack gum or Wintergreen Lifesavers for us and her cookie and candy jars on the kitchen counter always had something good in them. She made us Easter baskets, made crafts with us and took us shopping in Sioux Falls. We got to go to the Good Friday Ladies Luncheon at church with her. She made us our favorite foods: potato patties made out of leftover mashed potatoes for me and Mounds bars for Michelle. She once bet me a dime that I couldn't eat all the potato pats on the platter. I ate nine of them and won that dime from her! We loved having breakfast, a big delicious dinner at noon, a light lunch and then supper and cookies or a dessert were served with every meal! She kept coloring books on hand for us and boxes of Mom's old paper dolls. I loved the old brown doll buggy and red cash register. She sent us out the door in the summer with jar lids and told us which flower heads we could use to decorate mud pies. She let us play with all the cats and she used to sling Nuisance over her shoulder on her way out to the barn.

When Michelle was in a high school psychology class and told Grandma that chickens could be hypnotized, Grandma caught us a chicken and laid a piece of black baling twine down on the ground in front of its beak and sure enough, the chicken just laid on the ground, absolutely still. Although it probably made doing the chores slower, she let us go with her and "help." Entering the dimly lit barn was always an adventure with the smell of hay bales and cows and then trying to balance on the t-shaped milking stool and attempting to squirt milk into the pail while Grandma and Grandpa guided us and smiled at our poor efforts. It was so much fun when they would let us go into the pen with the new-born calves, Peg and Meg, and play. Gathering eggs with Grandma was like reaching out and finding treasure (except for the time I grabbed an egg out from under a hen that didn't have a hard shell...that was just gross.) Grandma would wear an old jacket and her hair would be in bobby-pinned curls under a faded old bandana and she would have big muddy rubber boots that buckled and then, after she cleaned up, she would be transformed into my pretty Grandma wearing a dress, a string of pearls, soft curls, low-heeled shoes and Avon perfume. I can still open up one of her Avon perfumes and the memories come flooding back.

We were looking at pictures with her two weeks ago, and I'm always amazed how stylish she and her sisters were all through their lives. They had fur-collared coats, high heels and fancier dresses than I have ever owned. We looked through her piles and piles of aprons, one for every occasion. Everywhere you look in her house, you can see something she made. Grandma's life was filled with hard work and busy days. The only time I remember her sitting down when we were at the farm was if it was after supper, but even then she had some piece of stitchery in her hands while we watched t.v. shows with Grandpa like Let's Make a Deal or Lawrence Welk. She had us help her with some of her daily work, but she made that fun for us. We picked strawberries and peas from the garden but got to eat as many as we wanted while we shelled. Drying dishes or washing eggs went by quickly, because it was a time to talk. We played a lot of the board game, Aggravation, with Grandpa but Grandma would join in too.

Grandma and Grandpa introduced Michelle and me to some of their hobbies. They took us golfing at the Beresford golf course and bowling in Alcester. They were good dancers too. Grandma had so many more talents and skills than women of my generation. In addition to golfing, dancing, and bowling, she could embroider, sew, can food, make extraordinary quilts and even draw and paint which she continued in the nursing home and produced pictures with poor eyesight that I could never match with my 20/20 vision!

I remember Grandma doing stretches and exercises in the evening to stay strong. Years of hard work and eating good food raised on the farm helped her to live 96 long years. I remember 5 or so years ago, Michelle was bragging to Grandma about how she had been working out-swimming and lifting weights and that her arms were getting really strong. She had Grandma feel her strong biceps and Grandma did

Waking to Mourning Doves

but with a smile and a twinkle in her eye and then Michelle felt Grandma's muscle and let out a loud exclamation. Grandma's muscles as an elderly woman were still much bigger and stronger. We'll be lucky if we are ever as fit and strong as Grandma was!

When we weren't with Grandma she wrote long, detailed letters. Grandma was sentimental and kept the letters she exchanged with Mom and Michelle and myself and all of you. When we were kids, she would include little pictures she had drawn for us or a small puzzle to do. She also kept diaries all through the years. We always wrote in her white guest book every time we visited.

Having family and friends over was something Grandma really enjoyed. Mom says she never really felt like an only child because there were always kids around growing up and lots of get-togethers. I'm sure all of you can remember many of those times.

She loved being a great grandma too. Twirling the girls around in her living room, taking them out to her garden, reading a story with Rachel or Claire curled up next to her, tickling and teasing Nate to get him to giggle, celebrating the new millennium and making lefse with all of us until she was 94 were just a few of the things she enjoyed doing with her great grandchildren.

Being a good wife and mother were also very important to Grandma. She and Grandpa were married for 62 years and were partners working in the field, on the dance floor, raising Mom, and loving each other. I hope they are together somehow now.

Grandma lived her dreams through my mom's life. At age 15 she wrote in her diary that she wanted to go to college and be a Home Economics teacher. We didn't find out about this dream until 10 years ago. She convinced Grandpa Ray to sell 4 steers each fall for Mom to go to college to be a Home Economist. She also made sure Mom got the piano lessons she never had and paid the piano teacher, Daisy Dewey, with eggs, cream and chickens. She taught Mom all the skills and instilled her values by example. I know she was proud of everything that my mom did and encouraged her in all her endeavors.

She lived all her life within a four-mile radius, but was able to travel later in life when Mom took her and Grandpa on trips around the Midwest and touring the great parks of the West. She also traveled vicariously when Mom told her about all of her trips to Europe including finding the homes in Sweden of Grandma's parents.

Grandma loved coming to Minneapolis and staying with Mom and Dad at their home and going fishing and boating at their Wisconsin lake cabin. She counted on my mom and dad to help her out at the farm after Grandpa died, and looked forward to coming to Burnsville with them or having them spend time with her in SD, which they did often. When they stayed at her farm after she entered the nursing the home, she joined them there for overnights, a place she always loved.

I also know how much Grandma liked getting together with the rest of the family, whether it was a big dinner at George and Inez's or a celebration at Alice's house in Sioux Falls, inviting Clarence and Hazel over, or spending time and visiting with nieces, nephews, cousins, neighbors and friends. She had friendships that spanned decades and even inspired my cousin, Tom, to write and produce an award-winning play about her Friendly Hour Club. Visits from all of you on the farm and then later in the nursing home were so special to her. It was a comfort to her, I know, to have family like Karen and Norman, Janice and Cindy looking out for her and for her to know that her land was in Dad's and Allen Voegeli's capable hands.

Grandma lived her 96 years richly and fully. These were some of my good memories of my grandma. I'm sure all of you have stories to tell so maybe we can share them today and celebrate her well-lived life.

As a child, I liked the song *My Grandfather's Clock* which went *"90*

Waking to Mourning Doves

years without slumbering, tick tock, tick tock. But it stopped, short, never to go again, when the old man died."

A few days before Mom died, her kitchen clock stopped. When we returned to the house after her death, I glanced at the clock and realized it had stopped at the exact time of her death: 3:43 a.m.!

EPILOGUE

1940

2011

CHAPTER 43

Still Paddling

Some things do last a lifetime: friendship, mutual respect, drive, common interests, love and passion. Not always in that order in a 50-year marriage, but friendship and a passionate drive in all of our common endeavors has cemented our relationship for whatever the future holds.

Reflecting on our 50 years together as a gentle breeze propels the first golden leaves of autumn onto the Wisconsin cabin shoreline, I realize we have been blessed. As brilliant orange and red leaves swirl in the wind currents and drift into paths unknown, so have our years together. Ups and downs, highs and lows. like the leaves, have always landed us safely. River currents carry leaves in unexpected directions just as our careers and interests have. Snagged by our jointed Rapala fishing lures, errant leaves are reeled in. The tether of a basic friendship/love may be the hook that has kept us together.

Our 1960 honeymoon spent on a canoe and camping trip into the Boundary Waters Canoe Area (BWCA), a lake- and stream-filled wilderness along the Minnesota–Canada border, resulted in our motto for marriage: "Just keep paddling."

For the most part, the waters have been smooth for us: an amazing family, fulfilling careers, adventure and travel, building homes, sharing common interests and the freedom to explore our individual passions.

Since our first trip up the Gunflint Trail into the BWCA could never be considered a luxury, our family gave us a pampered anniversary package to Gunflint Lodge — a fitting finale to a golden anniversary celebration, which lasted most of the summer of 2010.

Although a bit less agile than in our prime in 1960, we realized some things are better with age. Reminiscing about our life together brought memories, most of them joyful, others poignant and a few sad.

We both grew up in strong, supportive families in the Midwest and our parents' values systems became ours: hard work, fairness, always doing your best and supporting those you care about. Not surprisingly, our parents became each other's good friends even though they lived 70 miles apart.

Past generations' value systems can be seen in our daughters and grandchildren. Dedication to family and work, striving to do their best and having fun together harkens back through the families we've come to know through our genealogy research.

Waking to Mourning Doves

Life leads us down divergent paths and mine have been strewn with good people. Now, as I conclude my memoir, I am thankful for a lifetime of love from family and friends.

CPSIA information can be obtained at www.ICGtesting.com
Printed in the USA
LVOW132016200513

334703LV00001B/11/P